International studies in the history of sport
series editor J.A. Mangan

Sport and the making
of Britain

Copyright © Derek Birley 1993

Reprinted in paperback 1996

Published by Manchester University Press
Oxford Road, Manchester M13 9PL, UK
and Room 400, 175 Fifth Avenue, New York, NY10010, USA

Distributed exclusively in the USA and Canada
by St. Martin's Press, Inc., 175 Fifth Avenue, New York, NY10010, USA

British Library cataloguing in publication data
A catalogue record for this book is available from the British Library
Library of Congress cataloguing in publication data
Birley, Derek.
 Sport and the making of Britain / Derek Birley.
  p. cm. — (International studies in the history of sport)
  ISBN 0–7190–3758–1. — ISBN 0–7190–3759–X (paper)
  1. Sports—Great Britain—History. 2. Sports—Social aspects–
 –Great Britain—History. 3. Sports— Political aspects—Great
 Britain—History. 4. Great Britain—Politics and government.
 I. Title. II. Series.
 GV605.B57   1993
 796'.0941—dc20   93–81

ISBN 0 7190 3758 1 *hardback*
ISBN 0 7190 3759 X *paperback*

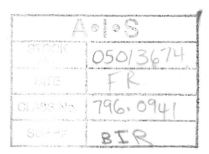
Photoset in Linotron Palatino by
Northern Phototypesetting Co Ltd, Bolton
Printed in Great Britain by Redwood Books, Trowbridge

Sport and the making of Britain

Sir Derek Birley

MANCHESTER UNIVERSITY PRESS
Manchester and New York

Distributed exclusively in the USA and Canada by St. Martin's Press

CONTENTS

List of illustrations   vi
Series editor's foreword   vii
List of abbreviations   viii

Introduction   1

1   Rude beginnings: AD 43–1199   8
2   'Christian service and true chivalry: 1200–1485   26
3   Upward mobility: 1485–03   48
4   Princes and people: 1603–1688   75
5   Politics and patrons: 1685–1756   99
6   Aristocrats and entrepreneurs: 1756–92   127
7   Watershed: 1793–1815   151
8   'Sporting personal': 1815–1637   172
9   Victorian dawn: 1837–51   200
10 Judicious bottle-holding:
    die-hards under pressure 1851–66   232
11 Judicious bottle-holding:
    glimpses of modernity 1851–66   245
12 The missionary spirit:
    tribal stirrings 1867–1888   262
13 The missionary spirit:
    Barbarian delights 1867–1888   284
14 The missionary spirit:
    Philistine perspectives 1867–1888   306
15 The missionary spirit:
    'Imperial Fiddlestick' 1867–1888   327

Index   343

LIST OF ILLUSTRATIONS

1 Ninth-century Saxon Chieftain on bear-hunting expedition (Cotton Library, Tiberius, Bv). Reproduced by kind permission of the British Library.
2 Wrestling: early fourteenth century (Royal Library, MS 2Bvii, folio 161v). Reproduced by kind permission of the British Library.
3 Glove fives: fifteenth century (Harleian MS 4375, folio 151v). Reproduced by kind permission of the British Library.
4 Compleat Angler: Izaak Walton. Mary Evans Picture Library.
5 Painting of Godolphin Barb by George Stubbs; early eighteenth century. Mansell Collection.
6 Engraving of Lord William Bertie at a cockfight, 1751: Hogarth, four stages of cruelty. Copyright, British Museum.
7 Painting by T. Stothard RA of the presentation of colours to the Bank of England Volunteer Corp, 2nd September, 1799 at the first Lord's. Copyright, Governor and company of the Bank of England.
8 Portrait of Tom Cribb. Copyright, British Museum.
9 Photograph of golfers at St Andrews, c.1850. Reproduced by kind permission of the University of St Andrew's Library.
10 'Drawing the Stumps'. 1862. Mansell Collection.
11 Young W. G. Grace. Reproduced by kind permission of Marylebone Cricket Club.
12 'The Death' by J. F. Herring. From a set of prints published by Ackerman & Sons Ltd., 1867.
13 Football match at the Oval, England v. Scotland, 1878. Reproduced by permission of the Hulton Deutsch Collection.
14 Renshaws v. Clarks (USA) in the 1883 Lawn Tennis Championships. Reproduced by kind permission of The Wimbledon Lawn Tennis Museum.
15 Arthur Shrewsbury. Reproduced by kind permission of Marylebone Cricket Club.

SERIES EDITOR'S FOREWORD

The purpose of this series is to relate sport in society to the political, cultural, economic, spiritual and aesthetic movements, trends, fashions and demands of the time in which it is considered by the contributors.

Earlier monographs and collections in the series have made this their central concern and they have mostly focused on a specific period.

This volume is a departure from general past practice. The intention is to provide a highly readable overview of the evolution of sport in Britain. Derek Birley takes the long view and covers a wide range of activities. What emerges from his survey is the continuous role that politics, religion and economics have played in the development of sport in Britain. Kings, aristocrats, clerics, merchants, preachers and industrialists have exerted mostly self-interested pressures, made for the most part successful demands and more often than not determined major developments. Their influence has been paramount.

While the mass of the British people has not been without some influence, unsurprisingly, as Birley reveals, the making of the *recorded* – perhaps this is an important caveat – history of sport in Britain, has been mostly the work, purposefully or otherwise, of the powerful, privileged and wealthy.

What Birley also reveals, however, are the various motives behind this effort. National defence, social order, religious zealotry, social privilege, 'caste' snobbery, secular morality and entrepreneurial motive, as well as personal enthusiasm, have been the main factors which have determined, in varying degrees at different moments, the nature of British sport down the centuries.

Sport is more than simply play!

J. A. Mangan

ABBREVIATIONS

AAA	Amateur Athletics Association
AAC	Amateur Athletics Club
ARA	Amateur Rowing Association
ASA	Amateur Swimming Association
BC	Boxing Club
FA	Football Association
GAA	Gaelic Athletics Association
ICAC	Irish Champion Athletic Club
LTA	Lawn Tennis Association
MCC	Marylebone Cricket Club
MFH	Master of Foxhounds
MSCA	Metropolitan Swimming Clubs Association
MRA	Metropolitan Rowing Association
NYYC	New York Yacht Club
R and A	Royal and Ancient Golf Club
RFC	Rugby Football Club
RFU	Rugby Football Union
RYA	Royal Yacht Association
RYS	Royal Yacht Squadron
YMCA	Young Men's Christian Association

To my wife, Norma, with much love

ACKNOWLEDGEMENTS

The footnotes to each chapter list my principal literary creditors, living and dead: I am deeply grateful to them all. For their help in procuring texts and tracing references I owe much to many librarians, and in particular those of the University of Ulster. I am also indebted to Pat Simpson, Sadie Faulkner, Margaret Connolly, Julie Cummins, Mandy Coult and Jane Lissaman for monumental patience and metaphrastic skills. Special thanks are due to Dr Bill McNeill, for philosophical and golfing advice, and to Lord Grey of Naunton, for encouragement and learned journals. And finally I should like to thank Tony Mangan for his enthusiastic support and shining example.

INTRODUCTION

I

'In order to form a just estimate of the character of any particular people it is absolutely necessary to investigate the sports and pastimes most prevalent amongst them.'[1] The uncompromising opening sentence of Joseph Strutt's pioneering work of 1801 overstates the case, suggesting perhaps an anxious author seeking to justify serious study of what may have seemed a frivolous topic. Readers today, when sport and leisure occupy so much of our daily lives and command so much scholarly attention, may need less persuasion. And the British have set such store by their prowess in athletic pursuits, devising complicated team-games and drawing weighty often self-congratulatory conclusions about their moral and spiritual value, that they seem specially suitable subjects of enquiry.

Trying to form a just estimate of the British character would, however, be a daunting not to say thankless task, and this book has more modest aims. It looks at developments in sport in relation to the emergence and growth of Britain as a whole, an interplay of cultural and social forces of a stimulating, if not always harmonious kind. It begins with the Romans' valiant though largely unavailing attempt to bestow the benefits of their way of life on the unsuspecting islanders and ends towards the close of the nineteenth century with Britain, precariously and imperfectly united but an imperial power herself, dominated by England and looking to English supporting traditions – and especially those of cricket – to sustain her missionary efforts.

II

Before plunging in with the Romans, however, we should look at the broader context, both of Britain and of sport.[2] Insularity, for all its protective strengths, has its drawbacks. Even the exposure of the Piltdown forgery has not wholly convinced the stauncher patriots that the first man was not, after all, an Englishman. But the stark fact is that when *Homo sapiens* arrived in southern Europe about 30,000 BC Britain was still firmly and frozenly attached to the mainland. The ice-cap was retreating but another 25,000 years elapsed before it dissolved into the channels and seas that created the British Isles. Even then it was a cultural irrelevance; much more significant things were happening further south.

As for sport it is not only older than the British Isles but older than man. Its basis, play, is a vital survival mechanism. Games help young animals to master their own bodies by pitting themselves against obstacles or against other youngsters in comparative safety. Mature animals also use games to settle disputes and determine hierarchies: it is a help to individual survival if young hopefuls need not go to the lengths of killing their rivals in order to establish dominance. The need to sublimate lethal impulses was sharpened by man's discovery of how to kill at a distance, which helped improve the food supply and fend off predators but posed a threat to his own species.

Fortunately what the mind creates the mind can control, and play, essentially, is not what the body does but what the mind makes of it. Hence the importance of the advance made by the people who inhabited the rocky valleys of southern France and northern Spain some 17,000 years ago, in visualising the significance of hunting, their principal means of life-support. Unlike their successors these men did not claim lordship over the rest of animal creation. Indeed the cave art they left behind – magnificent paintings of wild horses, cattle, bison, deer, ibex, lion, bear and woolly rhinoceros – suggests a religious reverence for fellow-creatures admired for their speed and strength. Such a lifestyle had none of today's cut-and-dried distinctions between work and play. Life itself was a ferocious game, one in which men compensated for their physical shortcomings by manual dexterity and superior brain-power and human advance depended on improvements in hunting techniques – better tools and weapons; domesticated dogs trained to hunt other animals; new ways of catching fish and fowl – and on more sophisticated forms of play.

Then sometime before 6,000 BC men began to domesticate draught animals and to cultivate crops. These dramatic developments brought to the inhabitants of the valleys of the Tigris, Euphrates and Nile a more leisured existence which gave rise to new religions and other forms of imaginative activity. Permanent settlement and the acquisition of property led to trade, but it also attracted barbaric attention, and the emerging cycle of conservation, attack and defence stimulated the arts of warfare and bred a new militaristic aristocracy. All these changes had their effect on the evolving pattern of preparation for life through play.

For one thing games became increasingly cerebral, putting a premium on the art of divination. Rolling astragali, sheep's ankle bones, to discover the will of the gods was the forerunner of dicing, which originally had sacred as well as secular purposes. In one of the new religions, indeed, the gods themselves were gamblers: an Egyptian myth of the origin of the calendar tells how Thoth, the god of wisdom, diced with Sin, the moon god, and won a 72nd part of his light, five days, which increased the total number of days to 365. Gambling's reputation has declined somewhat in religious circles since those days but dicing was a potent emblem of evolutionary advance. Dice were also used in the board games that were popular in the earliest civilisations. They were abstract versions of physical encounters and so surrogates for killing at the second remove from reality.

Dicing implied a code of honour: a cerebral game loses its point if at the end the loser slits the winner's throat. By the same token strict adherence to the rules was needed in the militaristic games which now came to the fore in civilised societies. One of the earliest records of an organised game – a fencing match depicted on the wall of a temple of Rameses III about 1190 BC – shows umpires carrying feathered wands. The fencers also had face masks and narrow shields and their swords were tipped. Such precautions could not prevent foul play but the regulations at least helped to identify and isolate non-conformists.

In any event followers of codes of honour tend to expect lower standards from outsiders. The Greek inheritors of Egyptian cultural leadership, who were inclined to be priggish about the Achaean Ideal, made a positive virtue of being underestimated by the uncouth or effete. Thus Homer recounts with relish how Odysseus, driven by homesickness and sensitivity to weep at an old minstrel war song and accused of softness by a young Phaecian, put the upstart firmly in his place when he roused himself to take up the challenge.[3]

The Greek code is of particular relevance to the story of British sport because of its powerful influence throughout the west, both directly as a philosophical concept and indirectly through the Roman Empire. It is essentially both pre-Christian and anthropomorphic. The Greeks believed in loving their friends and hating their enemies and they thought it a virtue to be lucky: success came to those who were on the right side of the right gods. In Patroclus' funeral games in *The Iliad* when Odysseus, whose renowned cunning was a gift of the gods, fell behind in the footrace he made a quick prayer to Pallas Athenae, his patroness, and she intervened by putting his opponent's foot in a cowpat.[4]

III

With civilisation and leisure came the creation of elite classes and occupational specialisms from kings, priests and generals down to slaves; and sport became a status symbol. It was a recipe for degeneration: the palaestras (wresting schools) and gymnasia which had traditionally provided the core of Greek military training were criticised by Aristophanes in *The Clouds* (423 BC) as mere social centres and Euripides complained[5] that the athletes, successors of the heroes who performed in the celebrated Olympic and other religious festivals, were useless both in war and in economic life. Whereas the Spartans had called their first year aspirants to manhood *sphairais*, ball-players, the *sphairisteria* (ball-playing rooms) in the Athenians' gymnasia dwindled to places for the exercises with a small ball commended by Galen, the second century physician.

Under the Romans the degeneration grew worse. The games were retained for political reasons but metropolitan taste was more for gladiatorial contests, wild beast shows and spectacle, while the chariot race, once dedicated to Apollo, became the outlet for fanaticism and a way for slaves to become rich. In first century Rome the ball-courts at the baths were used by the better sort to work up an appetite for dinner and the more effete were assisted by a slave or by the pilicreps, ball-rattler, who hung about keeping the score, acting as ball-boy and offering practice and tuition.

Civilisation also transmuted hunting, once a vital occupation, into a sport for the privileged. It retained traces of its religious significance into Neolithic times and beyond, which added to its gravity and social esteem as kingship and priesthood became separate but interrelated professions. Yet for Tutankhamun (c1350 BC) hunting was not only a social obligation for a monarch but also a recreation: in the paintings and carvings of his tomb the king is seen in his chariot in pursuit of the royal beast, the noble lion, but also hunting humbler creatures like the ostrich, hyena and onager, and wild-fowling and fishing, evidently for fun. Greek and Roman aristocrats were addicted to hunting sport and produced text books on the subject, but many urbanites found it more convenient to sublimate their primitive impulses by watching fights between cocks or quails and the more robust tradition owed much to the atavistic outlook of the horse-loving founders of high barbarian cultures like the Assyrians who terrorised Babylon and Egypt and the Macedonians who overran Greece in the fourth century BC.

Thus Philip of Macedon set great store by the traditional athletic festivals and his son Alexander was brought up on Homer, but their reinvigoration of the Hellenic ideal was essentially barbaric. Philip's conquest was achieved with the aid of a feudal cavalry élite known as the Companions, who spent their lives either in battle, wrestling, spear-fighting and similar contests or in hunting in which the wild boar was the ultimate test. Conversely the prelude to Rome's supremacy was her reaction to Hellenistic pressures, both military and philosophical, and the Empire proved a more successful bulwark against warring tribes than against the effete values of urbanism. By the first century BC Julius Caesar was remarking disapprovingly of the Germans that their whole life was composed of hunting expeditions and military pursuits.

IV

A similar spirit imbued the leaders of the southern British tribes whom Caesar's seventh legion encountered when it landed on the Kentish coast in 55 BC seeking to punish the local tribal chieftains for sending warriors across the Channel to help Caesar's enemies in northern Gaul.

By this time wave after wave of settlers had come from the mainland to the islands – dark-skinned Iberians, Beaker people, Battleaxe people, the Wessex chieftains, Urn people – all bringing distinctive skills to augment the original hunting, fishing, gathering way of life. Most significantly about 1000 BC the first Celts had arrived, bronze-workers and farmers but also notable warriors and later on highly skilled users of iron tools and weaponry. The Celts loved hunting, the boar had a special significance for them, and they were great horsemen. The spread of hill-forts in the south suggests a military aristocracy dominating the farmers, craftsmen and traders. Their methods and instruments of fighting, though ferocious, were old fashioned – such as the two-wheeled chariot – and they were doubtless sustained by ideals that made conservatism romantic. Such societies are characteristically led by an élite, motivated by noble striving, leading lives in which courage, virtue and honour go hand in hand.[6]

That militaristic opportunists should encumber themselves with notions of honour is explicable only in terms of the basic evolutionary importance of play as a survival mechanism. By the same token, the code of honour not only survived but permeated the institutions of civilisation, and, as we shall see, it was not threatened but strengthened by the stark, bloody reality brought by war, for under such codes the bereaved assuage their grief and the victors purge themselves of guilt through elaborate fables of heroic sacrifice. Hence the great efflorescence of art and poetry at times of social upheaval and hence, in the intervals, the pursuit of sporting surrogates. The honour codes of sport parody those of the great game of war and are devised by the same sort of people.

The chivalry of medieval Europe was the forerunner of many later British codes. The Dutch scholar Huizinga has pointed to the direct line from the knight in armour to the *honnête homme* of the seventeenth century and the modern gentleman.[7] There is a related continuity in the successive conventions – the etiquette of the Forest and the tournament, 'fayre lawe', 'shooting flying', Broughton's rules, the laws of cricket, the Jockey Club's rulings, public school regulation of football – that sustained British sport in its formative years. They were devised by privileged groups narrowly concerned with their own interests, as in the conventions of society as a whole.[8]

The tone was set by the Norman kings who kept the regulation of their hunting preserves outside the common law and maintained in later centuries by magnates who framed and used Parliamentary law to protect their own sporting privileges. The self-perpetuating oligarchies that governed fashionable sports exploited the talents of the lower orders and when this involved rubbing shoulders with them still kept them in their place socially. The mechanism of the gentleman's club, a voluntary association, allowed sporting legislators' arbitrary edicts to prevail over the law of the land, notably in the case of the Turf.

Yet the very venality of those who framed these élitist codes, especially when gambling was involved, obliged them to make room for wealthy vulgarians and ambitious professionals from the lower orders. The story of how sport assisted the emergence and rise to prominence of the British nation is not one of revolutionary fervour strengthened by the joy of athleticism (an alien concept if ever there was one) but rather of a common addiction, to gambling as well as sport itself, that perforated class barriers without actually removing them. Trevelyan's celebrated dictum – 'If the French noblesse had been capable of playing cricket with their tenants their chateaux would never been have burnt' – is an epigrammatic reminder of how love of sport helped to stave off overt revolution in Britain.'[9]

Indeed it helped to preserve the notion of caste and feudality. When eventually new sporting ideals arose in the reorganised public schools, the pure doctrines of muscular Christianity, team spirit and the 'white man's burden' were somewhat alloyed by the fact that the old attitudes still flourished. In particular the legislators felt obliged to spend a great deal of time trying to reconcile old notions of gentlemanly privilege with the emergent idea of amateurism. Sport, amongst other things, is a dream-world offering escape from harsh reality and the disturbing prospect of change.

V

It follows, then, that the chronological pattern of this book has no connotations of progress but is merely intended to allow events, and the actors involved in them, to tell their own story more comprehensibly. If we go along with Strutt to the extent of agreeing that a people's sport and pastimes can give important clues to its character then the unfolding of its sporting history can help to explain how it became that way. As Toynbee put it, 'We live in a mental time-stream, remembering the past and looking forward – with hope or with fear – to an oncoming future.'[10]

The story begins with the Romans' return to the British Isles in AD 43. They had been forced to retire in embarrassment in 55 BC and when Caesar went back a year later it took a massive force, assisted by tribal rivalry, to subdue the

Catuvellanni and oblige their leader to pay an annual tribute, thus allowing Caesar to withdraw gracefully, and no doubt gratefully, from the scene. It was nearly a century later, after the Catuvellani had greatly enlarged their territory in breach of their treaty obligations, that the Emperor Claudius, needing a spectacular military victory to establish his shaky throne, took advantage of an appeal for help from the King of the Atrebates and persuaded his reluctant troops to embark on the outlandish task of conquering the troublesome British. As reward they hoped to collect booty in the form of gold, silver, and other metals and of prisoners to be taken hostage or sold as slaves. That conquest would be good for Britain went without saying.[11]

Notes

1 Joseph Strutt, *Glig-gamena angel deod: or The Sports and Pastimes of the People of England*, London, 1801; new edition 1903, reprinted Bath, 1969, p. xv.

2 Some useful background works are (a) Early sport: E. B. Tylor, 'The History of Games', *Fortnightly Review*, London, 1879, pp. 735–47, reprinted in E. M. Avedon and B. Sutton-Smith, *The Study of Games*, New York, 1971; E. N. Gardiner, *Athletics of the Ancient World*, Oxford, 1930; H. A. Harris, *Greek Athletes and Athletics*, London, 1969. (b) Particular games: J. Arlott, *Oxford Companion to Sports and Games*, Oxford, 1976. J. A. Cuddon, *MacMillan Dictionary of Sport and Games*, London, 1980: (c) Function of games; R. Caillou, *Man, Play and Games*, London, 1962, J. Huizinga *Homo Ludens*, Leyden, 1938, English translation, London, 1971. (d) Prehistory and the ancient world: R. E. Leakey, *The Making of Mankind*, London, 1987; W. H McNeill, *The Rise of the West*, Chicago, 1963; C. S. Coon, *The History of Man*, Harmondsworth, 1967; H. D. F. Kitto, *The Greeks*, Harmondsworth, 1951; J. Carcopino, *Daily Life in Ancient Rome*, London, 1937.

3 Homer, probably tenth century BC, *The Odyssey*, Book VIII, translation E. V. Rieu, Harmondsworth, 1946.

4 *The Iliad*, Book XXIII, translation E. V. Rieu, Harmondsworth, 1950.

5 In a fragment of a lost play *Autolycus*, c440 BC.

6 For general background see V. G. Childe, *The Prehistoric Communities of the British Isles*, Edinburgh, 1947; A. Ross, *Pagan Celtic Britain*, London, 1967.

7 J. Huizinga, *The Waning of the Middle Ages*, Amsterdam, 1919.

8 See the early criticism, for example, of William Paley, *Principles of Moral and Political Philosophy*, 1785.

9 G. M. Trevelyan, *English Social History*, London, 1944, p. 408.

10 A. Toynbee, *A Study of History*, one volume edition, London, 1988, p. 10.

11 For the Romans' motivation, see P. Salway, *Roman Britain*, Oxford, 1981, pp. 24–5, 65–72.

CHAPTER ONE

Rude beginnings
AD 43–1199

The inhabitants of the British Isles came slowly and gingerly to civilisation. Indeed they showed few signs of gratitude to the Romans who first tried to extend its benefits to them. Even in the more settled south and east of the bigger island, where inter-tribal conflict and political machinations weakened resistance, it was a long and sometimes bloody struggle. Around the Pennine chain the Brigantes, at first compliant, turned hostile and hindered expansion to the north. The southern part of what was to become Scotland was extensively occupied for a while but was eventually given up, and the Highlands remained unsullied. To the west, 'Wales', before and after conquest, was a centre of Brittonic resistance; no attempt was made to instil imperial virtues into the Irish Gaels.[1]

Within its limits, however, the Pax Romana worked out quite well. With peace came prosperity, of a sort, largely based on disposal of natural resources. The army's roads and bridges became useful links between the slave plantations of the Romano-British villas and the new urban centres of commerce that replaced earlier native settlements. The principal exports, the first century Greek geographer Strabo noted, were 'corn, cattle, gold, silver, iron . . . hides, slaves and clever hunting dogs'.[2] Before long basketry and wool cloaks joined the list of value added products, but it was on these dogs, which even attracted the attention of the fashionable epigrammatist Martial, that the British reputation chiefly rested. In a second century treatise on hunting Oppian grew lyrical about 'a valiant breed of tracking dogs, small indeed but as worthy as large dogs to be the theme of song, bred by the wild tribes of the painted Britons and called by the name of Agasseus' – an ill-favoured creature, dull-eyed but crafty and mighty sharp in tooth and claw.[3]

Britain was no place for the genteel but it was a hunting paradise. There were still forest bulls, descended from the great Stone Age aurochs, for pursuit or for use in sacrificial ceremonies, baiting or other arena sports. By the end of the fourth century the court poet Claudian was commending the British bulldog. Bears, a common enough quarry for Claudian to depict the typical north British female clad in bear skins, were also exported live to Rome, where they were in demand for sport of various kinds including the rectification of criminals. The most prestigious adversary was the boar, famous in Celtic mythology and fierce as they come. Wolves were a menace rather than an amenity, but the local wolf hounds were much admired: seven Irish dogs sent to the aristocrat Symmachus by his brother caused a stir in Rome in the late fourth century.

If the native breeds – bulldogs, mastiffs, boar-hounds – were noted for strength rather than speed or grace, other specialisms developed to meet new hunting fashions amongst the aristocracy. A favourite theme of the drinking cups turned out in quantity by British potteries was the pursuit of deer or hare by swift greyhound-types. In the south-west a Roman shrine to Diana, goddess of the chase, had stone reliefs of hunters carrying home deer as well as boar and a mosaic showing a doe slung by its legs from a pole.[4] A less idyllic contribution from the colonists was the sword-fight, another popular theme of the drinking cups and doubtless a big attraction in the amphitheatres the Romans built in Britain. Originating in the savage rituals for renewal of the god in primitive vegetation ceremonies and the source of sacrificial offerings in Etruscan times these *munera* (gifts to appease the wrath of the gods) had been institutionalised by the Romans, first as proxy offerings by hired performers at aristocratic funerals and later as state-sponsored gladiatorial contests.

Chariot-racing, which aroused great passion in imperial Rome, and which also appears on the cups and other remains, was undoubtedly brought to Britain. What else was on offer in the amphitheatres we can only surmise, but almost certainly there was wrestling, boxing and pankration (an all-in affair), perhaps horse-racing and foot-racing, as well as animal shows – cock-fighting, bear-baiting, wild beast shows, armed men against boars, bulls, wolves or whatever. Equally speculative are the ball-games the Romans may have brought. At home they played *harpastum*, based on a Greek original, a game with a small ball similar to that later called hurling in the west country, and *pila paganica*, village ball, with a small ball stuffed with feathers, and they had a ball called the *follis*, an inflated bladder in a leather case, and presumably they introduced these to the British. But the nineteenth century attributions of surviving folk-football games to the colonists are apocryphal, and intrinsically improbable.

It seems more likely that these mass encounters (such as the Haxey, Lincolnshire, hood game, at Epiphany and the Shrove Tuesday games at Derby, Ashbourne and Chester, and their Fasten's E'en counterparts at Scone, Perthshire, and elsewhere in Scotland) were of native origin. The Celts certainly played a similar game, *la Soule* or *la Choule*, in Normandy. And in primeval times it probably derived from fertility or sacrificial rites, a reminder that play is a survival mechanism.[5]

Whatever their sporting interests the early Britons were obviously not yet ready for urban civilisation. In most towns public buildings – forum, basilica, balneae – lasted only as long as the Roman occupation. The decline of the balneae, or public baths, had a double significance for they were not only places to bathe, a practice that might in itself be thought worth encouraging, but leisure centres, with physical exercise and games halls and places where you could play board games like 'twelve lines', 'soldiers' and the dice-game 'tables'. The baths were an emblem of the Graeco-Roman ideal of a healthy mind in a healthy body, a balanced concept that held little intrinsic appeal for the local tribes.

The word and the sword

The Britons were no more urbane in spiritual than in temporal matters. The Romans, pagan, polytheistic and inclined to emperor-worship, tried to suppress the more outlandish manifestations of British druidism but otherwise allowed the local gods, Nordic as well as Celtic, to co-exist and even cohabit with their own pantheon. By contrast native fervour and intolerance found a new outlet in Christianity – probably brought in by enthusiasts in the army who had picked it up in Gaul – and this had become the most popular religion in Britain by the third century. It was still a tender plant, however, and when in AD 410 the Romans, under barbarian attack at home, left the province to fend for itself the Christian church was one of the immediate casualties, something of an irrelevance in the next two hundred years.

The opportunistic north European tribes who moved in as the grass grew over the products of Roman technology brought no new religious ideas. Indeed they reasserted older values: their gods – Woden, Thunor, Tia, Frig and the rest – were commemorated in days of the week along with the elemental forces of moon and sun and the influential Saturn, who presided over the mid-winter festival the Norsemen called Yule and the Romans Saturnalia. Many Roman holidays were also retained and absorbed. In the first century the Roman calendar already had 159 public holidays (93 of which featured publicly or privately sponsored games) and in AD 213 all free-born provincials were given Roman citizenship with attendant privileges.

Once granted, such liberties are not easily removed. In 597 when the cultured monk Augustine was asked by Pope Gregory to lead a missionary venture from the now-Christianised Rome to the former province he advised Mellitus, chosen as Bishop of London, not to forbid animal sacrifices and other heathen practices but to try to make them over, declaring 'If the people are allowed some worldly pleasure in this way, they will more readily come to desire the joys of the spirit.'[6] This may have been good theology but it was bad psychology, and it proved hard to turn holidays, with their fairs and other opportunities for licence, into holy days. Before long Augustine, baffled by the insular outlook of local bishops, was obliged to withdraw and the eventual Christian conquest of Britain was as much a political as a moral affair.

To say that it had a unifying effect would be misleading. Bede declared Britain to be a land of four nations – English, British, Scots and Picts – each

11

with its own language but united in their study of God's truth by a fifth, Latin.[7] But the church in Ireland, from whose north-western corner the Scots went to try to convert the heathen Picts of Caledonia, and whose missionaries penetrated south Wales, clashed with that of England, which was Romanised politically as well as spiritually. By the ninth century Anglo-Saxon colonists, pagan, Germanic and militaristic, controlled the land from the river Forth to the south coast and as far west as the Dee and Tamar. Within this territory during the periods of dominance enjoyed in turn by Northumbria, Mercia and Wessex between AD 600 and 1000 conquering kings found Christianity increasingly helpful to the maturing arts of holding on to and exploiting land and property, and they made generous expiatory gifts in return.

This expedient arrangement was all very well, but it had to reconcile opposing philosophies. The society of the Angles who gave their name to the emergent England and the fierce Saxons who set its tone depended on the principle of loyalty – between the king and his thanes and between them and the cheorl and slave classes – traditionally sustained by the blood feud and the duty of vengeance. This was hard to square with the Christian teaching of forgiveness. The church authorities, nevertheless, threw a cloak over the blood-letting by sanctifying the oath of allegiance to a lord.[8]

The veneer was pretty thin. Thus the epic poem *Beowulf* has a Christian message and periodically cites the scriptures, but its prevailing tone is of bleak ferocity mellowed only by Homeric echoes. The minstrelsy and feasting are given due ritual weight and the honour code by which Beowulf lives is exemplified not only in fending off marauding Danes and fearsome monsters but in sport. In a passage reminiscent of Odysseus in Phaeacia Beowulf puts a local blowhard in his place when taunted with losing a swimming match. His honour impugned, he describes how he came to accept the challenge, a rugged affair in which the competitors had swum in the open sea for five days and nights, carrying swords for protection against whales, until eventually the waves threw them apart and Beowulf was waylaid by sea-monsters. He fought them off, killing nine before being washed up exhausted on a beach. Then, with due modesty, the hero explains that he has spoken out not to brag but to contrast this kind of healthy sporting outlet with the evil ways of his accuser who had stained his blade with the blood of his brothers and who dare not face the monster Grendel.[9]

Our knowledge of British sport in the Dark Ages is limited. The ninth century Welsh scholar Nennius refers to boys in the fifth century quarrelling over a ball game (*ludus pilae*) which he does not describe.[10] An Anglo-Saxon didactic poem *The Endowments of Man* lists equitation, swimming, running and archery as fitting sports for training young men for the rigours of war. A *Rhyming Poem* writes of a horse, gaily caparisoned, carrying a young nobleman 'with long strides delightfully across the plains'. A *Runic Poem* describes the horse as 'the joy of princes' and 'the solace of the restless'. *Beowulf* tells of courtiers, returning from the monster's lair, racing whenever the ground is suitable. At places subject to Scandinavian invasion, place-names record horse-racing; Anglo-Saxon places commemorate horse-fighting. The church tried to control the misuse of holy days. In 747 the Council of Clofeshoh forbade sports and horse-racing on Rogation Days.[11]

What it could not control was hunting, the supreme sporting experience, the truly royal sport. It was a passionate addiction of the new rulers of Europe, including Charlemagne, the founder of western Christendom, and such men expected and got the imprimatur of the church. Charlemagne's tutor, the high-minded Alcuin of York, warned the monks of Wearmouth and Jarrow not to let young clergy go digging out foxes from their earths or coursing hares; but they took little notice, and built up the wrath of the Lord in consequence. They were aping their betters. Bishop Asser wrote of the concern of Alfred of Wessex (877–99) that his young courtiers should have formal education whilst preparing for 'hunting and other pursuits which are fitting for noblemen'. And Alfred himself used field sports in the introduction to a religious work as an allegory for earthly anticipation of heavenly bliss: 'every man when he has built a homestead on land leased to him by his lord . . . likes to . . . go hunting, fishing and fowling'.[12] Such imagery was fashionable. When Alfred, seeking help for his educational reforms, sent a present of choice hunting dogs to Archbishop Fulco of Rheims, the prelate's reply compared using such dogs to drive away 'the fury of visible wolves . . . with which our country graciously abounds' to the Christian task of fending off spiritual evils.[13]

This was somewhat disingenuous. Wolves were not what the best people chased. And the upper clergy was to the fore in hound-breeding, a highly sophisticated art dedicated almost entirely to the pleasure principle. But above all hunting was socially prestigious. Around the end of the tenth century when the homilist Abbot Ælfric, in a *Colloquy* to help students learn Latin, included the king's huntsman amongst his examples, he presented an heroic picture. Some beasts were driven into nets and stabbed but the fleet-footed were chased and brought down by hounds. The boar was the dangerous one, needing to be ambushed and speared. The kill went to the king who in return fed and clothed the huntsman and gave him presents of horses and rings. 'I hold first place in his hall', the huntsman proudly claimed.[14]

Ælfric's fisherman was of lower status, lacking royal patronage, working in rivers and estuaries (others went into the open sea, even whaling), using nets, hooks, bait or creels to catch trout, lampreys, eels and pike, which sold readily in the town. The fowler was equally eclectic in method, trapping with nets, snares or bird-lime, or using decoy whistles. The prestigious end of his job was training hawks for the aristocracy, to many of whom hawking was true bliss. Hawks, indeed, figured frequently in treaties between kings and their vanquished rivals, and in deals with thanes obligated by land-grants or with ecclesiastical or secular authorities who were required to provide hospitality and entertainment as the monarch moved around his realm with his vast retinue of 'feasting men'.

Bear-baiting (for which the city of Norwich, for example, was obliged to supply a bear and six dogs on the king's visits) was an indispensable feature of royal entertainment. Sometimes it was possible to buy exemption from such open-ended commitments. In 855 the Bishop of Worcester paid three hundred shillings to be rid of an obligation which included 'feeding of any hawks or falcons or any huntsman of king or ealdorman'. (Ealdormen were the king's regional deputies.) The Domesday Book later recorded many financial hang-overs from the past: for instance, six counties were each paying ten pounds a year to fulfil their duty to provide hawks.

Systems and survival

During the ninth century the balance of cultures in the British Isles – and the dominance of the Anglo-Saxons – was rudely shattered by the Vikings. Coming first in their long ships as raiders Norsemen set up trading posts at Dublin, Cork, Waterford and Limerick, bringing the first taste of town life to the Irish, and Danes colonised much of eastern Britain, bringing the first experience to the Anglo-Saxons of what it felt like to be second-class citizens in what had become their own country. The Danes also brought a new pagan challenge to the English church. King Alfred led the resistance and Wessex became a rallying point for nationalistic Christianity. Nevertheless the Danelaw left a lasting mark on Britain.

The Irish had their own anti-Viking hero, Brian Boru, whose dynasty, the O'Briens, became new-style regional kings of Munster, contending with their counterparts in Leinster, Connaught and Ulster, all of them forging alliances with the church in the hope of supremacy. The Welsh, also carving out kingdoms, had less trouble with Norsemen than with the Saxons of Wessex, but the Vikings occupied the northern and western isles off the Caledonian coast and penetrated mainland Caithness and Sutherland, driving together the Picts and the Scots whose king annexed the Pictish throne in 843 to form the kingdom of Alba.

The Danelaw appeared in a new guise under Cnut (1016–35) a Christian magnifico who made England the base for his European operations. He brought greater system to its affairs, replacing the old Anglo-Saxon ealdormen by his own earls, establishing new hierarchies, clerical as well as lay, in return for unquestioned obedience. His game laws, which earned a reputation for extreme severity but essential justice, were written to his specification by Wulfstan, Archbishop of York.

After Cnut, the succession fell on Edward the Confessor (1042–60) the least improbable of many contenders. Edward, brought up in exile with time on his hands, had devoted much of it to hunting, and despite a later reputation for piety his youthful passion remained. His chronicler put a brave face on it:

> And so with the Kingdom made safe on all sides the most kindly Edward passed his life in security and peace, and spent much of his time in the glades and woods in the pleasures of hunting. After divine service, which he gladly and devoutly attended every day, he took much pleasure in hawks and was really delighted by the baying and scrambling of the hounds. In these and such like activities he sometimes spent the day, and it was in these alone that he seemed naturally inclined to snatch some worldly pleasure.[15]

The notion that hunting was a fitting sport for a Christian king, a deserved reward when his military and social obligations had been discharged, fitted well with feudalism, an élitist code of honour masquerading as a mutual benefit scheme.

This was developed further by the Norman conquest. Duke William of Normandy and his henchmen, descended from Viking invaders, not only swept aside the aristocracy but imposed their own laws and adopted language on Britain, bringing it forcibly into the mainstream of European social and economic development. William drove a hard feudal bargain, taking all the land into his own possession and rewarding those who had delivered the conquest with generous baronies – called fees or honors – in return for military allegiance but on lease and scattered about the country to discourage private empire-building. This assisted a colonising process that followed military conquest by skilful economic exploitation, setting the new aristocracy above and across the four emergent nation states. The conquest of Wales, hard upon that of England, paved the way for the later invasion of Ireland where the great slices of land appropriated by Norman grandees like the Earl of Pembroke were subsequently put under royal control. The first history of Ireland was written by an ambitious Pembroke courtier, Giraldus Cambrensis.[16] The process was less direct in Scotland whose eleventh and twelfth century kings increasingly ruled with Norman aid, bringing in many Anglo-Norman families and rewarding them with lands and offices.

The code the Normans brought, though feudal, was not yet chivalric. The barons' lieutenants were armour-clad cavalry men sitting proudly astride their destriers, the great war-horses which had taken Europe by storm, but they were a miscellaneous bunch, often specially recruited by the barons to discharge the obligation they owed William. They owed their title, knights, to a scornful nickname arising from their peace-time duties of attendance on their lords: the disgruntled English aristocracy called them cnihtas, serving lads. Some were given or acquired land, but there were always plenty of knights bachelor looking for a chance of fame, and perhaps a ransom or two in battle. If there was no foreign war they looked for adventure at home.

In Normandy bloodthirsty private fights between barons and knights had long been a menace that defied control. Single combat had become an authorised method of settling disputes under the code of laws issued by the influential King Gundobad of Burgundy in the Dark Ages. But the mêlées and skirmishes that were rife on the continent were held in check by the force of William's personality and his judicious distribution of largesse.

William I brought not only feudal order but passion to the regulation of hunting. As William of Malmesbury put it, 'the King loved the tall deer as if he were their father'[17] and to demonstrate this paternal affection he kept great tracts of woodland for his own use and under his own private jurisdiction. Some English shires, like Kent, were already too much infiltrated by agriculture to be good hunting territory; Norfolk and Suffolk also escaped, but these were the exception. In the north Sherwood Forest in Nottinghamshire, High Peak and Macclesfield in Derbyshire, North York and Pickering, huge areas of Northumberland, Allerdale and Inglewood in Cumberland and Lonsdale and Amounderness in Lancashire came under Forest law. Further south was the great forest between Oxford and Stamford Bridge. Around London, nearly all Essex was royal forest and to the west the royal preserve ran from Windsor to the New Forest of Hampshire and on down to the coast.

Forest law was not based on landownership but on privileges granted by the king; even barons who owned land in the forest could only hunt on it by royal favour. William I's sparing and shrewd award of hunting privileges, designed to secure the co-operation of the concessionaires in the control of poaching, was chiefly aimed at conserving deer. By then the more rugged kinds of hunting, such as facing a boar on foot with a spear, were losing their popularity with the nobility. Indeed it was a difficult task even for the professionals – Edward the Confessor had given his huntsman, Nigel, an estate for killing a boar. Deer were a much less dangerous quarry: they could be attacked from a safe distance with a crossbow and were much more fun to chase since they offered great scope for strategy and tactics involving the use of several types of dog. Hound-breeding was already a highly-developed science, in monasteries as well as manor-houses.

In earlier times the church had tended to dominate the state. William I, though a devout Christian, was an autocrat who put the preservation of his own territory and rights first, even against the Pope. He naturally expected his lords spiritual to exercise the same feudal authority and to render him the same service as lords temporal. In return they were given the same privileges. Those who accepted these conditions were not greatly admired by home-grown subordinates. It also caused great offence that churches were destroyed for the sake of the New Forest, and the deaths of two of the Conqueror's sons on the hunting field were widely believed to be acts of divine retribution.[18]

After the Conqueror

The sons were a strange lot. The eldest, weak and lazy, had been packed off to Normandy. The second, William 'Rufus', despite being groomed for the succession by his father's faithful supporter Archbishop Lanfranc, was a blasphemer with little interest in anything but hunting, military exercises and nameless depravity. As William II he had more need to reward friends and placate enemies than his father and it was he who granted Cranborne Chase, full hunting rights over some 300,000 acres, to Robert FitzHaymon. The third son, Henry I, who came to the throne in 1100, probably got there by conspiring to kill Rufus, and he showed the same ruthlessness in putting down an early baronial revolt and ensuring peace in the realm for the next thirty-five years.

His forest laws were as harsh as those of Cnut and he granted few privileges to anyone else, even rights of warren (permission to hunt lesser animals like hare, fox, wild-cat and badger). And he forbade all private battles, including the new-fangled tourneys or tournaments that were rife in Flanders, France and Germany. These events, which the Council of Clermont, banning them, called 'detestable markets or fairs at which knights are accustomed to meet to show their strength', had, ironically, been given a boost by Pope Urban II's call to arms which led to the First Crusade in 1095.[19] Apart from legitimising violence the Crusades introduced the cavalry tactic of the couched lance and also popularised the quintain (a post for tilting at) as a training device.[20]

So, early in the twelfth century, mêlées starting with a mass cavalry open fight and developing into close-quarter sword and mailed-fist tussles were all the rage. They spread to Britain eventually in the confused aftermath of Henry I's death: King Stephen, a fighting man with no talent for politics and a romantic view of knighthood, shared his barons' enthusiasm for the new sport. It was in Stephen's time that Geoffrey of Monmouth wrote a fanciful history glorifying the legendary King Arthur and his gallant knights.

Geoffrey's fictional account of a tournament had everything – pageantry, feasting, drinking, sex – and all conducted in a sporting spirit:

> Britain had reached such a standard of sophistication that it excelled all other
> kingdoms in its general affluence, the richness of its decorations and the
> courteous behaviour of all its inhabitants. Every knight in the country who
> was in any way famed for his bravery wore livery and arms showing his own

distinctive colour: and women of fashion often displayed the same colours. They scorned to give their love to any man who had not proved himself three times in battle. In this way the womenfolk became chaste and more virtuous and for their love the knights were even more daring.

Invigorated by the food and drink they had consumed, they went out into the meadows outside the city and split up into groups ready to play various games. The knights planned an imitation battle and competed together on horseback while their women folk watched from the top of the city walls and aroused them to passionate excitement by their flirtatious behaviour. The others passed what remained of the day in shooting with bows and arrows, hurling the lance, tossing heavy stones and rocks, playing dice and an immense variety of other games: this without the slightest show of ill-feeling. Whoever won his particular game was then rewarded by Arthur with an immense prize.[21]

In reality the knights were sometimes far from chivalrous. William of Malmesbury told of an incident in 1141 when King Stephen and his supporters, confronted by the Earl of Gloucester's knights with whom they were in conflict, started to perform 'the prelude to battle, which they call a joust, because they were skilled in the art', but were ridden down by their opponents who just wanted to get on with the battle.[22] Chivalry was perhaps in the eye of the partisan beholder: these same boorish fellows were acclaimed in another account for their daily expeditions to perform gallant deeds whilst besieging Winchester.[23] More to the point, Stephen's enthusiasm for the tournament undoubtedly contributed to the near-anarchy of his last year at the helm.

Discipline returned in 1154 with the twenty year old Henry II. This remarkable young man was not only King of England but, through inheritance and marriage, Duke of Normandy, Count of Anjou and Maine and Duke of Aquitaine, which no doubt contributed to his self-assurance and sense of style. His soldierly skills, shrewd administrative know how and feel for legislation enabled him to impose his rule throughout the British Isles, subduing not only local chiefs but his own magnates, by a mixture of firmness and expediency. He was scarcely out of the saddle, either hunting or endlessly patrolling his territory, and although of the thirty-four years of his reign only eleven were spent in Britain, his impact on this somewhat backward region was tremendous. One of his most successful innovations was the jury system, in which twelve freeholders or knights heard evidence before the king's travelling justices, which not only curbed baronial power but brought a less explosive and more rational alternative to trial by combat. Accepting scutage, shield money, in lieu of military service, left him scope to hire mercenaries and helped to discourage private armies. In hunting, his generosity in granting rights of warren, usually on magnates' own estates but occasionally in the Forest, helped control poaching and also kept down vermin such as fox, hare, wild-cat, badger and squirrel which in various ways incommoded game birds and beasts of the chase – red deer, fallow deer, roe deer and the dwindling numbers of boar.

The king and his barons were at one in the restriction of the lower orders: by this time only the coney (rabbit) was fair game for everyone, apart of course from the old enemy, the wolf. Naturally, however, contemporary critics were more inclined to blame the magnates. As John of Salisbury complained 'hunting and hawking are esteemed the most honourable employments of our nobility and . . . they prepare for them with more solicitude, expense and parade than they do for war'. He reckoned hunting a poor hare lowered men almost to the level of animals and thought it outrageous that poor farmers tilling their land and tending their flocks should be harassed by heedless grandees crashing into their fields.[24] The nobility, of course, had to operate under the common law whilst Henry enjoyed the exclusive use of the Forest. This privilege was justified by apologists such as Richard FitzNeale, the Royal Treasurer: 'The Forest has its own laws, based not on the common law of the realm but on arbitrary regulation by the King.' This was justified, he reckoned, by the mounting pressures imposed by the feudal bargain: 'In the forests are the secret places of the Kings and their great delights. To them they go for hunting so that they may enjoy a little quiet. There, away from the continuous business and incessant turmoil of the court they can for a little time breathe in the grace of natural liberty.[25]

One of the attractions of colonising Ireland to magnates such as the Earl of Pembroke was the hunting. Giraldus Cambrensis offered a mouth-watering prospect – stags 'that are not able to escape because of their too-great fatness', a uniquely abundant supply of boars and pigs (though admittedly 'small, badly-formed and inclined to run away') and 'none but the best breed of falcons'.[26] More to the point it was outside the royal Forest. But very little escaped Henry II's notice. In 1171, after two preliminary ventures by Pembroke and others, he went to Ireland himself to accept their homage and that of the more biddable Irish chiefs.

Urban stirrings

Hunting was one of the favourite pursuits of the young Thomas Becket who was to become Henry's Archbishop of Canterbury. Becket, a well-connected merchant's son, found the sport a social asset on his way to the top and as Chancellor he frequently joined the King in this and other courtly amusements. As Archbishop, however, he began to aspire to sainthood and gave up such worldly vanities. His transformation sharpened the edges of the quarrel with the King over the precedence of canon or common law which led to his exile and eventual murder.

Christian folk everywhere were outraged and though Henry lived down the scandal, a coded but barbed attack was made on him towards the end of his reign by the martyred Archbishop's biographer. Theology apart, the clash between Archbishop and King reflected the aspirations of a new, grammar-school educated urban bourgeoisie for whom the church was the best available route to power. Becket was also a Londoner. London was a threat to the doctrine of feudalism. Its gilds, originally fraternities of knighthood, had extended the principle of mutual benevolence to trade and London's prosperity and consequent independence of outlook was a thorn in the flesh of central government. So William FitzStephen was trailing his coat by including a glowing account of London's amenities in the preface to his biography.[27]

He noted for instance that London citizens enjoyed the ancient privilege of hunting in Middlesex, Hertfordshire, all Chiltern and Kent as far as the river Cray – in fact just outside the royal Forest – where there were wild beasts such as stags, fallow deer and wild bulls. Every week at Smithfield – a 'smooth field' just outside the City gates – there was a market at which earls, barons, knights and other citizens came to inspect the fine array of horses for sale, including magnificent and costly destriers, and races were held to demonstrate quality. There were also contests with lance and shield which sound suspiciously like tournaments.

Politics apart, FitzStephen also offers a rare glimpse of the pleasures of ordinary folk. He describes in glowing terms the public cook-shop with its wine, roast, fried and boiled meats and fish great and small. Naturally it was the coarser food for the poor, the more delicate for the rich such as venison and poultry. The wine seems to have been a special attraction, for FitzStephen later says that the only plagues of London are the immoderate drinking of fools and the frequency of fires.

No doubt a good deal was drunk at the holiday sports, which were many and varied. At Easter there were water-sports, including one using boats from which the contestants tried to hit a target with a lance as they passed. In summer there were jumping, wrestling, casting the stone, archery, spear-throwing and sword-fighting for the men and dancing for the women, whilst on winter feast days there was bull- bear- or boar-baiting, and when the Moorfields marshes froze over men strapped bones to their shoes and propelled themselves with pointed sticks across the ice.

Shrove Tuesday, the great carnival before Lent, was a special day for schoolboys. In the morning, on receipt of his cock-penny, the master would cancel lessons so that his pupils could match the fighting cocks they had trained for the occasion.[28] This educational custom survived for many years and its passing was bemoaned by traditionalists. Cock-fighting itself remained a fashionable and popular diversion, declining in reputation as the squeamish middle classes grew in influence but still an attraction to the raffish, rich and poor alike, in the nineteenth century.

For the medieval students of London and their counterparts in industry the holiday was not over. After lunch they went to play 'the famous game of Ball' (*ad ludum Pilae celebrem*) on a level ground near the city (probably Smithfield). 'Scholars from every place of learning and workers in the various occupations of the town played their own games of Ball, whilst older men, fathers and rich men from the city on horseback, watched the young men's contests, being young along with them in their own way, showing a natural excitement at so much action and sharing in the uninhibited pleasures of youth '[29]

We are told no more about these games but they may have included football which was so prominent in the later history of Shrove Tuesday sport. Annual tussles, village against village with the ball being captured and carried home in triumph, or married versus single, with the ball provided by newly weds, were part of ancient manorial custom. They were tolerated and even encouraged by parish clergy, some of whom provided the ball, as part of the pre-Lenten carnival, a good way of letting off steam. Lords of the manor were often hosts at the celebrations. And later, in more urban communities, Shrove Tuesday football matches were sponsored by the various craft gilds with special reference to the initiation of apprentices.

Modelled on earlier gilds of knights, the craft and trade gilds were now becoming prominent in urban social and economic life. They sought to exercise monopolies, often purchasing royal or baronial permission to exact local tolls: these were collected from stallholders at weekly markets and bigger seasonal and annual fairs which were also a focal point for professional entertainers and for popular sporting contests. Nationally the gilds' influence grew with the increased output of agricultural products and especially wool. The cloth industry eventually built up such strong gilds of weavers, fullers and the like that their tariffs provoked first domestic and then international reprisals. (One disagreeable result was heavy duty on imported wine, which was far better than the local product. Drinking, on its own or as an essential part of festivals and sporting activities, was the principal British leisure pursuit.)[30]

Urban and commercial life was still essentially a support to that of the countryside in which 90% of the people lived, working mostly as farmers and fishermen. The Domesday survey of rural England in 1087 had revealed, beneath the tiny group of feudal aristocrats who lived sumptuously on the rents the farmers paid, a stratified society. Some 14% were freemen holding 20% of the land, 40% were villeins holding 45%, 32% borders and cotters held only 5%, and the 9% who were serfs had none at all. There was no dramatic change in this as the population slowly grew from perhaps 1.5 million in 1066 to about 2 million in 1200.

But there was some increase in trade and industry. Shipping flourished as exports grew – in wool, cloth, timber, salt, grain and wine. Industrial growth mainly centred on mining, which had languished since Roman times, and pottery, most of it fairly crude but hinting at latent manufacturing skill. Yet there was nothing like the extent of urbanisation of Flanders, the chief market, and until the Gascons and Italians came to the fore in the thirteenth century, the chief centre of the import–export trade and banking.[31]

The crusading spirit

Britain's urban and mercantile wealth was eventually to undermine feudalism – but not yet. Indeed local trade monopolies were a rich source of income for the aristocracy. Many boroughs in Scotland, Ireland and Wales were virtually little colonies run by Flemish or English immigrants who enjoyed royal or baronial support. This, together with the sanctions of religious and military obligation to the king, underpinned the Norman hierarchy. Henry II tightened his grip in the Assize of Arms, 1181, which required service according to rank, each man providing his own, appropriate weapon and accoutrements, and the Assize of the Forest, 1134, which required even earls and barons to attend swanimotes, the forest courts called to try offenders against vert and venison, the greenwood and the game.

But the last years of his reign were clouded by quarrels between his four sons over the disposition of the territories they were to inherit. The second son, Richard, allocated Aquitaine, bore down so heavily on his rebellious barons that the third, Geoffrey, allocated Brittany, and the eldest, Henry, who was to inherit Anjou, Normandy and England, joined the barons against him. In the event Henry and Geoffrey both died – one from a tournament wound, the other from dysentery – and Richard scooped the pool. He did not stay long in England, returning to Aquitaine and then embarking with the King of France on the Third Crusade, in which he achieved great success against the dreaded Saladin. Crusading was now the ultimate test of the chivalric ideal, and Richard I won great renown throughout Europe.

During his reign, as a result of his obsession with his sacred mission, Britain was not so much neglected as exploited. He sold offices of state, called royal privilege into question by licensing assarts (pockets of Forest woodland converted to arable use) and even selling Forest land, and he designated five official tournament sites in England. This risked conflict with the pope, for the church, despite its militancy against the infidel, continually – though not surprisingly with little effect – threatened to excommunicate those who took part in tournaments and to deny Christian burial to those killed in them.

According to William of Newburgh his motives were sound: 'The famous King Richard, observing that the extra training and instruction of the French made them correspondingly fierce in war, wished that the knights of his kingdom should train in their own lands, so that they could learn from tourneying the art and custom of war'.[32] In fact he did it for profit: he charged fees – a flat rate of ten marks for a licence and a performing fee on a graduated scale according to rank, from twenty marks for an earl to two marks for a landless knight. He also no doubt hoped to moderate the effects of the tournament by institutionalising it. With this in mind he did not allow French knights to compete and he authorised tournaments only on condition that 'our peace shall not be broken, the power of our justiciar shall not be threatened and loss shall not fall on our royal forests'.[33] The special oath he demanded required contestants to respect the royal rights of vert and vension.

The effects were profound, for politics and for sport. On the one hand tournaments became something of a badge of defiance for disaffected magnates. More positively, though, English kings soon felt obliged to join in the sport themselves and those who took pleasure in doing so not only won local popularity, but became part of the European élite. By contrast the rulers of France, who tried to enforce prohibitions of tournaments in accordance with papal wishes for another century, set themselves apart from their nobility.[34]

The chivalric code, in which every knight had to have a lady whose integrity he defended and for whom he carried out valorous deeds, was both a secular version of the spreading cult of the Virgin Mary and a sentimentalising of the old warrior code of honour in which truth and justice were put to the test and decided by combat. The reality of the tournament was cruder. It was still essentially a mass activity, a mêlée or free-for-all, and, apart from an emphasis on capture rather than killing, there was little to distinguish it from the real thing. Successful practitioners like William the Marshal, a veteran of the French circuit who was to become Regent of England, regarded them as professional opportunities rather than emblems of chivalry: William's concern was more with ransom money than impressing ladies.

Yet the powerful mythology of the age was not that of the old scop or glee-man with his tales of battles in strange lands but of the troubadours, Provençal lyricists rhapsodising about courtly love and the chivalric ideal. The dominant cultural influence was French: the first surviving appearance of King Arthur's famous Round Table is in a French enhancement of Geoffrey of Monmouth's Latin text, fifty years before the first known English version.[35] In practice Richard I's captivity and death in the Crusades left

England in a tangle. But the French poets gave him the dashing romantic image that still survives. And the Lionheart's brother, John, who tried to take over the throne while Richard was held captive, never lived it down.

Notes

1 See P. Salway, *Roman Britain*, Oxford, 1981, Chapter 4–8; I.A. Richmond *Roman Britain*, Harmondsworth, 1955, Chapter 1; H. Kearney, *The British Isles*, Cambridge, 1989, Chapter 2.
2 *Geographia*, AD c20, ed. H.L. Jones, Cambridge, Mass., 1917, IV v.2.
3 *Cynegeticus*, AD c80, ed. A.W. Moir, Cambridge, Mass., 1928, p. 69.
4 Richmond, *Roman Britain*, esp. pp. 162–4.
5 For a discussion of the various theories see M. Marples, *A History of Football*, London, 1954, pp. 1–18.
6 Bede, *History of the English Church and People*, AD 731, ed. L. Sherley-Price, Harmondsworth, 1955, Book 1, Chapter 30.
7 Ibid., Book I, Chapter 1.
8 D. Whitelock, *The Beginnings of English Society*, Harmondsworth, 1952, Chapter 2.
9 *The Lay of Beowulf*, prob. mid eighth century, trans. C.W. Kennedy, 1940, extract in F. Kermode and J. Hollander (eds.), *Oxford Anthology of English Literture*, 2 vols., Oxford, 1973, vol. 1 pp. 41–3.
10 *Historia Brittonum*, c850, trans. J.A. Giles, London, 1912, p. 402, quoted in F.P. Magoun, *History of Football from the Beginnings to 1871*, Cologne, 1938. Magoun's copious references have been drawn on freely by all later writers: in these notes such use is indicated by adding his name in brackets.
11 See R.I. Page, *Life in Anglo-Saxon England*, London, 1970. Hesket, Cumberland and Hesketh, Yorkshire and Lancashire derive from Old Norse hestaskeith = race track for horses: Follifoot and Follithwaite, Yorkshire from Old English folage-feocht = horsefight. For the poems see *The Exeter Book of English Poetry*, London, 1933.
12 'St Augustine's Soliloquies' in *Alfred the Great*, ed. S. Keynes and M. Lepidge, Harmondsworth, 1983, p. 139.
13 Ibid., p. 184.
14 Whitelock, *Beginnings* p. 105
15 *Life of Edward the Confessor*, c1066–75, ed. F. Barlow, London, 1962, quoted in C. Brooke, *The Saxon and Norman Kings*, London, 1963, p. 62.
16 Gerald of Wales (Giraldus Cambrensis), *The History and Topography of Ireland*, 1185 onwards, ed. J. O'Meara, Harmondsworth, 1982.
17 *Gesta Regum Anglorum*, c1130, ed. W. Stubbs, London, 1887, quoted in Brooke, *Saxon and Norman Kings*, p. 68.
18 For the social and cultural background see Brooke, *Saxon and Norman Kings*, Chapter 3 and D.M. Stenton, *English Society in the Early Middle Ages*, Harmondsworth, 1951, passim.
19 See R. Barber and J. Barker, *Tournaments*, Woodbridge, 1989, p. 17, the standard modern work.
20 The quintain was a suspended dummy figure, often in the guise of a Saracen, at which the lancer rode: properly struck it fell down; otherwise a counterweight swung round to hit the rider.
21 *The History of the Kings of Britain*, c1136, ed. L. Thorpe, Harmondsworth, 1966, pp. 229–30.
22 *Historia Novella*, c1190, ed. K.R. Potter, Oxford, 195, pp. 48–9, quoted in Barber and Barker, *Tournaments*, pp. 18–19.

23 *L'histoire de Guillaume le Maréchal*, ed. P. Meyer, Paris, 1901, II 175–8, quoted in Barber and Barker, *Tournaments*, p. 19.
24 *Polycraticus*, c1159, ed. J. Dickinson, New York, 1927, pp. 135–6.
25 *Dialogus de Scaccario*, c1170, ed. C. Johnson, London, 1950, pp. 59–60.
26 Giraldus, *Ireland*, pp. 47–8.
27 Preface to *Vita Sancti Thomae*, c1185, trans. H.E. Butler in *Norman London*, ed. F.M. Stenton, 2nd edn, London, 1934.
28 Cockpence, originally awarded to pay for housing and keeping the fighting cocks, became a perquisite for schoolmasters. The custom survived long after the schools stopped staging the fights, particularly in the north of England where school-masters' reluctance to give up this augmentation of their salaries kept it going until the nineteenth century. *Oxford English Dictionary*, 2nd edition, 1989.
29 Translations of the relevant paragraphs from the original Latin, which is con-veniently printed in P.M. Young, *The History of British Football*, London 1973 edn, p. 32, are generally unhelpful, and the original is somewhat terse. The paraphrase given here may be more helpful.
30 Apart from wine, ale, a north European speciality, was drunk in vast quantities, especially in rural areas and amongst the lower orders. It was cheap, brewed locally (from malt until the sixteenth century) and its consumption was increased not only by fear of polluted water supplies but by the ale-drinking contests, such as scotales, which featured in every holiday celebration. See A.L. Poole, *From Domesday Book to Magna Carta*, Oxford, 1954, pp. 60–2 (ale consumption) and 93 (wine tariffs).
31 J. Gillingham, 'The Early Middle Ages' in *The Oxford Illustrated History of Britain*, ed. K.O. Morgan, Oxford, 1984, pp. 157–63.
32 *Historia Regum Anglicarum*, c1180, in *Chronicles of the Reigns of Stephen, Henry II and Richard I*, ed. R. Howlett, London, 1889, vol. 2 pp. 422–3.
33 T. Rymer, *Foedera*, London 1816, vol. I, p. 65.
34 For the importance of Richard I in the history of tournaments see Barber and Barker, *Tournaments* pp. 24–7.
35 R. Wace, *Li Romans di Brut*, c1155, Layamon, *Brut* c1200.

CHAPTER TWO

'Christian service and true chivalry'

1200–1485

Magna Carta, the Great Charter King John was made to sign in 1215, sought to put limits on the prerogatives of the crown, but the result satisfied neither side. After John's death the barons saw an opportunity to grab more power, for his successor, Henry III, was a child. But there were royalist earls as well as rebels and they included old William the Marshal, now Earl of Pembroke, who became regent. He and his associates, along with the papal legate, not only scotched the rebels' schemes but revised the Charter to shift the balance of power back a little in their protégé's favour. They also prohibited tournaments, which were both a symbol of defiance and a cover for plotting rebellions.

This was rather like forbidding adultery. Making it illegal did not stop the practice: indeed even the appearance of the Archbishop of Canterbury at a tournament in Staines had no effect. At first the young King, who was nervous, pious and aesthetically inclined, went along with the prohibition but after he came of age he was put under great pressure by friends as well as enemies and began to vacillate. In 1228 he not only interceded with the Pope to allow a tournament but ordered his own household knights to attend it. In 1232 he authorised four. Then, following a rebellion, he changed his tack and tried to stop tournaments altogether. The only effect was to encourage less orderly, unlicensed events. In 1236 an encounter between northern and southern knights turned into a real battle requiring the intervention of the Papal Legate. And in 1242 the Earl of Atholl was murdered in his bed by an opponent he had unhorsed in a Scottish versus English hastilude at Haddington.[1]

The tournament and the code

Yet, however bloody, the tournament and the code on which it was based had a powerful appeal that lifted it above the merely prudential values of politics. After the King's marriage in 1236 dozens of his new Queen's Savoy and Provençal relations came over, many of them into royal service. Their influence infuriated the barons, notably the young Earl of Gloucester, to whose forefather Geoffrey of Monmouth had dedicated his book and whose father had been part of the committee set up to implement Magna Carta. Gloucester was a fierce though volatile tournament fighter and it was an embarrassment when one of the king's half-brothers, Guy de Lusignan, challenged him. Henry forbade it, fearing for Guy's life, but was persuaded to allow his younger half-brother, William of Valence, to accept Gloucester's invitation to a celebratory tourney on Ash Wednesday 1248, at Newbury. There was no mayhem. William acquitted himself well, and when he was dumped from the saddle by the English veterans, took it in good part, as he did the clubbing he was given afterwards, treating it as a welcome to the knightly circle. The code allowed him a return match, and he persuaded the King not to interfere. By the time the weather allowed it to take place, at Brackley in the summer of 1249, Gloucester had decided to switch his political allegiance and he helped William and his team to victory.

Gloucester's defection intensified the bitter hostility between the English and French camps, which had some nasty and rather unsporting side-effects; at Rochester in 1251 the barons not only put the enemy to flight but set their squires to ambush them. Even the training game, the quintain, could bring trouble, as when the champions of London beat the King's courtiers in a challenge match. Anarchical or not, tournaments could not be prevented when the code of honour gave a man beaten in one contest the right and duty to a return engagement. Gloucester himself went abroad in 1252 to salvage the family honour after his brother had lost his horses and arms in a tournament. In 1260 Henry III's twenty-one year old son, Lord Edward, took a great company of knights abroad seeking adventure. They lost everything they had, and when the Prince went back for revenge two years later, on borrowed money, he not only lost it all but was badly wounded.[2]

Win or lose, however, by then the tournament was accepted as part of a knight's training, and princes and kings who did not come to terms with this were unlikely to succeed. Yet it was too much like the real thing to be called sport and of little use for training purposes. There were milder versions such as the béhourd. This was a friendly affair in which the contestants wore padded suits instead of armour and used blunt, lightweight lances. But this lacked glamour. It was time for something more stylish, less of a free-for-all. As early as 1232 Henry III had banned an event described as a Round Table but no more was heard of it until twenty years later Matthew Paris referred approvingly to an occasion 'when knights from north, south and abroad gathered at Walden not in that sport vulgarly called the tournament but rather in that game of chivalry called the Round Table'.[3] This, in principle at least, was a polite affair consisting of a series of individual jousts with blunt weapons. Tables were set round for feasting, and minstrels, heraldic devices, fine costumes, colour and ceremony were important features. The process of institutionalisation was underway.

The Forest Charter

The vexed question of the King's hunting rights was also addressed in the aftermath of Magna Carta. As a result of royal irresponsibility and greed, the administration of Forest law had become not only arbitrary but corrupt. Forest eyres, the circuit courts authorised to dispense justice, met infrequently, leaving a virtually free hand to the chief foresters. These hereditary or opportunistic sinecurists with their bevy of assistants were fiercely hated and the magnates secured three clauses in Magna Carta, later expanded into a separate Forest Charter, designed to curb their powers.

One of the more liberal provisions of the Charter was the King's pledge that 'in future no-one shall lose life or limb for our venison.' Henceforth deer-stealing entailed a heavy fine, or for a man who lacked the wherewithal a year and a day in prison. Afterwards if he could promise good behaviour the Charter provided that 'he shall go out of our prison, but if he cannot, let him abjure the realm of England'.[4] It was a great concession that the magnates won the privilege of taking one or two beasts as they passed through Forest land provided they were in view of the foresters or, in their absence, blew their horns. Each such individual act of royal generosity was duly recorded.

The magnates in turn policed their own territories, sometimes over-zealously. The Earl of Arundel, who was scheduled to act as butler at the coronation of Queen Eleanor in 1236, could not do so because the Archbishop of Canterbury had excommunicated him as a punishment for seizing the archbishop's hounds which had strayed into the Earl's forests. In the normal course of events prudent magnates granted rights of warren freely as an aid to supervision: anything beyond this was exceptional.

Legal arguments about the Forest grew more not less after the Charter and so did popular resentment against the foresters. Poachers could usually rely on the silence of law-abiding fellow-citizens. Nevertheless the foresters, wits sharpened by the new procedures, caught a good many red-handed and the outlaw population grew apace. Whatever their internal disagreements, furthermore, the magnates and the monarchy were generally at one in seeking to preserve the privileges of their traditional style of landownership not only against poachers but against the inroads of modernity, whether through agriculture, urban spread or democracy. Yet for an increasing number of their social inferiors land was not a divinely bestowed or romantically acquired emblem of privilege but a hard-earned source of present livelihood and future profit.[5]

Knighthood and the lower orders

Similarly knighthood might be a glamorous notion in the minstrel gallery but it was an irrelevance and a potential distraction to many an industrious peasant who had acquired enough property to qualify. Burdensome duties such as jury service were particularly unpopular. In 1234 Henry III instructed his sheriffs to convey the royal displeasure to these shirkers. Fifty years later his more assertive son actually obliged those qualified to become knights whether they liked it or not. But he also set them a shining example of what a true knight should aspire to.

Lord Edward, who became Edward I in 1272, was two years into a crusade and did not return to occupy the throne for another two. He was the archetypal chivalric hero graduating from tournaments through baronial civil war and tussles with the Welsh and Scots to the holy war. At thirty-five experience had subdued his hot temper but had further strengthened his will. He was a formidable opponent at wrestling and all the martial arts and a magnificent horseman but he was also good at chess, a game the Crusaders had brought back. He was never happier than when hawking or hunting but he loved music, poetry and architecture. To the task of kingship he brought a capacity for hard work and a lively mind, and though he was no scholar he had an acute grasp of the fundamentals of finance and an ability to pursue the intricate legal arguments so characteristic of the age.

Beyond all this, though, he brought a love of the old chivalric stories, particularly King Arthur and the Round Table. To such a man tournaments, so far from being a threat, were essential to the training of the knights on whom the country's future depended. He encouraged them, and indeed joined in. In Edward's time they were rarely undisciplined, and his own personal involvement led to a number of changes that helped the trend towards individual jousts rather than mêlées and the growth in popularity of first the béhourd and then the Round Table. In 1278 for instance there was a béhourd at Windsor in which the contestants wore leather suits and used whalebone swords and wooden shields; and in 1284 victory over the Welsh was celebrated by a Round Table at Nevin in which the most celebrated knights in Christendom jousted with great ceremony and pageantry – an Arthurian victory celebrated in Arthurian style.[6]

The Welsh campaign was no mere assertion of English nationalism but part of the continuing Norman conquest. Similarly Edward I's wars in Scotland and in France were more to do with overlordship and vassalage than nationalism. The Scottish King Alexander III paid homage to Edward in 1278 but in the power struggle after Alexander's death Edward's protégé, though successful, could not persuade his colleagues to support Edward in defending

Gascony against the French, provoking harsh reprisals. Most of the Scottish barons were of Norman descent, including Robert Bruce, who after declaring himself King at Scone began to harass his Gaelic subjects. Discontented Anglo-Norman overlords later joined with Ulster chieftains in inviting Bruce's brother to assume the Irish crown, and though the result was defeat and disillusionment, the episode showed how much the King of England's hold on Ireland depended on the ambitions of the great earls who held it for him.

Meanwhile Edward I had to put his own house in order. The civil wars of his father's time had left a legacy of violence, and now gangs of disbanded soldiers from the Welsh affair were beating up travellers and breaking into houses: burglaries, rapes and arson were common, and murders went unpunished, some through ineptitude or evasion of responsibility and others through benefit of clergy in which not only ordained priests but students, school masters and professional men, anyone who could translate a Latin psalm known as the neck-verse, were protected under canon law.[7] This exemption remained but Edward tightened up communal responsibility for the administration of justice. In every shire trusted knights and landowners were appointed as keepers of the peace acting through elected petty constables. These were soldiers as well as policemen, required in time of invasion, riot or rebellion to see that every able-bodied man turned out at the sheriff's summons for national service.

Edward's Statute of Winchester of 1285 specified that freemen worth £20 to £40 a year were to come as knights, those worth £15 as troopers with horse, lance and armour and the rest, except for serfs, as foot-soldiers. These, in four classes, were to provide themselves or be provided by the constable with iron headpiece, quilted jacket, spear, dagger and bow and arrows – increasingly not the crossbow which shot arrows into the air from a string pulled to the chest but the longbow of Gwent, first used by the Welsh in border clashes, a formidable weapon whose string, drawn to the ear, could fire from a vast distance wooden arrows tipped with steel that could pierce chain mail.[8] The humble rustics assigned to this task were to transform the art of war, but however celebrated the longbow became it could not match the sword and the lance socially. The English archer remained a yeoman, and cavalrymen and their chivalric sports were the height of fashion.[9]

London needed special attention. In 1285 after years of political dissidence, corruption and violent crime Edward I manoeuvred the civic authorities into a situation where he could impose direct rule on the city. He immediately banned tournaments and sword-play. The statute, referring to 'fools who delight in their folly', prohibited the teaching of swordsmanship in the city on pain of forty days' imprisonment. It did not close the fashionable fencing schools but it drove them underground, confirming their reputation as hotbeds of drinking, gambling and brawling. Nothing of course could prevent sword-fights when it was the right and duty of every freeman to bear arms. Military swords were too cumbersome for pedestrian use and the classes obliged to go on foot carried staves for protection and support, especially in the country or on journeys. Daggers, of varying length, were widely used, either openly or concealed. In a ball-game, probably football, at Ukham, Northumberland on Trinity Sunday 1280, Henry de Ellington was accidentally killed when, jostling for the ball, he impaled himself on another player's knife. [10]

But ball-games could be dangerous even without knives. Three years earlier a ten year old boy killed a twelve year old companion by hitting him on the ear after a clash of sticks in a hockey game (*ad pilam ludendo altercantes*). [11] And there was growing fear of public nuisance especially in towns. In 1303 an Oxford student from Salisbury was killed – allegedly by Irish fellow students – whilst playing football in the High. [12] By 1314, calling for restraint during Edward II's forthcoming absence in the resumed wars with the Scots, the Lord Mayor of London issued a proclamation on the King's behalf forbidding rumpuses with large footballs (*rageries de grosses pelotes de pee* in Norman French) in the public fields. [13]

King Arthur and Robin Hood

There was, for one thing, a generation gap between the leading barons and his twenty-three year old son. Edward II was a constant source of annoyance to his father's old cronies, not least because of his antics with Piers Gaveston, a Gascon adventurer. The new king was big and strong but utterly self-indulgent with no enthusiasm whatever for the disciplines of knighthood, still less the ascetic approach to military campaigning his father had followed. As a young prince he had attracted disapproval from the orthodox by his idleness and frivolity, constantly seeking some new pleasure. He had a taste for fine but bizarre clothes and he was known to enjoy acting and playing the kettle drums. Along with Gaveston the fifteen year old prince played what the wardrobe accounts for 1299–1300 called creog, probably an abbreviation of creaget, which some equate with a French word criquet and reckon must be the same as cricket. [14] If it was cricket it was heard of no more for some three hundred years, and any self-respecting medieval knight would have regarded it as childish frivolity.

Edward II had some chivalric attributes: he liked horses and hunting and enjoyed wrestling, swimming and other physical pursuits. But he lacked knightly dignity. With his father away campaigning he had grown up in the society of grooms, blacksmiths, huntsmen and the officers and clerks of the household. Then later, under the influence of Gaveston, he had surrounded himself with jesters, jugglers, actors and singers. It added insult to injury when soon after coming to the throne he allowed Gaveston to arrange several tournaments against the English lords – and beat them. When, trying to win the barons over by joining in their martial pursuits, he sponsored an event at Kensington in 1308 with himself as 'King of the Greenwood' he was snubbed.[15]

The barons drove home their point the following year by complimenting Giles de Argentine, a renowned tournament figure, on his success in the same role at an event at Stepney, and before presenting to Parliament their many grievances against Gaveston they held a tournament at Dunstable whose roll of arms listed two hundred and eighty knights. Three years later, in 1312, they used tournaments as a cover to raise an army that captured and murdered Gaveston. Not surprisingly Edward II thereafter authorised few tournaments, Round Tables or other forms of hastilude.

Gaveston's murder provoked a royalist reaction and a split in the barons' ranks. But the feckless king plunged into further trouble when, having assembled the biggest army in English history, he lost to the Scots at Bannockburn in 1314. Meanwhile the common people were suffering intense misery. Torrential storms in 1315 which destroyed the crops reduced many to eating horses and dogs and there were reports of cannibalism in Ireland and elsewhere. Famine and discord continued: London was close to anarchy. Edward II was eventually forced to abdicate in favour of his fifteen year old son.

Edward III, obliged to surrender his claim to Scotland and to bow the knees to the French because of the machinations of his guardians, determined to get rid of them. He was a precocious and self-confident youth. Even the plotting was done with style. A few months before he struck, he and his allies took part together in a three-day tournament at Cheapside having ridden through the London streets, dressed as Tartars and dragging ladies dressed in ruby velvet by silver chains, challenging allcomers. Processions, ceremony and lavish costumes were a feature of the tournaments that greeted the new regime. The conquest of Scotland and the quarrels with France were resumed with enthusiasm, not least amongst the nobility, which included six newly-created earls friendly to the king, eager to prove themselves as good in battle as they were in tournaments and thereby to impress their ladies by chivalric deeds.[16]

The Arthurian legend, suitably glamourised, on which Edward III's philosophy was based, was sylvan rather than truly rural. The knights lived in castles which were in the country but not of it, and the thick woodland into which they plunged, questing after mythical beasts, was a mere backdrop to chivalrous deeds. No peasants obtruded themselves into this dream-world, nor did real life outlaws. But the Greenwood, the wild places the Norman kings had made into the Forest and the modern nobility were turning into deer-parks, had its own legend, that of Robin Hood. Robin had the same quasi-historical status as Arthur and an equally powerful romantic appeal. The two never clashed in mythology, despite their very different relations with authority.

That Robin Hood was popular with the aristocrats on whose patronage the minstrels depended owed much to the fact that he did not exist. He exemplified the free-born, plain spoken English yeoman but he resembled no actual yeoman: the bold strokes by which he overcame aristocratic, bureaucratic and mercantile opposition were not likely to be so effective in practice. Similarly yeoman expertise with the longbow, though honoured in song and story, brought little tangible reward. Armoured knights on mighty horses were the ones with prestige and the crossbow favoured by the French, though less deadly and slower to reload, became the officer's weapon. Military status remained much as it had been defined in the Statute of Winchester. An earl who brought a retinue got eight shillings a day and his officers were paid proportionately: four shillings for experienced knight-commanders, two shillings for knights bachelor and one shilling for mounted men at arms. The yeoman class of archers, who usually rode to battle on ponies, got six pence if they provided their own transport, otherwise three pence, a penny more than the spearmen.[17]

Emergency measures

Recruitment was made easier by a change in the public perception of foreign wars which for the first time were seen as something more than princely disputes about possessions and inheritance. The reason was the wool trade with the weavers of the Low Countries who were so restricted by the Counts of Flanders that they rebelled, looking to England for aid against their oppressors and their aristocratic French allies. So it was not only the chivalric classes who supported the King when in 1337 he called a muster and forbade all other games and sports except archery in preparation for war with France.

The city merchants who supplied the King had much to gain from a war which protected their interests. Though most of the population – now grown to some 4 million or more[18] – still lived and worked in the country, the prosperity of the better sort was increasingly based on trade. London, a city of some 50,000 people, was booming. It was a leading port at a time when the value of the sea, in war and peace, was being rediscovered, and a rich source of capital. London merchants were not yet able to match the bankers and cloth merchants of Florence and Lombardy, but they had money to invest for a noble cause. Crown and city forged a new alliance. Edward III built up the power of the navy which helped to protect trade as well as wage war. The Staple, his ingenious monopoly agreement with leading wool merchants, imposed taxes on exports which they passed on to the consumer and which gave him a ready and flexible source of revenue. The deal was not popular with the smaller wool merchants, a pressure group of growing influence, but it allowed the leading capitalists to infiltrate the upper reaches of society.

The war was costly in lives as well as money. Yet the chivalric myth suffused the mayhem with a poetic glow: the bloody exploits of the Black Prince were wrapped in a cloak of romance. At Windsor in 1344, after six years of futile struggle, the King and nineteen of his best knights took on all-comers for three days in a splendid tournament. Religion played its part, too. After mass, Bible in hand, Edward took a solemn oath to establish a permanent Round Table, and the Earls of Derby, Salisbury, Warwick, Arundel and Pembroke pledged support. This piety was rewarded by military success against the Scots who had crossed the border as a diversionary tactic and against the French. Nevertheless, the emblem of the victors of Crécy, a lady's garter, displayed at twenty tournaments in 1348, did not please the moralists. Henry Knighton ascribed the incessant rains of that year to divine displeasure at the loose behaviour of ladies ogling knights who 'lavished their possessions and tired their bodies on fooleries and wanton buffoonery'.[19] He prophesied even further doom.

The Black Death which struck that very August must indeed have seemed like a visitation from above, so sudden and mysterious was it in origin, so devastating in effect. Yet as a divine device to improve morality it achieved little. A few prudent souls repented of their past crimes, but as one monastic chronicler wrote 'The people for the greater part became even more depraved, more prone to every vice.'[20] By the following spring it reached Norfolk and by autumn north Yorkshire. The Scots called it 'the foul death of England', thoroughly deserved, until it struck them hard the following year. In 1352 it ravaged the Welsh valleys. In Ireland, similarly, it struck first against the English settlers on the lower plains, but the Irish who lived in the uplands and believed themselves exempt were smitten at last in 1357.

The manpower shortage called for special measures, notably the Statute of Labourers (1351) which sought to freeze wages at pre-plague levels. And with an eye to the war, which he waged with undiminished enthusiasm, the King wrote to his sheriffs in London in 1349 ordering them to stop idle games in the city on feast days so that all able-bodied men could practise with bows and arrows, pellets or bolts as appropriate. The warriors themselves – or at least their noble leaders – managed to combine business with pleasure. As the French chronicler Froissart recorded, when Edward III led an expedition to Calais in 1359 he took with him 'thirty mounted falconers and their loads of birds and sixty couples of big hounds and as many coursing dogs',[21] an example followed by many accompanying nobles and other rich men.

The curb on civilian sports continued. In 1369 the King sent his sheriffs throughout England a list of the games they were to ban.[22] As well as cock-fighting these included *jactus lapidem, lignum et ferrum*, throwing stone, wood and iron. Casting the stone we have already encountered in FitzStephen's account of London amenities. Such tests of strength were amongst the earliest and most basic of sports: reputedly early Irish and Scottish chieftains would keep a rock or two by their doors for the purpose. Throwing a lump of iron (called a diskos) was one of the events in Patroclus' funeral games in *The Iliad* when iron-working was part of the new technology and *jactus ferrum* no doubt included contests with shot, discus or quoit.

Similarly, throwing wood could include tossing the caber (Celtic = beam) or the more domesticated (English) axle-tree. The chances are, however, that the terms also embraced bowling and skittles and such variants as loggats, kayles and cloish, prohibited by name in later statutes. Bowls itself was traced back to the thirteenth century by Joseph Strutt, who illustrates three types: players trying to hit each other's bowl, bowling at small cones and bowling to a jack in the modern manner.[23]

The other main category of prohibitions was that of games *ad pilam manualem, pedalem et baculoream, et cambucam*: handball, football, club-ball and cambuck. This last, also called cammock, may have been, as a contemporary commentator believed,[24] a game in which a small wooden ball was propelled forward with a curved stick or mallet (and thus an ancestor of golf, pall mall and croquet); or, equally likely, an early form of hockey, also known as bandy, shinty, hurling and camogie, games that were played with the bent or knobbed stick from which cammock got its name.[25] From the law enforcement point of view, of course, it did not matter if the categories were overlapping: overlap was better than underlap. Thus *pila baculorea*, club-ball or stickball, could also refer to the hockey group of games. Club-ball, however, was the term later used to denote the rounders-type game illustrated in early manuscripts and believed by Strutt (but not his later editors) to be the source of cricket.

The two remaining games in the prohibition were to cause the authorities great concern over the years. Football, *pila pedalis*, was banned, as Strutt put it 'not, perhaps from any particular objection to the sport in itself, but because it co-operated, with other favourite amusements, to impede the progress of archery'.[26] Handball, *pila manualis*, no doubt took many forms about which the same could be said. The kind that caused most trouble later, however, was the French game *jeu de paume*, later known as tennis, played in an open quadrangular space, making use of surrounding roofs, buttresses and grilles.

Monastic cloisters, occupied by frustrated young men wit
hands, were used as well as the domestic variety (in 1286 the E
complained about fellow-prelates joining in Easter games
ordinates in monasteries or in their palaces).[27] The French no
pose-built courts made on the original idiosyncratic model, b
played anywhere and everywhere in simplified form, by teams o   ....uals,
across a rope or against a wall.

Restrictive legislation was also imposed on the Anglo-Norman community
in Ireland in the Statute of Kilkenny, 1367:

> Also, whereas a land, which is at war, requires that every person do render
> himself able to defend himself, it is ordained and established, that the com-
> mons of the said land of Ireland, who are in divers marches of war, use not
> henceforth the games which men call hurling, with great clubs at ball upon the
> ground, from which great evils and maims have arisen, to the weakening of
> the defence of the said land, and other games which men call quoits, but that
> they apply and accustom themselves to use and draw bows and throw lances,
> and other gentle games which appertain to arms, whereby the Irish enemies
> may be the better checked by the liege commons of these parts.[28]

By then there had been two further outbreaks of the plague and a quarter of
the population had been wiped out – a great worry to Parliament which was
finding it harder and harder to enforce the Statute of Labourers. Rents had
fallen sharply as land lay unused. And the war was taking a disastrous turn.
There was another bout of the plague in 1369, reducing the population still
more. Edward III escaped retribution through some celestial oversight but he
was growing senile. The Scots, though weakened themselves, stubbornly
hung on to most of their country, and forced the English to recognise their
King. There was trouble in Ireland over unlawful taxes. Worst of all, the Black
Prince, the English national hero, was stricken with dysentery and came home
to die. With the King sunk in squalid dependence on his mistress English
hopes were pinned on his second son, John of Gaunt, Duke of Lancaster. But
he failed in France, scandalised the nation by flagrant immorality and upset
the House of Commons – the burgesses of the towns and the knights of the
shires – by trying to tax them to pay for his mistakes.

'This happy breed of men'

People had high hopes of Richard II, the Black Prince's young son, but they
were short-lived. The new King was high-handed and priggish. Things got
worse in France and invasion was feared. Then came trouble at home. The
Peasants' Revolt of 1381 was the first time rebellion had come from outside the
circle of privilege. The immediate cause, a sharp increase in the discriminatory

poll-tax to finance the French war, concealed a deeper discontent. While the Commons complained of impoverishment by the outrageous wages demanded by labourers and their failure to honour feudal commitments, the peasants were concerned at the erosion of common land. Hunting rights were also an issue. Amongst the petty restrictions most resented by the peasant class was a ban on hunting rabbits, and a rabbit skin on a pole became a rebel emblem. Fishermen and fowlers from the Fens were the first to take action. Theirs was not a political grievance, but the Essex rebels wanted the abolition of serfdom and freely negotiated wages. The establishment closed ranks behind the young King, and the peasants were easily defeated. At the height of the insurrection Richard bought time by listening with apparent sympathy to their demands but then, with danger averted, told them 'Villeins ye are still, and villeins ye shall remain.'

Parliament had been given a fright and clamped down even harder on the peasants. In 1388 hunting laws were introduced which applied not just in the royal Forest but throughout the land. Noting that 'artificers and labourers and servants and grooms' were in the habit of keeping 'greyhounds and other dogs' and that 'on holy days, when good Christian people be at Church' they went hunting 'in parks, warrens and coneyries of lords and others, to the very great destruction of the same', the new law forbade, on pain of a year's imprisonment, laymen with holdings worth less than forty shillings and clerics with benefices less than ten pounds a year to keep greyhounds or other hunting dogs or to use 'ferrets, hayes, rees, hare-pipes, cords and other engines to take or destroy the deer, hares or coneys'. The legislation also renewed the ban on 'importune games' with particular reference to the servant and labourer class, forbidding all ball-games whether handball or football, together with quoits, dice and casting the stone.[29]

The King's overriding problem was with the magnates who did not like his willingness to end the French war short of victory. It was a measure of his unpopularity that his support for the tournament won him no friends or political influence. In an effort to canalise the continued tension with Scotland he issued general licences for use against unspecified enemy knights. After an epic encounter between four Scots and four Englishmen, first on horseback with lances and then on foot with short swords, at London Bridge in 1390, the King presented the prizes to the Scottish victors, and three years later presided when the English got their revenge. In 1390 Richard also sponsored an elaborate tournament which attracted French nobility as well as many English contestants. It was an event of great splendour but when he attempted to re-capture its glory in 1398 with a festival at Windsor in which forty knights and their squires would take on all-comers, few of the better sort attended because of their growing antagonism to the King.[30]

For one thing Richard was too conscious of his dignity to carry weight with men brought up on the Arthurian myth. He and his household lived in luxury beyond even that of Edward III's time, indulging a refined taste in costume, ornament, heraldry and the trappings of rank. Richard's own patronage of the arts, though magnificent, was always ostentatious, as in the three great glories of the age – the new, vast Westminster Hall, the portrait of Richard in Westminster Abbey and the celebrated Wilton Triptych.[31]

In the tournament he was too aloof, too much the sponsor, too little the participant to carry conviction. By contrast his cousin, Henry of Lancaster, was renowned for his skill at the joust. It was a serious error of judgement when he banished Henry and kept him from inheriting John of Gaunt's vast fortune. Apart from his over-reliance on the doctrine of the divine right of kings Richard II also failed to recognise that a new nationalistic spirit was arising, even amongst the nobility whose interests in Europe had often hitherto taken precedence over patriotism. Henry of Lancaster tapped the spring of Englishness.

But sporting attitudes, often an escape from reality, are slower to change than political ones. At the beginning of the century when handbooks on hunting began to appear, orthodox opinion was formed in France. William Twici, Edward II's huntsman, who produced an early treatise (1328), wrote in Norman French and though it was soon to be 'Englished' as *Maister of the Game* by John Gyffard, it was French works such as *Les Livres du Roy Modus et de la Reine Racio* on stag hunting and the poem *Romans des Deduits* about falconry (both c1300) that were regarded as the true authorities.

The great pundit by the end of the century was Gaston, Comte de Foix (known as Phoebus because of his flame-coloured hair), author of the celebrated *Livre de Chasse* (c1400) and a considerable expert on hound-breeding and the tactics of the hunt. These he felt should centre on the hounds: he was an advocate of the style known as *par force de chiens* and he believed the supreme experience was hunting the hart, which required a special breed of dog, called a lymer, to detect the quarry. Phoebus was against over-elaboration to impress fine ladies or foreign visitors. In particular he did not much care for modern 'bow and stable' hunting. In earlier times even royal hunting had involved no more than six men, say three archers and three horsemen, with a single hound. Nowadays up to twenty men, known as a stable, might lie in wait to act as beaters and a great number of assorted hounds drove as many stags as could be mustered past the tryst, a vantage point behind a tree where the hunting party lurked trying to get a bow shot in as a deer rushed by. Another set of dogs was available to assist the noble archers if they should miss. A hunting party of this kind could be a fairly static affair with dogs doing most of the work.

But although Phoebus believed the true hunter should actively follow the hounds, his reverence for the hart was based on the sophisticated methods needed to seek it out and bring it down. The fallow buck, meatier and tastier if smaller than the noble hart, was an acceptable substitute, but the techniques for catching it were less complicated and so it was accorded somewhat lower status. Early the next century *The Master of Game* by Edward Plantagenet, Duke of York, though heavily indebted to Phoebus, showed a touch of independence. The hare held a special place in English affections (Twici and Gyffard regarded it as a marvellous beast) and Edward altered Phoebus' chapter order to put the hare first. This modest amendment was a challenge to hierarchical conventions, for hare-hunting was the most common sport amongst the less affluent gentry and the minor clergy. Similarly many Englishmen liked to hunt the roebuck, though it lacked the prestige of the hart and the taste of the fallow buck, because of its great capacity to prolong the chase through cunning and courage.[32] Here, in fact, was the first hint of that English addiction to sport that was to soften otherwise rigid class attitudes, and, in later years, some would say, help stave off revolution.

Meanwhile English nationalism burgeoned. Throughout the second half of the fourteenth century Francophobia gripped the nation, swelling with every victory and act of revenge. In 1362 Parliamentary proceedings opened in English for the first time and it was decreed that all legal pleadings be in English since French was too little known for plaintiffs or defendants to understand what was being said about them. When Richard II tried to revive the old sense of kinship between Plantagenets and Valois he soon had to drop the idea. His French marriage and avowed admiration for French culture set him aside from his people as much as his absolutist attitudes. There was an inevitability in his overthrow by Henry of Lancaster in 1399, and the new King took his coronation oath in English.

A more positive reason for the advance of the English language was that it not only matched French but showed fresh, flexible possibilities, notably in the work of Chaucer. Chaucer was an establishment figure, who served both Richard II and Henry IV, and though he poked fun at hypocrisy, notably in the church, he did not question the social order, as the Prologue to the *Canterbury Tales* makes clear. The comedy of manners, debunking pretension and hypocrisy, was the oldest and most enduring British joke. This kind of humour, of which Chaucer was a master, was another way, along with sport, in which the starker aspects of hierarchy could be transmuted into amiably idiosyncratic foibles.

The emergent English ascendancy was strengthened under Henry IV. Having seized the throne by lawless means he was much concerned to preserve law and order, so that rebellions, border raids, crushing the Scots and

Welsh and fending off the French kept him busy throughout most of his reign. Disorder at an Epiphany tournament soon after his coronation dampened his enthusiasm for his old sport, and he sponsored only a few events on special occasions such as the visits of foreign dignitaries. His son, Henry V, was even less enthusiastic. Though trained in tournament skills he found his true métier in Welsh and Scottish expeditions and French raids.

Henries IV and V regularly renewed Edward III's bans on popular sports, with new Acts in 1401, 1409, 1410 and 1414, and they tried to apply the same disciplinary standards to the upper classes of society as to the lower orders. Henry V was particularly puritanical in this respect. After his marriage to Catherine of France in 1420, when his allies proposed a celebratory tournament, Henry told them grimly that they would be better employed by laying siege to the stronghold of Monterau where they could joust and tourney as much as they pleased. As for ball-games, his obsession with the game of war left no room for such frivolity. Thus when the Dauphin sent him a 'barrell of Paris balles' the joke misfired. Henry's terse response, promising the Dauphin 'some London balles that should break and batter down the roofs of his house about his ears', was the prelude to the siege of Harfleur and the great victory of Agincourt.[33]

Chivalric twilight

English sea-power was reasserted and the longbow reigned supreme but the result – after Henry's death from dysentery and the accession of a nine month old baby – was another costly stalemate. The enthusiasm of the merchant classes, whose backing for foreign wars was now essential, was not yet exhausted, however, for they and many of the older aristocracy had done well out of the prolonged struggle with France.

Evidence of the wealth of the nobility and gentry survives in the artefacts of the period. Patronage of the arts was fashionable and gave increasing scope to the work of English artists and craftsmen. In ecclesiastical architecture, the chief beneficiary, there was a shift from the French-inspired Gothic to the distinctive perpendicular style. As patronage increased so too did the cult of the personality: many stained glass windows included portraits of their donors. Sculpture began to flourish, chiefly in carvings on tombs or other effigies of the great. Domestic architecture also flourished: lavish tapestries, covers and cushions offset the functional severity of baronial residences. The office of royal tapestry-maker dating back to Edward III was a by-product of the burgeoning wool trade. There were other signs of secularisation. The much admired English embroidery had traditionally been the work of nuns whereas under patronage it increasingly depended on professional seamstresses. Illuminated manuscripts, previously hidden away in monasteries, were bought by wealthy laymen and new ones were commissioned. The only commonly accessible paintings were on the walls of chantries, but a few rich patrons were beginning to prefer pictures to tapestries in their houses. The results, unfortunately, were not bursting with imaginative life, but it was a start.

Lower down the social scale pious but secular patrons appeared in the rising middle classes, notably in the work of the gilds who were beginning to dominate both municipal administration and urban leisure activities. Their most celebrated achievement was the promulgation of the miracle plays which, having developed out of the illustrative episodes of parts of the mass introduced by evangelistic clergy, outgrew church services, outwore the patience of ecclesiastical authority and took on a life of their own in pageants, dramatising Bible stories acted on mobile scaffolds. In some towns these became episodic cycles of the Christian story, lovingly and poetically presented, though with popular embellishments that did not always please the church.

The same might be said of the gilds' sponsorship of sport, which put a secular seal of approval on activities that the church was in two minds about. A Tudor recollection of Chester noted that each year on Shrove Tuesday from 'time out of man's remembrance' the Shoemaker's Company had presented a football, worth three shillings and four pence, to the Draper's Company 'at the Cross upon the Rood Dee' in the presence of the Mayor before the annual encounter.[34] This compared favourably with the largesse of the Prior of Bicester, Oxfordshire, who in 1425 authorised donations not exceeding four pence for a St Catherine's Day match.[35] The London footballers seem to have had a thriving social side as well as plenty of money. The accounts of the Brewer's Company in 1422–3 include hiring charges for dinners in the hall 'by the football players twice . . . 20 pence'.[36]

Yet, outside special occasions, football was still often banned in favour of archery. James I of Scotland, released in 1424 from captivity in England, took a leaf out of his captors' book, ordaining that 'na man play at the foot ball under pain of iiijd.' That the fine was to be collected by the 'Shariffe of the land, or his Ministers, gif the Lordes will not punish the trespassors'[37] indicates reluctance in some quarters to implement royal policies. This was a problem in England, too – a lack of fervour for war-like pursuit in districts not immediately affected by foreign invasion. Yet officialdom was increasing in its efforts to seek out backsliders and exact retribution.

Local authorities often had their own by-laws, for the purpose of maintaining law and order and discouraging moral turpitude. In 1450 Halifax justices imposed a shilling penalty on players of idle games, in which they included bowls along with dicing and football. Played on gracious surroundings bowls was becoming fashionable, played in alleys, which might be narrow strips of turf b were sometimes long narrow spaces between buildir When in 1455 the young Henry VI was persuaded to remov bowling in London, the city was soon full of greens, and even fuller of a outdoor and indoor, spawning the evils of gambling, drink and disorder.[38]

Idle games were, however, like perennial weeds in a garden: as fast as one was eradicated another sprang up. In 1457 James II felt it necessary to suppress a new distraction from military duties, ordering that 'the fut bal and the golf be utterly cryit downe and nochte usit'.[39] Golf or golfe, gouff, goite or gowfe as it was variously called, after a Scottish dialect word meaning to clout or clump, may have been of foreign origin, a variant of the Dutch game *kolven* adapted to the terrain in the part of Scotland where it began, the links land around Musselburgh. Certainly Dutch herring fishermen regularly called at this port in the Firth of Forth in the fifteenth century. But the Scots made it their own.[40]

Meanwhile in England the church was particularly concerned at the loose habits of junior clergy. In 1364 the Synod of Ely forbade its clergy to play games, and some years later the Prior of Lilleshall, issuing moral guidance, urged parish priests not to cast stones or axle trees and to banish 'ball and bar and similar games' from their churchyards.[41] In 1385 the Bishop of London denounced the playing of ball games at St Paul's both inside and outside the cathedral.[42] *Jeu de paume* was a particular problem. As an aristocratic pursuit the fashion had been encouraged a century earlier by the advocacy of moderate ball-games for princes of the royal blood by the educator Giles of Rome,[43] but now less distinguished citizens, clerical as well as lay, were playing it, often in simpler versions using church walls and churchyards.[44]

By 1400, under the name tenetz or tennis, after the call made by the server (*tenez*, hold), *jeu de paume* was already sufficiently well-known to be used to illustrate the need for a never-say-die spirit:

> Of the Tenetz to win or lose a chace
> Mai no lif wite er that the bal be ronne.[45]

At Lydd on the Kent coast the first of several similar items in the town accounts link it with fear of the French. '1429: Paid to a man crying the watch to be kept by the seaside and that no man should play at the tenys'.[46] And in 1447 the Dean and Chapter of Exeter Cathedral complained to the Mayor that ungodly people, usually young, were using the cloister for 'unlawful games as the toppe, queke, penny prykke and most atte tenys', defouling the walls and making 'the glas wyndowes all to brost'.[47] Six years later after a petition to Henry VI tennis balls were added to the list of restricted French imports.[48]

By this time the failure of the French campaign was clear. In 1431 Joan of Arc had been burnt and the boy Henry crowned King of France, but these were futile gestures and the French artillery thereafter revealed the vulnerability of the British archers. In 1450 Normandy fell, the royal debt came to £400,000, corrupt and incompetent officials infuriated all the tax-paying classes, and Jack Cade's rebellion, though quickly put down, showed the strength of middle class feeling. The old dynastic quarrels resumed amongst the nobility, some of whom were now prodigiously rich. Both Houses of Parliament became instruments of class privilege and personal rivalry. A strong king could perhaps have restored the situation but Henry, though pious, was volatile and feeble-minded.

The various discontents were subsumed in the claims of Richard of York against the Lancastrian usurpers. In 1453 Gascony fell and the King went mad under the pressure of events. Two years later the country was engulfed in civil war. The Wars of the Roses put another nail in the coffin of the Anglo-Norman realm. It was already weakened by the Hundred Years War and the alliance between France and Scotland, and the Black Death had not only lessened the pressure for land, weakening the urge to colonise, and the supply of man-power for the great estates of Wales and Ireland, but unleashed market forces that undermined their feudal self-sufficiency. Wales became more Anglicised as the native population seized the economic opportunities that came their way, but Scotland had won a precarious independence at the expense of locating a more powerful military aristocracy in the lowlands and widening the culture gap with the Highlands. In northern Ireland one of the great dynasties, the O'Donnells, aligned itself with Scotland and its traditional rival, the O'Neills, with England. Both there and in the south, where the Earls of Kildare, Desmond and Osmond were keeping down the Gaels, Westminster control was nominal. The Wars of the Roses allowed them more scope for strategic manoeuvres: Ireland was a potential power base for claimants to the English throne. Both the pretenders, Lambert Simnel and Perkin Warbeck, were to play the Irish card.

The domestic upheavals also weakened the English will and capacity to resume the French wars. Richard of York's son who made himself Edward IV in 1461 was a dashing chivalric hero in his youth but in office, though he retained the sportsman's affability, he became self-indulgent and money-conscious. He saw more sense in trade than in war, and he not only made common cause with the merchants, he became one. When he finally went to war with France in 1475 it was with the aid of a big grant from Parliament, and he came out of it, after concluding a not very favourable peace treaty, with his personal fortune increased by 75,000 crowns and a 50,000 a year pension. Though the foreign military situation began to change with the advent of artillery the pike and the bow were what counted in wars against the Welsh, Scots and Irish, and he issued edicts forbidding idle sports for the protection of archery in 1474 and 1477 on the same lines as those that had followed the Peasants' Revolt – restoring, for example, the ban on bowls, with fines of up to £10 and prison for up to two years for defaulters, and £20 fines for green- or alley-keepers who broke the law. (Similarly James III of Scotland again prohibited football and golf in 1471.)

Edward IV's departure from the canons of chivalry was a sign of things to come. The trend was masked, and delayed somewhat, by the obsession of his younger brother, Richard III with fulfilling his dynastic mission, of which he had a very strong sense. Richard's violent and crooked methods consigned him to a thoroughly old-fashioned life of intrigue and murder until he met his death at the battle of Bosworth in 1485. But then in the long years of peace after Henry Tudor's accession chivalry found itself increasingly out of place in the real world, though it took refuge in the dream-worlds of poetry and, of course, sport. The destrier, once a fearsome engine of war, now became a showhorse in the tournament, and the tournament itself became more and more a matter of spectacle. Less and less was heard from the church authorities in Rome about its potential value in training the defenders of Christendom and in Britain, whose prodigious appetite for the great game of war was temporarily satisfied, other forms of diversion began to appeal to the aristocracy.[49]

Notes

1 Hastilude, literally spear-play, was the generic name for tilting, jousting, or melées in tournaments or Round Tables. See R. Barber and J. Barker, *Tournaments*, Woodbridge, 1989.

2 The main contemporary source for these events is Matthew Paris, *Chronica Majora*, 1235–1259, ed. H. Luard, London, 1872–3, vols. III and IV, summarised in D.M. Stenton, *English Society in the Early Middle Ages*, Harmondsworth, 1951, pp. 86–9.

3 Paris, *Chronica Majora* vol. V p. 138.

4 W. Stubbs, *Select Charters*, Oxford, 1870, pp. 344–8.

5 See Stenton, *English Society*, pp. 106–10.

6 For Edward I see A. Bryant, *The Age of Chivalry*, London, 1963, Chapters 1 and 2.

7 The ecclesiastical courts dealt with a wide range of civil affairs and had wide and sometimes over-riding powers in criminal matters affecting the individual rights of clerics. The neck-verse was Psalm 50 of the Vulgate Bible. Bryant, *Age of Chivalry*, p. 365.

8 Ibid., pp. 101–3.

9 Yeoman, probably from youngman, a servant, meant an armed retainer, later a farmer, tenant or otherwise, and later still a land-owning peasant OED.

10 *Calendar of Inquisitions*, Miscellaneous I, p. 599 (Magoun).

11 Ibid., p. 592.

12 H.E. Salter, (ed.) , *Records of Medieval Oxford*, Oxford, 1912, vol. II, col. 1(e) (Magoun).

13 H.T. Riley (ed.), *Munimenta Gilldhalliae Londoniensis*, London, 1859–62, vol. III, app.

ii, p. 439 (Magoun).

14 *OED* allows the possibility, but quotes no earlier reference to cricket than 1598. For the theory of French origin see R. Bowen, *Cricket*, London, 1970, p. 30; refuted in H. Leonard, *Journal of the Society of Archivists*, vol. 4, No. 7 (April 1973) pp. 579–80.

15 R. Barber and J. Barker, *Tournaments*, Woodbridge, 1989, p. 31. King of the Greenwood was a sylvan version of King of the Castle.

16 Bryant, *Age of Chivalry*, pp. 239–40.

17 Ibid., p. 282, pp. 303–4.

18 For the widely varying estimates of population see J. Gillingham, 'The Early Middle Ages' in *The Oxford Illustrated History of Britain*, ed. K.O. Morgan, Oxford, 1984, p. 161, and M McKisack, *The Fourteenth Century*, Oxford, 1959, p. 13.

19 H. Knighton, *Compilatio de Eventibus Angliae*, c1366, ed. J.R. Lumby, London, 1889–95, quoted in Bryant, *Age of Chivalry* p. 379.

20 William Dene of Rochester, quoted in Bryant, *Age of Chivalry*, p. 390.

21 J. Froissart, *Chronicles*, 1395–1400, ed. G. Brereton, Harmondsworth, 1968, p. 165.

22 *Calendar of Close Rolls* (Record Office) pp. 534–5.

23 Strutt, *Sports and Pastimes*, 1969 edn, p. 216.

24 T. Rymer, *Foedera* etc., 1816, vol. 1, p. 417.

25 For 'cammock' see *OED*. Sir Guy Campbell, 'The Early History of English Golf' in *A History of Golf in Britain*, ed. B. Darwin, et al., London, 1952, pp. 44–5, gives helpful references to cambuca and offers this as a pointer to the origin of golf.

26 *Sports and Pastimes*, p. 94.

27 See Lord Aberdare, *The Story of Tennis*, London, 1959, p. 12.

28 Carew MS 603 in Lambeth Palace Library issued in translation by the Gaelic Athletic Association, Dublin, 1978.

29 Rymer, *Foedera*, vol. II, p. 57.

30 Barber and Barker, *Tournaments*, pp. 36–7.

31 D. Pearsall, 'The Visual World of the Middle Ages' in *The New Pelican Guide to English Literature*, ed. Boris Ford, vol. 1, Part One, pp. 290–317.

32 For French and British tastes see J. Cummins, *The Hound and the Hawk*, London, 1988, esp. Chapter 1, 2, 5 and 7.

33 R. Holinshed, *Chronicles*, 1577, the source for Shakespeare's *Henry V*, Act I, ii.

34 J. Hemingway, *History of the City of Chester*, Chester, 1831, pp. 207–8.

35 W. Kennet, *Parochial Antiquities*, 1695, 2nd edn, Oxford, 1818, p. 259.

36 Quoted in F.P. Magoun *History of Football from the Beginnings to 1871*, Cologne, 1938, pp. 11–12.

37 *Acts of the Parliament of Scotland* (1424–1567) II (1814) 51, Chapter 18 (Magoun).

38 P. Sullivan, *Bowls: The Records*, Enfield, 1986, pp. 10–11.

39 Campbell, 'Early History of English Golf', p. 46.

40 R. Browning, *A History of Golf*, London, 1955, pp. 7–28, discusses the matter at length. For an irreverent corrective to nationalistic theories see 'How Golf invented the Scots' in P. Dobereiner, *The Glorious World of Golf*, New York, 1973. A good short account is in W.H. Gibson, *Early Irish Golf*, Naas, 1988, pp. 1–5.

41 *Instructions for Parish Priests*, John Mirc, 1403, ed E. Peacock, London, 1902 edn, p. 11 (Magoun). 'Bar' was the children's game known as prisoners' base or relievio.

42 D. Wilkins, *Concilia Magnae Britanniae*, 1787, III, 194, quoted in Strutt, *Sports and Pastimes*, p. 81.

43 *De Regimine Principum* c1280, quoted by H. Gillmeister, 'Medieval Sport' in *International Journal for the History of Sport*, May 1988, p. 59.

44 Strutt. *Sports and Pastimes*, p. 82.

45 J. Gower, *In Praise of Peace*, c1400, in G.C. Macauley (ed.), *Collected Works of John*

Gower, 4 vols., Oxford, 1899–1902.

46 Aberdare, *Story of Tennis*, p. 45.

47 J. Shillingford, *Letters and Papers*, 1447–50, Camden Society, 1871 quoted in E.A. Freeman, *Exeter*, Exeter, 1887, p. 161. The toppe = whip and top; queke = checkers; penny prykke = penny prick, aiming at pennies on the tops of sticks.

48 Under the Lancastrian kings almost all legislation arose through petitions. See McKisack, *Fourteen Century*, pp. 409–11.

49 H. Kearney, *The British Isles*, Cambridge, 1989, pp. 95–103.

CHAPTER THREE

Upward mobility
1485–1603

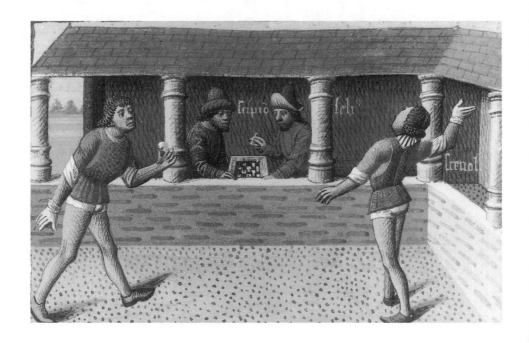

The new peace and prosperity offered great scope for the ancient art of mutual back-scratching. The crusading spirit went commercial, and to a large extent, private. The Company of the Staple, which handled the all-important wool trade, was kept under government control but the Merchant Adventurers, set up by the opportunist Perkin Warbeck, were into everything else in Europe and beyond. The nobility and gentry discovered that trade, despite its unchivalric image, had its advantages. Land was still the measure of social esteem and the usual investment for successful military men, but money values, eroding those of feudalism, increasingly obtruded themselves.

The trick was to make land more profitable, and sheep farming was the most popular option. Inconvenient villages were destroyed to make way for sheep and thousands of acres, particularly in the south of England, were enclosed for pasture, breaking up the old open-field system and further undermining feudal relationships. Though the ravaged population did not begin to recover until the second quarter of the sixteenth century, unemployment, the great weapon of market economies, mounted with the advent of this less labour-intensive use of land. Small farmers found their rents dramatically increased and many were evicted when they could not pay. Farm labourers set off for the towns in search of work.

By contrast clothiers grew rich, becoming a chartered organisation of such power that the new king was able to negotiate a highly favourable commercial treaty with the Low Countries. Under Henry VII improved exports, economies brought by more efficient administration and the end of foreign wars made Britain prosperous. And his renowned assiduity in collecting his dues gave him the personal prosperity to provide the display and pageantry which enhanced the monarchy and sublimated the urge to conquer France.

The medieval hierarchy was thus preserved in the new age by the scope offered to the upwardly mobile. This applied to spiritual as well as secular matters. Literacy fomented religious discontent and the anti-clerical temper of the greatest scholar of the age, Erasmus, was echoed by popular writers who reached a new public through the English language. Nevertheless the church still kept a firm grip not only on spiritual matters but on the civil service. The clergy extended its influence on education, through new colleges in Oxford and Cambridge and new schools. Winchester (1382) was founded by Bishop William of Wykeham and Eton (1440) as a pious benefaction by Henry VI. Above all churchmen were shrewd enough to recognise that, with the magnates and Parliament still reeling from the shocks of the Wars of the Roses and their aftermath, the King was the only effective power.

It was an irony that Henry VII, who inaugurated a new era of English, as distinct from Anglo-Norman, domination of the British Isles, was Welsh by origin and upbringing. But ancient tribal impulses had been sufficiently made over by the clarion call of his ancestry to make Welsh support decisive at Bosworth and judicious appointments afterwards strenghthened his grip. The end of the French wars put a brake on Scottish ambitions and after a period of tension a peace treaty was signed in 1502. In Ireland, the Earl of Kildare's support for the two pretenders to the English throne, Lambert Simnel and Perkin Warbeck, brought reprisals, and though the administrative costs of replacing him proved too great, he was more circumspect thereafter.

Domestically the most urgent problem was the host of 'sturdy beggars', fit to work but idle, their ranks swollen in the general climate of unemployment by the disbanding of baronial armies after the Wars of the Roses, and the great increase in robberies and murders. Though keen to suppress private armies – and to exact fines from defaulters – Henry VII looked to honorary justices of the peace, chosen carefully from men he could trust, to administer the law. Voluntary service was demanded according to rank and not suprisingly justice was administered on similar principles. The laws were framed for the benefit of people of substance: hence restricting ball-games in favour of archery, though it was obsolescent in military terms, was retained as a means of preserving the privileges of rank and keeping down the costs of defence.

Sporting fashions

Ball-games – of an individualistic kind – were much more fashionable in the new society. Bowling greens were a standard feature of country estates, some of which even aspired to tennis courts. Tennis, popular throughout Europe, had become an accepted part of royal hospitality for visiting dignitaries. When the young Philip of Burgundy, on his way from Holland to claim his Spanish inheritance in 1506, was marooned by shipwreck in England, Henry VII, combining business with pleasure, arranged a hunting trip for him during which Philip played tennis with the Marquess of Dorset. He used a racquet and gave the Marquess, who played in the old style, with the hand, fifteen points a game.[1]

Tennis was played with a hard, leather ball and racquets, originally gloves with netting stretched across them, were an effete development. Their Latin name, *reticula*, allowed Erasmus to deploy his celebrated wit in a collection of exercises (like those of Abbot Ælfric only funnier) one of which was devoted to sport. One of the players who thinks tennis more suited to winter than summer, says 'We'll sweat less if we play with a racquet' to which the other replies, 'No, let's leave the net to fishermen. Using your hand is finer.' They go on to play, scoring in the already traditional fashion, fifteen, thirty, forty-five, and then enduring two ties before reaching game.[2]

Erasmus goes on to tell us, in short space, a good deal about schoolboy sport, evidently modelled on sophisticated adult practice though with a good deal of improvisation, scratching base lines 'with a shell or stone or with your cap if you prefer', and so forth. First he describes some other popular games of the time. There is casting the stone, apparently a version of putting the shot, since there is a debate about choosing stones of equal weight and distance seems to be an objective, with an intriguing reference to a 'damned little brick' getting in the way of an otherwise winning throw. There is jumping, which has many types, hopping, vaulting, running, boxing (not approved despite Virgil's commendation) and swimming (also scorned as 'a frog's life': in spite of being 'anciently regarded as noble sport' it was merely utilitarian, useful for those who 'have to flee in war'). And there is a game of ball and mallet, in which the ball had to go through a hoop, which was clearly an ancestor of the game pall mall which was to become fashionable in London under the influence of James I and his courtiers, steeped in French culture.

Beyond this, however, we learn about the attitude to sport of the pupils and their masters, which, though Erasmus' scene was Parisian, was much the same throughout Renaissance Europe. For a start the masters needed a lot of persuading to allow pupils time to play and when reminded of their own teachings, in which 'moderate play' is commended by Quintilian as refreshment for tired brains, retorted that there was no reason for some brains to get tired since they were preoccupied with play and demanded better performance in study as a condition of release. They also forbade drinking, which was nevertheless part and parcel of the boys' sport, as was gambling; drinks all round or a feast were considered the honourable way to spend one's winnings. Erasmus' own view seems to have been that honour, not money, was what should really be at stake – in one sketch the contestants play for their countries' honour – and similarly, though he joked about it as he did about most things, that cheating defeated its own objective which was to demonstrate superior skill. Bearing the vicissitudes of fortune was also important.

The tennis Erasmus' pupils played was obviously of a simpler kind than fashionable court tennis and they played, from choice, in teams. But they served on to a sloping penthouse roof, à la mode, and they paid for the hire of balls. There were in England as in France, outdoor versions: *longue paume* sometimes called 'bord and cord' played outdoors with a rope for a dividing line between teams, and *courte paume* played against a wall. Similarly in British bowls, as in *boule* in France, there were less formal types adapted to the terrain and the circumstances, like alley bowls, outdoor and indoor. It was these simpler games, which could be staged at commercial venues such as inn-yards, that were the chief target of the current legislation which linked bowls and tennis with closh, dice and cards as games forbidden to labourers and artificers and to servants except at Christmas in their employers' households.

Fear of English attacks led to a Scottish ban on 'futbawle, gouffe or uther sik unprofitaball sportis' in the interests of 'bowlis and schutting' by James IV in 1491. This was relaxed as uneasy truce was followed by more lasting peace, and the Scottish royal household records six years later show payment of two shillings (= two English pence) to a James Dog for footballs.[3] It seems unlikely that the 27 year old monarch, a traditionalist who loved hunting and hawking and held splendid tournaments, would have lowered his dignity by playing football himself. It was, according to a contemporary English account, a game in which 'young men, in country sport, propel a large ball not by throwing it in the air but by striking and rolling it along the ground and that not with their hands but their feet', a game 'abominable enough and . . . more common, worthless and undignified than any other kind of game'.[4] The royal purchase may have been a gift for a junior member of the household rather than a personal addiction.

Golf was a different proposition. In 1502 James IV paid thirteen Scottish shillings 'to the bowar of Sanct Johnstown for Clubbs'. (Scottish bow-makers were more fortunate than their English counterparts in finding a peace-time sideline). The following year he drew thirteen shillings 'to play at the golf with the Earl of Bothuile' and nine shillings for 'clubbis and ballis that he play it with'.[5] Some at least of the balls, made either of wood or sheepskin filled with cow's hair, were imported from Holland. Nevertheless royal patronage from this time ensured the standing of the sport in Scotland.

In England the peace brought anxieties about the uses ex-service men might find for their war-like skills. Poaching was a particular problem. Yet the law of 1504 restricting the use of crossbows to the nobility, gentry and landowners with 200 marks or more also required lesser ranks to continue to practise regularly with the longbow, and the price of yew wood, mostly imported from Italy, was kept down by a statute of 1488. The fact was that Henry VII did not like new methods of war such as the master-weapon, artillery, which he rarely used, or regular soldiers. Nor was it just economy that led him to rely instead on the stout right arms of the ploughmen called up by commissions of array: his own personal protection was in the hands of the yeomen of the guard, a company of longbowmen he created in 1485, already an anachronism and rarely if ever called on to perform more than ceremonial duties.

There were plenty of those. Too prudent to engage in foreign wars, too canny to keep a standing army, too parsimonious even to maintain the naval strength that had served Britain so well, Henry VII nevertheless loved the pageantry and traditions of the good old days. Easter, Pentecost and Christmas began with religious observance but were followed by sumptuous feasts. Lavish costume and elaborate display marked special occasions. The splendid ceremonial for the arrival of Catherine of Aragon in 1501 included tilting in New Palace Yard, sanded to keep the horses from slipping; there were stages for the King and his court at one side and for the mayor and leading citizens at the other. These citizens, according to an antiquary of the next era, had to hire their seats 'at great price and cost' and they were not, of course, invited to the evening revels in Westminster Hall.[6]

Henry VII also enjoyed the annual May games in the royal park at Greenwich. They lasted several weeks, every afternoon except Sundays, with horse-racing, tilting, archery, sword-play, wrestling, a mock battle and casting the bar 'both heavit and hight'.[7] None of this bore any relation to the modern realities of knighthood or to soldiering, both of which were guyed unmercifully by Erasmus.[8] His knight emerges as a snobbish popinjay, concocting his coat of arms, trying to forget his obscure ancestry, surrounded by sycophantic followers, and scorning to pay debts to poor tradesmen and innkeepers. He is secure in the 'soldierly creed that nothing survives a man but his corpse'. In another sketch soldiers lie about their exploits, turning injuries incurred whilst running away into heroic wounds, plundering, looting and violating nuns under the protection of hypocritical priests.

Henry VII himself, though pious, as his great monument the chapel at Westminster shows, laid up a fortune in plate and jewels. Awareness of the value of possessions had been tainting the motives of noble patrons of the arts for some time. Edward IV in exile had seen the wonderful artefacts created under the patronage of the Dukes of Burgundy and as soon as he could he began collecting Flemish manuscripts. Vanity was another motive. The Yorkist kings and Henry VII all commissioned portraits of themselves and their loved ones (usually from Flemish artists since the English court had not so far done much to encourage local endeavour). The English talent lay more in crafts like cabinet-making, metalwork and embroidery. Statuary was still largely funerary, but whether in tombs or wall-niches it testified to growing, secular individualism.

The tastes of the rich and powerful laity also influenced book production, hitherto under church control but now threatened not only by Erasmus' humanism but by printing. Neither could exist without money. Erasmus moved uneasily from patron to patron, and William Caxton, who introduced printing to England, used it to publish material of a lucrative highly conservative kind – translations of favourite medieval romances, the collection of saints' lives known as the *Golden Legend*, the works of Chaucer, Lydgate, Gower – and his most famous publication, Malory's *Morte d'Arthur*, gave added resonance to the chivalric myth. The new printing presses were also put to the service of two particularly conservative groups – those who sought guidance on etiquette and lovers of sport.

The two came together in 1486 in the *Boke of Hawking, Hunting and the Blazing of Arms*, usually known as the *Boke of St Albans*. Its longest section, the *Liber Armorum*, based on earlier compilations, was about heraldry and its theme was that gentle lineage inclines men to virtue, citing as an example Jesus Christ himself, presented as a gentleman entitled to wear the coat armour of his ancestors. This same outlandish snobbery characterised the section on hunting, though not without humour, as in its enumeration of species of hounds. 'First ther is a Grehownd, a Bastard, a Mengrell, a Mastyfe, a Lemor, a Spanyell, Rachys, Kenettys, Terorres, Bocheris houndes, Mydding dogges, Tryndeltayles, and Prikherid curris, and smale ladies popis that beere away the flees.'[9]

Likewise the traditional hierarchy of beasts is presented with folkloric licence:

> 'Bestys of venery
> . . . Fowre maner bestys to venery there are;
> The first of theym is the hert; the secunde is the hare;
> The boore is oon of tho; the Wolff and not oon moo.
> Bestys of the Chace
> And where that ye cum, in pleyne or in place,
> I shall you tell which be beestys of enchace.
> Oon of theym is the Bucke, another is the Doo;
> The Fox and the Martron and the wilde Roo.

The section on falconry pursues the notion of hierarchy to absurd lengths, beginning with eagle, vulture and kite (supposedly used only by emperors and in practice used by no-one) through gyrfalcon, falcon gentle, falcon of the rock, 'Bastarde', saker and sakeret, lanner and lanneret, used respectively by king, prince, duke, earl, baron, knight, squire, lady and youngman (a novice) down to the birds allowed to the baser sort:

> There is a Goshawke, and that hawke is for a yeoman. Ther is a Tercell. And that is for a powere man. Ther is a Spare Hawke, and he is an hawke for a prest. There is a Muskyte, And he is for an holiwater Clerke.[10]

As a modern critic explains, the musket, the male sparrow hawk, 'would suit the holywater Clerk because it hardly eats anything and because its neurotic behaviour would drive a profane layman to perdition'.[11] The poor holywater Clerk was, of course, the butt of many jokes, the recognised emblem of low status.

The *Boke of St Albans*, with its mixture of conventional wisdom, medieval folklore, religious symbolism, jokes and outrageous snobbery, was highly popular, and ten years later it was reprinted, this time with a new chapter, 'The Treatyse of Fysshinge with an Angle', the first of its kind and one of the sources, at second-hand, of Izaak Walton's *Compleat Angler*. The new section had a delightful introduction in a format that was to become familiar, setting out the claims of fishing compared with hunting (too laborious), hawking (too chancy) and fowling (too cold). But angling, though scarcely yet refined, was the genteel end of fishing: traditional methods relied on nets. Even if he caught no fish the angler had 'at least his wholesome walk, and merry at his ease . . . the sweet savour of the mead flowers that maketh him hungry, the melodious harmony of fowls', and 'if the angler take fish, surely then is there no man merrier than he'.[12]

Renaissance: English style

Henry VIII, not quite eighteen when he succeeded his father in 1509, was already a commanding figure, sure of himself and well-prepared for the task in hand. He had learned the arts not only of statecraft and finance but theology. He was a fair Latin scholar and he knew Froissart and Malory, and read and wrote poetry. Handsome and expensively clothed, he looked every inch a king. He took the tournament seriously and was a skilled performer; he was a fine and tireless horseman, whether hunting or riding 'the great courses' at the May games; and he was as good an archer as any in the kingdom. The physical sports in which he excelled – wrestling, high-jumping, pole-vaulting – he undertook not merely for pleasure but to harden his muscles. He was more open-handed than his father, whose carefully husbanded wealth the new King spent freely in a ceaseless round of pageantry, masques, music – he played the lute and harpsichord and sang – jousts and sports, whilst he dazzled the gaping throng with his finery. He gave his father-in-law, the King of Spain, the impression that he was interested only in girls and hunting, but his ambitions were far more complex.

Strongly supportive of the Pope, he saw himself as the most chivalrous prince in Europe, the protector of the Holy Grail: contemptuous of the Scots and jealous of the French, he sought military adventure in the old style. First building up the navy, he designed a war machine to be led by a coterie of captains who would command either on land or sea. These gentlemen guards, known as the King's Spears, were like himself masters of the tournament and they followed his lead in wanting to show they could be just as good in battle as in sport. The archers were an important part of the elaborate array of supporting troops and it was no surprise when in 1511 Henry forbade idle games that got in the way of practice at the butts. His resumption of hostilities with France, bringing fresh Scottish troubles, diverted the nobility from domestic squabbles but cost many lives, much of his inheritance and Parliamentary money as well.

When the war fizzled out internal disorder began again and as Martin Luther preached Reformation in Germany and Calvin set out his stall in Geneva, anti-papal feeling began to grow in England. This was strongly discouraged by Cardinal Wolsey the careerist butcher's son who was Henry's early mentor. He had guided the young King in his early adventures, fostered his romantic illusions and profited from supporting Henry's French campaign by becoming in quick succession Bishop of Tournay, Archbishop of York, Cardinal and Papal Legate. Henry now looked to Wolsey to curb domestic unrest, and allowed him to pursue the cause of European peace, whilst he indulged himself in post-war pleasures.

Sport and luxury were not only enjoyable in themselves but ways of impressing both his latest mistress and the foreign ambassadors who came in train of Wolsey's diplomatic efforts. In his pageants of 1517 and 1518, the jousts were decked out in more colour and opulence than ever before with gold baudekin, silver chains on the horses and trappings which were half of gold embroidery, half of purple velvet embroidered with gold stars. Henry astounded onlookers by his boundless energy and prowess, leading pages and other cavaliers in feats of horsemanship requiring frequent changes of mount which he seemed to make fly not merely jump. And in the evening after the banquet and its accompanying music there were two hours of dancing, at which the King excelled, using the occasion to display his energy and skill in leaping.

The climax of this phase was the month-long festival of the Field of the Cloth of Gold in 1520. In this the French sought to win England as an ally against the Holy Roman Empire through a festival that was to include every kind of knightly tournament and chivalric courtesy. Henry set out to out-do the French hosts in lavish entertainment, in spectacle, in sporting achievement, in energy – indeed in everything that mattered. He succeeded quite well but overdid it. Everyone was impressed by his sporting skills and his gorgeous clothes. His rough, jocularly intended but sudden gesture in putting a wrestling grip on King Francis I of France was a mistake. Francis was a big man and, startled out of his best behaviour, he threw Henry to the ground.

No-one was surprised when two years later Henry joined forces with the Emperor against France. The protean Wolsey's task was now to find money for the war. Taxation apart, his zeal and moral fervour for the cause were hard to bear. Thus in 1526 a proclamation deploring the decline in the 'exercising of longbows and archery of this realm' ordered that 'no person within the realm of what estate, degree or condition he or they be, do play or use the said unlawful games'.[13] This was as unpopular as the war itself. As the royalist historian Edward Hall commented, 'the people murmured against the Cardinal saying he grudged at every man's pleasure saving his own, but the proclamation small time endured'.[14]

Two years later with peace restored Wolsey introduced a revised measure which whilst equally draconian was more socially selective. It gave the county commissioners appointed under his 1526 legislation power to enter private houses in search of illicit crossbows and handguns, and to enter hostelries, inns and alehouses to 'take and burn . . . tables, dice, cards, bowls, closhes, tennis balls' and other instruments of the devil. Tennis was forbidden only if courts were not properly conducted: similarly bowls was condemned 'because the alleys are in operation in conjunction with saloons or dissolute places' which denied it the status of a true sport.[15]

Wolsey's removal when he balked at Henry's wish to divorce Catherine of Aragon who had failed to give him an heir led to the breach with Rome and the establishment of the Church of England. Henry was now able to extract funds not only from the citizenry but from the Roman Catholic Church by the dissolution of the monasteries. The land was mostly sold to pay for Henry VIII's renewed dreams of conquering France. The beneficiaries included opportunist courtiers, aspirant gentry, ambitious merchants and yeomen and not a few crafty lawyers. These transactions started a wave of land speculation in which rents and prices spiralled, bringing further economic trouble for poorer and less adroit peasants, and adding to their social decline.

It was an uncertain and anxious time, triggered by a sudden expansion of population – in England from about 2.25 million in 1525 to over 3 million in 1550 and in Wales from about 250,000 to 300,000 in the same period – which added to the employment problems. Inflation, fuelled by the gold and silver that flooded in from the New World, reduced the value of the traditional coinage and forced up the cost of goods and services. Prices, which had been stable for centuries, doubled and in the case of wheat, trebled. As well as the sharp division between rich and poor there was one between north and south. The short-lived uprising of northern English gentry known as the Pilgrimage of Grace (1536) was as much a protest against interference by the Londoner Thomas Cromwell, Wolsey's successor as chief minister, as support for the papacy. In Ireland, Cromwell's moves against Kildare to assert direct rule from Westminster aroused similar anti-southern feeling. Even after her defeat at Flodden in 1513 and invasion by an English army thirty years later, Scotland still looked to the 'auld alliance' with France for ultimate victory. And in Wales, where the Acts of Union of 1536 and 1542 introduced English common law and the use of English as the official language, the old feudal relationships were destroyed, the church was reformed and its lands passed into the hands of aspirant laymen, the gulf between the country people and their Anglicised if not English gentry and clergy grew wider.[16]

Meanwhile Henry VIII, flushed with success, found it increasingly hard to distinguish between his own whims and the country's needs. His sporting enthusiasms were translated into patriotic virtues. The archery lobby was not slow to take advantage: for instance, the bowyers and fletchers of Salisbury petitioned the King, complaining that the decline in archery, which was adversely affecting trade, was being accelerated by popular indulgence in games which 'might be tolerable to eminent inhabitants for their recreations' but were clearly not meant for the lower orders.[17] Henry agreed, condemning the 'customable usage of match-play at bowls' by 'subtil, inventative and crafty persons'. In 1541 legislation restricted bowls to noblemen or citizens worth £100 a year or more on their own greens or alleys: their servants could play at Christmas, but to all others bowls was banned, and keeping alleys or greens for profit was forbidden.[18]

Protecting archery was becoming harder to justify. The longbow had clearly had its day as a serious military weapon. Yet the government, so long as there was no standing army, was always torn between the need for trained man-power and the danger of putting powerful weapons into the hands of the populace. The ban on handguns for those worth less than £100 a year was lifted in 1544 during the Scottish wars but reimposed at the truce two years later. Nevertheless the advance in military technology had unexpected side-effects. Once gunpowder showed full armour to be a costly irrelevance, swords came into their own again for close-quarter work. The new military need was for short, light weapons such as the Italian rapier. The 'foyne' or thrust with which this fashionable blade was associated was, however, alien to English tradition, and the King, a notable exponent of the old two-handed sword, disapproved.

The London salons, trying to copy the great fencing schools of the continent, had been restricted but not eliminated by medieval prohibitions. Henry sought to discourage their resurgence by granting letters patent to an English Corporation of Masters of Defence. These sturdy patriots taught the two-handed sword, pike, bastard, dagger, back-sword, quarter-staff and sword-and-buckler. Sword-and-buckler in particular proved highly popular and soon, ironically enough, as fencing schools sprang up in every town, there were to be complaints that the new fashion was contributing to the neglect of archery.

Renaissance: European style

Henry VIII's forceful assertion of his own preferences was a major factor in the emergence of peculiarly English, as distinct from European, ideas of sport. Yet the context, for Henry himself as well as his sycophantic followers, was the mainstream of Renaissance thought. One of the most important influences was Castiglione's *The Courtier* (1516). Castiglione's ideal courtier was a good soldier, but also a diplomatist, well-read, familiar with the arts, easy in manners and conversation and proficient in suitable games and recreations. It followed that these athletic activities were not merely military preparation – dancing and tennis were commended as well as horsemanship and sword-play – but only if they were suited to gentlemen. Thus gymnastics were allowed but not tumbling and rope-climbing, which were associated with low-grade professional performers.

All was part of a preordained chain of being. 'Hath not God set degrees and estates in all his glorious works?' asked Sir Thomas Elyot, an English admirer of Castiglione. Hunting and baiting animals fitted easily into this theory, not only because such exercises kept the beasts in their place but because they allowed men to establish their own hierarchy: Elyot reckoned 'daunting a fierce and cruel beast' a spectacle that 'imparteth a majesty and dread to inferior persons'.[19] The Castiglione doctrine enabled Elyot to gloss over the tricky question of whether the martial arts were still of practical value. He commended the convenience of the sword and the battle axe for a gentleman, and praised wrestling, running and swimming as useful skills currently little practised by the nobility but of impeccable classical lineage.[20] Similarly, he emphasised the social and psychological advantages of archery, lauding it as a valuable and healthy activity 'moderate and mean beyond every extrimity.'[21]

Horsemanship was very important to Elyot's scheme of things, the chief exercise of men of rank, and he was scornful of less active forms of hunting. Like Gaston Phoebus he criticised bow and stable methods. 'The hunting of red deer and fallow,' he reckoned, 'might be a great part of semblable exercise used by noble men . . . if they would use a few number of hounds only' to rouse the game and indicate its flight, 'the remnant of the disport to be in pursuing with javelins and other weapons in manner of war.' Fox-hunting (which involved digging out quarry that dogs had run to earth) was lacking in 'commodity of exercise' and hare-hunting was merely 'a right good solace for men that be studious, or them to whom nature hath not given personage or courage apt for the wars' or 'gentlewomen which fear neither sun nor wind for appairing of their beauty'.[22]

Hawking, despite its antiquity, was similarly dismissed – 'measurably used, and for pastime' it would give a man a good appetite for his supper and might keep him from 'other dalliance or disports dishonest' – but it was better than netting or liming, which gave rise to concern lest 'within a short space of years our familiar poultry shall be as scarce as now be partridge and pheasant'.[23]

self became more interested in hawking as he grew older,
ect falconry, and a 1542 law forbade the taking of hawks or
.n a fine of £100 and possible imprisonment as penalty and a
.0 for informers.[24]

.requent references to moderation reflected Renaissance admiration
.sical perspectives – reason in all things – and for the Castiglione notion
.sy mastery, but also revealed a growing awareness of cause and effect in
matters of health. Archery, according to its laureate Roger Ascham, was better
for you than tennis in which the labour was 'too vehement and unequal'.[25]
Elyot thought tennis a fitting pursuit for young men but admitted that it was a
violent game 'by reason that two men do play . . . if the one strike the ball
hard, the other is then constrained to use semblable violence'.[26] There was
great concern about sweating as Erasmus' reference to tennis suggests. There
were several notable instances of royal persons, after a bout of tennis, catching
chills that led to serious illness or worse. (They wore too many clothes when
playing and neglected to bath and change afterwards.)

Sweaty or not, the King loved the game, which had become very popular as
a spectator sport for fashionable ladies. One of his young courtiers, the Earl of
Surrey, whose chivalric verses exalted the tournament, also wrote of

> The palm-play where, despoiled for the game,
> With dazed eyes oft we by gleams of love
> Have missed the ball, and got sight of our dame
> To bait her eyes which kept the leads above[27]

Henry's tennis professional became a standard member of his retinue on trips
as far afield as Calais (still an English possession) and he built new courts at
several palaces, notably Hampton Court. Henry enjoyed bowls, too, and the
household accounts record bets won and lost in the company of Ann Boleyn.
But tennis undoubtedly had more cachet because of its popularity with the
fashionable Europeans. In 1522 the king played with Emperor Charles V at
'the Bayne' (the Baths), Blackfriars, and in 1532 he lost a substantial bet to the
Cardinal of Lorraine. By 1542 William Griffiths was authorised to keep a court
for use by foreign visitors and the following year Richard and Elizabeth
Kynwolmershe were authorised to keep a court restricted to lords, knights,
gentlemen and merchants.[28]

A glimpse of team games

Little was yet recorded of the great team-games for which the British were to
become celebrated. Cricket was being played by schoolboys – and probably by
country men – in the south of England, but showed no signs of rising above

the other members of the club-ball family. Football, though its status was ambivalent, was much more socially significant. In Ireland, for instance, when in 1527 the Common Council of Galway used its powers under Royal charter to legislate for the protection of civically worthy sports like archery, long- and cross-bow, and throwing javelins and spears, it added a clause that discriminated in favour of football. No citizen, it said, was 'to engage in the hurling of the little ball with hockey sticks or staves, or use the handball for playing outside the walls, but only to play with the great football', on pain of a fine of eight pence.[29]

Football, institutionalised as in the traditional Shrovetide encounters, was seen to have social value as a purgative. For centuries throughout Europe at Carnival (as Shrovetide was called) and other festival times the custom was to allow normal authority to be set aside for a brief span before the penitential days ahead or as a midwinter break on the lines of Saturnalia. By the later middle ages English kings and lord mayors employed lords and abbots of misrule to preside over the revelling. The custom of electing a boy bishop was one of the many ways in which youth was allowed to relieve its frustrations. Football, which was a form of mêlée without armour and weapons, was one of the more harmless manifestations.

That football matches often took the form of bachelors challenging their married seniors further emphasises the valuable social role of these encounters. The period of apprenticeship for artisans, like the squire's preparation for knighthood, was one of bachelorhood but with fewer opportunities for relief than in the upper reaches of society. Violence, with or without drink, was an easier outlet than sex and in football the violence could be institutionalised not only by the rules, descended from the old honour code, but by the rituals before and after the game. Thus the Freeman Marblers of Corfe Castle marked the initiation of their apprentices by a Shrovetide football match at which the previous year's graduates, by now wed, treated the novitiates to a feast.[30]

Territory was another basic fact of life. The Corfe Castle game was played over land to which the Marblers laid claim, through custom and practice, by paying the Lord of the Manor a pound of pepper. Parish or village identity was a prime source of rivalry some of whose frustrations could be expunged through football. The annual encounters between the parishes of St Peter's and All Saints in Derby, which became the name for any keenly fought local contest, seem to have come close to licensed mayhem.

For some romantic scholars the game had a rustic charm in its own right. In 1514, Andrew Barclay, a Scottish Benedictine based at Ely, offered this tribute:

The sturdie plowman, lustie, strong and bolde
O'ercometh the winter with driving the football
Forgetting labour and many a grievous fall.

He made it sound very agreeable, in an unsophisticated sort of way:

in the Winter, when men kill the fat swine,
They get the bladder and blow it great and thin,
With many beans and peasen put within.
It ratleth, soundeth, and shineth clear and fayre.
When it is throwen and cast up in the ayre,
Each one contendeth and hath a great delite
With foote and with hande the bladder for to smite.[31]

However, polite society took a dimmer view. Elyot dismissed football in 1531 as 'nothing but beastly fury and extreme violence, whereof proceedeth hurt and consequently rancour and malice do remain with them that be wounded'.[32] There were grave disorders at Chester in 1533 and six years later the Shoemakers' Company withdrew their backing from the traditional Shrovetide game, offering the Mayor and Corporation six gleaves of silver for a foot-race instead. It may be that when Elyot in 1541, recommending for health reasons games 'compound of violent exercise and swift as dancing galliards, throwing of the ball and running after it', conceded that 'football play may be in the number thereof', he was thinking of the more ordered and orderly games played by the Italian nobility.[33] In England, however, 1540 was another bad year: the Saddlers' Company followed the Shoemakers' lead at Chester, donating a silver bell for a horse-race.[34]

In Scotland, too, though football had its respectable side, abuses were causing concern. In 1511 the Privy Council heard a complaint that Perthshire youths had swarmed the 'ball-green of the lands of Campbell' armed to the teeth under the cloak of a game of 'wood futeball', mad football.[35] Twenty-five years later the poet Sir David Lindsay satirised a football-mad minister.[36] On Fasten's E'en, which was beginning to be celebrated in much the same way as in England, the municipal authorities of Glasgow paid for the footballs in the annual game.[37] But in 1546 the Company of Hammermen at Perth threatened over-enthusiastic players with a penalty of a pound of wax (for candles to their patron St Eloy).[38] And soon there were reports of 'moss-troopers' using the football games in border towns as a cover for their activities.[39]

Blood-letting, animal and human

The death of Henry VIII left a power vacuum. Then the pendulum swung between the extreme Protestantism of the boy Edward VI (1547–53), who completed his father's asset-stripping of the Roman church by dissolving the chantries, and the avenging Catholicism of his equally pious half-sister, Mary (1553–8) who burnt at the stake some 300 enemies of the faith. There was no apparent conflict between religious belief and personal cruelty.

At Christmas 1550 the saintly Edward had publicly rebuked Mary for observing popish practices like 'conjured bread and water': then after dinner on the feast of the Epiphany he watched a bear-baiting with the seventeen year old Princess Elizabeth. When, as Queen, Mary was persuaded by her devious husband, Philip of Spain, to visit Elizabeth at her country house at Hatfield she was treated to a bear-baiting, with which 'their highnesses were right well content'.[40] And when Elizabeth herself became Queen in 1558 it was natural that the entertainment she offered to foreign ambassadors would include bear-baiting.

This bloodthirsty streak is a reminder of the realities that lay behind Renaissance rhetoric. Elizabeth's tutor Roger Ascham summarised the ideals of courtly education in splendidly decorous prose:

> To ride comely, to run fair at the tilt or ring, to play at all weapons, to shoot fair in bow or surely in gun, to vault lustily, to run, to leap, to wrestle, to swim, to dance comely, to sing and play of instruments cunningly, to hawk, to hunt, to play at tennis and all pastimes generally which be joined with labour, used in open place and on the daylight, containing either some fit exercise for war or some pleasant pastime for peace, be not only comely and decent, but also very necessary for a courtly gentleman to use.[41]

Yet Ascham himself was addicted not only to gaming but to cock-fighting.

In 1574 one of Elizabeth's courtiers described how a bear was savaged 'by a great sort of ban-dogs' for the delectation of Her Majesty on a visit to Kenilworth Castle:

> It was a sport very pleasant to see the bear, with his pink eyes leering after his enemies, approach; the nimbleness and wait of the dog to take his advantage; and force and experience of the beast again to avoid his assault: if he were bitten in one place, how he would pinch in another to get free; that if he were taken at once, then by what shift with biting, with clawing, with roaring, with tossing, and trembling, he would work and wind himself from them; and when he was loose, to shake his ears twice or thrice with blood and slaver hanging about his physiognomy.[42]

The royal family had its own private bear gardens but there were public bear gardens in London of which the most famous was behind the Globe Theatre, Bankside. Because of their cost bears were usually kept alive (it was the dogs that died) but as they grew battle-scarred they could expect no mercy, as a German visitor pointed out: 'to this entertainment there often follows that of whipping a blind bear, which is performed by five or six men, standing in a circle with whips, which they exercise upon him without any mercy'.[43]

Bulls were more readily available, and expendable, though if they fought well they too might be retained for further service. They could do a lot of damage with their fearsome horns and the trick was for the bull-dog to get in underneath and grab the muzzle, the dewlap or 'the pendant glands'. If it got a hold it clung on, and either tore the flesh away and fell or had to be pulled off, with the aid of flour blown up the nostrils to make it let go. This tenacity so inspired the populace that the bull-dog became an emblem of the British character. There was a convenient superstition that bulls needed to be baited to improve the taste of beef and in some parts of the country by-laws required this to be done.

The Puritans found the whole idea repellent: 'What Christian heart can take pleasure to set one poor beast to rent, tear and kill another, and all for his fiendish pleasure?' asked Philip Stubbes in his *Anatomie of Abuses* in 1583. The answer was a great many. Cock-fighting was perhaps the most popular variety, since game-cocks were easier to obtain than bears or bulls and since it combined blood-letting with the excitement of gambling. 'Cocks of the game', said the chronicler John Stow, were 'cherished by divers men for the pleasures, much money being laid on their heads when they fight in pits.[44] A later development was the Welsh main, an uncomplimentary English description of a battle-royal, in which eight pairs of cocks were set in the pit together, the winner being the sole survivor. And everywhere in England on Shrove Tuesday there was cock-throwing in which a stake was hurled at a captive bird.

None of these delights were, of course, English inventions, but the sporting pundits took pride in one native innovation, coursing. George Turberville concluded his *The Noble Art of Venerie* (1575) with the statement that, though he could find nothing in the foreign books he had translated about coursing with greyhounds, the English set great store by coursing them 'at Deare, Hare, Foxe, or such like.' This happy circumstance enabled the Queen herself to make a contribution to the British reputation, at least among themselves, for sportmanship. Early in her reign, it was said, she had instructed the Duke of Norfolk, the Earl Marshal, to draw up 'laws of the leash' to regulate coursing matches.[45] One of them, 'Fayre Lawe', reo uired the quarry to be given a start. Sportsmanship apart, this provided better entertainment. In 1593 on a splendid occasion at Lord Montacute's seat at Cowdray, Sussex, the 58 year old Queen entered her bower, took her crossbow and slew, to the accompaniment of music, several of the thirty deer assembled for her pleasure. (The Countess of Kildare, in attendance, was allowed to take one beast.) Then, in the evening, the ladies looked down from a turret to see 'sixteen bucks, all having fayre lawe', pulled down by greyhounds.[46]

The growing population – by 1600 it had reached some 4 million in England, 380,000 in Wales, and perhaps 1.5 million in Scotland and Ireland – needed to be fed, which meant improved agriculture, more emphasis on tillage. The government's efforts in this regard were certainly not helped by the enthusiasm for hunting which, as the topographer William Harrison pointed out, wreaked havoc with the crops. Nevertheless Elizabeth remained a passionate adherent all her life. In 1600 when she was sixty-seven she was still at it. 'Her Majesty is well', wrote a courtier, 'and excellently disposed towards hunting, for every second day she is on horseback and continues to sport long.'[47]

Such moral ambiguity was no disadvantage in political life. Her expedient alliance with France, whose ruler Henry IV converted to Catholicism, led to a shaky peace. The somewhat fortunate, though much-acclaimed, defeat of the Spanish Armada in 1588 was followed by quarrels with her Dutch allies over the cost of the war. Her attempts at reformation in Ireland failed and threats of a Spanish invasion there led to bloody, long drawn-out and much-resented full-scale conquest. She was fortunate in Scotland, where the church, still rich and unplundered, was first infiltrated by careerist lairds and then reformed to their financial advantage, and where the French alliance, which meant support for the old church, began to splinter. The English Act of Supremacy in 1559, putting the church under Crown control and requiring Edward VI's prayer book to be used for worship, was followed in 1560 by the Scottish Parliament's abolition of papal authority and John Knox's Calvanistic crusade against Catholicism and the claim to the throne of Mary Stuart, brought up at the French court. To the Protestants France was the enemy and England an ally.

Throughout Britain Elizabeth's religious settlement left the Catholics isolated and thus potential traitors, requiring fierce anti-treason measures. Still progress towards union – that is southern English domination – continued. Abroad, English ambition was boundless: the merchant venturers exploring new markets in Muscovy, the north-west passage to Cathay; the Levant and India; Spanish inroads in America sparking plans to 'plant' the New World (killing two birds with one stone by getting rid of undesirable elements in the community) and the efforts of the hapless Sir Walter Ralegh and Spain's dashing arch-enemy, Sir Francis Drake. At home ambition was bounded by the lingering assumptions of medieval hierarchy but nevertheless backed by entrepreneurial flair. The people, including the deserving poor, were fed, improvements in housing were available to the aspirant at all levels, inflation was checked by currency reform and labour was organised through a Statute of Artificers which linked entry to the professions, trade and agriculture to manpower needs and restricted it by standards of property and wealth. Only chaotic taxation and persistent disorder marred the scene.

The cultural achievements of the age were impressive. In painting, apart from the miniatures of Nicholas Hilliard, the British were better-known as collectors than creators. And there was much mediocrity in sculpture and public building: only in domestic architecture, a surviving glory, was there distinction. The sacred music of William Byrd, Thomas Tallis and Orlando Gibbons, the madrigals of Thomas Morley and the songs of John Dowland had spontaneity and charm as well as technical skill. But English literature was unsurpassed, from the historians and topographers to the poets, pastoral in Sidney and Spenser, dramatic in Marlowe and Shakespeare, and the host of prose-writers, revelling in a new-found freedom of language, sometimes flowery, sometimes sinewy, always confident.[48]

Confidence was the keynote. Indeed, amidst the ferment of new aesthetic, geographical, philosophical and scientific discoveries, the English had become complacent – and more than a little xenophobic. This went far beyond hostility to the French and Spanish: elaborate foreign styles of speech and dress aped by the fashion-conscious brought the scorn of satirists and Puritan pamphleteers alike. Many hated Italians for political and religious reasons as the seat of Catholicism. Elizabeth was excommunicated by the Pope in 1570 and the following year an attempt on her life was made by the Florentine merchant Ridolfi.

Italians were also blamed for effete new fashions of sword-play. The old ones seem to have been in need of reform. As Stow put it:

> Untill the twelfe or thirteenth yeare of Queen Elizabeth the ancient English fight of Sword and Buckler was only held in use . . . the Buckler then being but a foote broad, with a pike of four or five inches long. But then they began to make them full half-ell broad, with sharp pikes ten or twelve inches long.[49]

According to the cosmopolitan Fynes Morrison, 'nothing was more common with them, than to fight against taking the right or left hand, or the wall, or upon any unpleasing countenance'.[50] The 1572 legislation which declared 'fencers, bearwards, common players in interludes and minstrels' who did not obtain baronial patronage or special licence rogues, vagabonds and sturdy beggars, did not discriminate between types of sword-play but it was, according to Stow, the Italianate fashion for 'long Tucks and long Rapiers' that led to a decree of 1580 limiting swords to three feet and daggers to one foot in length, inclusive of handles.[51]

The decree had little effect on the disorder: duelling was the fashionable virile sport. Ben Jonson, afterwards Poet Laureate, was tried for murdering a man in a duel in 1598 and escaped hanging only because he knew enough Latin to recite the neck-verse and claim benefit of clergy. Shakespeare a few years earlier in *Romeo and Juliet* had given a vivid picture of the manners of Italian gallants like Tybalt who kept 'time, distance and proportion . . . the very butcher of a silk button'. By 1599 in *As You Like It* the target of his wit was Vincente Saviolo, a Paduan whom the Earl of Essex had taken into his service and who became the leading London master of the reviled Italian style. Saviolo was the author of a treatise which dealt not only with sword-play itself but the elaborate, sub-chivalric courtesies and challenges surrounding the duel. The various stages in the gentlemanly quarrel were guyed by Touchstone as the Retort Courteous, the Quip Modest, the Reply Churlish and so on.[52]

One of the characters in a popular satirical farce complained that 'sword and buckler fight begins to grow out of use; I am sorry for it; I shall never see good manhood again; if it be once gone the poking fight of rapier and dagger will come up'.[53] Nostalgia and xenophobia combined powerfully in the impassioned pleas of George Silver for the British to abandon the fantastic Italian, Spanish and French styles and stick to the true art with traditional British weapons.[54] Such sentiments could, of course, be turned to commercial advantage. The Four Ancient Maisters of the Science of Defence who presided over Henry VIII's foundation had developed an elaborate system of progress from novice to scholar, thence to provost, assistant master and master through competitions with various weapons from back-sword (a stick with a hilt), back-staff, two-handed sword, bastard, pike and sword-and-buckler. They held those contests in public using such venues as the Bull, Bishopsgate and the Belle Savage, Ludgate for the lower grades and for masters' trials the prestigious Artillery Grounds, Leadenhall or even Hampton Court. The aspirant in these trials was said to be 'playing his prize' and the contests, known as prize fights, were extremely popular and ripe for commercial exploitation.

Sport in a changing society

The code of honour was in need of refurbishment if not repair. The martial arts were now in disarray, victims of technological as much as social change. The tournament was little more than a piece of nostalgic ceremonial: the last judicial joust took place in 1571. And the waning assets of archery dwindled still further in 1595 when local militias were required to change their bows for calivers and muskets.

Wrestling, the oldest of the martial arts, had lost sporting appeal as well as socio-military cachet. The annual festival in London had shrunk to a single afternoon. Even in country districts it was beginning to die out. Richard Carew, High Sheriff of Cornwall, where the tradition was strong and the style ferocious, reckoned that much of its old prestige was gone: there were no silver hatbands for prizes proudly worn by travelling musclemen.[55] The pastoral tradition helped preserve an aristocratic veneer: the wrestling feats of Sir Philip Sidney, the cynosure, was commemorated in Spenser's *The Faerie Queene*, and there is a good-humoured episode in *As You Like It*, based on a passage in Saviolo in which the oafish professional, Charles, is beaten by the dashing amateur Orlando.[56] The gifted noble amateur, defeating the crafty or brutish base-born with apparently effortless ease, was an appealing Renaissance theme that stood the test of time.

Wrestling itself, however, was too slow and undramatic in its violence to stay in fashion, and in later centuries it was to give way to pugilism, which grew out of the prize-fights with sword and quarter-staff. Fynes Morrison, in the next age, detected signs of advance beyond the Elizabethen sword-and-buckler gallants 'of an idle brain who for ridiculous or trifling causes run the trial of single fight' and who quarrelled in the street rather than making 'private trial of their differences' or fought with 'men of base condition', or – coming closer to modern ideas of sport – 'with disparity of numbers assailed one man'. Nevertheless he hoped that a better way could be found 'to preserve reputation than this of single fights.'[57]

Meanwhile Tudor licensing laws were much concerned with keeping out 'men of base condition' from fashionable games like tennis and bowls. In 1592 Thomas Bedingfield, seeking permission to keep houses in London and Westminster for dice, cards, tables, bowls and tennis, proposed exemplary rules: no play before noon on weekdays or during hours of religious service on Sundays, no swearing or blaspheming, and 'none but noblemen, gentlemen and merchants, or such as shall be entered in the Book of Subsidies at £10 in land or goods'.[58]

The schools, which in future years were to become important influences on the honour code of sport, were not yet willing or able to contemplate such a role. The development of secondary education had been set back by Edward VI's pillaging of the chantries. It was now recovering; not by any acts of crown or Parliament but by private enterprise, notably endowments from rich merchants, industrialists, brewers and clothiers and even idealistic well-to-do clergy. Before Elizabeth's reign was over almost all towns of any size had their grammar school, some of which, like Repton, Merchant Taylors', Rugby, Uppingham and Harrow were to achieve celebrity. But the ethos behind their foundation, opening doors of opportunity for the sons of aspirant parents, left little room for leisure activities. The classical curriculum with Latin at the core was under great pressure from arrivistes who wanted to introduce commercially relevant subjects like arithmetic and English, so that even the most trendy schoolmasters were not likely to find time in the crowded day for anything that might be considered frivolous.

There were certainly no organised games: at most the pupils were allowed a 'play-day', a half holiday, in their six days a week, forty-odd weeks a year annual cycle and on these they were required to confirm rigidly to the authorities' idea of appropriate relaxation. The headmaster of newly founded Harrow allowed only whip-and-top, handball and archery. John Brinsley, head of Ashby de la Zouch, made it clear in his treatise on the curriculum that the part of one afternoon he allowed each week for recreation was strictly conditional on the pupils' hard work and good conduct and on their writing verses on the experience afterwards. It was axiomatic that 'all recreation and sports of the scholars would be meet for gentlemen: clownish sports, or perilous ones, or playing for money' were not acceptable.[59]

The most unusual advocate of physical recreation was Richard Mulcaster, master first of Merchant Taylors' and afterwards of St Paul's. He was a progressive in other ways, for instance in supporting the idea of teaching English, but he was never able to achieve this in practice and there is no reason to suppose that he was any more successful in introducing games, least of all football about which he waxed so eloquent. Mulcaster did not challenge accepted social conventions. His support, he made clear, was not for the football 'now commonly used, with thronging of a rude multitude, with bursting of shins and breaking of legs' but for more disciplined encounters under the control of neutral arbiters. His argument was rather that the game could not have reached its present 'greatness' nor 'have been so much used, as it is in all places' had it not been found valuable to health and strength. Provided there was a curb on 'rash running' or 'too much force' which might cause some internal damage or rupture it could help 'weak hams by much moving' and 'simple shanks by thickening the flesh'. Football, properly used, he claimed 'strengthened and brawneth the whole body, by provoking super-fluities downwards it dischargeth the head and upper parts, it is good for the bowels and to drive down the stone from both the bladder and the kidneys'.[60]

There was in fact a stylised version of football in effete Italy *gioso del calcio* (the kicking game) played by the Florentine nobility, with limited numbers of players. And it was doubtless a game of this sort that was played by the sprigs of Scottish aristocracy. The seventh Earl of Argyll, chief of the Campbell clan, had been a player in his youth and there were accounts of a match in which the fourteenth Earl of Sutherland, Lord Willougby and some of their servants played a team of local countrymen.[61] And there are detailed accounts from other Celtic parts of Britain of regional games organised by landed gentry.

The local game in Cornwall, known as hurling, was, according to the High Sheriff, Richard Carew, of two types. In the western part of the county there was a game, hurling to country, with neither 'comparing of numbers nor matching of men' with goals three miles apart and some players on horseback. (Carew commended this for 'manhood and exercise' and found it 'not destitute of policies' and therefore 'semblable to feats of arms', but he also thought it 'rude and rough'.) On the other hand in the east of the county 'hurling to goales' had equal teams of fifteen, twenty or thirty aside with each man marking his opposite number according to strict conventions: 'The Hurlers are bound to the observation of many lawes, as that they must hurle man to man, and not to set upon one man at once: the Hurler against the ball must not butt nor hand-fast under the girdle, he who hath the ball must butt onely in the others brest.'[62]

There are evident traces of the chivalric code of honour. A Pembrokeshire magistrate, describing the Welsh game, knappan, a notoriously violent affair, whilst noting the mayhem and opportunities for grudge-fights was impressed that the players should contend 'not for any wager or valuable thing but strive to the death for glory and fame which they esteem dearer than any worldly wealth'.[63] Indeed it was often this vulgar parody of the gentlemanly code that made it a target for the satirists. In Robert Greene's mock-heroic *Eclogue* of 1587 a shepherdess tells her rustic lover:

> Within thy cap 'tis thou shalt wear my glove,
> At football sport thou shalt my champion be.

Footballers found it hard to shed this oafish, bumpkin image. In Chapman's *Sir Giles Goosecap* of 1591 the eponymous hero, asked why he intends to marry, replies, 'Why, Madam, we have a great match of football towards, married men against bachelors, and the married men be all my friends.'[64] They also had to face the broadsides of the Puritans. To Philip Stubbes football was more 'a friendly kind of fight than a play or recreation', more 'a bloody and murderous practice than a fellowly sport or pastime': was not the idea to lie in wait for an adversary and 'pick him on his nose'? It invited 'envy, malice, rancour, choler, hatred, displeasure, enmity' and sometimes led to 'fighting, brawling, contention, quarrel-picking, murder, homicide and great effusion of blood'.[65]

So it was somewhat unusual to find an Elizabethan schoolmaster recommending such a socially dubious and definitely sweaty exercise. However, Mulcaster was an unusual man, with a prose style as spiky as his opinions, who thought nothing of giving his book a title twenty-seven words long. Another of his idiosyncratic interests was the education of girls. He had reservations about their capacity – 'their brains be not so much charged neither with weight nor with multitude of matters as boys' heads be, and, therefore, like empty casks, they make the greater noise' – and his views on their physical education laid stress on seemliness.[66]

But decorum, as we have seen, was highly important to the Elizabethans.

Once it was assured, even the lower orders and their sports could find a place in the scheme of things, and though urban pursuits still needed oppressive legislation, rustic ones could be tolerated and even admired. The pastoral convention, popular amongst fashionable poets, was a vehicle for romantic declarations and moral reflections. Thus Sir Philip Sidney has a country girl say in one of his poems:

> A time there is for all,
> My mother often says,
> When she with skirts tucked very high
> With girls at stool-ball plays.[67]

This simple game, called after the milking stool at which the pitcher aimed, was a favourite – and decorous – country pastime amonst boys as well as girls. More virile versions, variously call stop-ball, stow-ball or stobbal, were popular in the West Country and further north. In the south-east they used a wicket – a kind of gate – as a target and called the game cricket. The first record of this version, in a law suit about a piece of land, showed that it was being played on the land in question in the mid sixteenth century by boys of the Free School at Guildford, Surrey.[68] If adults played it their games did not find their way into the records either as nuisances or important social occasions.

The reasons for cricket's eventual change of fortune were complex, but they had much to do with the role of sport as an escapist dream-world. Sport was to be an emblem of wealth and leisure for the better sort and a source of profit for the upwardly mobile but its appeal was based on romantic notions of past glories and past virtues, real and imagined. The mythology of rural, heart of oak England, peopled by the solid yeomen of popular imagination, was to flourish in sport even as it dwindled in the new, sophisticated real world of monopolies and money-making.

Notes

1 J. Strutt's editor (*Glig-gamena angel deod: or The Sports and Pastimes of the People of England*, London, 1801; new edition 1903, reprinted Bath, 1969), pp. 85–6, citing Cotton MS Vesp. c. xii, Fol. 281, gives interesting background information, but gets the date wrong. For details of the visit and the flavour of the times see A.F. Pollard, *The Reign of Henry VII from Contemporary Sources*, 3 vols., London, 1913–14, vol. 1 pp. 263–85.

    Tennis's singular method of scoring, preserved in modern lawn tennis, may derive from the four quarters marked by the minute hand of a clock. Sixty was a significant medieval number and the movement of a pointer in a circle a good graphic way of showing the progress of a game. A crown, introduced to England under Wolsey's direction in 1526 in imitation of the French coinage, had sixty pence, and it was a common wager in tennis matches.

2 *The Colloquies of Erasmus* written 1495–9, first printed 1518, trans. C.A. Thompson, Chicago, 1965, pp. 22–30.

3 M. Marples, p. 39. *A History of Football*, London 1954.
4 R.A. Knox and S. Leslie (eds.) *The Miracles of Henry VI*, Cambridge, 1923, pp. 130–2 (Magoun).
5 Sir Guy Campbell, 'The Early History of English Golf' in *A History of Golf in Britain*, ed. B. Darwin, et al., 1952, p. 47, citing Scottish Lord High Treasurer's accounts.
6 J. Leland, *De Rebus Britannicis Collectanae*, v. 357, quoted by J.D. Mackie, *The Earlier Tudors*, Oxford, 1952, p. 192, a good introduction to the period. See also S.T. Bindoff, *Tudor England*, Harmondsworth, 1950.
7 Strutt, *Sport and Pastimes*, pp. 278–9, 'Heavit and hight' = for distance and for height.
8 *Colloquies of Erasmus*, pp. 11–15, 'Military Affairs'; pp. 424–31, 'The Ignoble Knight'.
9 *Boke of St Albans*, facsimile in R. Hands, *English Hawking and Hunting*, Oxford, 1979, p. 80.
10 Ibid., pp. 54–5.
11 J. Cummins, *The Hound and the Hawk*, London, 1988, p. 188.
12 Extract, with modernised spelling, from T. Satchell (ed.), *The Treatyse of Fysshinge Wyth an Angle*, London, 1883 p. 1.
13 R.W. Heinze (ed.), *Proclamations of the Tudor Kings*, Cambridge, 1976, p. 91.
14 Hall, 'The Union of the Two and Illustrious Families of Lancaster and York', 1550, in Heinze, *Tudor Kings*.
15 Heinze, *Tudor Kings*, p. 93.
16 For the population and economic changes see J. Guy, 'The Tudor Age' in K.O. Morgan (ed.), *The Oxford Illustrated History of Britain*, Oxford, 1984, pp. 223–30. For the north–south divide see H. Kearney, *The British Isles*, Cambridge, 1989, pp. 106–13.
17 Heinze, *Tudor Kings*, p. 90.
18 D. Brailsford, *Sport and Society*, London, 1969, p. 31.
19 *The Boke of the Gouvernour*, 1531, ed. F. Watson, London, 1907, p. 78.
20 Ibid., pp. 73–9.
21 Ibid., p. 112.
22 Ibid., p. 82–3.
23 Ibid., p. 84.
24 Heinze, *Tudor Kings*, pp. 181–2.
25 *Toxophilos*, 1545.
26 Elyot, *Boke of the Gouvernour*, p. 112.
27 *Poems of Love and Chivalry*, XV, 1557.
28 Lord Aberdare, *The Story of Tennis*, London 1959, p. 55.
29 *Statute Book* (1485–1710), in library of University College, Galway: modernised version issued by the Gaelic Athletic Association, 1987.
30 N. Elias and E. Dunning, 'Folk Football in Medieval and Early Modern Britain' in *The Sociology of Sport*, ed. E. Dunning, London, 1970, p. 20.
31 Eclogues, V, quoted in Strutt, *Sport and Pastimes*, p. 94.
32 *Boke of the Gouvernour*, p. 113.
33 *The Castell of Helth*, 1541, Fol. 50(V) (Magoun). The most famous Italian game was *calcio* played by the Florentine nobility. See page 69 below.
34 M. Marples, *A History of Football*, London, 1954, p. 46.
35 *The Register of the Privy Council of Scotland*; ed. D. Mason, X, p. 301 (Magoun).
36 *Satire of the Three Estates*, c1535–40, ed. F. Hall, London, 1869, p. 505 (Magoun).
37 Extracts from the *Records of the Burgh of Glasgow* (1573–1642), 1876, I, p. 149, (Magoun).
38 *Early Burgh Organization in Scotland*, D. Murray, I, 1924, p. 233 (Magoun).

39 Marples, *History of Football*, p. 61. 'Moss-troopers' were free-booting border raiders.
40 Strutt, *Sports and Pastimes*, p. 205.
41 *The Scholemaster*, 1530, ed. J. Upton, London, 1743, p. 62.
42 J. Nichols, *Progresses and Pageants of Queen Elizabeth*, London, 1788–1800, vol. i, p. 40, quoted by Strutt, *Sports and Pastimes*, p. 206.
43 P. Hentzner, *Itinerary*, 1598 (trans. Lord Orford) quoted by Strutt, *Sports and Pastimes*, p. 20.
44 J. Stow, *Survey of London*, 1598, quoted by Strutt, *Sports and Pastimes*, p. 224.
45 Strutt, *Sports and Pastimes*, pp. 18–19.
46 Nichols, *Progresses and Pageants*, vol. II, quoted by Strutt, *Sports and Pastimes*, p. 9.
47 Rowland Whyte to Sir Richard Sidney, 12 September, 1660, quoted by Strutt, *Sports and Pastimes*, p. 9.
48 Two contrasting accounts of the period are A.L. Rouse, *The England of Elizabeth*, London, 1950 and J.B. Black, *The Reign of Elizabeth* (2nd edn), Oxford, 1959. For the literary and artistic background see *The Age of Shakespeare* ed. B. Ford (vol. 2 of *New Pelican Guide to English Literature*), Harmondsworth, 1982.
49 Strutt, *Sports and Pastimes*, Chapter 2.
50 Fynes Morrison, *Itinerary*, 1617, quoted in J. Dover Wilson, *Life in Shakespeare's England*, Harmondsworth, 1944, p. 102.
51 For the legislation see F.E. Halliday, *Shakespeare and His Critics*, London, 1949, p. 83.
52 *Vincente Saviolo and his Practice*, 1585. *Romeo and Juliet*, II iv. *As You Like It*, V iii.
53 Henry Porter, *Two Angry Women of Abingdon*, 1599, quoted in Strutt, *Sports and Pastimes*, p. 210.
54 *Paradoxes of Defence*, 1599.
55 *The Survey of Cornwall*, 1602.
56 *The Faerie Queene*, Book IV, Canto IX, verses 13 4, *As You Like It* I ii. It should be noted, however, that Sir Calidore (= Sidney) is the only one of Spenser's knights to show such prowess.
57 Morrison, *Itinerary*.
58 Aberdare, *Story of Tennis*, p. 59.
59 J. Brinsley, *Ludus Literarius*, 1612, ed. E.T. Campagnac, Liverpool, 1917. For a full discussion see Brailsford, *Sport and Society*, pp. 89–91.
60 *Positions: Where in those primitive circumstances be examined which are necessary for the training up of children either for skill in their books, or health in their bodie*, 1561, ed. R.H. Quick, London, 1881, Chapter 27.
61 P.M. Young, *The History of British Football*, London, 1973 edn, p. 64.
62 Carew MS 603, Lambeth Palace Library, pp. 75–6, quoted at length in E. Dunning and K. Sheard, *Barbarians, Gentlemen and Players*, Oxford, 1979, pp. 27 and 35
63 Sir George Owen, *The Description of Pembrokeshire*, 1603 ed. H. Owen, Cymmrodorion Society Research Series no. 1, 1892, pp. 270–82 quoted by Dunning and Sheard, *Barbarians*, p. 28.
64 Young, *History of British Football*, p. 64.
65 *The Anatomie of Abuses*, 1583, ed. F.J. Furnirall, London, 1879. New Shakespeare Society, series VI, no. 6 I, p. 137 (Magoun).
66 Mulcaster, *Positions*, p. 175.
67 *Dialogue between two Shepherdesses*, 1586.
68 *Guildford Book of Court*, 16 January 1598, records the testimony of John Derrick, aged 59 'or thereabouts' that in his youth he and other scholars of the Free School 'did runne and play . . . at Crickett and other Plaies' on a disputed piece of land. There is reference on p. 370 to John Florio's *A Worlde of Wordes*, London, 1598, which

defines the Italian word *sgrillare* as 'to make a noise as a cricket, to play cricket-a-wicket, and be merry'. This gives a clue as to how it was played: a cricket was, amongst other things, a foot-stool; a wicket was a small gate: either would make suitable targets. That it was a children's game is clear. As late as 1611 Randle Cotgrove's *A dictionary of the French and English Tongues* defines 'crosse' as 'the crooked staff wherewith boyes play at cricket'.

CHAPTER FOUR

Princes and people

1603–88

The alignment of England and Scotland in the Protestant cause exposed and widened social and cultural divisions. In Scotland, the gulf between Highlands and Lowlands grew as Puritan emphasis on Bible-reading in the literate south contrasted with the oral traditions of the north. The Highlanders themselves were torn by the rift between the Campbells, who accepted the Reformation, and their arch-enemies, the MacDonalds. In the Lowlands the episcopalian, hierarchical society north of the Tay contrasted with the south, where lairds and townsmen joined in support of Presbyterianism, and the rural south-west where the small farmers associated inherited wealth with sin, taking strong exception to both. It added fuel to the fires of Ireland (where collapsing feudalism was at odds with the Crown and its urban supporters and the legislators imposing the English common law) by introducing Protestant planters from Scotland as well as England.

The most dramatic consequence, however, was that when Elizabeth died James VI of Scotland became King of England. James, an arch-manipulator of the factions in the Scottish nobility, misjudged the size of his new task particularly in its European dimensions, but he was sustained by a vast conceit and a strong sense of his own destiny. In his month-long journey south to London he made good first impressions by his affability and his enthusiasm for hunting. But longer acquaintance showed him to be arbitrary, arrogant and, behind the lecturing and pedantry, rather foolish.

He was not physically appealing. He was spindly-legged. He never washed his hands, preferring to oil them, and he was forever fondling youthful courtiers. He had big, wet blue eyes and a tongue too big for his mouth, which led to sloppy eating and drinking habits: the strong, sweet Greek wines he liked would dribble down his chin. He drank a lot, though he was rarely as drunk as his mumbling speech, Scottish accent, rolling eyes and peculiar gait made him seem. He would talk, confidently and often wittily, on all manner of subjects in private but he lacked dignity in more formal gatherings.[1]

Basilicon Doron

James saw himself as the embodiment of Renaissance virtues. He compiled several books from his omnivorous youthful reading, unoriginal but given force by the pithy, authoritarian views with which he laced them. One such, dedicated to his son, Henry, was *Basilicon Doron*, the Royal Gift (1599), a collection of precepts for the proper education of his son, Prince Henry. Its tone was lofty, redolent of Greek notions of all-round excellence and moderation in all things, the Roman ideal of *mens sana in corpore sano*, the chivalric concept of noblesse oblige, and the emergent English code based on 'fair law'.

James expounded the conventional wisdom that 'it becometh a prince best of any man to be a fair and good horseman', and advocated horseback sports 'such as the tilt, the ring and low-riding for handling of your sword'. He listed 'exercises of the body most commendable to be used by a young prince, in such honest games . . . as may . . . maintain health' enabling a king to 'exercise his engine' lest it rust through inactivity, and making the royal body 'durable for travel': these included running, leaping, wrestling, fencing and ('moderately, not making a craft of them') dancing and 'playing at the caiche', but excluded 'rumling violent exercises' like football, which were more suited to laming people than building them up. Some games could properly be played for their own sake or 'for banishing of idleness, the mother of all vice', but a young prince should eschew all 'such tumbling tricks as only serve for comedians and gysairis to win their bread with'.[2]

James favoured hunting of the traditional kind 'with running hounds' rather than the modern 'thievish form' with guns. He spent much of the year at one or other of his hunting lodges in the Home Counties. In daylight hours he would stay in the saddle for hours on end, closely attended by a cup-bearer. The kill excited him greatly and he delighted in plunging his legs into the beast's steaming entrails (a ghoulish habit that may have had something to do with the belief that stag's blood would strengthen weak limbs). As he grew older and less active he increasingly preferred his vast deer-park at Theobald's, Hertfordshire, the scene of many orgies and drinking sessions, hawking and the politer forms of hunting. In old age he would have himself carried in a litter to the forest, and not long before his death he defied doctor's orders to go from Royston to Newmarket to see some choice birds.

James and his courtiers also spent a great deal of time horse-racing. This was by no means a new sport in England. Matching the speed and endurance of horses was a sport for aristocrats in *Beowulf*, a source of disobedience amongst monks in Bede, a natural concomitant of horse-dealing in FitzStephen, and the sport to which the Saddler's Company in Chester, deploring football hooliganism, transferred their allegiance in 1540, offering a silver bell as a prize.[3] Yet the Scottish nobility were particularly enthusiastic about it. That same year, 1540, the poet Sir David Lindsay was castigating the young bloods careering along the sands at Leith.[4] In 1552 Lord Seytoun, probably reviving an ancient custom, presented the Provost and Bailies of nearby Haddington with a silver bell for an annual horse-race, and soon every lowland town of any size had its gold or silver bell.[5] And it was James I and his cronies, much taken with the Newmarket terrain, who sparked off a new aristocratic enthusiasm in England.

The new fashion greatly stimulated horse-breeding, hitherto a somewhat neglected art in Britain. It also aroused great interest in foreign bloodstock. Arabs and Barbaries were renowned for their speed and manoeuvrability: the ponderous north European destrier was manifestly useless at racing, and native breeds, such as the Irish hobbies, were assumed to lack the requisite class.[6] Gervase Markham, an early expert, did well out of importing Arabs, reputedly selling one to the King for £500. An important task James gave his Master of Horse, George Villiers, was to seek out fine horses abroad and bring them back (in Royal Navy ships).

Villiers, later Duke of Buckingham, was the light of James' middle-aged life. Under Buckingham's influence the King hankered after European adventure and when Parliament denied him the money for it sought new sources of revenue. Thereafter his manipulation of trade monopolies was a constant source of tension. In particular the disposal of the alehouse concession took away a customary perquisite from landowners at a time when James was trying to get them to stay in the country and pay more attention to the duties of magistracy.

A less publicised monopoly south of the border was the golfball concession. In the month of his accession to the English throne James had appointed one William Mayne his club-maker for life suggesting a serious intention of keeping on with the game in England.[7] To what extent he did so is not clear, though anecdotal evidence has him striking out at Blackheath. He certainly played pall mall, a 'Frenchified' cross between golf and croquet, an expensive recreation which required a specially constructed and carefully groomed alley with side walls half a mile long, and which gave its name to the superior avenue where it was played, Pall Mall.[8] Back home golfball manufacture was a serious issue. Dutch balls had been imported for a century or more and the usual modern variety made of leather fetched a good price. James' accession to the English throne gave him a firmer grip on such matters and in 1618, noting that 'no small quantity of gold and silver' was 'transported yierly out of his Heines' Kingdom of Scotland' James granted a monopoly for twenty-one years to James Melville and associates, subject to a maximum price of four shillings (= four English pence)[9] which was as much as some of the new capitalist employers paid their workers for ten or twelve hours work.

The 'Book of Sports'

The games working people played were beginning to cause problems in hitherto untroubled country districts, now turning to manufacture. As early as

1608 in Manchester, which was just emerging from its manorial origins to become a textile centre, the Court Leet reported 'grave disorder in our town' with 'glass windows boken . . . by lewd and disordered persons' resulting in fines of twelve pence for playing football in the street.[10] Tennis and bowls, especially in London, were being taken up by artisans, a danger to morality and the social proprieties. London, of course, was in a category of its own. Tudor licensing arrangements for fencing schools had broken down. The Masters of Defence were largely a front for commercial prize-fights, stakes were growing and violence was on the increase at their events. They might start decorously enough, with protected blades, but then the crowd would cry 'sharps' and the blood would flow. Duelling was frequent, a drunken parody of the chivalric code of honour.

Yet it was old religious allegiances that brought sport to the centre of the political stage requiring the intervention of the king himself. There was a new twist to the old concern about the way the lower orders spent their leisure time. Now that archery practice had ceased to be thought desirable they were supposed to spend it reading the Bible or thinking improving thoughts. Catholic magistrates generally allowed games-playing after divine service, but this was thought outrageous and provocative in Puritan circles, which were widening all the time. In Edinburgh games 'sic as Gof' had been banned all day on the Sabbath since 1592. On a tombstone at Llanfair church, South Wales, appeared the warning

> Who ever hear on Sunday
> will practis playing at Ball
> It may be before Monday
> The Devil will Have you all.[11]

In 1607 young men of Aberdeen were arraigned for profaning the Sabbath by 'drinking, playing football, dancing and roving from parish to parish'.[12] At Guisborough, Yorkshire, in 1616 a man was charged with 'making a banquet for football players' on a Sunday.[13]

The question for Puritans, as expressed by Stubbes, was whether 'the playing at foot-ball, reding of mery bookes and such like delectations' profaned the Sabbath day.[14] They had only one answer. But Puritanism was essentially a middle class movement. A day of quiet contemplation each week was all very well for those who had leisure on weekdays for more exciting activities, but a bit hard on the average man in the fields. Matters came to a head in Lancashire, a county of extremes. Many of the aristocracy and their rustic followers clung obstinately to the old faith but Puritanism was also strong. Sunday sport was an inevitable source of conflict. In 1616 the Manchester justices banned 'piping, dancing, bowling, bear- and bull-baiting' or any other 'profanation' at any time on the Sabbath and similar restrictions were imposed in surrounding districts.

The following year as James was returning from Scotland a party of Lancashire villagers met him at Myerscough with a petition complaining about the attempt to ban their customary amusements. The King made an impromptu speech promising them protection. They took him at his word, and the following Sunday there were complaints from churchgoers in the vicinity that their worship had been disturbed by music, piping, dancing, shouting and laughter outside. The outcome was a declaration drawn up on the King's instructions by the local bishop to be read from pulpits throughout Lancashire. It was a rambling document but it answered the purpose, which was compromise. The King rebuked certain 'Puritans and precise people' for interfering with the people's 'lawful recreations' and ordained that after divine service on Sundays and other holy days piping, dancing, archery, leaping and vaulting and other harmless recreations were to be allowed. Yet he maintained existing legislation which forbade bear- and bull-baiting and interludes on Sundays and bowling 'for the meaner sort of people' at all times.[15]

James was so impressed by the success of his Solomon-like judgement in Lancashire that in 1618 he ordered an expanded version to be read in every pulpit in England and Scotland, adding approval of May games, Whitsun ales, Morris dances and the like 'in due and convenient time' to his bounty. James's *Book of Sports*, as it came to be known, was a setback for extreme Puritanism. Its arguments, taken at face value, were hard to counter – the people would turn from the church if it allowed them no amusement; they would be 'less able for war'; if denied sport they would spend more time in the alehouse. Most telling of all when would 'the common people have leave to exercise if not upon Sundays and holy days, seeing they must apply their labour and win their living in all working days?'[16]

The *Book of Sports* gave pause to extremists but otherwise only appealed to the converted. The moderate Puritan William Perkins concluded that the common people should have time for recreation during the week and the idiosyncratic Oxford cleric Robert Burton suggested that 'if one half-day in a week were allowed to our household servants for their merry-making by their hard masters . . . they would labour harder for the rest of their time.'[17] No such dangerous experiments were tried, however, and in truth workers' rights were not even remotely the central issue. The Declaration was a gambit in the political struggle between their betters.

Sir Symonds d'Ewes, for instance, noted in his diary how the Declaration had been celebrated by students at Cambridge University, as a goad to Puritan dons. The rebels indulged in 'foppish recreations', even invading the Fellows' bowling green. To celebrate the first anniversary of the Declaration they played football (at which d'Ewes broke his shin), bowls, jumping, running, pitching the bar, and – his own favourites – tennis, shovel-groats and cards.[18] They made plans for sports meetings on the Gogmagog Hills lasting a month or more to be designated the Olympic Games but this was a political gesture in honour of the Cotswold 'Olympicks' founded by Captain Robert Dover, an intensely Royalist Catholic lawyer, in 1604. Conducted in great splendour and ceremonial, with Dover parading on a white horse, the Olympicks offered a vast array of uplifting and inspiring activities – cudgel-play, wrestling, the quintain, leaping, pitching the bar and the hammer, pikestaff, leap-frog, windball, acrobatics, smock-races for the girls, country dancing by virgins, hare-coursing and horse-racing. There was feasting on traditional lines and generous prizes were awarded in a somewhat self-conscious attempt to recreate 'merrie England'.

Students were the last people to care much about how the common people found time for recreation. The universities had become great breeding grounds for snobbery. The poor scholar, once revered, was now an object of derision, and the games he played revealed his inferiority: 'A mere scholar is an intelligible ass, or a silly fellow in black . . . The antiquity of his university is his creed and the excellency of his college (though but for a match at football) an article of his faith' was how one of James' more flamboyant courtiers put it.[19] A special brand of satire was directed at university footballers: in a popular play a Bachelor of Arts called Hammershin was 'sent for far and near by the valiant of the parishes to play matches at football . . . not a serving man can keep an arm or a leg whole for him'.[20] By contrast a sketch of 'a young gentleman of the university' by a future bishop of Worcester concluded: 'The two marks of his seniority is the bare velvet of his gown and his proficiency at tennis . . . of all things he endures not to be mistaken for a scholar.'[21]

Towards the end of James' reign a fully-fledged authority on etiquette appeared. This was Henry Peacham, whose The Compleat Gentleman, first published in 1622, went through many editions. (Johnson used its heraldry section in compiling his Dictionary.) Peacham's line was that certain intrinsically noble sports and games found a response in noble youth, thus fortifying nature with nurture, and conversely that such gentlemanly amusements were not suited to the lower orders and might indeed be damaging to their moral fibre. It was Basilicon Doron enlarged and improved.

Civil War

The gap between Jacobean theory and reality was, however, beginning to show and to matter. The country's economic state was widely blamed on

James' extravagance and he had caused a shortage of bullion by giving the gold and silver thread monopoly to the Villiers family. Spanish invasion of Holland led to a war that brought the cloth trade to the brink of collapse, sharply reduced land values and greatly encouraged emigration. When Charles I came to the throne in 1625 relations with Parliament were at a low ebb, and unable to tolerate his priggish absolutism, Parliament dissolved itself and refused him funds for overseas wars. From 1629 to 1640 he stubbornly ruled without Parliament; showing great resource in unearthing ancient, alternative sources of revenue such as Ship Money, a levy for coastal defence. He used it wisely for the most part, restoring the navy, neglected by his father, and protecting schemes of emigration and colonisation. Royal income was buoyant, at a time when the country was reeling from inflation: from the £350,000 a year James I inherited it had risen to over £1 million by the late 1630s. Charles was wilful, however: he upset the London merchants by sponsoring rivals to existing overseas monopolists such as the East India Company; and he extended the monopoly system to include everyday things like soap, starch and salt to the general chagrin whilst his raids on Ship Money for his own purposes led to tax strikes and court cases.

The country's basic problem was that the population was rising faster than food resources – from about 6 million in 1600 to 7.5 million in 1650, of which 5.5 million were in England. There were severe food shortages, even starvation in places, until a variety of factors combined to ease matters: improved agricultural production, mainly through enclosure of land; better communications; better credit arrangements; and eventual levelling-off of population growth. The worst problem was inflation: prices had risen to eight times their 1500 level by 1640, and wages by less than three times. Yet there was surprisingly little violence, and though the Scots were restive, James' plantation policy in Ulster, spearheaded by a London consortium which transformed Derry into Londonderry, seemed to be working.

Policies apart, however, Charles I lacked the common touch. He had none of his father's gifts for back-slapping rough bonhomie. He followed the precepts of *Basilicon Doron* too rigidly. Newmarket was an interest: he kept up the Royal stables and in 1627 inaugurated the Spring and Autumn meetings which have been going on every since. He greatly enjoyed riding as an exercise, extending Richmond Park for the purpose, but he somehow always seemed somewhat aloof. His interest in hunting was real enough and his tastes were less crude than his father's. Yet he was unsportingly keen to establish his rights, invoking medieval Forest law and strictly enforcing it through Special Commissions. At Rockingham and Waltham Forest, the New Forest and the Forest of Dean ancient boundaries were reinstated – Rockingham, for instance, was extended from six square miles to sixty. This was not popular, and Charles's circle of friends grew smaller and smaller.

The new movement towards enclosure of land forced land prices and rents up, creating a smaller if more prosperous yeoman class. The squire class grew and extended its interests into manufacture and trade, often putting its younger sons into lucrative professions, notably law, or even turning them into master-craftsmen. At the other end of the scale landless labourers suffered badly not least because there was a time lag between higher prices and higher wages. Enclosure also affected common land and its privileges, restricting opportunities for ordinary folk to catch coneys or woodcock and to play games. Similarly the drainage of the fens, for the purpose of reclaiming arable or pasture land, held no appeal for the locals, who preferred a free supply of pike or duck. In 1638, a game of campball, an East Anglian version of football, was used as a cloak for the destruction of drainage ditches – one of many similar incidents that were to disturb the authorities in the troubled times to come.

Charles was still plagued by the political arguments over Sunday observance. In 1625, on assuming office, he had signed an Act of Parliament forbidding people to take part in Sunday sport outside their own parishes; and he stiffened the penalties for law-breakers. But whatever credit this gave him with Puritan magistrates was soon outweighed by his later measures in which he was much influenced by Bishop William Laud, a leading Arminian – a group that supported royal absolutism in return for reciprocal recognition for the church – who later became Archbishop of Canterbury. First, in 1632 Charles renewed his father's order rusticating the gentry. Then the following year he forbade Chief Justice Richardson (publicly insulted by Laud for showing too much leniency to Puritan magistrates in Somerset who failed to implement the law) to travel the Western Circuit. Finally Charles, contemptuously rejecting a petition from the magistrates to curb Sunday sport, resurrected his father's Declaration, causing it to be read from every pulpit once again.

The Declaration did not apply to Scotland, where it was regarded as evidence of the King's softness towards Catholics. Charles was finding it increasingly difficult to govern his native land from London. His authoritarian, conformist soul led him first to challenge the lairds' authority over, and title to, the land they had grabbed from the church, then to try to impose the English prayer book on Scotland. His attempt at a punitive invasion was undermined by Parliament's reluctance to trust him with troops and it was the Scots who invaded England, occupying Newcastle in the autumn of 1640. In the subsequent negotiations Charles lost his privileges with such bad grace that Parliament began to consider stronger measures. When Ulster Catholics rebelled, and their efforts to disarm their Protestant oppressors spilled over into a massacre of some 3,000 of them – one in five – Parliament would not entrust the King with raising an army to quell the rebellion.

The resulting Civil War was an odd affair, with old arguments over ideals and policies now subsumed in a struggle for power. Neither side had a clearly defined membership, though the Royalists (Cavaliers) included most of the nobility, some country gentlemen and most town authorities outside London, whilst the Parliament side (Roundheads) included most members of the Commons, virtually all the middle class Puritans, most merchants, some lawyers and a few dissident courtiers. London was divided.

The war began slowly and fitfully, but the Roundheads were able to suppress the Cavaliers in London, the seaports and the manufacturing towns, and they soon controlled Kent, Surrey and Essex, and East Anglia was shortly in the grip of Oliver Cromwell, a gentleman farmer with a business brain. In many districts Puritan magistrates began to assert or reassert their authority: events like the Cobb Ale at Lyme Regis and Dover's Cotswold Games came to an end. In 1642 the London authorities decided to close the play-houses, which, of course, meant closing the bear-gardens as well.

Bear-baiting was a potent symbol of the old order, but there was at least a suspicion that, as Macaulay put it 'The Puritan hated bear-baiting not because it gave pain to the bear but because it gave pleasure to the spectators.'[22] This reputation lost them sympathy at all levels of society. In 1643, Charles' Queen, Henrietta Maria, a French Catholic, coming back from the continent to support her husband, brought with her a collection of particularly baitable bears and distributed them en route. When Cromwell's men found a bait in progress they tied the bears to a tree and shot them. This earned them no friends; nor, indeed, did wringing the necks of fighting cocks.

As in most wars ordinary frivolous human pursuits continued, and indeed a new one emerged from obscurity. Cricket, not mentioned in the *Book of Sports*, had been moving up the age-range – and the social scale – ever since. In 1622 six parishioners of Boxgrove, Sussex, were charged with disturbing the peace by playing cricket in the churchyard on Sunday, breaking windows and endangering the life of a small girl.[23] In 1628 the eight Sabbath-breakers punished at nearby East Lavant included one also guilty of multiple adultery.[24] In 1629 Henry Cuffen, a curate at Ruckinge, criticised for playing cricket, claimed in defence that it was played by persons of repute and quality.[25] And in 1646, at the height of the Civil War, a cricket match at Coxheath led to a lawsuit over a gambling debt.[26]

The Commonwealth

After the war Cromwell's regime did not greatly disturb the leisure pursuits of the rich; but the old popular festivals were abolished and Roman holidays were replaced by a day a month to be set aside for prayer and fasting. Cromwell clamped down on alehouses and inns, which needed special attention once the monopolies were ended, not only for their encouragement of drink and tobacco (an Elizabethan innovation which had become London's biggest import by 1640), but for their consequent stimulation of wild political and religious enthusiasms. Similarly sport amongst the lower orders was now suspect not only in urban bowling alleys and tennis courts because it encouraged gambling and drink but also in the country where, 'under the pretence of football matches and cudgel-playing and the like', there were 'suspicious meetings and assemblies . . . of very disaffected persons'.[27]

The executioners of Charles I had no great collective urge towards radical social reform. The Council appointed to govern 'the Commonwealth or Free State' included many idealists and religious extremists, but their prospectus left little room for egalitarianism or anarchism. Cromwell himself set about ruthlessly reconquering Ireland before bearing down on the Scots, afterwards disbanding the surviving Rump of the old Parliament. For a few months the country was ruled by a nominated body – Barebones' Parliament – intended as an Assembly of Saints. But sanctity fell foul of human pragmatism and they soon gave way to a Protectorate, with Cromwell sharing power with an elected Council. Election to this body was not by popular suffrage but by property owners worth £200 or more. Hence an early priority was to control the seething mass of 'masterless men', from itinerant preachers and rural squatters on commons and wastes to rogues, vagabonds and beggars, prowling the countryside or lurking in the London streets.

A government that behaved as arrogantly and sanctimoniously as Cromwell's invited charges of hypocrisy. At school and at Cambridge, one critic said, Cromwell had been 'more famous for his exercises in the fields than in the schools . . . being one of the chief match-makers and players at football, cudgel or any other boisterous sport or game'.[28] There was also a rumour that Cromwell and other members of the Council had in 1655 watched a hurling match in Hyde Park played by 150 Cornishmen, one side wearing red caps, the other white.[29] What was certain was that his government took sabbatarian purity to inordinate lengths, and their use of soldiery to discover breaches of the law went beyond anything Wolsey's commissioners had ever attempted. An ordinance of 1654 requiring schoolmasters to be examined for undesirable practices made popery a dismissible offence along with adultery and profane behaviour: other serious misdemeanours were card-playing, dicing and support by word or deed of Whitsun ales, wakes, morris dancing, Maypoles, stage plays or such like licentious practices. If soldiers entering private homes was particularly resented, chopping down Maypoles and disrupting popular festivals was thought petty and vindictive; both were counter-productive.

In 1655 Cromwell divided England and Wales into eleven districts, each supervised by a Major-General, to implement Sabbath day laws and to stamp out idle and dissolute behaviour generally. Bear-baiting, cock-fighting, horse-racing and any other sport that might attract unlawful assemblies were to be suppressed along with drunkenness, blasphemy, gambling, play-going and frequenting brothels. In Scotland all boisterous games were banned 'for the better observance of the Lord's Day'. In Ireland in 1656 cricket was specifically forbidden and all 'sticks' and balls were to be confiscated for burning by the public hangman. In Cheshire, where some two hundred alehouses were suppressed, an ordinance of 1656 forbade fiddlers and minstrels from making music in any inn, alehouse and tavern.

The major-generals had their work cut out. 'I am much troubled by these market towns everywhere', reported one, 'vices abounding and magistrates fast asleep.'[30] Their oppressive rule, resented by local authorities as well as by citizens, did not last long. Meanwhile resourceful sinners kept one jump ahead when the troops searched kitchens in search of forbidden emblems of popery like plum pudding, and the celebrations resumed once they had left. When Parliament met in 1656 on what was no longer supposed to be Christmas Day conscientious members recorded their anger that many shops were closed. But they spoke to a thinly-attended House.

Apart from the ending of monopolies, the transition was not marked by any democratic share-out of the spoils of victory. Crown and church lands went to the state or were sold to private citizens, mostly leading Republicans, successful soldiers or merchants looking for speculative ventures: otherwise little property changed hands. Royalist squires were relieved of government office – sometimes without regret – but not of their lands. They paid heavy taxes and fines for 'malignancy' but were mostly able to cling on to their estates. John Evelyn, the Cavalier diarist who returned to England after visiting the court in exile, recorded no disastrous losses, bankruptcies or changes of ownership in his friends' country estates.

Indeed he had a high old time hunting deer in Wiltshire, hawking in the Midlands, watching a coach race in Hyde Park, playing bowls at Tower Green and seeing a famous rope-dancer perform in the London streets.[31] London, the great Parliamentary stronghold, had in practice been unable or unwilling to press restrictive legislation too far. The Vere Street tennis court, for instance, had remained open throughout the Civil War, despite its Royalist reputation. The court-keeper, Charles Gibbons, had been reported by an escaped Royalist prisoner as a man 'unto whose house noblemen resort there and eat' but Vere Street continued to be a venue for plays, and for illicit actors, after the ban on theatres. The plays were eventually stopped – on information received – but no action was taken against Gibbons, who indeed sought to open a second tennis court under the Commonwealth. In 1654 John Tilson 'and others' petitioned the Protector and Council 'to prohibit Charles Gibbons, a tennis court keeper near Lincoln's Inn Fields, from erecting another tennis court, to the disturbance and ill example of others in this time of reformation'. But the second tennis court went ahead, later becoming, as fashion changed, the Lincoln's Inn Theatre.[32]

The Major-Generals knew the score. One of them, having authorised the Earl of Exeter to proceed with arrangements for the Lady Grantham Cup at Lincoln, reported afterwards to Cromwell that he had assured the Earl 'that it was not your highness's intention in the suppressing of horse races to abridge gentlemen of that sport, but to prevent the great confluence of irreconcilable enemies'.[33] Yet horse-racing was not only a dubious activity in itself but had a bad effect on serious horse-breeding. Long before the civil war Sir Edward Howard petitioned Charles I to improve cavalry mounts, severely criticising the indifference of the nobility to military needs in contrast with their lavish spending on race-horses. Cromwell, a noted horse-lover, had shown great interest in his early years in breeding for farm-work and for field sports. He became a fine cavalry commander and as Army Commander in 1648 he had confiscated the fine Arab and continental stock in the Royal Stud and sent many of the best to Ireland to be crossed with coarser breeds. Afterwards as Lord Protector he built up a stud, small but distinguished, using judicious Arab imports (his stallion, the White Turk, was famous) for utilitarian purposes. Yet he did little to curtail horse-racing.

Another legacy of aristocratic decadence was the destrier, originally bred for war and a campaign-winner in its time but trading on its reputation for centuries, and a doubtful quantity even as a sporting horse now that jousting had become an antiquarian interest. Enthusiasts for the Great Horse nevertheless maintained that sophisticated techniques of equitation could overcome the problem of its unwieldiness on the battlefield. These included 'airs above the ground' like the curvet, the volte, the half-piroutte and the capriole (leaping in the air kicking with front and hind legs). William Cavendish, Duke of Newcastle, exiled in Europe during the Civil War, had used the time to promulgate his own system of horse management.[34] He was a flamboyant and influential advocate. Nevertheless the Great Horse faded into insignificance, until its eventual reappearance in the circus ring.

The aristocratic passion for horse-racing, by contrast, was to prove irresistible. Fashionable horse-breeders also began to look for speed and agility because of the changing pattern of hunting. Many deer parks had been broken up during the Civil War, and post-war conditions – the accelerating pace of enclosure, new systems of agriculture and the incursion of iron-works and other industrial enterprise into the countryside – led to more intensive and localised cultivation of crops and improved animal husbandry, which meant that people who wanted to hunt would in future need horses that could jump fences.

In general, the old values survived. The stag was still the noble and the hare the gentlemanly quarry. Foxes were well down the social scale, and were, of course, also inedible. If hawking declined it was not because the Commonwealth government thought it distasteful – it was one of Cromwell's favourite relaxations – but because shooting and netting were more popular. Izaak Walton's *Compleat Angler*, which first appeared in 1653 about the time of the Assembly of Saints experiment, proved more durable, meriting a second edition in 1655. Walton, a city ironmonger of high church Anglican Royalist leanings, came in for criticism, though not for encouraging the unbridled pursuit of pleasure. The book's chief critic, a retired Cromwellian trooper, Richard Franck, who had served in Scotland, was scornful of Walton's ignorance of salmon-fishing and accused him of plagiarism.[35]

High-minded hypocrisy administered by Major-Generals was not a successful formula, but even after its abandonment the campaign to purge the common people of sin continued. The policy offered diminishing returns, and after Cromwell's death in 1658 increasingly lacked conviction. In Bristol, on the day before Shrove Tuesday, 1660, the bellman's reading of the annual proclamation forbidding cock-throwing, dog-tossing, street football and the rest, caused a riot. It was emblematic of the end of the Commonwealth, which brought an invitation to assume the throne to Charles I's dissolute son.

The Restoration and the Puritan legacy

On the day of Charles II's triumphal entry to London John Evelyn wrote 'I stood in the Strand and beheld it and blessed God.'[36] Charles accepted the gift of a Bible and swore to live by it. In fact he changed his life-style not at all. His womanising since early youth had become a byword throughout Europe and he was fortunate to be blessed with a strong constitution. This gave a new and more realistic slant to the precepts of *Basilicon Doron*. Charles II kept himself fit for work and sex by intense athletic activity: riding, hunting, swimming and tennis. By his mid-thirties, Samuel Pepys noticed, he was having a steel-yard carried to the tennis court, weighing himself before and after the game.[37] Though deplorable, however, Charles II was no mere rake. He was an opportunist and a shrewd and supple politician, and he needed to be to survive the vicissitudes of his early life. He had the common touch his father lacked, nurtured during his spell as a fugitive, and an ingratiating manner developed over nine years of exile in Europe. He recognised that England wanted the form and style of monarchy but not a tyrant or a pursist who sought to control Parliament by edict or prerogative.

He also realised that people were hungry for pleasure. Tennis had never lost its attraction and now it regained social cachet: Charles' visits to the court drew admiring crowds. Pepys had mixed feelings about this, remarking on one occasion 'to see how the King's play was extolled without any cause at all, was a loathsome sight, though sometimes, indeed, he did play very well and deserved to be commended.'[38] This match was at Hampton Court Palace. Charles had another court built at Whitehall (though according to Pepys, it was built so badly that it fell down). The aspirant nobility, like Lord Sandwich, also had new courts. Commercial courts were challenged by rival attractions, notably the theatre, and were sometimes converted.

Yet there was good money to be made at tennis, if not by court-keepers, then by players. Contemporary memoirs describe, for instance, Richard Bouchier who, 'if he could have lived upon two or three hundred a year, the tennis court might have maintained him'. Bouchier's need for money evidently led him into devices later associated with crafty professionals from the lower classes: he 'won a pretty deal of money . . . not so much by his skill, as his dexterity in hiding it.'[39] Bowls also retained its ambivalent reputation. Royalty and the aristocracy and gentry enjoyed it, as did Pepys and his lady wife; but it was blemished, the current pundit Charles Cotton reckoned, by 'swarms of rooks'.[40] Tennis was debased by the social laxity of public courts and simplified versions played by artisans. Pall mall was more exclusive: Pepys noted the patronage of the Duke of York (the King's brother and the future James II) and marvelled at the meticulous preparation the alley required.

Another expensive fashion was introduced by Charles II himself. During his exile he had been presented with a 66 foot pleasure boat, known as a yacht, by the Dutch East India Company, and in 1661 he and brother James staged a race for £100 from Greenwich to Gravesend and back. Evelyn, on the King's boat, proudly noted that 'there were diverse noble persons and lords on board, His Majesty sometimes steering himself.[41] When in 1665 war broke out (against the Dutch, largely for commercial reasons), Charles' yachts went into naval service which greatly enhanced the sport's reputation: Charles built 14 new ones during the 1670s and his life-long interest not only stimulated naval recruitment and ship design but ensured an aristocratic following for the sport.

Charles had also learned ice-skating during his exile. In England skating had hitherto been mainly confined to the artisans of the Fen country as a means of transport in winter. Nothing had been heard of it in London since FitzStephen's twelfth century description of young men propelling themselves with sticks across the frozen marshes of Moorfields on sharpened bones. In Holland, however, it was not only a general means of winter locomotion in the country and a standard skill for the military but a fashionable leisure activity. Now in the exceptionally cold winter of 1662 Charles patronised a display on the new canal in St James's Park. Both Pepys, who thought it 'a very pretty art', and Evelyn – impressed by the 'strange and wonderful dexterity of the sliders . . . performed before their Majesties' – witnessed the spectacle.[42] The weather afterwards limited ice-skating's popularity in London, though twenty-one years later when the Thames froze over for three months it enjoyed a brief but spectacular revival.

But Charles, like all the Stuarts, above all enjoyed riding horses. He greatly enlarged Cromwell's stud, importing many fine Arabians and commissioning the Levant Company to acquire ten horses a year for him. His interest in the cavalry was mainly for ceremonial purposes and he did little for English or Irish breeds, or for hunters – he preferred hawking, possibly because it was more suited to the ladies. But no-one was keener on racing. In 1665 he inaugurated the Town Plate at Newmarket, the first race for which rules have survived. Disputes were to be settled by the noblemen and gentlemen who had contributed to the prize 'but more especially' by a judge elected by majority of contributors. When the King was present he, of course, acted as judge. Yet he was no mere patron: he chiefly enjoyed the actual riding. In 1670, in his mid-forties, he rode his horse Woodcock to victory in the Town Plate, defeating amongst others the 22 year old Duke of Monmouth, reputedly Charles' illegitimate son, a future aspirant to the throne. And ten years later Charles was still winning races when his opponents might well have included illegitimate grandchildren. His fondness for a particular horse, Old Rowley – an 'ill-favoured stallion . . . remarkable for getting fine colts' – gave rise to much humour. Charles enjoyed the joke of the shared nickname and the Rowley Mile was named in honour of both.[43]

On 25 July 1663 Pepys noted that 'having intended to go this day to see a famous race at Banstead Downs . . . hear it is put off, because the Lords do sit in Parliament to-day'. In later years Parliamentary business was to be either rearranged or neglected when such a clash arose. Meanwhile Charles would not miss the Autumn meeting at Newmarket and important committees were scheduled with this in mind. As Theobalds was to his grandfather, Newmarket was to Charles. The royal lodge was the scene of great feasts and orgies, and all manner of sporting activities. As the versifier Tom D'Urfey put it:

> Let cullies that lose at a race
> Go venture at hazard to win,

> Or he that is bubbl'd at dice
> Recover at cocking again.[44]

Puritanism did not disappear. The Commonwealth had failed to translate Puritan ethics into legally ordained national purity but the ethics themselves had sunk deep into the national consciousness. The discouragement of idleness in the lower orders was a notion dear to the heart of the governing classes. And there were also many Puritans amongst the workers. Frustrated members of the new sects of the Commonwealth years, denied meaningful political and social change, plunged even more fervently into soul-searching. One celebrated moralist the tinker John Bunyan, actually saw the light whilst playing a game. He had been an immoderate lover of hockey, dancing, ballad-reading and, not least, tip-cat. One day, though he had heard a sermon against dancing and games, he had nevertheless fallen into temptation. 'But . . . as I was in the midst of a game of cat and having struck it one blow from the hole, just as I was about to strike it a second time a voice did suddenly dart from heaven into my soul, "Wilt thou leave thy sins and go to heaven or have thy sins and go to hell?" '[45] There was only one choice.

But Puritanism lost much of its political clout, not only in Parliament but in the magistracy. The powerful alliance between squire and parson forged by the Corporation Act of 1661 strengthened the position of the gentry in the boroughs, and the Act of Settlement of 1662 expelled nearly two thousand clergy from the established church into legal but down-trodden Dissent. The old House of Lords was re-created as if the Commonwealth had never been. One of the casualties of the new dispensation was the old legislation against Sunday sport. It was 1667 before new laws 'for the better observation of the Lord's Day' were enacted and they were not specifically directed at sport.

Gambling – and worse

Indeed when in 1664 a law was passed against 'deceitful, disorderly and excessive gaming' the preamble declared that, properly used, games were innocent and moderate recreations: it was when they were misused that they promoted idleness and dissolute living and the circumventing, deceiving, cozening and debauchery of many of the younger sort. Even the most pre-judiced could hardly sustain the view that it was simply a matter of keeping the lower orders in check. There were plenty of stories like that of Bob Weed, brought up in fashionable circles but 'forced to follow gaming for a livelihood' frequenting 'some tennis-court, or the bowling green at Marylebone where by betting and playing he won a great deal of money'.[46] Gaming obviously increased the risk of sharp practice. Charles Cotton's *The Compleat Gamester*, highly critical of certain bowls-players, also warned of the hazards of horse-racing, the 'many subtilties and tricks there are used in making a match, the craft of the setters' and 'the knavery of the riders'. Gentlemen riders were known as jockeys, a reference to the jostling skills and chicanery needed to win, their professional assistants being called grooms. D'Urfey's song suggests where the corruption began:

> Let jades that are founder'd be bought,
> Let jockeys play crimp to make sport.
> Another makes racing his trade,
> And many a crimp match has made
> By bubbing another man's groom.[47]

There was immorality and greed at all levels. In a diatribe against the uncontrolled behaviour of crowds on Easter Sunday, 1678, a North Country parson blamed the rapaciousness of town councils for assisting the spread of drinking and gambling: 'One race begets another, that at Rastrick begot one at Halifax . . . it was given out that many races would be run to gather the country to drink their ale, for it was hoped it would be as profitable to the town as a fair'.[48]

London remained the trend-setter. Evelyn described a 'wrestling match of £1,000' – with side bets – 'in St James's Park, before his Majesty, a world of lords and other spectators, 'twixt the Western and Northern men, Mr Secretary Maurice and Lord Gerard being the judges'.[49] And though the old Masters of Defence had failed to survive the Commonwealth there were now out-and-out commercial prize-fights in bear-gardens and theatres. Pepys described one in 1663:

> I with Sir J. Minnes to the . . . New Theatre, which since the King's players are gone to the Royal one, is this day begun to be employed for the fencers to play prizes at. And here I came and saw the first prize I ever saw in my life; and it was between one Matthews, who did best at all points, and one Westwicke who was soundly cut both in the head and the legs that he was all over blood.[50]

This was a so-called 'private quarrel' (many professional contests were not 'in good earnest') which ensured bloodshed and therefore drew a good crowd: 'Strange to see what a deal of money is flung to them', Pepys commented. Of another 'at Beargarden Stairs' he complained, 'the house so full there was no getting there, so forced to go through an ale house into the pits where the bears are baited, and upon a stool did see them fight, a butcher and a waterman'. But it was worth it. Each had their factions. The butcher slashed his opponent's wrist after he had dropped his sword and 'Lord! to see in a minute the whole stage was full of watermen to revenge the foul play and the butcher to defend their fellow': the ensuing fracas was 'pleasant to see'.[51] Another London vogue was running. In 1660 Pepys went to Hyde Park 'and saw a fine foot-race three times round the Park between an Irishman and Crow that was once my Lord Claypoole's footman'.[52] And three years later

> The town talk this day is of nothing but the great foot-race run this day in Banstead Downs, between Lee, the Duke of Richmond's footman, and a tiler, a famous runner. And Lee hath beat him, though the King and Duke of York, and all men almost, did bet three or four to one upon the tiler's head'.[53]

That so many of the participants were 'footmen' was because these organised contests grew up from impromptu challenges amongst the nobility who employed servants to run messages and to run in front of coaches on bumpy or dangerous roads. London, however, offered many new ways in which working class young men of all trades could augment their income through sport. These were, for instance, contests on water between the liveried watermen of the nobility when boats were a social necessity in the days when the Thames was spanned by only one bridge.

Few gentlemen actually took part in these strenuous sports themselves: a more congenial new game for the better sort was cricket. Early Stuart edicts requiring country gentry to stay at home to look after their estates may well have helped bring it to the fore as a vehicle for gambling. We have noted that adults – including persons of quality – played cricket before the Commonwealth period, and by the Restoration its commercial possibilities began to be realised. In 1668 the proprietor of 'The Ram' at Smithfield paid rates for a cricket field and the magistrates at Maidstone licensed the sale of beer at a 'kricketing'. But it flourished chiefly because of noble patronage. In 1677 the Earl of Sussex drew £3 – presumably for betting – from his treasurer to go to 'the crekitt match at the Dicker'; and his countess, marooned at Hurstmonceaux, confessed to boredom with 'the prevailing amusements – hunting, hawking, ninepins, cricket'.[54]

In the bleak north of Britain golf was the comparable leisure pursuit. After the ending of monopolies every Scottish town of any size that had links land to play on soon had its own ball-maker; and the bowyers made many more clubs than bows. A humbler trade was club-carrying for the great (the carriers were later called 'cadets', as an insult to Frenchified courtiers, pronounced 'caddies'). In 1672 Sir John Foulis of Ravelston paid a boy four shillings to carry for him in a game with Sir Archibald Primrose, the Lord Register and Sir John Baird of Newbyth.[55] Some of these lads, like Andrew Dickson who carried clubs for James, Duke of York, the King's brother, at Leith in 1682 when the Duke was Commissioner to the Scottish Parliament, went on to be equipment makers. There was even money to be made by playing. The shoemaker, John Patersone, for instance, who successfully partnered the Duke in a grudge match, was rewarded with half the royal winnings, enough to buy a substantial house.[56]

The Restoration also brought a great revival in the old blood-letting sports. Neither Pepys nor Evelyn approved, but they both went to see for themselves. Pepys described a bull-baiting at Southwark when a dog was tossed into the spectators as 'a very rude and nasty pleasure'.[57] Evelyn went

> to the Bear Garden, where there was cock-fighting, dog-fighting and bear- and bull-baiting, it being a famous day for these butcherly sports, or rather barbarous cruelties . . . One of the bulls tossed a dog full into a lady's lap . . . Two poor dogs were killed and so all ended with an ape on horseback and I most heartily weary of the rude and dirty pastime.[58]

Bears, which had higher social status and did not toss dogs about, were in shorter supply. Bulls were therefore the standard fare, not only for baits but for rustic variants such as the traditional bull-running at Stamford and the bizarre goings on at Tutford. The lowest level of baiting was of badgers, all that could be afforded in some country districts.

The connoisseur's sport was cock-fighting. Charles Cotton grew lyrical:

> Cocking is a great sport or pastime so full of delight and pleasure that I know not any game . . to be preferred before it, and since the Fighting Cock hath gained so great an estimation among the gentry in respect of this noble recreation I shall here propose it before all the other games of which I have afore succinctly dismissed.[59]

Fighting cocks had metal spurs tied to their heels, often of silver, fashioned by expert craftsmen, proud to engrave their name on each pair. Cockspur Street in London took its name from this sophisticated craft. Huge sums were wagered on choice birds by the highest in the land.

There were more vulgar enthusiasts. Pepys at the new cockpit at Shoe Lane commented 'Lord! to see the strange variety of people, from a Parliament man by name Wilder that was Deputy Governor of the Tower . . . to the poorest 'prentices, bakers, brewers, draymen and what not; and all these fellows one with another cursing and betting'.[60] An even less savoury survival was the cock-shy, a traditional Shrove Tuesday schoolboy pastime. In 1661 Pepys recorded laconically: 'very merry and best fritters that ever I eat in my life. After that looked out at window; saw the flinging at cocks.'[61] Others were less complacent: a French character in one of Davenant's plays sardonically related English courage to their 'military pastime of throwing at cocks'.[62]

A rich source of comedy

The English talent for satire was honed to a sharper edge in Restoration times. The superficial fastidiousness of the nobility and gentry was matched by increasing subtlety in diplomacy and government. There were intellectual and

cultural advances – the founding of the Royal Society, new styles of architecture, the first public library, higher standards of classical scholarship. Yet
the age lacked deeper moral purpose and concern for honesty and trust: these
were distinctly unfashionable as the plays and poetry of the period attest. It
became an age of high but sour comedy.

Charles II's own manoeuvrings – secret treaties with the French and so forth
– have to be seen in the context of increasingly devious Parliamentary political
activity. These were years of strict government censorship, the Cabal and the
rise of the supple Earl of Shaftesbury at the head of a hard-faced Country
Party. Religion, though still powerful, was increasingly tribalised and it was
from tribes that the emerging political parties took their names – the Whigs
from fiercely Protestant Scottish covenanters and the Tories from Irish Catholic brigands who preferred Crown to Parliament.

The old values were gradually being modified by commercialism. Foreign
wars centred on colonial possessions and trade, and domestic policies on
materialism. The nobility, including the royal family, took shares in the new
joint stock enterprises – East India, Royal Africa, Hudson's Bay – and the
merchants further infiltrated the upper classes. Divisions between town and
country were still sharp, despite the growth of attractive spa towns like Bath,
Buxton and Harrogate and the incursions of industry into rural Warwickshire,
Durham, Northumberland, Scotland and Wales. Above all, London's spread
continued. The Great Plague was only a temporary set back whilst the subsequent Great Fire enabled the City to be rebuilt in handsome brick, in even
starker contrast to the slum districts outside the walls. Interest in agriculture
declined amongst the bigger landowners, and the enclosure movement
slowed. However, rents went on rising and the Parliamentary squires looked
after their own interests by restricting imports of foreign and Irish corn and
offering bounties for export.

Many of the working classes also benefited from the new commercialism:
skilled men got higher wages and increased further the gap between English
and European standards. Yet the burden of the Poor Law increased and the
Settlement Act forbade the movement of paupers between parishes. Older
rural values also declined. Yeoman freeholders were socially divided by a new
Game Act of 1671. For many years all freeholders outside royal Forest areas
had been allowed to take any game that crossed their own land. But conservation became more important as shooting became the gentlemanly norm
(the lower orders used netting, liming, snaring and trapping and heaven
knows what else) and the new Act restricted hunting privileges to those with
holdings worth over £100 a year. This was to be another source of hypocrisy –
and blander social comedy – in the Augustan age to come.

Notes

1 For James I's social and sporting habits see J.P. Kenyon, *The Stuarts*, London, 1958, and for political and social background G. Davies, *The Early Stuarts*, Oxford, 2nd edn, 1959, J. Morrill 'The Stuarts' in K.O. Morgan (ed.), *The Oxford Illustrated History of Britain*; Oxford, 1984, and H. Kearney, Chapter 7.

2 *Basilicon Doron, 1599*, in C.H. McIlwain, *The Political Works of James I*, Cambridge, Mass., 1928. 'The Caiche', or catch-ball, the Scottish name for tennis, was popular with the Scottish nobility, reflecting French influence. 'Gysairis' – mummers.

3 The precise date is uncertain. See the slightly different accounts in P.M. Young, *The History of British Football*, London, 1973 edn, p. 40 and J. Strutt, *Glig-gamena angel deod: or The Sports and Pastimes of the People of England*, London, 1801; new edition 1903, reprinted Bath, 1969, p. 33. The choice of a bell as a prize in racing probably stemmed from the fact that the leading sheep in a flock carried a bell. Chaucer used the phrase 'to bear the bell' and in the Wakefield Second Shepherds' Play (c1440) it is used to mean 'win the prize'.

4 'Complaint'.

5 Lanark claimed to have had such a bell in 1160.

6 The word 'hobby', which originally meant a small hawk, gradually came to mean any small, swift creature. Hence its modern meaning, from hobby-horse, which was used to mean a frivolity that becomes an obsession in Lawrence Sterne's *Tristram Shandy (1760–1)*.

7 R. Browning, *A History of Golf*, London, 1955, p. 3.

8 D. Brailsford, *Sport and Society*, London, 1969, pp. 108–9.

9 Browning, *History of Golf*, p. 3.

10 J.P. Earwaker (ed.), *The Court Leet Records of the Manor of Manchester*, Manchester, 1955, pp. 239–40 (Magoun).

11 M. Marples, *A History of Football*, London, 1954, p. 58.

12 Ibid., p. 59.

13 Ibid., p. 55.

14 *Anatomie of Abuses*, quoted in F.P. Magoun, *History of Football from the Beginnings to 1871*, Cologne, 1938, pp. 29–30.

15 L.A. Govett (ed.), *The King's Book of Sports*, London, 1890, pp. 24–5, 29–30.

16 Ibid., pp. 38–40.

17 *The Anatomy of Melancholy*, 1621, 6th edn, reprinted in Everyman's Library, London, 1932, vol. II, p. 85.

18 J.H. Marsden (ed.), *College Life in the Times of James I*, Cambridge, 1851, pp. 94–6.

19 Sir Thomas Overbury, *Characters*, 1614–16, quoted in J. Dover Wilson, *Life in Shakespeare's England*, Harmondsworth, 1944, pp. 77–8.

20 Peter Hausted, *The Rival Friends*, 1632, quoted in Young, *History of British Football*, pp. 61–2.

21 John Earle, *Microcosmographie*, 1625, quoted in Dover Wilson, *Life in Shakespeare's England*, pp. 75–6.

22 *History of England*, vol. 1, 1849, Chapter 2.

23 Easter Bill of Presentment, noted in Sussex Records Society, vol. XLIX, 1947–8, Part 1, ed. Hilda Johnstone, reprinted in *Sussex Notes and Queries*, vol. 12, Lewes, 1950.

24 Parish records cited by T.J. McCann, 'Seventeenth Century Cricket: East Lavant 1628' in *Journal of the Cricket Society*, vol. 15, no. 1, Autumn 1990.

25 R. Bowen, *Cricket*, London, 1970, p. 45.

26 Manuscript held by Corporation of Maidstone: Nicholas Hunt sued William Wood for twelve candles.

27 A.R. Bayley, *The Great Civil Wars in Dorset*, Taunton, 1910, p. 349, quoted by D.L.

Brailsford, *Sport and Society*, London, 1969, p. 135. For the background see C. Hill, *The World Turned Upside Down*, London, 1972, esp. Chapter 3.

28 Young, *History of British Football*, p. 65.

29 Ibid.

30 M. James, *Social Problems and Policy during the Puritan Revolution*, London, 1930, p. 293.

31 *Diaries*, ed. E.S. de Beer, London, 1955, quoted with dates in Brailsford, *Sport and Society*, pp. 138–9.

32 W. McQueen Pope in *Oxford Companion to the Theatre*, ed. Phyllis Hartnell, 3rd edn, Oxford, 1951, p. 825, and Lord Aberdare, *The Story of Tennis*, London, 1959.

33 James, *Social Problems*, p. 21.

34 *A General System of Horsemanship*, 1658.

35 Andrew Lang, introduction to Everyman's Library edition, London, 1906.

36 *Diaries*, 29 May 1660.

37 *Diaries*, ed. R.C. Latham and W. Matthews, London, 1970–85, 2 September 1667. Charles lost 4½lbs.

38 Ibid., 4 January 1664.

39 Theophilus Lucas, *Memoirs of Gamesters*, 1714, quoted in Brailsford, *Sport and Society*, p. 212.

40 *The Compleat Gamester*, 1674, reprinted in *Games and Gamesters of the Reformation*, London, 1930, p. 21.

41 Evelyn, *Diaries*, 1 October 1661.

42 1 December 1662.

43 J. Granger, *Biographical History of England*, 1769. For Charles II see Kenyon, *The Stuarts*; for the period generally, with special reference to England's relations with Scotland and Ireland, see G.N. Clark, *The Later Stuarts* (2nd edn), Oxford, 1956; for Restoration society see Pepys *Diaries*.

44 'New Market' in *Pills to Purge Melancholy*, 1719 (4th edn) vol. ii, p. 53, quoted in *Glig-gamena angel deod: or The Sports and Pastimes of the People of England*, London, 1801: new edition 1903, reprinted Bath, 1969, p. 36.

45 *Grace Abounding to the Chief of Sinners*, 1646. Tip-cat was a rounders-type game. The cat was a short piece of wood tapered at the ends, which had to be tipped into the air then struck as far as possible. There were variants such as trap-ball, cat in the-hole and cat and dog. The two last were children's games 'invented' in Scotland and thought by some to be ancestors of golf and cricket. See Strutt, *Sports and Pastimes*, p. 104 and for a full discussion H. Barty-King, *Quilt Winders and Pod-Shavers*, London, 1979, pp. 9–17.

46 Lucas, *Memories of Gamesters*, pp. 238–9.

47 *Pills to Purge Melancholy*.

48 Quoted in R.W. Malcolmson, *Popular Recreations in English Society, 1700–1850*, Cambridge, 1973, pp. 271–2.

49 19 February 1667.

50 1 June 1663.

51 27 May 1667.

52 10 August 1660.

53 30 July 1663.

54 Sir Thomas Barrett-Leonard, *An Account of the Families of Lennard and Barrett*, published privately, 1908, p. 317. The Dicker was a common.

55 Sir Guy Campbell, 'The Early History of English Golf in *A History of Golf in Britain*, ed. B. Darwin et al., 1952. pp. 52–3.

56 Ibid., pp. 49–50.

57 11 August 1666.
58 16 June 1670.
59 *Compleat Gamester*, pp. 100–14.
60 21 September 1663.
61 26 February.
62 'First Day's Entertainment at Rutland House', 1656, *The Dramatic Works of Sir William Davenant* (1873 edn), vol. III, p. 221.

CHAPTER FIVE

Politics and patrons
1685–1756

The social and political patterns shaped in the years following the Restoration were to endure until Victorian times. The Tories sought to preserve the old rural values: the Whig landowners were in closer touch with commerce and readier to support economic change. Religion complicated the situation. Anglicanism, the faith of the upper classes and their followers, represented conformity. The Dissenters included some wealthy merchants but their strength mainly stemmed from the ranks of the urban artisan. The few surviving Roman Catholic gentry were excluded from the corridors of power and their lower orders were low indeed.

Nevertheless the convoluted politics of the time allowed the Duke of York, who had turned Catholic, to succeed his brother as James II. Once on the throne, however, the wiliness that had got him there deserted him, and his blundering attempts to settle old scores aroused the fury of Puritans, dismayed the Whigs and alarmed even moderate Tories. When he produced an heir the prospect of a permanent Catholic monarchy led to all-party overtures to Prince William of Orange. Both William and his wife Mary had family claims to the English throne and William saw it as a convenient base for his life's work, rescuing Europe from domination by the despotic Catholic French monarchy. So after a skilful invasion in which James was forced to re-group in Ireland William and Mary became England's first constitutional monarchs, striking a bargain with Parliament that was given the somewhat extravagant title of the Glorious Revolution.

Dutch courage

It was not a comfortable reign. For one thing William was too efficient. The Tories, especially those with Jacobite leanings, resisted his attempts to systematise the country's primitive finances – founding the Bank of England, increasing land taxes to offset trading losses as imports from the American colonies increased, and raising loans to reduce the national debt. His Protestant crusade also meant that England was to be engaged off and on for sixty years in European wars. Even the Whig landowners whose interests he advanced did not like King William. The antipathy was mutual. William declined to align himself with either party, for he disliked the devious politics of his adopted country as much as its haphazard life style.

In Scotland, where there were many rich and powerful Jacobites, the increased authority the Revolutionary Settlement gave to Parliament would inevitably have spelled trouble for any intruding monarch. William was personally unpopular because he was thought insufficiently supportive of Scottish trade, and his stock plummeted when he signed an order against a Jacobite chieftain, MacDonald of Glencoe, that led to massacre. Ireland was even more hostile. Her chief export was cattle, a source of competition to English and Scottish breeders and hence much hampered by regulatory restriction. James II's overt support for Catholics had caused deep resentment amongst the dominant Protestant minority, and like every one before and since William failed to square the Irish circle.

In fact he wasted little time trying. After a brisk military campaign he turned his attention to France and left affairs in Ireland to surrogates who were mostly concerned to get their own back by ousting James' appointees and by screwing down Catholics generally. Catholics could not, for instance, enter the learned professions, bear arms, buy land or even own horses of any great value.

This last was a far from trivial matter. In 1673 the English diplomat Sir William Temple had successfully proposed to the Lord Lieutenant an annual event in Dublin – three days of racing followed by a horse fair – as an aid to breeding and exporting horses, which were in plentiful supply.[1] From 1684 there were a series of King's Plates for horse-races – prizes of £20 or £30 to help breed 'large and serviceable horses' with a minimum weight for riders of twelve stones. Under William and Mary horse-racing, which in England was to draw the social classes together, became a source of division in Ireland.

What brought the English together was the profit motive. Captain Robert Byerly, who served under John Churchill, later Duke of Marlborough, at the Boyne, rode an Arab horse he had captured from a Turkish officer in Hungary, which was known as the Byerly Turk. On his return he put it to stud in the north of England where through its son, Jig, it bred famous stallions like Herod, The Tetrarch and Tourbillon, initiating the first great English thoroughbred racing bloodstock line. Even William, who had little time for frivolity, liked a gamble and the prospect of profitable investment whether in art or on the turf. He made a shrewd move when, about 1695, he appointed Trigonwell Frampton as Keeper of the Running Horse.

Frampton, the fifth son of a Dorset squire, was typical of many younger, sons brought up to the life of a country gentleman but impoverished by primogeniture and so obliged to try to make a living from his knowledge of horseflesh. (Gervase Markham was another.) Frampton himself became a successful if unscrupulous trainer, breeder and match-maker, in the service of three successive monarchs. In 1675 when he first moved into the Newmarket scene he was 'a gentleman of some £120 rent . . . engaged £900 deep'.[2] But although he had some losses he also had some big wins at cocking and coursing as well as horse-racing. His approach to gambling was steely-nerved

– in 1676 he had two bets of £1,000 in the same week – and his reaction was the same whether he won or lost.

By 1700 Frampton was getting training fees amounting to £1,000 for the season, apparently based on £100 for each horse in training. This, even allowing for the cost of stabling, fodder and wages was very big money. A contemporary survey showed that half the population of England subsisted on £15 a year or less and only one in every two hundred had £1,000 a year or more. (Some 200 noble families averaged £3,000 a year, 1,500 baronets and knights £800, 2,000 merchants £400 and 1,200 gentlemen £280.)[3] The averages of course concealed great variations – the Duke of Newcastle's rents brought him £40,000 a year. So too amongst the lower orders: a skilled artisan in London might aspire to fifteen or eighteen shillings a week, but the labouring class, 400,000 or so, got between five and seven shillings and a similar number of cottagers only half that.[4]

Yet there seems to have been little serious class conflict. For one thing love of sport offered other outlets. Henri Misson de Valbourg, a Huguenot refugee who came to England in 1685, noted the 'many persons of fine quality' at Newmarket, adding that it was 'pretty common for them to lay wagers of £2,000 upon one race', but he also noticed the unusually free mixing of the social classes. He found a rougher example in London; where 'even two little boys quarrelling in the street would draw a crowd not only of other boys, porters, and rabble, but all sorts of men of fashion, some thrusting by the mob that they may see plainly, others getting upon stalls, and all would hire places if scaffolds could be built in a moment.'[5] Furthermore the better sort were not above a scrap themselves. Gentlemen disputing the fare with coachmen would offer to fight them for it: the coachmen were usually beaten. 'I once saw the late Duke of Grafton at fisticuffs in the open street with such a fellow whom he lambed most horribly.' wrote de Valbourg. In France, he concluded, such rascals would be punished with a cane or the flat of a sword but to use a weapon on an unarmed man was unthinkable to an Englishman and would not be tolerated by passers-by.

He drew similar charitable conclusions about street football – though he found it a little simple-minded perhaps – but to the English themselves it was a serious menace. Edward Chamberlayne in his survey of London found it 'very uncivil, rude and barbarous'.[6] In later editions Chamberlayne marvelled at working-class enthusiasm for games: 'The Natives will endure long and hard labour, insomuch that after twelve hours hard work they will go in the evening to football, stoolball, cricket.'[7] But there was great concern about the amount and nature of leisure. One of the new breed of experts known as economists worked out that every public holiday cost the nation £50,000. And the old fear of sport as a cloak for anarchy was by no means dead: opponents of Fenland drainage, for instance, used football or campball matches as cover for destructive behaviour. The context was constant anxiety about law and order, heavily dependent on parish constables elected by their neighbours. This was the golden age of the highwayman.

England, her England

Parliament blamed the Dutchman, William. The 1701 Act of Settlement required future sovereigns to be in communion with the Church of England and foreign-born ones not to engage in wars or even travel abroad without Parliament's approval. William's sister-in-law Anne made it very clear in her first speech after succeeding that she was thoroughly English and would make England her prime concern. During her long wait in the wings the unsophisticated Anne had been cultivated by the protean Marlborough and dominated by his wife Sarah and for some years after her accession party politics were overridden by a kitchen cabinet arrangement. But Marlborough's victories in the War of the Spanish Succession were followed by disasters, recovery was costly and by 1710 the Whigs lost office and the Queen had had enough of Sarah.

Anne was still mourning her husband, Prince George of Denmark, two years after his death, and her grief fortified her determination not to be put upon. In the early years of marriage she and George had taken almost as much pleasure in riding to hounds as in conjugality. They were both inclined to stoutness but Anne, a true Stuart, was a fine horsewoman before abortive pregnancy disabled her. Now, at the age of forty-three with a serious weight problem, she had a special two-wheeled vehicle constructed, had wide tracks cut through Windsor Forest and drove up to sixty miles a day in pursuit of game. Swift, who was at court in 1711, reported that: 'she hunts in a chaise with one horse, which she drives like Jehu and is a mighty hunter like Nimrod.'[8]

That same year she built a new race-course a few miles from Windsor on Ascot Common. It cost as much as a good horse (£555 19s 5d, plus £15 2s 6d for posts and £2 25s for painting them), though Anne had once defied Sarah Churchill to spend a thousand guineas on an Arab stallion, Leedes, as a birthday present for Prince George. (Arab influence on British bloodstock – and its prices – had increased with the importation of a great stallion in 1705 by Thomas Darley, English consul in Aleppo.) Anne endowed a new Queen's Plate at Ascot and she later used secret service funds to found races there and at Newmarket. This was an enjoyable way of marking George's memory and, shrewdly advised by Trigonwell Frampton, she found another in successful race-horse ownership.

Royal Plates, which ranged from £100 to £20, were valuable prizes but much more could be won by betting. Gambling was feared by the moralists as a besetting sin that could undermine society, and, in an era of Protestant revival, sins were again a matter for public concern. The Society for the Reformation of Manners, which included Dissenters but had a respectable leavening of established churchmen, issued tracts not only against gambling, but drunkenness, swearing, 'vice', and Sunday trading. (Sunday, after all the political upheavals, was now officially a day of rest on which very little was legal.) Hundreds of charity schools sprang up to educate poor children not only in reading and writing but to inculcate the true doctrines of the church. The Society for Promoting Christian Knowledge published cheap Bibles and prayer books for schools, the armed forces and the colonies.

In the upper reaches of society, however, reform meant improving manners rather than saving souls. At the new spas refined conduct was now expected. The dandy Beau Nash, ex-officer and gambler, became Master of Ceremonies at Bath, where the balls were of great splendour but also very polite (no smoking in front of the ladies for instance). There were also two potentially civilising but ambivalent new influences amongst the urban middle class trend-setters – coffee-houses and newspapers. Tea, coffee, cocoa and chocolate were now being imported in quantity and the coffee-houses were the latest fashionable resort, congenial places for conversation, business and political intrigue. Different groups tended to frequent particular houses. Lloyd's shipping business began in a coffee-house. Will's was the literary venue, Truby's that of the clergy, the Grecian of scholars; Whigs went to the St James's and Tories to the Cocoa Tree; White's, a chocolate house, was for the smart set, with a dubious reputation for crooked gambling and loose women. Coffee-houses helped diminish drunkenness, though not smoking, a highly fashionable vice.

They also assisted the circulation of newspapers, which proliferated after the repeal of the Licensing Act in 1695, usually in single sheets. These precariously financed affairs mostly went to the wall after the government introduced stamp duty and advertising tax in 1712. Meanwhile, however, *The Tatler* (1709–11) and *The Spectator* (1711–12) brought a new style of social journalism, specialising in satirical comment on the manners of the day, that was to have lasting influence.

The Spectator offered an array of fictional rural stereotypes for the entertainment of the sophisticated urban middle classes. Its most famous character, Sir Roger de Coverley, had in his hot-blooded youth been a man about town – 'what you call a fine gentleman', dining with the scandalous Restoration wits Lord Rochester and Sir George Etherage and 'fighting a duel with Bully Dawson in a public coffee-house for calling him youngster'. Now he was a pillar of respectability, a country square and magistrate so learned that he had once gained universal applause by reciting a passage in the Game Act.[9] Sir Roger greatly disliked the erosion of social distinctions in this Act. His neighbour, though respectable enough – 'a very sensible man, shoots flying and . . . several times Foreman of the Petty-Jury' – is a 'Yeoman of about an hundred pounds a year' coming 'just within the Game Act, and qualified to kill a hare or pheasant. He knocks down a dinner with his Gun twice or thrice a week and by this means lives cheaper than those who have not such a good estate as himself. He would be a good neighbour if he did not destroy so many partridges.'[10]

Squires, *The Spectator* pointed out, were highly experienced in conservation. It was 'usual for a man who loves country sports to preserve the game in his own grounds and divert himself upon those that belong to his neighbour'. Sir Roger would go two or three miles before 'beating about in search of a hare or partridge' leaving untouched his own estate 'where he is always sure of finding diversion if the worst comes to the worst'. This practice gave the squire's own game time to increase and multiply, whilst he was on more distant territory facing a bigger challenge where the game was scarcer: 'For these reasons, the country gentleman, like the fox, seldom preys near his own home.'[11]

Fox-hunting still had an ambivalent social status, but as deer grew scarcer it was increasingly favoured by sportsmen of relatively limited means in its new style of chasing the quarry across open country. In the past Sir Roger had earned the eternal thanks of the neighbourhood 'on account of his remarkable enmity towards foxes, having destroyed more of those vermin in one year than it was thought the whole country could have produced', his secret being that he imported them and released them at night. Later, having grown too old for this modern fox-hunting, a strenuous business, Sir Roger had sold his beagles and bought a pack of stop-hounds for hare-hunting. They were chosen, *The Spectator* reckoned, mainly for the musical qualities of their baying. The same elaborate irony noted how the farmers' sons were pleased to open the gate for dear Sir Roger as he traversed their land with kindly nods and enquiries after their families.[12]

A more direct urban critic of country sport was the rising poet, Alexander Pope:

> See! from the brake the whirring pheasant springs:
> And mounts exultant on triumphant wings:
> Short is his joy; he feels the fiery wound,
> Flutters in blood and panting beats the ground.[13]

Pope deplored particularly 'that savage compliment our huntsmen pass amongst ladies of quality' in the deer-hunt, handing them the knife to cut the throat of the cornered beast.[14] The truth was that the English were, as Trevelyan put it, 'a race that had not yet learned to dislike the sight of pain inflicted'.[15]

Hanging and whipping were greatly enjoyed as public spectacles, and what the literary set saw as cruelty in sport enthusiasts saw as a desirable emblem of virility. Thus cock-fighting was proclaimed a valuable way of diverting the English gentry from effeminate dancing, whoring and drinking 'which are three evils grown almost epidemical' and a more manly occupation than 'to run whooting after a poor, timorous hare'.[16] Its ancient lineage was generally cited in its favour and at least one writer, a Scottish fencing master, cited Aristotle, with salacious intent.[17]

Such populism did not impress the coffee-house wits. 'It will be said', wrote Dick Steele in *The Tatler*, 'that these are the entertainments of the common people . . . It is true, but they are the entertainments of no other common people.'[18] *The Spectator* made fun of most country sports – wrestling, football – and of the ludicrous mock-ferocity of the prize-fighters at the Bear Garden at Hockley-in-the-Hole, Clerkenwell. Cricket was in a different category: favoured by public school and university men this once-rustic game had achieved the distinction of a description in Latin verse,[19] and had become an important vehicle for gambling. During the newspaper boom promoters used the size of bets to advertise 'great matches' and to attract spectators. Their excesses were inhibited by the 'Qui Tam' Act of 1710 which reduced the legal limit of bets from £100 to £10 and allowed informers to sue for four times the amount of illegal transactions. The ban was clearly not meant to apply to private matches amongst the aristocracy and gentry, but cricket now attracted great public interest. The great men who played it were frequently urged to set a better example, especially by political opponents and their hacks. Great matches apart, a broadsheet in 1712 condemned a multiple offence by the deposed Duke of Marlborough. He and his friend Viscount Townshend were censured for corrupting the 'innocent sports of those inferior in age and grandeur' by playing cricket with two boys in Windsor Forest on the Sabbath and betting twenty guineas on the result.[20]

Private and public morality

The Tories were jubilant over their success in 1713 in concluding the advantageous Treaty of Utrecht which increased British colonial possessions – Gibraltar was to be of lasting importance – and hence trading opportunities. But when George, Elector of Hanover, came to the throne after Anne's death the following year the Whig architects of the Act of Settlement came back into power. They acted swiftly and vindictively against the Tory leaders for knuckling under to the French. They needed a new Riot Act to cope with active dissidents and, despite the 1707 Act of Union with Scotland, were faced in 1715 with a Jacobite rebellion. It was a pathetic affair: the support the High-landers had counted on from English Tories and French allies failed to materialise, and it was sternly put down, but the bitterness lingered on.

This bumpy start inaugurated nearly half a century of Whig rule. They had a natural majority in the House of Lords, and though the Commons had had vastly more power since the civil war, the Whigs had so much money and land that they could now control election to the lower House. Their support included not only well-to-do parvenus but rich Dissenters and, not least, the merchants who had financed the war to the tune of some £50 million and who feared repudiation of this 'national debt' if the Stuarts came back. The Whigs made sure that State patronage gave them full control of important central and local government agencies, the Poor Law and the militia. The confusion between public and private interests reached new heights with the meteoric rise and fall of the South Sea Company, monopoly-holders for the Pacific trade who had offered to take over the national debt. The King's chief minister and adviser at the time the bubble burst was Sir Robert Walpole, who had made a fortune by selling at the right time and had seen to it that the royal family also did not suffer.

George I, who spoke little or no English and therefore rarely attended Cabinet meetings, became increasingly reliant on Walpole. Their main area of disagreement was the extent and manner of British involvement in European affairs in support of the Hanoverian cause, which had no great appeal for Walpole. They had many more areas of mutual self-interest. An important one, which they used the law to protect, was hunting. Walpole's addiction was well-known, and well-publicised by Walpole himself to demonstrate political nonchalance. He put it about, for instance, that even as Chief Minister letters from his huntsman were opened before official correspondence. He kept a pack of harriers at his Norfolk estate and there, each November, he held a 'hunting congress'. In town he had a pack of beagles at the new park in Richmond where he built himself a house. In the season he hunted on one week-day and also on Saturdays – a practice which is said to have influenced Parliamentary time-tables and inspired the notion of the week-end, reputedly an English invention.

The King's approach was anything but nonchalant. Throughout Anne's reign she had only once, in 1708, summoned Windsor Forest's Swanimote, otherwise relying on her personal hunting trips to discourage poaching. George I's ideas were very different. He was not impressed by Windsor, preferring (if he had to be in England) the better-stocked parks at Hampton and Richmond which offered sport more like the orderly proceedings in Hanover. His main aim for Windsor was to introduce discipline and pro-fitability. He called a swanimote in 1717, at which his steward, heading the numerous sinecurists and outmoded specialists who still ran the Forest, made charges alleging manifest destruction of vert and venison by denizens of the purlieus. The medieval phraseology was that of actual laws still on the Statute books, such as those forbidding hunting on the Sabbath or in 'fence-time', or between sunset and sunrise, and those restricting the use of dogs, nets, snares and guns. George I not only insisted on severe penalties but required railings, deer-pens and vermin-traps to be provided by his tenants at their own expense.[21]

It was not surprising, then, that the King and his circle joined with Whig ministers, who themselves had similar axes to grind, to introduce in Parlia-ment an anti-poaching Bill of a severity unprecedented in modern times. The poachers undoubtedly gave genuine cause for social concern. As Parson Gilbert White later noted: 'towards the beginning of this century all this country went wild about deer-stealing. Unless he was a hunter . . . no young person was allowed to be possessed of manhood or gallantry.'[22] This apart the shotgun was to change the ecology of the countryside.

Giles Jacob, the current authority, noted the decline of hawking since sportsmen were 'arrived at such perfection in shooting, and so much improved in the making of dogs'.[23] Organised attacks on game by groups of mounted armed men were becoming a serious menace, provoking retaliation from gamekeepers who confiscated dogs and equipment and even searched houses. This was deeply resented and it encouraged, in turn, the revival of a practice – 'blacking' for disguise – that had been a felony in medieval times but had long lain dormant. Predictably the offenders were tagged as Jacobite rebel sympathisers and in 1723 Parliament, without debate, passed the Black Act, greatly extending the Game Laws, with severe penalties for disguised or armed poaching, adding fifty new capital offences.

Pleasure and profit

'What merchant is so conscientious that he will refuse to sell a thread satin to a highwayman's harlot?' asked Bernard de Mandeville, commenting on the mercantile values of the age.[24] As a physician he was particularly concerned at the appalling effects of the 'infamous liquor', juniper or gin for short, that flooded the market. Ale had been the traditional people's drink in England but restrictions on distilling were removed during the 1720s and though this, as Daniel Defoe pointed out, was good for agriculture since it consumed corn, it had devastating social effects especially in urban areas.

Some had hoped for better things from Protestant freedom than this sour reality. In 1715 the 24 year old Irish actor, Thomas Doggett, displayed a poster on London Bridge offering an orange coloured livery with a badge 'representing Liberty' to commemorate His Majesty's 'happy accession to the throne'. This was to be the prize for a race from there to Chelsea to be rowed for by six watermen who had finished their apprenticeship in the previous year. ('It will be continued on the same day for ever', it concluded with remarkable confidence and prescience.)

Politics apart, Doggett's gesture was characteristic of a new age of pleasure and profit in which we begin to hear of individual sportsmen earning a good living and gaining some celebrity from their skills. One of the first was Jack Broughton, an early winner of Doggett's Coat and Badge, though his fame came from pugilism and stemmed only incidentally from his trade. Watermen were amongst the growing class of workers, sometimes liveried sometimes not – sedan chairmen, porters, footmen, linkmen, coachmen, butcher boys, coal-heavers and so on – who transported people or goods around London and other cities and frequently found themselves confronted by rival groups. In 1728 the Swiss traveller Caesar de Saussure affirmed Misson de Valbourg's observations of Londoners' eagerness to fight with their fists in public: when two of them quarrelled they would 'retire into some quiet place and strip from the waist upward. All who see them preparing . . . surround them, not in order to separate them, but on the contrary to enjoy the fight . . . The spectators sometimes get so interested they lay bets.'[25]

Early in George I's reign a fenced enclosure had been set aside in the Park as the recognised arena for dust-ups, and the commercial possibilities of pugilism were later exploited by James Figg, a professional swordsman and cudgel-player. Figg was brought from an Oxfordshire village under the auspices of the Earl of Peterborough and he made his name in and around the metropolis by issuing challenges at fairs, such as the annual event at the Bowling Green, Southwark, where he put up a booth and took on all-comers. In 1719 he declared himself champion and set himself up at an 'academy of arms' alongside an old coaching inn. His business card – designed for him by a young admirer, William Hogarth – read 'Master of the Noble Science of Defence in Oxford Road near Adam and Eve Court – teaches gentlemen the use of the small backsword and quarterstaff'.

Fist-fighting was only the middle one of three stages in the battle for the championship, and it was sword- and cudgel-play that chiefly appealed to the *cognoscenti*. In 1727 the amphitheatre was crowded – some thousand seats around the raised circular platform as well as a hundred in the gallery – for a contest between Figg and Ned Sutton, a pipe-maker from Gravesend. Amongst the spectators were Walpole, the poets Pope, Swift and Colley

Cibber and many fashionable ladies. (Women were not just spectators. Bob Stokes, champion of London, partnered his wife against Ned Sutton and a Kentish heroine in a battle at Figg's in August, 1725, in which there were a £40 prize for the person inflicting most sword-cuts and £20 for most cudgel-hits.) Figg excited the passions and remained the master in all three arts of defence and, above all, he was a great entrepreneur.

The same entrepreneurial spirit was invading the favourite aristocratic sport, horse-racing. By this time imported Arab stallions were showing ever more exciting possibilities of speed as well as stamina. The Byerley Turk's progeny were already making their mark and Darley Arabian stock came to the fore when Flying Childers, owned by the Duke of Devonshire, beat the Duke of Bolton's Speedwell in a match for 500 guineas. Both were six year olds, the normal racing age, but competitions for four year olds began in 1727 at Hambleton in Yorkshire. The year George I and Isaac Newton died, 1727, was also the end of an era for racing: Trigonwell Frampton, working to the last, died aged eighty-six.

The new age was marked by the appearance of John Cheney's *Horse Matches*. For five shillings Cheney offered not only 'an agreeable amusement for gentlemen to divert themselves in the midst of winter' but also practical information. 'From hence 'twill always be discoverable what old horses are dropping . . . what young horses are every year coming up . . . which must render gentlemen capable of reducing their calculations nearer to perfection.'[26] Races for three year olds began at York in 1730, and the great vogue was for speed. In 1737 the Earl of Godolphin acquired an Arab stallion from the estate of an entrepreneurial northern landowner, which – as the Godolphin Barb – joined the Byerley Turk and the Darley Arabian as the third pillar of the English thoroughbred line. 'Our noble breed of horses,' complained the *Gentleman's Magazine* in April 1739, 'is now enervated by an intermixture with Turks, Arabians and Barbs, just as our modern nobility and gentry are debauch'd with the effeminate manners of France and Italy.'

Cheney had listed 112 race-courses in England and 5 in Wales. The numbers continued to grow. Even tiny villages like Shalstone in Buckinghamshire stated meetings. Many were low-level affairs and there was strong support for a bill in the House of Lords 'to restrain and prevent the excessive increase of horse races'. Its preamble explained that 'horse-racing for small prizes or sums of money hath contributed very much to the encouragement of idleness, to the impoverishment of many of the meaner sort' and prejudiced 'the breed of strong and useful horses'. In 1740 the government banned races of lesser value than £50 (except at Newmarket and Hambleton). It also laid down minimum weights, but this did not suit the speed fanatics and it was scrapped in 1745.

In later years élitist ideas about breeding and protective legislation were to be shaken, notably in Ireland, where the restrictions on native breeders boomeranged. Racing was an addiction of the Anglo-Irish ascendancy. Sir Edmond O'Brien, for instance, named a village on his County Clare estate Newmarket-on-Fergus and laid out a race-course nearby. Their English friends loved to come over to the Curragh. On one famous occasion young John Douglas, Earl of March and future Duke of Queensberry, 'Old Q', the anti-hero of many stories of eccentricity, sharp practice and extravagance, matched his Bajazet against Sir Ralph Gore's Black-and-All-Black reputedly for a wager of 10,000 guineas. Theoretically, Irish Catholics would never have been able to produce horses of this calibre but horse-breeding is not entirely a matter of theory and the native population were delighted when a locally-bred mare, Irish Lass, at long odds beat Black-And-All-Black, the costly ascendancy favourite.[27]

Hunting retained much of its old cachet, but it too was changing: the invention of the deer-cart in 1728, allowing beasts to be rounded up in advance and released as convenient, somewhat revived royal interest in hunting but the monarchy's importance in this once exclusively royal sport was diminishing. It was the hunts of the great aristocrats that now became famous. In 1730 the Duke of Rutland and four companions subscribed £150 each to found a pack of hounds named after his castle, Belvoir, and in the same year the Duke of Richmond and Lord de la Warr acquired the Charlton Hunt from the Duke of Bolton with the avowed intention of making it the finest in England. Tom Johnson, Richmond's huntsman, who paraded a hundred horses a day in the season, was perhaps the leading professional sportsman of the day. At the other extreme Squire William Draper of Beverley, Yorkshire, was showing how an energetic fox-hunter could get good sport on an income of £700 a year, but socially the fox-hunt still had some way to go.[28]

Sylvan attractions: cricket and football

Walpole's supremacy was only briefly threatened by the death of the old King. George II, waiting impatiently in the wings, had gathered round him a group of disaffected Whigs who were resentful of Walpole's dominance: he brought as many into office as he could and thereafter a shifting band of allies who operated across party boundaries were a constant threat to the old order. But Walpole hung on for another fourteen years. The country meanwhile paid the price, with growing urban squalor the most tangible sign of the effects of unbridled profit making.

Gin was the chief contributor to the soaring death rates in London, where burials far exceeded the number of baptisms, but poor sanitation also took its toll there and in other centres of urban growth. The water supply may have been better than continental alternatives but the British were not conspicuously keen to put it to the test. Instead they preferred to dose themselves with painkillers such as laudanum which unborn children took in from their mothers' bloodstreams and infants from their breasts. Laudanum and gin undoubtedly accounted for much of the alarming rate of infant mortality and may have advanced the tendency towards melancholia. 'I was surprised,' wrote de Saussure, 'at the light-hearted way in which men of this country commit suicide.'[29] He wrote with feeling for he himself was gripped by melancholy and had to get out of London to the country village of Islington, famous for its fresh bread and milk.

London had some 300 private lunatic asylums of which Bedlam was the foremost and the great attraction for sightseers. The manifest effects of poor sanitation and gin sent out such shock waves of compassion particularly in relation to children as to encourage philanthropy and to help medical science to advance beyond medieval superstition. But the enlightened were a small minority, and it was not an age of government intervention, except for the protection of the interests of the ruling classes.

De Saussure's rustication led him observe, and marvel at, the great enthusiasm for cricket in the counties around London: 'they go into a large open field' he wrote, 'and knock a small ball about with a piece of wood'.[30] In 1720 Revd John Strype, updating Stow's *Survey of London*, listed cricket as a diversion of the more common sort of people, along with football, wrestling, cudgels, nine-pins, shovelboard, throwing at cocks and 'lying at alehouses'. But devotees took it seriously: a match in 1719 at White Conduit Fields, Islington for a guinea a man had led to a law suit with costs estimated at £200. And in 1726 a similar situation arose at Chingford, Essex (where that same year a magistrate, suspecting the gathering of a mob for mischievous purposes, had taken a constable to a cricket field and read the Riot Act).

One of the reasons for the disorder was that wealthy patrons were beginning to assemble their own teams: both law suits involved groups from Kent led by Mr Edwin Stead, of Stede Hall, who found cricket an agreeable way of gambling away his patrimony. It was in fact the requirements of gentlemanly gambling that led to the first rules of cricket. In Sussex in 1727 Charles Lennox, Duke of Richmond, made an agreement with Mr Alan Brodrick of Peperharowe in Surrey, for two matches, home and away, for stakes of twelve guineas (a guinea a man). Umpires were to be appointed and if any of the 'gamesters' – apart from the two principals – were to 'speak or give their opinion on any point of the game' they were to be 'turned out and voided'. And the umpires themselves were subject to the jurisdiction of the two principals who were to settle any disputes about umpiring decisions 'upon their honour'. This was to be one of the cornerstones of cricket for nearly two and a half centuries: the gentlemen controlled the game according to the prevailing honour code of the time and were thus able to play with skilled hirelings from the lower classes who acted under their orders.[31]

Football had no such sponsors, although in a mock-heroic poem in 1720 an emigrant Irishman described a six-a-side match between Lusk and Soards, villages near Dublin, where the local gentry offered Holland caps with ribbons for the winners, gloves for the losers and 'a cask of humming beer' for all.[32] This was no mere kick-and-rush affair: indeed the humour was directed at the sophisticated approach of these rustics. Various techniques were required – catching, kicking, passing, running with ball – and there were rules (by whomsoever determined). Violence was used to advantage – players were adroitly tripped, brought down, even laid out: Dick the Miller, 'toss'd down', refused to play for a while. The Soards team had a veteran, Felim, the object of supporter's prayers:

> Practice and years to thee the knack impart
> To shift with cunning and to trip with art.

Lusk had two imported Ulstermen

> Neal and Cabe, whom poverty sent forth
> From the black regions of the rugged north.

They had been given a special diet and 'With strengthening turnips fed and fatning pease' were ready for anything. And footballers like other sporting heroes attracted the girls:

> What monarch's envy might not Terence move,
> So crown'd with conquest, and so pleas'd with love.

And the game was well-enough known to be used as a metaphor for the vicissitudes of life in sermons and moral essays.[33] An elaborate example appeared in The *London Magazine* in March 1735. In many rural areas it remained a cherished – or at least tolerated – tradition on festival occasions, such as Shrove Tuesday, Christmas or Plough Monday.[34] As time went on more and more localities put an end to them as unfitting for modern, polite society, but they often met determined opposition: when Baillie John Grey of Duns in Berwick tried the stop the annual 'effusion of blood' on Fasten's E'en by confiscating the summoning drum he started a riot.[35] Nor were the sanctions of family discipline in Bible-loving rural Wales strong enough to stamp out atavistic urges. For that we have the testimony of a farmer's daughter, Anne Beynon, describing with relish the Christmas Day match in 1719 between the parishes of Llandyssul and Llanwenog in Cardiganshire.[36]

Welsh ancestral pride – and Welsh accents – had been guyed in a song, with harp accompaniment, in Tom D'Urfey's play *The Richmond Heiress* in 1697, beginning 'Of noble race was Shenkin' and including the verse.

> Hur was the prettiest Fellows (trum, trum etc.)
> At Bandy once and Cricket (trum, trum etc.)
> At Hunting Chase, or Prison-base (trum, trum etc.)
> Cot's plut, how hur could nick it![37]

Miss Beynon, writing to her married sister who had emigrated to Delaware, farming land assigned to non-conformists by William Penn, lifts the veil a little from sporting passions that drew their intensity from local, tribal loyalty and the virility cult.

She despised her brother Siencyn (= Shenkin, Jenkin) as 'an old flannel' who thanked their God-fearing father for steering him away from such a violent encounter whilst she herself had defied parental warnings and gone to support the village against the renowned men of Llanwenog. 'I wish I were a boy instead of him to fight for the parish', she wrote. She preferred Evan Bwlch Gwyn, with whom she was keeping company and who got so drunk during the noon-day break for bread and cheese and beer that he could not defend himself and had to be dragged away to safety. It had been a close contest in the morning with Llandyssul just on top, but then it degenerated into a brawl:

> It was said that one youth of Llanwenog had been killed. He was insensible for a time but he came to and is now well. Twm Penddol was kicked rather badly because he was too drunk to take care of himself. There is much talk of the battle everywhere, and the two parishes threaten to go at it again with cudgels sometime in the summer. They say that the Llanwenog men are very ugly with the cudgel . . .
>
> Lewis, the minister, spoke very severely of the thing . . . afterwards. He cried like a baby, while father and mother and the chief people were crying with him. They have since had a good many prayer meetings to pray for the young people, but I do not see the young people one whit the better after they have been prayed for.

Nineteenth century publicists and popular antiquarians were wont to ascribe the passionate loyalties such games continued to evoke to their origins as clan feuds or struggles against invaders. This same Llanwenog was noted also for grudge-matches within the parish between the Bros, or 'Paddy' Bros, from the hilly parts and the Blaenaus from the valley, a survival of clan warfare.[38] At both Kingston upon Thames and Chester, the annual games were said to commemorate a victory a thousand years before when the head of a Danish leader was kicked around the streets.[39] And in Derby the notorious inter-parish battles were said to mask a victory over the Romans in AD 217.[40] Whatever their origins, they evoked loyalties and emotions that led the participants and their friends to stout resistance to all attempts at prohibition.

Nevertheless opposition to football grew, not only for its lack of decorum but for fear of what it bred, idleness, and what it could conceal, subversiveness. In England football was sometimes a symbol of resistance to authority or to change, like the rabbit-skins carried on poles in the Peasants' Revolt. In East Anglia, which had its own popular variant, campball, it frequently marked objections to Fenland drainage schemes or enclosures. There were tense battles to retain 'camping closes' and the loss of one, as at White Roding, Essex, in 1724 could be the signal for a riot.[41] Change affected all classes, but it naturally hit some much harder than others. Some small farmers, for instance, faced with land taxes and rent increases, sold up and started out again in the colonies: others frittered away the proceeds. Throughout it all the lesser squires and yeomen freeholders felt a burning hatred for the Whig landowners and the Hanoverian court.

Cricket forges ahead

Amidst this turmoil cricket was better suited both to gambling and to the preservation of the social order. Indeed the Duke of Richmond's social standing brought lustre to the game and even to the professionals he hired to play with him. On 6 September 1729 the *London Journal*, in an account of a match for 100 guineas played at the Earl of Leicester's seat at Penshurst Park, Sussex, between Sir William Gage's team and 'Kent, headed by Edwin Stead, Esq.', noted that 'a groom of the Duke of Richmond signalised himself by such extraordinary agility and dexterity, to the surprise of all the spectators, which were some thousands' that "tis reckoned he turned the scale of victory, which for some years past has generally been on the Kentish side'.

That he was the Duke's groom was all-important; his name, Thomas Waymark, was not mentioned. This honour was grudgingly accorded the following year when his prowess was such that a match against Sir William Gage 'was put off an account of Waymark, The Duke's man, being ill'. Other early plebeian cricketers survive only as names, like Joseph Budd, or even more meagrely Pye and Green. Not all were servants of the great men; some were itinerant tradesmen augmenting their incomes from cricket, like Stephen Dingate, a barber born in Surrey who had played for Kent as a 'given man' before moving to Sussex to play for the Duke.

Such a situation, in which sponsors played alongside their hirelings, must often have called for great tact by professionals on the field and sycophantic journalists off it. One of the first incompetent but rich and enthusiastic sponsors was no less a person than the monarch's eldest son Frederick Louis, Prince of Wales. 'Poor Fred' did not enjoy the confidence of his father, to whom he had been a trouble since his arrival from Hanover in 1728, idling about the place and, worse, consorting with opposition politicians. Yet he had the saving grace of wanting to be English.[42] He had learned cricket with imported equipment as a boy and though he was no great player, he loved the game, and relished the opportunity to become a patron.

He began modestly. In 1731 he attended a match between teams from Surrey and Middlesex at Mowlsey Hurst when he was pleased to award a guinea to each man in appreciation of their dexterity. Two years later he gave a silver cup for a game in which 'the Prince's men' played Edwin Stead's Kent. Up to this point the great matches in London had been played for moderate stakes, but in July 1735 there was a dramatic change when Frederick's Surrey team played one from Kent (led by the Earl of Middlesex, the son of the first Duke of Dorset!) for £1,000 a side. The prince lost both this and the return game at Bromley Common two weeks later but his enthusiasm was undiminished.

In 1737 at a game on Kennington Common a pavilion was 'created for His Royal Highness who was accompanied by several persons of distinction'. The opposing leader for Kent this time was Lord John Sackville, another son of the Duke of Dorset. (The Sackvilles of Knowle were to be amongst the strongest, if most erratic, supporters of cricket.) The high stakes and the swells brought in the crowds. 'The press was so great on this occasion that a poor woman by the crowd bearing upon her, unfortunately had her leg broke, which being related to His Royal Highness, he was pleased to order her ten guineas.'[43]

The banners under which the teams fought varied haphazardly between the names of their patrons, the counties for whose honour they fought, 'England' if they were a miscellany, 'London' if they were metropolitan, and even villages. When the Duke of Richmond returned to cricket in 1741, after a hunting accident and assorted domestic problems, it was to lead Slindon, a Sussex village. Slindon's star performer was a new kind of professional. Richard Newland was from the middle reaches of society, of yeoman farmer stock, and a good enough cricket player to spend his early summers at it, making good profits out of shrewd bets and perhaps a share of the gate, which no doubt helped him set himself up in due course as a surgeon, a cut above Stephen Dingate one might say.

Soon Slindon were challenging the leading metropolitan teams, 'London' and 'Surrey' who played at the Artillery Ground at Finsbury. This old archery field was not a splendid stretch of green sward in the modern manner but a rather smelly badly drained affair. Yet what it lacked in environmental purity it made up for in social prestige. The Honourable Artillery Company was a snobbish crowd, renowned nowadays more for wining and dining than for military prowess, but its ground offered privacy as well as social cachet.

Slindon came to grief there and then lost at home, and though they sought return matches no-one was interested: their moment of glory had gone. Newland, on the other hand, rose to new heights. The following July he led Three of England against Three of Kent at the Artillery Ground for a £500 wager in front of 10,000 spectators.[44]

Rules to make money by

Gambling was not quite so far advanced in Scotland, perhaps because of native frugality and caution. In 1724 what the newspapers called a 'solemn match of goff' for twenty guineas was thought 'an affair so remarkable on account of the stake that it was attended by the Duke of Hamilton, the Earl of Morton and a vast mob of the great and little besides'.[45] Golf was still played on public links lands and there were as yet no organised societies although there were embryonic groups at Bruntsfield Links, Musselburgh, and Leith near Edinburgh as well as at Carnoustie and St Andrews further up the coast. Whether they had club meetings or not they had no clubhouses. Entertainment after the game meant repairing to the nearest tavern, and even the great men of Edinburgh society – afterwards known as the Gentlemen Golfers – had no clubhouse: a private room at Luckie Clephan's served the purpose.[46]

Inns and Innkeepers had, of course, been a vital element in the spread of sport everywhere in Britain. Innyards were early venues for tennis, bowls and boxing matches with the innkeeper the stakeholder or matchmaker. Publicans sponsored sport of all kinds – cock-fighting, bull-baiting, cudgel-playing, wrestling, football, cricket, even bell-ringing contests. When The Swan at Highworth, Wiltshire staged a wrestling match between teams from Berkshire and Gloucestershire in 1740 the newspapers announced that 'for the encouragement of the gamesters the landlord will give two guineas to that side which shall throw three falls out of the five and half-a-crown to every man that throws a fall' and 'if any persons are inclin'd to lay any sums of money against the Berkshire boys, they may have bets'.[47]

The food and drink concession was also important. In 1736 three Gloucestershire publicans took out an advertisement warning the opposition at a forthcoming race meeting that they had 'taken the field, so that all persons not concern'd are to bring no liquor there for sale.'[48] Some travelled around: George Williams of the White Lion, Streatham had a specially-designed marquee, with barmaids and waitresses in smart red uniforms, that he took to Ascot races and various cricket grounds in the London area. A 1742 advertisement by Adam's Coffee House, Holborn, offered 'a complete Tennis Court with a Tambour . . . at a charge of one shilling a hand, six pence for a set of double'.[49] And melancholia victims could visit Robert Bartholomew at White

Conduit House, Islington, where the old inn had been rebuilt and tea-rooms added: 'My cows eat no grain, neither any adulteration in the milk and cream. Bats and balls for cricket and a convenient place to play in.' Experts could test the assertion of Francis Ludgate, mine host of the Rising Sun and Sportsman', Marylebone, that his cricket bats and balls were 'of the right sort, and no others in town as they pretend'.[50]

Entrepreneurs met all tastes. New-style football promoters took advantage of the new advertising media – the *Suffolk Mercury* of 17 October 1735, carried the challenge of '12 Norfolk men to play against 12 of any county or country whatever' – and running footmen sought opponents in the *Westminster Gazette*.[51] For polite society there was the metropolitan wonder of the Pleasure Gardens at Ranelagh, opened that same year, to challenge the older creation at Foxhall, or Vauxhall, where Pepys had taken the air. Ranelagh had a rotunda, a promenade with fashionable shops, a Chinese pavilion and facilities for concerts, masquerades and firework displays.[52]

The politeness of early Georgian society was, however, a thin veneer, though it may be thought a sign of progress that 'prize-fighting' gradually came to mean pugilism. Figg's amphitheatre continued to stage the animal shows so much enjoyed by the young Duke of Cumberland (the King's second son, who had been given the benefit of an English education at Eton, where at the age of nine his rank had given him the privilege of striking the first blow in the climax of the annual ram hunt, clubbing the animal to death),[53] but it was increasingly popular for its exhibitions of pugilism.

By 1730 Figg himself was done with serious fighting and was looking to his protégés to draw in the crowds. One of them, Bob Whittaker, was the victor in a spectacular contest against a Venetian gondolier, watched by George II himself from a specially constructed royal box. Another, the great Jack Broughton, sparred with Figg in exhibitions after serious contests. It was a third protégé, George Taylor, who took over the business when Figg died in 1734. He declared himself champion but he was soon beaten by Broughton who for eight years was the main attraction at Taylor's Booth. Broughton also brought in aristocratic pupils through his skilled tuition and such thoughtful gestures as devising 'mufflers', primitive boxing gloves, for their protection. One of these was the adolescent Cumberland, an eager practitioner of the noble art of defence as preparation for his desired career as a great soldier.[54]

With Broughton came the birth of a national myth – the British preference for fisticuffs as a blunt, straightforward, honest solution to disputes compared with the sneaky methods of foreigners. This flourished in the highly charged atmosphere of 1739 when Spanish searches of English trading ships, allegedly resulting in a Captain Jenkins losing his ear, forced the reluctant Walpole into a declaration of war, which spread through Bourbon family compact to

France. The conflict was proceeding by fits and starts when, in February 1741, the portly Prince of Wales and the more athletic Cumberland took time out from public affairs to watch Jack Broughton face a challenge from a brash former coachman from Yorkshire, George Stevenson.

Stevenson had challenged Broughton in the extravagant language popularised by the Masters of Defence in imitating the courtly traditions of the past. Thus John Francis, the Jumping Soldier, declared himself unimpressed by the 'Irish Bragadoccio' of an opponent, Patrick Henly. And Patrick for his part claimed that he had 'never refused anyone on or off the stage' and that he fought 'as often for the diversion of gentlemen as for money'.[55] By the same token the infrastructure of pugilism was a vulgar parody of the time when the clash of swords was daily music in London. John Francis' credentials included fighting 'several bruisers in the street', the first rung on the professional ladder. Another bill advertised 'bye-battles', supporting bouts, involving 'the noted Cock-eye from Brick Street and the Sailor that made so terrible a battle the day the Battle Royal was fought'. (A Battle Royal was a pugilistic version of the old armed mêlées in which newcomers could take their chances.)[56]

Stevenson's challenge to Broughton read: 'I will meet you a month from to-day. If you don't come up you are a coward. If you don't dust me you are a humbug. If I beat you are a dead man.'[57] In fact it was Stevenson who died a month after the fight following a blow over the heart. For Broughton, who had a reputation for tough but honest fighting, as well as his backers the death of a challenger was undoubtedly a great embarrassment. For a time the shock seems to have put a damper on patrons' enthusiasm and Broughton vowed never to fight again.

The war was also going badly and, exasperated with Walpole, the Prince of Wales toured the country trying to work up patriotic fervour as crowds sang the new song 'Rule, Britannia'. Walpole eventually resigned, on a matter unconnected with the war, giving way to the meteor Carteret who indulged the King's martial inclinations. These included taking the field himself at Dettingen in 1743, the last time a reigning British monarch led his troops into battle. The result was a military success but at great cost and to no strategic purpose. Cumberland accompanied the King and acquitted himself well enough to intensify the envy and enmity of the Prince of Wales who as heir to the throne had been kept at home.

Broughton, having in the meantime quarrelled with Taylor, was so far recovered in spirits as to set up his own establishment. He took the precaution however of securing the approval of his backers to a set of rules 'agreed by several gentlemen at Broughton's amphitheatre, Tottenham Court Road, August 16, 1743'.[58] They were crude enough, permitting wrestling moves like the hold in chancery and the cross-buttock throw, hitting below the belt and hair-pulling, but they barred hitting a man when he was down, even when he dropped to his knees tactically, or seizing him by 'the ham, the breeches or any part below the waist'. Furthermore the ring was to be kept clear when fighting was on, and half-a-minute recovery time was allowed after a knockdown or drop down. And finally the fighters were to choose two umpires to settle disputes.

Thus formal rules were introduced in pugilism before politer sports, such as racing and cricket. The latter was increasingly thought to be in need of regulation, however. In September 1743 the *Gentleman's Magazine* criticised the game on social and legal grounds:

> Noblemen, gentlemen and clergymen have certainly a right to divert them-
> selves in what manner they think fit, nor do I dispute their privilege of making
> butchers, cobblers or tinkers their companions, provided they are gratified to
> keep them company. But I very much doubt whether they have any right to
> invite thousands of people to be spectators of their agility.

This was an act of social irresponsibility: 'The time of people of fashion may be, indeed, of little value, but in a trading country the time of the meanest man ought to be of some worth to himself and to the community.' This apart, these public cricket matches were 'a most notorious breach of the laws' which gave 'the most open encouragement to gaming, the advertisements most impudently reciting that great sums were laid'.

The law on gaming was renewed and reinforced in 1744, but that very same year the Artillery Ground staged 'the greatest cricket match ever known' before 'their Royal Highnesses the Prince of Wales and Duke of Cumberland, the Duke of Richmond, Admiral Vernon and many other persons of distinc-tion'. This game, between Kent led by Lord John Sackville and England under Newland, inspired a mock-heroic poem by the pseudonymous James Love satirising the curious social mix which included Bryan, 'whose cautious hand could fix, / In neat dispos'd array the well pil'd bricks'.[59]

The poem also portrayed the ground-keeper, George Smith, keeping the crowds back by plying 'with strenuous arms the smacking whip'. More pro-saically, according to the *Daily Advertiser*, 'it was observed by the noblemen and gentlemen present that there was great disorder so that it was with difficulty that the match was played out'.[60] Admission charges were put up sharply from two pence to six pence, which had a disastrous effect on atten-dance, but kept out the riff-raff.

It was in these troubled times that the nobility and gentry decided to standardise the playing conditions. The earliest surviving 'laws' of cricket appeared on the border of a commemorative linen handkerchief with no indication of authorship. When reprinted in a polite magazine they were headed 'The game of cricket, as settl'd by the Cricket Club in 1744, and play'd at the Artillery Ground London'.[61] This Cricket Club was not, however, a playing club but a gathering of élite members of various teams around the metropolis: when the laws were reprinted in booklet form they were offered 'as settled by the several cricket clubs, particularly that of the Star and Garter in Pall Mall', which was where the leading lights of sport foregathered.[62]

The age of the Butcher

One of them was the egregious Duke of Cumberland, who was attracted for a while into cricket sponsorship by the ingratiating Earl of Sandwich. (The quick snack called after him – meat between two slices of bread – was a device to allow more time at the gaming table, and he is said to have impressed Cumberland by showing him how to hunt and throw dice at the same time.) Meanwhile, however, his hopes of military glory were revived when he was called once more into action in Europe, as Captain-General no less. The subsequent defeat at Fontenoy was a humiliation and a betrayal of Britain's allies. It also encouraged Charles Edward, the Stuart pretender, to make a bid for the throne: he landed in Scotland in 1745 and the Highlanders rose in support. This was Cumberland's chance to make amends, for his father sent him to deal with the situation. The way he did so earned contempt in England and the hatred of Scots of every political persuasion.

Since the Act of Union, England and Scotland had, nominally at least, been one British nation, but Scotland was very much the lesser partner. Her electoral system was even less representative than the English and she was greatly under-represented at Westminster. The chief benefit of union was that of sharing in English trading arrangements with a consequent spur to agricultural advance and industrial development. Of Scotland's one million inhabitants, nine-tenths still lived in the country: Edinburgh had 36,000 people, Glasgow 12,000–13,000 and none of the other towns had more than 7,000. The union was the making of Glasgow: the first Glasgow-built and -owned ship crossed the Atlantic in 1718 and the town and eventually the lowland region were transformed.

Religion still troubled Scotland, but economic advance was about to offer some consolations for the disaffected. In Ireland, five-sixths of whose 2 million people were Catholics and subject to callously repressive legislation and economic hardship, there was no such prospect: indeed the Scots now joined in the discriminatory trade practices that squeezed the life out of any Irish initiatives. All the top posts, civil and ecclesiastical, went to English nominees and the office of Lord Lieutenant, two of whose occupants never set foot in Ireland, was a convenient shelf on which to park ministers who were out of favour but too important to be sacked outright. Supplying the English with food, linen and cheap laughs seemed the Irish fate.

If there was no hope for Ireland the price of Scottish advance was to widen the gulf between the culture of the Lowlands, which were largely reconciled to the Union, and of the Highlands, a backward region, dependent on cattle-raising and riven by feuds amongst the clans, of whom only one (albeit the biggest, the Duke of Argyll's Campbells) supported the government. At the time of Bonnie Prince Charlie's landing much depended on the goodwill of Duncan Forbes, Lord President of the Court of Session, hitherto a loyal supporter of George II. Forbes was a fanatical golfer – when the Leith links were under snow he played on the sands – and he had featured in a mock-heroic poem of 1743, somewhat like Edward the Confessor in his forest:

> . . . patron of the just
> The dread of villains and the good man's trust,
> When spent with toils in serving humankind
> His body recreates, and unbends his mind.[63]

He belonged to the Gentlemen Golfers, superior citizens on whom in 1744 Edinburgh Council had bestowed a silver club to be played for annually at Leith, and the following year Forbes took part in the competition before hurrying north to dissuade the rebels. He failed, with disastrous results.

The Highlanders were put down so brutally at Culloden in 1746 that Cumberland was called 'the Butcher' from then on. The nickname, spitefully encouraged by his brother, clouded Cumberland's triumphal homecoming. One of the spoils of Culloden was the rangership of Windsor Great Park including residence in what became known as Cumberland Lodge. The Butcher spent much time extending and improving the park and building bigger stables. But his hunting was of the deer-cart variety and twice a week in season, Tuesdays and Saturdays, 1,200 deer were assembled for his pleasure from all over the country. As Gilbert White put it, 'His Highness sent down a huntsman, and six yeomen prickers, in scarlet jackets laced with gold . . . ordering them to take every deer in the forest alive, and convey them in carts to Windsor.'[64]

The outbreak of peace in Europe in 1749 brought a celebratory Hogarth painting *The Gate of Calais* contrasting French government tyranny over their starving masses with the liberty enjoyed by the beef-eating citizens of Old England. There was a lavish firework display at Ranelagh and at the Hockley-le-Hole bear-garden the advertisements promised fireworks tied to animals. In the hierarchy of British vices cruelty came first, but there were other serious claimants. The profit motive was limitless in its scope. Human excrement was a valuable commodity: 'Those who sell this dirt are said to receive large income from it', noted a Dutch traveller.[65]

Drink and drugs were a deadly menace; Hogarth's beef-eating Britishers appeared in a less flattering light in his 1751 prints contrasting the past pleasures and plenty of Beer Street with the modern miseries of Gin Lane. Gambling was another menace. A poignant detail of another Hogarth print showed the blind Lord William Bertie preoccupied with a cock-fight he could not even see and having his pocket picked as a result. The print was one of a series that Hogarth called *Four Stages of Cruelty* (1751) and there are no more graphic horrors in all his work than the vicious examples he gives.

The crudeness of the prize-ring fitted easily into this context. In 1750, now aged forty-six, Jack Broughton was persuaded to return to the ring by a challenge from a rough-and-ready fellow called Jack Slack. Slack made no secret of his scorn both for Broughton's rules (which had cost him a fight on what he reckoned was a technicality) and for the champion himself. Broughton's backer and old pupil Cumberland was so confident of the outcome that he gave the Earl of Chesterfield odds of twenty-five to one against Slack – £10,000 to £400. Unfortunately Broughton's confidence took the form of not bothering to train, and he paid the penalty. After a few minutes of early mastery he got a blow between the eyes from which he never recovered.

Thereafter the fight game in the fifties was dominated by Slack, to whom Cumberland switched his allegiance, and it sank further into brutality and dishonesty. Cricket too was in the doldrums. The old strongholds of Sussex and Kent, already undermined by the vogue for the Artillery Ground, were seriously weakened by the death of the Duke of Richmond in 1750 and by the family problems of the Sackvilles of Knowle Park.

The latest preoccupation at the Star and Garter was Newmarket. In 1751 the auctioneer John Pond published a *Sporting Kalendar* which included rules for match-making and the conduct of races, and a year later it was announced that these rules would govern 'a contribution Free Plate . . . to be run for at Newmarket. . . by horses the property of the noblemen and gentlemen of the Jockey Club at the Star and Garter in Pall Mall'.[66] The precise membership of this group is as shadowy as that of the 'Cricket Club' but they were much the same men with much the same motives.

Meanwhile, however in Scotland legislative advances in the emergent national game owed less to the demands of gambling. At the small coastal town of St Andrews a group of noblemen and gentlemen led by the Earl of Wemyss and the Earl of Elgin decided the time was ripe for organised competition there. They bought the by now traditional silver club as a trophy and drew up a set of rules, 13 in all, based on those of the Gentlemen Golfers of Edinburgh. This dependence does not, however, seem to have prevented them when inviting the Edinburgh golfers to take part in their inaugural competition from calling their society 'the ALMA MATER of the GOLF.' The rivalry that ensued was, of course, of an entirely gentlemanly kind.

Notes

1 *Essay upon the Advancement of Irish Trade*.
2 Article by Alsager Vian in *Dictionary of National Biography*.
3 Gregory King's Tables, 1688, printed in G.M. Trevelyan, *English Social History*, London, 1944, p. 277.
4 For the relative prosperity and prospects of the classes and the masses see M. Ashley, *England in the Seventeenth Century*, Harmondsworth, 1967, pp. 17–25.
5 *Travels over England*, 1698, trans. J. Ozell, 1719, pp. 254–5.
6 *Angliae Notitia*, 1669, p. 86.
7 Ibid. 1694 ed. p. 52.
8 31 July 1711, in *Journal to Stella* (1710–13), ed. H. Williams, Oxford, 1948, vol. 1.
9 *The Spectator*, no. 2, 2 March 1711 (Richard Steele).
10 Ibid., no. 122, 20 July 1711 (Joseph Addison).
11 Ibid., no. 135, 31 July 1711 (Joseph Addison).
12 Ibid., no. 116, 13 July 1711 (Eustace Budgell).
13 *Windsor Forest*, 1712.
14 *The Guardian*, 1713.
15 *English Social History*, p. 281.
16 *The Royal Pastime of Cock-fighting*, by R.H., 1709.
17 William Machrie, *An Essay upon the Royal Art and Recreation of Cocking*, 1705. 'Sadness seizeth on every creature after coition except the cock'.
18 The Tatler, no. 134, 1709.
19 *In certamen pilae* by William Goldwin, scholar of Eton and King's College, Cambridge, printed in *Musae juveniles*, ed. A. Baldwin, 1706, translated by Harold Perry in 'Etoniana' December 1922. The original and the translation are printed in R.S. Rait-Kerr, *The Laws of Cricket*, London, 1950.
20 J. Barker, *The Devil and the Peers* or *The Princely Way of Sabbath-breaking*, 1712.
21 E.P. Thompson, *Whigs and Hunters*, Harmondsworth, 1977, pp. 28–44. 'Fence-time' was the fawning season.
22 White, *The Natural History of Selbourne*, 1789, Letter VII, to Thomas Pennant.
23 *The Complete Sportsman*, 1718, quoted in J. Strutt, *Glig-gamena angel deod: or The Sports and Pastimes of the People of England*, London, 1801; new edition 1903, reprinted Bath, 1969, p. 25.
24 *The Fable of the Bees*, 1723. For the Walpole era see P. Langford, 'The Eighteenth Century', K.O. Morgan, *The Oxford Illustrated History of Britain*, Oxford, 1984, pp. 362–74, and for the period generally B. Wiliams, revised C.H. Stuart, *The Whig Supremacy 1714–60*, Oxford 1962.
25 de Saussure, *A Foreign View of England*, trans. Mivan Muyden, London, 1902, pp. 281–2.
26 R. Mortimer, *The Jockey Club*, London, 1958, p. 8. For the classic account of the early turf by the editor of *The Field* see T. Cook, *History of the English Turf* (2 vols.), London, 1901–4.
27 For early Irish racing see S.J. Watson, *Between the Flags*, Dublin, 1969.
28 Packs exclusively for fox-hunting were started at Cheshunt, Hertfordshire (1725) and Stapleton, Dorset (1730), Strutt, *Sports and Pastimes*, p. 15.
29 *Foreign View of England*, p. 196.
30 Ibid., p. 275.

31 For the Duke of Richmond see J. Marshall, *The Duke who was Cricket*, London, 1961, and for early cricket generally J. Ford, *Cricket: A Social History 1700–1850*, Newton Abbott, 1972.

32 M. Concannen, *A Match at Football*, quoted in P.M. Young, *The History of British Football*, London, 1973 edn, pp. 78–83.

33 M. Marples, *A History of Football, London, 1954*, pp. 90–2 gives examples.

34 Plough Monday was the first Monday after Twelfth Night, when the return to work was signalled by farm labourers dragging a Fond Plough (i.e. a foolish one, often decked with flowers) from door to door seeking 'plough money' for a party.

35 Marples, *History of Football*, p. 84.

36 *Notes and Queries*, 16 May 1931, quoted in Young, *History of British Football*, pp. 75–8.

37 Variation (second line = 'At football or at cricket') quoted in Strutt, *Sports and Pastimes* p. 101. Cot's plut = God's blood, Prettiest Fellows = likeliest lads, nickit = hit the mark, score.

38 C.L. Gomme, *The Village Community*, London, 1890, quoted in Young, *History of British Football*, p. 77.

39 W.D. Biden, *The History of Kingston-upon-Thames*, London, 1852; M. Shearman, *Football*, London, 1899, cited in Marples, *History of Football*, p. 7.

40 S. Glover, *The History of Derby*, 1829.

41 R.W. Malcolmson, p. 115. *Popular Recreations in English Society, 1700–1850*, Cambridge 1973, p. 115.

42 Williams, *Whig Supremacy*, pp. 338–40 which notes his influence on his son, the future George IV, also a staunch patriot. Unfortunately remembered in the rhyme circulated in court circles at his death: 'Here lies Poor Fred / Who was alive and is dead', etc. There has been some debate amongst sports chroniclers about whether his death came from his having been struck in his youth by a cricket or a tennis ball.

43 *London Evening Post*, 16 June 1737.

44 Newland also featured in a celebrated mock-heroic poem, in which he is called 'the Champion'. See note 59 below.

45 Sir Guy Campbell, 'The Early History of English Golf' in *A History of Golf in Britain*, ed. B. Darwin et al., 1952, pp. 53–4.

46 For Mrs Clephan's establishment and its counter parts, such as Baillie Glass's in St Andrews see R. Browning, *A History of Golf*, London 1955, pp. 45–51.

47 Malcolmson, *Popular Recreations*, p. 77.

48 Ibid., p. 73.

49 The tambour was a projection from the wall of the court designed to offer variety of play. For a discussion of the varying fortunes of tennis in the eighteenth century see Lord Aberdare, *The Story of Tennis*, London, 1959, pp. 78–9.

50 Ford, *Cricket*, pp. 115–6.

51 *The Tatler*, 14 September 1710 (Joseph Addison).

52 J.H. Plumb, 'The Commercialisation of Leisure', Stenton Lecture, University of Reading, 1972.

53 H.C. Maxwell-Lyte, *History of Eton College*, London, 1911, pp. 302–3. The custom was abandoned in 1747.

54 For Cumberland in action see J. Prebble, *Culloden* London, 1961. For early boxing see B. Lynch, *The Prize Ring*, London, 1925; J. Ford, *Prizefighting*, Newton Abbot, 1971; D. Brailsford, *Bareknuckles: A Social History of Prizefighting*, Cambridge, 1988.

55 Handbill for Taylor's Booth, 4 May 1742.

56 Handbill for 'the Great Booth at Tottenham Court Road 1742'. For the style see *The Spectator*, no. 436, 19 July 1712 (Richard Steele). For other examples including women prizefighters see E.S. Turner, *The Shocking History of Advertising*, London,

1952, pp. 30–1.

57 D. Batchelor, *The Big Fight*, London, 1954, p. 18.

58 Reproduced in facsimile in S. Andre and N. Fleischer, *A Pictorial History of Boxing*, New York, 1987, p. 12.

59 J. Dance, *Cricket: An Heroic Poem*, London, 1741 (6th edn ed., F.S. Ashley-Cooper, Nottingham, 1922).

60 19 June 1744.

61 *The New Universal Magazine or the Gentleman and Lady's Polite Instructor*, vol. II, November 1752.

62 'The Game of Cricket', 1755.

63 T. Matheson, *The Goff, an Heroi-Comical Poem in Three Cantos*, Edinburgh, 1743, quoted in Browning, *History of Golf*, p. 36.

64 White, *Selbourne*, Letter VI to Thomas Pennant.

65 P. Kalm, *Account of his visit to England*, 1748 trans. J. Lucas, London, 1892, p. 143, quoted in D. Jarrett, *England in the Age of Hogarth*, London, 1974, an admirable account of the social life of the next age.

66 Mortimer, *Jockey Club*, p. 10.

CHAPTER SIX

Aristocrats and entrepreneurs
1756–92

The political parties were not yet strong enough either in philosophy or in organisation to formulate distinctive policies and translate them into action. Both Whigs and Tories shared the view, articulated by John Locke, that the chief function of government was the preservation of property and that men had the right to civil liberty within rules prescribed for that purpose. This still left plenty of room for disagreement for the rule-makers were all highly individualistic and most were self-seeking. They also had tribal prejudices especially in matters of religion. Not least they were much exercised by the question of how a constitutional monarchy should operate.

The first two Georges, militaristic and preoccupied with the claims of Hanover, had been kept in check by their dependence on native ministers who were adept at pulling the necessary Parliamentary strings and exacted an appropriate price. One of these was control over Crown patronage, used for many years by the Duke of Newcastle to sustain Whig domination. This cosy arrangement was threatened in 1756 when, with things going badly in the resumed tussle with France, Newcastle was obliged to turn to his Cabinet colleague William Pitt to retrieve the situation. Pitt, a powerful speaker in the House of Commons and 'the voice of Britain' in the public mind, was the man to save the nation, but it was a risk – to Newcastle because of his reputation for integrity and to George II because he was a former ally of his now defunct but not forgiven son, Frederick.

Pitt duly united the country, defeating the French at sea as well as on land and in the colonies as well as in Europe. Yet his unique mixture of high-mindedness and protection of trade made him absolutist and intransigent and he was elbowed out of office in 1761 by those, like Newcastle, who felt the cost of pursuing an all-out war to total victory was too great. The chief beneficiary was the new king, George III, Frederick's idealistic and patriotic son, who had marked his accession by a proclamation for the 'encouragement of piety and virtue', who announced in his first speech from the throne that he gloried in the name of Britain and who now took advantage of Cabinet disagreements as the war dragged on to play a positive personal role in concluding the Peace of Paris in 1763.[1]

New directions

George III's determination to rule, not merely reign, was assisted by his taking Crown patronage back into his own hands, an act which further alienated the

Whig grandees and made the King, willy-nilly, a party man. His move to centre stage, furthermore, brought him up against a new phenomenon, personified by a *nouveau-riche* rabble rouser, John Wilkes, whose youthful sport it was to press the constitutional cause to the brink of anarchy, and who exploited the potentially violent force of 'public opinion' through mass meetings, pamphlets and newspapers. The king found himself exposed to personal attacks that he could neither counter nor ignore, and the House of Commons, well-stocked with Tory squires of simplistic outlook, got little sympathy from the electors when they tried to suppress Wilkes.

Domestic politics apart, the monarch's romantic yearnings affected the large sectors of the globe now falling into British hands. After Pitt's successes in Canada and India, Australia was acquired simply by Captain Cook's landing there in 1770. The assumption was that if colonies were to be taken in they should benefit the mother country. George III's conviction that American colonists should be taxed led to confrontation. The Americans' sturdy defence of their rights, though admirable, was severely compromised by their own reliance on slavery. Indeed the clarion call for freedom increasingly heard on both sides of the Atlantic tended to drown the quieter voices of justice and compassion.

Thus 1776, the year of American independence, also saw the publication of *The Wealth of Nations* in which Adam Smith applied to political economy the philosophy adumbrated in earlier works. It conferred on capitalism the status accorded to feudalism in earlier centuries. The divine strategy of wealth distribution, it now appeared, was to make use of human greed and folly for charitable purposes. Self-seeking men bent on the 'gratification of their own vain and insatiable desires' were, Smith reckoned, often 'led by an invisible hand' to confer incidental benefit on society.[2] This convenient doctrine was thereafter to salve the consciences of landowners, tycoons, rakish sprigs of aristocracy, money-grabbing Dissenters, pious distillers, Quaker plantation-owners, sanctimonious bankers, owners of gambling dens, brothel-keepers and all who pandered to human frailty for profit. More immediately, it inspired a new breed of entrepreneur who, seeing that the demand for consumer goods in an increasingly prosperous Britain was not being met by the traditional domestic system, financed a new one based on technology.

The potential had been shown earlier in the century when Huguenot refugees and stolen Italian patents had transformed the silk trade. The Lancashire climate was eminently suitable for cotton and fustian manufacture. Yet there was a gap of thirty years before Kay's invention, around 1733, of the flying shuttle was matched by Hargreaves' spinning jenny and exploited by the humbly-born Richard Arkwright who rose to knighthood and a fortune of half a million pounds. In the interim new methods of smelting iron ore had made large-scale production practical, and Joseph Black's scientific discoveries paved the way for James Watt's improvements to the steam engine. The great expansion which followed took place not only in textiles but in pottery and engineering, great and small, pioneered by men like Josiah Wedgwood and Matthew Boulton who had already seen the benefits of standard design and manufacturing processes and were quick to see the further possibilities of steam-powered mass-production.

Communications also improved and became cheaper, mainly because of the network of canals begun in 1759 through the entrepreneurial enthusiasm of the Duke of Bridgewater and the engineering skills of an illiterate genius, James Brindley. The effect of all this on trade was dramatic. Exports, which had remained around £14 million between 1760 and 1780 rose to £23.7 million by 1792. Economic advance brought changes in employment patterns and profoundly disturbed traditionalists. Yet it was to be some time before social change followed. For one thing the people who made most out of the industrial revolution at first were the landowners whose rents and profits increased with the commercial value of their sites and who also benefited from the exploitation of mineral resources: by contrast the inventors and engineers all too often lacked the capital to take much personal advantage.

In agriculture, furthermore, which was still the basic industry, progressive landowners and big-scale farmers were in a better position to take advantage of scientific discovery; and the new methods of Viscount Townshend, known as 'Turnip' for one of his interests, and the Leicestershire stockbreeder, Robert Bakewell, sparked interest and emulation in a highly conservative profession, paving the way for the vast improvements (and profits) later in the century by such as Thomas Coke of Holkham, Earl of Leicester.

Field sports in transition

The old open-field strip system, the concept of common land and the mutual obligation of landlord and tenant were clearly obstacles to the onward march towards cost-effective land usage, as the growing frequency of Inclosure Acts testified. Legal but rarely used in Queen Anne's days, they had multiplied in Georgian times – there were 67 between 1721 and 1740, 204 between 1741 and 1760 and then, as corn prices rose, the number shot up to 1,043 between 1761 and 1780. So the countryside became a battleground and sport a major issue.

Hunting was an important status symbol. Few, of course, could aspire to the old style. Deer-hunting had almost disappeared with the destruction of forests, enclosure of wastes and the encroachments of arable farming. The old herds of wild deer had gone, except on Exmoor and a few other remote regions, and the deer-cart alternative could be afforded only by the very rich, and was preferred only by the insensitive (including the royal family and its foreign adherents). Most of the noble stags that roamed the parks of the nobility were shot, in season, as venison. Hare-hunting, never quite in the top drawer socially, suffered accordingly. Coursing was given social cachet by the creation of élitist clubs which offered the additional spice of gambling. The first was the Swaffham, founded in 1776 by the raffish third Earl of Orford, grandson of Robert Walpole: the Ashdown Park (1780) and Malton (1781) were on similar, if less idiosyncratic lines. By contrast modern landlords and their gamekeepers did not always encourage the traditional style.

Thus Rev James Woodforde, scholar of Winchester and sub-warden of New College, Oxford, having recently become the rector of Weston Longeville, Norfolk, was obliged to record in his diary, 'In the afternoon my dog Pompey came home shot terribly, so bad that I had her hanged directly out of her misery. My greyhound Minx who was with her did not come home and we suppose met with the same fate.'[3] They had been shot by Black Jack, gamekeeper to the landowner, Hon. Charles Townshend. The episode ended happily – Mr Townshend apologised and invited Woodforde to take a course on his land whenever he liked – but it was a sign of the times.

Shooting was the new vogue, gradually replacing hawking, netting and liming as a way of taking wild fowl – at least amongst those who could afford guns and were legally entitled to use them. Gilbert White reckoned that from the 1740s 'unreasonable sportsmen' shooting twenty or thirty brace a day were threatening to extinguish 'the heathcock, black game or grouse'.[4] Early sporting guns – flintlock and hammer – were difficult to handle and muzzle-loading was highly dangerous. Reloading took time and this gave the birds some respite. Nor were they yet 'driven' as in modern times. The long, hand-cut stubble of arable land made it easy for the sportsman, aided by his setter, to sneak up behind partridge and shoot them as they rose. Pheasants were flushed out of hedgerows and coppices by packs of spaniels and similarly despatched. Grouse were plentiful on the northern moors, and blackgame and duck abounded in their own terrain; ruffs and reeves, bittern, plovers, wheatears, landrails and other wild birds were shot whenever they offered themselves.

The notion of game as property fitted well into the modern scheme of things. Thirty-two Game Laws were enacted in George III's reign, and gamekeepers proliferated. Despite this – or perhaps because of it – poaching was rife. When the law made it illegal to buy and sell game both poachers and gamekeepers found it profitable to sell a few brace on the side. Animal predators, as ever, were a serious problem. Farmers' enemies, especially if they were edible like hares and rabbits, were more likely to be snared than shot, but for bigger nuisances, like the fox, either shooting or stopping up their earths and digging them out was common.

This did not accord with the evolving code of the fox-hunters, who saw themselves as the true inheritors of the 'fayre lawe' tradition, chasing something wholly inedible for the sheer pleasure of hounding it to death. Their claims had been enhanced by changes in the sport that added both to its excitement and its social acceptability. In earlier days fox-hunting had meant riding slowly some distance behind hounds that were bred for their sensitive noses. Once a discovered fox took off the only hope of their catching it was it had a fully belly (which meant that the hunt usually started out at dawn).

New possibilities had been shown by Hugo Meynell of Quorndon Hall, Leicestershire, who in 1753, aged only eighteen, took over a traditional pack and improved the breed, making it famous within a few years for speed as well as scent. Horse-breeding also adapted, producing mounts that were both faster and better able to jump over the growing number of hedges and fences: thoroughbred stallions were brought in. Under the new scheme of things hunts could begin in mid-morning, an obvious social advantage. In 1762 the Duke of Beaufort's Badminton pack changed over to fox-hunting, as did the Duke of Rutland's Belvoir (under the Duke's war-hero son, the Marquis of Granby, who featured on so many inn signs of the day). In 1766 the aspirant Viscount Lowther founded the Cottesmore specifically to hunt the fox.[5]

There were some less socially acceptable developments. Meynell's swift-moving pack began to attract a flashy type of rider that the more orthodox called 'first flight' or 'thrusters'. Their behaviour on the hunting field shocked the conventional, but they also encouraged vulgar competitive elements that purists found quite alien to the emerging tradition in which hunters were supposed to keep the same collective discipline as the pack they followed. Some of the thrusters, for instance, were much taken with a new sport that was taking shape in Ireland.

In its primitive beginnings a rider would set off cross-country choosing a route his opponent had to follow, until one or other came to a standstill. A more sophisticated version involved both riders racing towards some conspicuous object on the horizon by whatever route they could. Church steeples were a favourite target, hence the name steeple-hunting or steeplechasing. There were accounts of early Irish contests for wagers but the first significant event took place at Melton Mowbray.

This previously obscure little town began to achieve social status after 1787, when a Mr Ralph Lambton, one of the Quorn 'thrusters', took a house there. It was handy for the Belvoir and the Cottesmore as well as the Quorn and it soon became the fashionable centre during the hunting season. It was there that Lambton and his cronies founded the 'old club' which popularised the scarlet evening coat, afterwards to become the strident emblem of fox-hunting *nouveaux-riches.* And it was there, in 1790, that a seven mile steeplechase was started for a wager of a thousand guineas. The dangers were evident in the fact that the winning horse, in the fashion of flat-racing, was ridden by its owner's valet.

The Meltonians also made their mark on hunting itself. Meynell, who had controlled them fairly well at first, could no longer do so when he ran into financial difficulties and had to ask his members for a subscription. These, however, were as yet small clouds on the horizon. Meanwhile fox-hunting found a true laureate in Peter Beckford, a Dorset landowner, Member of Parliament and pretender to culture. His first sporting treatise in 1781 was produced anonymously, and the *Monthly Review*, assuming him to be a clergyman, took him to task for so urbane a presentation of so cruel an exercise. The book was as remarkable for its snobbery as its blood lust. 'The intemperance, clownishness and ignorance of the old fox-hunters are quite worn out', Beckford claimed, describing the professional huntsman as 'frequently a greater brute than the creatures on which he rides'. Yet at another point he could write:

> The whole art of fox-hunting being to keep the hounds well in blood, sport is a secondary consideration with a true fox-hunter . . . I confess I esteem blood so necessary to a pack of fox-hounds that . . . I always return home better pleased with an indifferent chase with a death at the end of it, than with the best chase possible if it ends up in the loss of the fox.[6]

Nevertheless Beckford made much of the honour code. It could not, for instance, countenance hunting pregnant bitches: 'A gentleman of my acquaintance who killed most of his foxes at this season was humorously called "the midwife of the foxes" ', he smirked. The book's success persuaded Beckford to abandon anonymity and his *Thoughts upon Hare and Fox-hunting* (reprinted in 1790 and 1820) made him famous. 'Never had fox or hare the honour of being chased to death by so accomplished a hunter', wrote Sir Egerton Brydges waspishly. 'He would bag a fox in Greek, find a hare in Latin, inspect his kennels in Italian and direct the economy of his stables in exquisite French.'[7] But though the literati might scoff, Beckford greatly impressed the squires.

Fishing, albeit more gently, began to generate its own snobberies. Technological advance led to greater fastidiousness amongst anglers: the reel revolutionised rod-making, and silk lines began to replace hair. In 1770 Onesimus Ustonson, the tackle-maker, advertised 'a fresh Parcel of superfine Silk Worm Cut, no better ever seen in England . . . the only thing for Trout, Carp and Salmon'. Fly-dressing, the latest art, evoked a good-natured sally from John Gay:

Around the steel no tortured worm shall twine,
No blood of living insect stain my line:
Let me, less cruel, cast the feathered hook,
With pliant rod across the pebbled brook.[8]

Such shafts of urban satire missed the target: less fastidious amateurs and rapacious professionals using nets had depleted the Thames. The Fishmonger's Company, responsible for the river since 1770, had concentrated, with little effect, on trying to prevent crime rather than on conservation. Some minor gentry were even more rapacious than the poachers. Parson Woodforde, who had a small fishpool in his yard for domestic use and a 'great pond' for angling sport, stocked both from the nearby river using nets, and enjoyed it greatly. Recording 'the best day of Fishing we ever had', he noted that

> We caught at one draught ... ten full Pails of Fish ... We caught about 20 Brace of Pike, but threw back all the small ones – also we caught about 15 Brace of Trout ... 3 brace also of Perch – one tolerable Tench and ... not quite five hundred Brace of Roach and Dace.'

He was not pleased when the riparian owner ordered his men off 'and behaved quite contrary to the opinion I had of him'.[9]

Woodforde was not, of course, the most progressive of men. Twenty years earlier he had witnessed a bear-baiting without distaste, and his moral attitudes towards blood sports had changed as little as those of society.[10] Bears had since become a rarity but bull-baiting thrived in spite of the magistrates. In 1778 the Duke of Devonshire was able to stop the Tutbury affair but ten years later the people of Stamford defied a proclamation by the Quarter Sessions and several were arrested in the skirmishing. In some places baiting remained an important political symbol. At Beverley, East Yorkshire, for instance, incoming mayors had to provide a bull for sport and bull-rings were set into the pavement outside aldermanic residences as a mark of distinction. At Liverpool the town provided a bull for the Mayor to inaugurate the baiting.

Cock-throwing was now forbidden in most places, but cock-fighting was as popular as ever. One reason was the Shrove Tuesday custom in the schools (reinforced by the retention of the cockpenny as the schoolmaster's perquisite) but this in turn stemmed from its popularity with the aristocracy and especially the race-going sort. The best-known enthusiast was the twelfth Earl of Derby who at one time owned 3,000 prime birds. His cockpit at his Penwortham estate was the finest in the country but he would stage a main anywhere, if the fancy took him, including the countess's drawing room.

The Turf: old and new values

Here were Adam Smith's theories in action. Whatever aristocratic patronage may have done for wealth distribution, however, it assisted social progress very little. In his last years Cumberland was the central figure of Newmarket society, not so much for his sporting achievements as for his rank: when racing colours were introduced in 1762 his royal purple was listed first of the seventeen. He had a vast stud and bred some good horses, though they somehow never ran as well for him as for other owners. But patronage and backing your fancy were all he understood. His last political manoeuvrings were conducted from his Newmarket base. Just before his death he actually held a political meeting in his stables.[11]

The Butcher was a special case, but his demise heralded no general advance in moral standards. His nephew, Henry, who succeeded to the title, was a notorious rake. He was cited in a divorce suit in 1770 by Lord Grosvenor to whom he was obliged to pay £10,000. Lady Grosvenor complained that her husband had brought the situation on himself by his absorption in racing and horse-breeding. Grosvenor certainly set store by his reputation as the most famous owner–breeder in the country, and his addiction extended to the patronage of the arts. In the age of Gainsborough and Reynolds, many aristocratic patrons commissioned portraits not only of themselves, their homes and landscapes but also their horses and dogs. Horace Walpole compared John Weston to Poussin and Lorrain, and also admired George Seymour and Francis Sartorius. But George Stubbs, son of an ostler and author of *The Anatomy of the Horse*, was supreme and his masterpiece was *The Grosvenor Hunt*.[12]

Adam Smith's 'invisible hand' could also be seen in the aristocratic support for new variants on their obsessive pleasures. The growing complexity of betting, breeding, sales and race-organisation were attracting professional men into the sport. Grosvenor's leasing of part of his Hyde Park estate to an auctioneer called Richard Tattersall was a landmark. Tattersall's auction rooms for horses and hounds were an immediate success, and soon the premises had to be extended and he adapted his house as a tavern, coffee-room and club room for the members of the Jockey Club to transact their business and their bets.

The old pattern of betting was based on bi-lateral wagers between owners: thus one of the features of the Newmarket Spring meeting in 1776 was a match between Mr Pigott's Shark and Mr Greville's Postmaster for £1,000. Sidebets, which often far exceeded the original stake, could be arranged at odds fixed by the interested parties with a gentlemanly stakeholder or through the services of a distinctly ungentlemanly bookmaker. For cup races, such as the Royal Plates, where there might be many entries, heats were run in pairs on a knock-out basis. This, reflecting earlier emphasis on stamina to service cavalry or commercial needs, meant that horses were not usually subjected to long distance races run several times a day before the age of five or six. The introduction of the sweepstake altered all that. Under this arrangement any number of horses could take part with owners each putting up a uniform stake; the race was run on a sudden death basis and the winner swept up the lot. As a result betting became a more complex, mathematical affair, and the concurrent trend towards shorter races for younger horses carrying lighter weights increased the uncertainties and complexities. It was some time before Newmarket adopted the fashion, but the pressure for change became intense with the advent of what became known as the classic races.[13]

These were further results of the insatiable quest for new and exciting forms of gambling. That the first of them was in the north was because the Wentworth Woodhouse estate of the Earl of Rockingham, twice briefly Chief Minister and a lifelong racing addict, was near Doncaster. Rockingham was the leading sponsor of a new race there in 1776, a 25 guinea sweepstake for three year old colts, called after its organiser, Colonel Barry St Leger. Its success led to two similar ventures, the Oaks and the Derby Stakes. In 1779 the Countess of Derby leased a country house called The Oaks at Epsom, Surrey, from her uncle, General Burgoyne, the loser at Saratoga. Epsom, an old spa town, had fallen behind the fashion when Bath and its imitators developed their Assembly Rooms and refined entertainments, and its magnificent Downs had not hitherto staged races of any distinction. Now, however, the idea arose at one of Lord Derby's houseparties of a counterpart to the St Leger – a sweepstake for three year old fillies called The Oaks after the house. It was repeated the following year by popular acclaim, together with another sweepstake for three year olds – colts or fillies – this time called after Lord Derby himself, reputedly by the toss of a coin.[14]

The loser of the toss was the winner of the first race, Sir Charles Bunbury, Grosvenor's great rival for the leadership of the Turf. Bunbury's was the decisive support behind the bid of the Newcastle lawyer, James Weatherby, to publish a *Racing Calendar* in 1769. The five year legal wrangle this entailed showed that more was involved than the right to list the dates of race meetings: the *Calendar* was the repository of the increasingly elaborate rules of racing and Weatherby's editorial status grew into that of secretary, solicitor, treasurer, and not least stakeholder to the Jockey Club.

The lucrative dynasties Weatherby and Tattersall founded were based on service to the nobility and gentry. But there were other, essentially anarchic, forces at work, stemming from the crude element of luck in gambling and the fundamental uncertainties of horse-breeding and training. One of the worst threats to accepted norms was Dennis O'Kelly. O'Kelly, of an Irish immigrant family, had begun his adult working life as a sedan chairman, graduating (after a spell in the arms of a rich admirer) from billiard-marker and tennis-court attendant to professional gambler, sustained by another social aspirant, Charlotte Hayer, a successful prostitute who became his wife.

O'Kelly went on to make a fortune on the Turf. His most celebrated deal was the acquisition of Eclipse, the greatest horse of the eighteenth century, bred by Butcher Cumberland and sold at his death to a Smithfield master butcher for seventy-five guineas. In 1769 when it first appeared in a race of any importance Eclipse immediately caught O'Kelly's eye: he took a share in it and eventually owned it outright. He was not merely interested in winning races. Indeed Eclipse was so good and O'Kelly so slippery that before long nobody wanted to race against them. Lord Grosvenor offered £11,000 for the horse but O'Kelly put it to stud where he earned some £25,000 in fees. O'Kelly had other good horses, one of which came second in the Derby, and he made a great deal of money, which he was quite ready to spend for social purposes, purchasing a commission and eventually a colonelcy in the Middlesex militia, and similarly progressing from a country house near Epsom to Lord Chandos' estate, Canons. That none of this secured him membership of the Jockey Club was nothing to do with morality, but everything to do with belonging to the right circles.

Rival attractions

For members of these circles who fancied themselves as sea-dogs there was sport to be had in yachting. Most early yachts – many of them state owned and used for carrying ambassadors or royalty – were scaled-down warships and their sporting activity was limited and ritualistic. The members of Cork Water Club, for instance, (c1720–65) spent their time manoeuvring and parading ceremonially. But in 1743 Lord Ferrars commissioned a more refined craft on which to entertain friends at sailing parties on the Thames. This encouraged a revival of interest in racing. In 1749 George III, still Prince George, had given a cup for a race from Greenwich to the Nore and back, but it was his brother Henry's cup, presented in 1775, for a race between 'Pleasure sailing boats from 2 to 5 tons burthen from Westminster Bridge to Putney Bridge and back' that started a new craze and the club formed afterwards was called the Cumberland Fleet in his honour.

This inspirational yacht race was itself inspired by the success of a rowing regatta held the previous month on the Thames near Ranelagh. Gentlemen oarsmen had for some years been making a sport of what the watermen did for employment and the memoirs of the young man about town William Hickey mention boat races at Walton in 1768.[15] The 1775 Regatta, based on Venetian models, was a splendid novelty and it was the talk of social and literary circles. The yachtsmen were not to be outdone. The *Morning Post*, indicating that 'only those boats which were never let out on hire' could enter the race, announced that 'the gentlemen, about 18 or 20 in number, who sail for the prize have come to a resolution to be dressed in aquatic uniforms'.[16] There were commercial possibilities in such elegance and a later sponsor was Jonathan Tyers, the proprietor of Vauxhall Pleasure Gardens, who gave a cup to celebrate the jubilee of the Gardens in 1786.

The quest for novelty was greatly encouraged by the newspapers which, costing three pence or four pence because of the tax, enjoyed a limited but influential circulation. 'The true old English game of cricket', pronounced the *Whitehall Evening Post* in 1767, 'is now going out of doors, and in the room thereof is instituted the Scotch game called Goff which is played practically every day upon Blackheath'. Prophesying such swings of fortune was meat and drink to journalists (often in more ways than one). Cricket was in no more danger then from golf than it was in September 1793 when the *Sporting Magazine* announced 'Field tennis threatens ere long to bowl out cricket' on the grounds that one patron had taken up the new vogue and another had dropped the old one.[17]. As for golf, the Blackheath golfers and a similar group of Scottish exiles and their cronies on Kersal Moor, Manchester, were the only two in England.[18] Even in Scotland there were only six clubs, all on the eastern coastal strip, until Glasgow, a little further west, was established in 1787, and no fewer than four were in Edinburgh.

All the early clubs were suburban, playing on common land. Their membership, apart from a sprinkling of the aristocracy, was middleclass: of Glasgow's twenty-five members in 1789, nineteen were merchants, two surgeons and four army officers.[19] On the 'fields called the Links' at Leith near Edinburgh race course, Smollett noted in 1771 'a multitude of all ranks from the Senator of Justice to the lowest tradesmen mingled in their shirts'; but it was the 'gentlemen of independent fortunes' eighty years old who 'never went to bed without each having the best part of a gallon of claret in his belly' that caught his eye.[20] Heavy gambling was not a feature of the golf clubs – unlike their English counterparts in cricket – but conviviality certainly was. At the Musselburgh Club founded in 1774 betting limits were set at ten shillings and sixpence a match and 'Dining, wining and fining (fines were paid in wine) formed the greater part of the Club regulations.'[21]

More truly popular sports – taking Scotland as a whole – were football (still played in its traditional form at Hawick, Berwick, Jedburgh, Inveresk, Kirkmichael and Scone, for instance), racing (where the Leith meeting Smollett attended attracted a more genteel company than any he ever saw in England and was followed by a dinner at which 'lords, and lairds and other gentlemen, courtezans and cawdies mingled together') and, more respectably, bowls and curling. Bowls – a Stuart rather than a Hanoverian enthusiasm – had never been banned in Scotland, except on Sundays, and had never caused the problems of gambling and drinking associated with the English alleys. Now every country town had its green, patronised by all ranks.[22] And in winter curling drew hundreds to the shores of frozen lochs and rivers, sliding flat stones towards a tee. Amongst its most passionate adherents were clergymen, one of whom became a member of the influential Dudington Curling Club (1795) at Edinburgh, and wrote the earliest book on the subject.[23] On the other hand the Kilmarnock curler, Tam Samson, whose death was mourned by Burns in 1786, had 'two fauts or maybe three': and he walked with 'bottle-swagger'.[24]

Golf, needing more costly equipment as well as space, was more exclusive. In Ireland, where Scottish settlers had reputedly played the game on the Ards peninsula in 1606, it had a similar middle class appeal and a similar emphasis on the social side. The earliest record of the game, in *Faulkner's Dublin Journal* of 23 October 1762, announced: 'The Goff Club meet to dine at the house of Mr Charles Moran at Bray on Thursday, the 28th October, at half an hour after three o'clock, ELIAS DE BUTTS, Esq. in the Chair.' And the following year an auctioneer's advertisement listed amongst the amenities of an 'enchanting country seat' an adjoining common 'famous for that manly Exercise called GOFF'.[25]

Meanwhile, though the vogue for cricket may have temporarily waned in London – which was as far as most journalists' horizon extended – it was about to become stronger than ever. The roots of the revival lay in public school rivalry. This stimulated some casual interest at the universities – Parson Woodforde played for 'the Winchester against the Eaton' at Oxford in 1760 – but, more immediately important, it underlay a lot of the 'county' challenges that restored the game to prominence. Surrey's foremost patron, the Earl of Tankerville, was an old Etonian and his flamboyant rival and crony, the patron of Kent, John Sackville, third Duke of Dorset, was an old Westminster. Another Kentish sponsor, Sir Horatio Mann, MP for Sandwich, was an old Carthusian, not quite in the inner circle, but with his own ground, and money to burn.

And just as Charles I's rustication of the gentry had first brought cricket to aristocratic notice so now a rusticated parson, Revd Charles Powlett, one of the fruits of the – eventually legitimated – liaison between the Duke of Bolton and the actress Lavinia Fulton helped to bring it back to fashion. Powlett, a Westminster with a taste for high life, was consigned in 1763, when still in his mid-thirties, to a curacy at Itchen Abbas in the depths of Hampshire. He enlisted the aid of fellow-Westminsters Philip Delaney, son of a wealthy Bristol merchant, and Charles Lennox, grandson of the pioneering second Duke of Richmond, to found a cricket club near the village of Hambledon. The club met at the Bat and Ball Inn, alongside the bleak Broad Half-penny Down, where the landlord Richard Nyren, nephew of Richard Newland of Slindon, acted as club secretary and team captain. Hambledon was for a time the foremost cricket club in England.

Lennox, Lord Tankerville and, slightly later, the Etonian George Finch, Earl of Winchilsea, were the best of Hambledon's gentlemen players, but the strength of the team lay in men of lower rank. They were not, of course, club members – a status requiring, for one thing, an outlay of three guineas a year subscription as well as bills for wining and dining. Indeed they were paid to play – four shillings if winners and three shillings if losers for a one-day home game – remuneration which, given the size of stakes for great matches (normally 500 guineas and sometimes 1,000) must have tempted them to look for profits on the side. Yet, according to John Nyren, Richard's son and the author of a celebrated tribute to the club, the Hambledonians were honest and, for all their down-to-earth rusticity, men of some independence of outlook, respectful but not subservient to their noble patrons.[26]

Nyren's book, written 'in association with' Charles Cowden Clarke, a man of letters, presents a romanticised picture of the great days of the club, not least in its social relationships. The professional players – gamekeepers, tradesmen, craftsmen, small farmers and their sons – are sometimes gauche, sometimes prickly, always honest and true. When the Duke of Dorset, hearing of the plebeian John Small's musical talents, sent him a present of two violins, carriage-paid, Small, who made cricket equipment, sent the Duke two bats and balls, also paying the carriage. Nyren senior, a 'thoroughbred old English yeoman' who 'placed a full and just value upon the station he held in society' and 'maintained it without insolence or assumption', was the middle man between the gentry and the rank-and-file. His judgement on matters of dispute on the field of play was never questioned, and if the Duke or Sir Horatio Mann were shown to have been wrong they would afterwards shake Nyren by the hand and thank him. Or so John Nyren would have us believe.

Writing in avowedly more cynical times Nyren claimed that the 'modern politics of trickery and "crossing" were as yet a sealed book' to the Hambledonians, and that it was a great disgrace when one of them 'sold the birthright of his good name for a mess of pottage'. Yet Nyren's defence of his father and the other professional stalwarts suggests that these paragons could never be sure of their own patrons' support when money was at stake. He recounts how once, when Hambledon, their bowling having been badly mauled by Minshull and Miller (gardener and gamekeeper to the Duke of Dorset) looked like losing, Powlett and Delaney 'began to quake and hedged off all their money'; and then, when Richard Nyren and John Small turned the tide, 'the backers came up to Nyren and said 'You will win the match and we will lose our money.'[27] The point of the story is how his 'proud old yeoman' father rebuffed the corrupt money-men, which is a pleasant variation on the honour code theme but perhaps an unreliable indicator of the true state of affairs.

The actual 'selling' or 'throwing' of matches by professionals only surfaced at a slightly later date but there were already players ready to take advantage of ambiguities in the rules, such as Thomas 'Shock' White of Chertsey who in 1771 sought to use a bat as wide as the wickets. It was apparently the prerogative of Hambledon, as leading club (after a bad patch around the turn of the decade) to modify the laws to forestall this. Other controversial issues, such as the vexed question of bowlers' actions, seem to have been settled by challenge and response. Bowlers had to bowl underarm but they did not all simply trundle the ball along the ground. For instance, Edward 'Lumpy' Stevens, one of Lord Tankerville's retainers, was renowned for his sharp eye for choosing a stretch of turf on which he could pitch it 'o'er a brow' to make it rear up. In response John Small began to make himself straighter bats than the normal type (hitherto something like a modern ice-hockey goalkeeper's implement), and in due course Hambledon brought in a tricky bowler of their own, David Harris, a potter, who could flick the ball from underneath his armpit to make it bounce and spin.

As crowds increased – a reputed 20,000 watched Hambledon play Sir Horatio Mann's Kent at his Canterbury ground in 1772 – it became obvious that some more organised and authoritative means of settling disputes was needed. Revised laws were agreed by a 'Committee of Noblemen and Gentlemen' at the Star and Garter on 25 February 1774. The reformers were not wholly successful, mainly because of the unscrupulous behaviour of some of their own number. The *Chelmsford Chronicle* that same year criticised the 'excessive gaming and public dissipation' of matches at the Artillery Ground by 'a set of idle fellows, or more properly a gang of dextrous gamblers, hired and maintained by a most noble Lord, at so little expense as £1000 a year'. This was the Duke of Dorset. Similarly his crony, Tankerville, who had once been summoned for assaulting a coachman, was attacked by the *St James's Chronicle* as 'renowned for cricket playing, bruising and keeping low company.'[28] Powlett and Delaney were undoubtedly as crooked as Nyren made out and the up-and-coming Earl of Winchilsea maintained the tradition. In this context no laws were likely to succeed and in fact things grew worse, often provoking violence as crowds and stakes increased. There was a riot at the Artillery Ground the following year when things began to go wrong for the Duke of Dorset's team against All-England, and soon the rural idyll of Hambledon was to end as fortuitously as it had begun.

God bless the Prince of Wales

American independence was the product of, and a spur to, religious and political dissent in Britain: it helped foster the emergent notion of 'class' and arouse a fierce backlash from the Establishment. Wales where 80% of the population were still Anglican, but uncomfortably so, ripe for religious reform and reluctant to share the faith of an élite minority, experienced a romantic revival of traditional Welsh culture, including the long defunct eisteddfod, that was particularly popular amongst Welsh exiles of whom London had a great many. In Ireland, where native culture had survived better, especially in the primitive west, the division between Anglicans, northern Presbyterians and the mass of the Catholic population grew wider. The social and material advances in Ulster, where Belfast began to flourish as a port and market town, in the dairy, cattle and sheep-rearing regions of the midlands and south and in Dublin (which, with a population of 150,000, twice the size of Edinburgh, was emerging from squalor to become a fine, gracious city) were mostly to the benefit of the Anglo-Irish ascendancy, who had secured a good deal of autonomy from Westminster and used it to feather their own nests. The emerging middle class of stronger farmers and landowners' agents, merchants and shopkeepers had enough political influence to achieve some easement of the economic grievances under which Ireland laboured, but they were socially disadvantaged, whilst the resentment of the long-suffering Catholic working people was reflected in sporadic outbursts of rural violence.

In Scotland by contrast, despite periodic Presbyterian alarm about the increase in popery, Catholicism was a tattered, scattered remnant. And after the failure of two successive Jacobite rebellions, with the Highland clans shorn of their traditional dress and deprived of their hereditary legislation, the lowland Presbyterians were on the box seat and the episcopalians bore the stigma of association with the deplorably licentious English. In the aftermath of Culloden, as Clydeside grew with the advance of external trade and agricultural reforms began to take effect, the main problem that remained was the insufferable assumption of superiority on the part of the English. Dr Johnson's reaction to Scottish objections to his criticism during his tour was to express 'wonder at the extreme jealousy of the Scotch, and their resentment at having their country described by him as it really was; when to say that it was a country as good as England, would have been a gross falsehood'.[29]

The British government, meanwhile, was led, for want of credible alternatives acceptable to the king, from 1770 to 1782 by the resilient but ineffective Lord North. Britain was embattled abroad – the American affair, growing anxiety about India and war with France, Spain and Holland over colonial possessions and trade. There was mounting pressure, lessened only partly by allowing colonial-style trading rights, for Home Rule in Ireland. In England despite (and in part because of) horrific repressive legislation public order was breaking down, assisted by the lack of proper police forces. Housebreakers, highwaymen and footpads operated at will. The climax came in 1780 when Lord George Gordon's anti-Catholic demonstration got so out of hand that in four days of rioting some 400 were injured or killed, many of them burnt to death or maimed as they lay drunk on looted gin.

North was finally forced out by defeat in Europe. He was followed by some improbable coalitions in which the peace settlement caused equal resentment. One of those who intermittently held the reins either from government or opposition was Charles James Fox, womaniser, gambler, racegoer and powerful orator, whom George III loathed. The King detested Fox not only for his slippery Whig policies but for his evil influence on his twenty year old son and heir whose latest escapade was to contract a form of marriage with Maria Fitzherbert, a Catholic widow. Both George III's brothers had contracted irregular marriages, and Henry Cumberland had added insult to injury by introducing Prince George to the attractions of the new resort Brighthelmstone, or Brighton, which included Faro, Loo, Macao and Hazard as well as loose women and drink. In fact Prince George needed little tuition and he revelled in his uncle's company, as well as that of Fox and his circle, not only for the delights of dissipation in themselves, but out of spite towards his father.

As Fox over-reached himself the King entered into uneasy but productive alliance with twenty-four year old William Pitt, Chatham's second son, a devotee of Adam Smith who saw increased trade with Europe as a way of offsetting the loss of the American colonies, sorted out the irregular affairs of the East India Company, reorganised the country's finances, brought many new peers into the House of Lords to challenge Whig supremacy and even tried – without success – to reform the system of election to the House of Commons. Pitt needed no coalitions and the Whigs' prospects of future power seemed to depend on the favours of the heir to the throne.

The Prince meanwhile had a high old time, surrounded by sybaritic cronies and opportunist adventurers. The current sporting vogue was coaching, aping the skills, dress and mannerisms of stagecoach drivers. Coach travel had become vastly more pleasurable as the new roads built by licensed turnpike companies came into commission and encouraged in turn faster and more comfortable vehicles. Their drivers, who needed courage as well as skill, were well paid – comparable with the best huntsmen who could earn up to £400 a year – and many of them used their affluence to live up to their image as 'swell dragsmen', dressing to the nines in a parody of their working clothes and parading the streets with a 'bit of muslin' on their arms. The most brilliant amateur Whip of the day was Sir John Lade, heir to a brewing fortune. Dr Johnson, who knew the family, had written some rousing if sycophantic verses to celebrate the lad's coming of age, but by 1783 Lade had frittered away his inheritance and was obliged to seek gainful employment. The Prince himself was already running into debt but he took Lade on to supervise his coaching establishment – as his coachman, the wits put it.

In 1784 the Post Office introduced the mail coach, with five horses and an armed guard, which travelled from Bath to London at seven miles an hour on its trial run. As the roads improved the target became ten. The charges, four pence or five pence a mile inside, two pence or three pence outside, were almost double those of the stage coaches but they were considered worth it. Mailcoach drivers and the liveried coachmen of the nobility were the admired models of the young bucks who liked to sit alongside them or better still take over the driving themselves. This offended the sense of propriety of those who shared the King's concern for the preservation of true values. The new royalist newspaper *The Times* rebuked a 'certain young gentleman near Brighton' for 'descending to the office of a coachman' and making his own lamplighter a partner at cricket.[30]

Sex and sport were the two great levellers. Lade married Letitia Smith, the former mistress both of Prince Frederick, Duke of York, and John Rann, the highwayman known as 'Sixteen String Jack'. The Prince's sexual exploits obviously interested the public prints. He was also much criticised for his misdemeanours at Newmarket, though when he first set up as an owner, his Uncle Cumberland having unloaded his own lavish stable on him, he was as much a victim as a villain. By 1786 he was obliged to sell up and find some cheaper form of amusement.

Pugilism briefly seemed to fill the bill. It was tip-toeing back into fashion after a long spell in the shadows. The end of Jack Slack's reign in 1760 had brought no relief from corruption: he was beaten by a protégé of the Duke of York, Bill Stevens (called 'the Nailer' after his mother who was a blacksmith), who threw a championship fight against the collier, George Meggs, tutored by Slack. During the seventies Dennis O'Kelly was a leading patron, principally with a view to arranging 'crosses' as in 1771 when Bill Darts, 'the Dyer', threw his championship bout with Peter Corcoran of Galway for £100.

However, the appearance as champion of Tom Johnson in 1783 helped revive interest. Johnson had decent instincts, a pleasant manner and some rudimentary pugilistic science. He also secured aristocratic backing including the hard-drinking Earl of Surrey and for a time the Duke of Hamilton. And another of Dr Johnson's somewhat improbable young friends, the Old Etonian Whig William Windham MP, eloquent in the cause of ancient manly virtues, missed a Parliamentary debate to see Tom Johnson win a return fight in 1787 against Michael Ryan. The champion was not entirely spotless, having needed the tactical intervention of his second, Richard Humphries, to win the first bout. Humphries himself, known as 'Gentleman' for his civil demeanour

– his father served in the household of one of the members of the Clapham Sect, moral and social reformers – had impressed the Prince of Wales in 1786 in a fight against Sam Martin, a butcher from Bath. The following year one of Humphries' stable-mates, a small but skilful Jew called Daniel Mendoza, was performing against Martin before the Prince when the contest was nipped in the bud by the 10th Dragoons, summoned at the behest of the local magistrates.

Nevertheless the Prince continued his support in 1788. It was a good year. Tom Johnson withstood the challenge of Bill Warr of Bristol. Humphries lost a return match against Mendoza, but another 'Gentleman', John Jackson, the nineteen year old son of a London builder, beat the giant William Futrell (who retained enough wit and capital from his ring career to publish the first boxing paper) in a contest witnessed by the Prince and graphically illustrated by the young James Gillray. Unfortunately the Prince happened to witness a death in the ring at a bout near Brighton, and although Windham was able to offset some of the bad publicity a repetition would not have been politically expedient. In November 1788 George III had aroused hopes of a Regency by stepping from his coach in Windsor Great Park and addressing an oak tree as the King of Prussia. Pitt temporised long enough for the King to recover his wits, but there were no more public prize-fights for the Prince for some years.

One of the fashions of the time was for the hooligan aristocracy to hire pugilists as bodyguards on their rampages. This was the pleasant custom both of the heir to the throne and one of his most unsavoury friends Richard Barry, Lord Barrymore, a young Irish peer, with a vast fortune and a great talent for spending it. Barrymore died after a shooting accident in 1793, when he was only twenty-four, but by then he had managed to get rid of most of his inheritance in a style sufficient to earn him the nickname 'Hellgate'. (His club-footed brother Henry was called 'Cripplegate', and his other brother, Augustus, a cleric and a compulsive gambler, 'Newgate'. Their sister, Lady Milfort, famous for her invective, was known as 'Billingsgate'.) Barrymore's 'cottage' near Maidenhead had its own private Opera House, built at a cost of £60,000. His coachmen, grooms and footmen were decked out in his racing colours in summer and in the hunting season in the style of Louis XIV's retinue at Fontainebleu, with four Negroes in scarlet and silver playing horns.[31]

Cricket, cock-fighting and boxing all attracted Barrymore's fitful attention, and he lost nearly as much in betting on the Ring as he did on the Turf. He married the daughter of Jack Rann's brother, who was a porter. On the fringes of this raffish circle was Colonel George Hanger, also Anglo-Irish, an older rogue whose patronage of sport was limited by his chronically modest means. Hanger had run away from Eton after an affair with a greengrocer's daughter to join the army, serving in America before retiring on half pay in 1780.

Thereafter he perfected the art of living beyond his means – £1,100 a year – largely through brazen effrontery but assisted by an occasional shrewd bet. Hanger fell from princely favour as his luck ran out and he went to the King's Bench prison for a spell.[32]

John Walter, editor of *The Times*, reportedly paid £300 a year by the King's Party, led the attack on the Prince for his dissolute behaviour, his links with Fox and his ambitions of Regency. A particular strong piece against all three royal princes, however, landed Walter in Newgate for a while. Fear of sedition mounted as the French Revolution broke out in 1789. The following year Edmund Burke published his *Reflections*, warning sternly of the dangers of the spread of Jacobinism and Tom Paine rushed off to his room at the Angel, Islington, to compose a reply.

The Prince chose this time to become embroiled in a scandal on the Turf. His finances temporarily restored during his father's bout of lunacy, he had returned to Newmarket as an owner, enjoying some success including winning the Derby. But keeping forty horses in training was too much both for his purse and his acumen and soon the wiseacres were pointing out that fewer and fewer of his fancied horses were winning. In 1791 his principal rider, Sam Chifney, skilful but dodgy, was the central figure in a sequence of events suggesting that he, at least, was more interested in winning bets than winning races. In a series of articles *The Times* hinted strongly at a conspiracy between owner and jockey in which the trainer, Warwick Lake, had been an innocent dupe and advised the Prince to avoid the 'blacklegs' in future.[33]

The wider question was whether horse-racing was a sport or just a racket. The Jockey Club's enquiry into the matter was restricted to the much narrower concerns of the honour code. They found the plebeian Chifney guilty as charged and Sir Charles Bunbury advised His Royal Highness that 'if he suffered Chifney to ride his horses no gentleman would ever start against him'.[34] As he was £400,000 in debt the Prince had no choice but to swallow the insult, sell his horses, and stay away from Newmarket.

This evasion of the issue by both parties was exposed in a searing attack the following year which lumped the Prince together with the rest of the Jockey Club circle. It was the work of Charles Pigott (nicknamed after his famous horse Shark), a former member of the club who had lost a fortune on the Turf. This had soured him to the extent of denouncing the system and commending the French Revolution, and first the publisher and then Pigott himself were imprisoned. Tom Paine was more fortunate. Charged with sedition for publishing *The Rights of Man*, he returned to France to take up his seat in the Convention from which vantage point he wrote a letter denying 'that the capacity of such a man as Mr Guelph, or any of his profligate sons, is necessary to the government of a nation'.[35]

18 B. Darwin et al. (eds.), *A History of Golf in Britain*, 1952, pp. 134–5.
19 R. Holt, *Sport and the British*, Oxford, 1989, p. 71.
20 *Humphrey Clinker*, reprinted Everyman's Library, London, 1943, p. 215.
21 *History of Royal Musselburgh Golf Club*, Edinburgh, 1974, quoted in W.H. Gibson, *Early Irish Golf*, Naas, 1988, p. 12.
22 P. Sullivan, *Bowls: The Records*, Enfield, 1986, pp. 16–17.
23 Revd J. Ramsay, *An account of the Game of Curling*, 1810, cited by Cuddon, *Dictionary of Sports and Games*, p. 264.
24 'Tam Samson's Elegy' in *Poems and Songs of Robert Burns*, ed. J. Barke, London, 1955, p. 176.
25 Gibson, *Early Irish Golf*, p. 9.
26 J. Nyren, *The Young Cricketer's Tutor and The Cricketers of My Time*, ed. C. Cowden-Clarke, 1833, revised edition, with introduction by J. Arlott, London, 1974, pp. 55–6.
27 Ibid., p. 67.
28 J. Ford, *Cricket: A Social History, 1700–1850*, Newton Abbot, 1972, p. 61.
29 James Boswell, *The Life of Samuel Johnson*, 1791, ed. R. Shewan, London, 1968 (2 vols.), vol. I, p. 502.
30 9 September 1788.
31 P. Somerville-Large, *Irish Eccentrics*, London, 1975, pp. 222–5.
32 Ibid., pp. 225–30.
33 R. Mortimer, *The Jockey Club*, London, 1958, p. 44. Blacklegs – book-makers, so called from the mud they acquired wading around paddocks.
34 Ibid., p. 44.
35 E.P. Thompson, *The Making of the English Working Class*, Harmondsworth, 1968, p. 119.
36 *Works*, 4 vols., 1790, vol. I, p. 93.
37 Known as the *Daily Universal Register* from 1785 to 1788.
38 22 June 1785.
39 2 May 1786.
40 31 October 1787.
41 J. Pycroft, *The Cricket Field*, 1851, ed. F.S. Ashley-Cooper, London, 1922, p. 134.
42 26 June 1787.
43 F.S. Ashley-Cooper and Lord Harris, *Lord's and MCC*, London, 1914, p. 21.
44 Ibid., p. 40.

Cricket versus revolution

The Gordon riots had, however, greatly reduced the support for radical solutions. London politicians were no longer confident that rebellious mobs were a safe weapon to use against an oppressive government. In any event a surprising number of people at all levels of society shared the belief of 'Mr Guelph' and the conservatives in the superiority of the British system. Was not the Habeas Corpus Act of 1679 a bulwark of freedom? They saw no comparison between the French people's necessarily violent rejection of tyranny and the wanton overthrow of their own flawed but accessible rulers. In this consensus sport played an important part.

It had its critics. As the moralist Soame Jenyns put it:

> England, when once of peace and wealth possest,
> Began to think frugality a jest,
> So grew polite: hence all her well-bred heirs
> Gamesters and jockies turn'd, and cricket play'rs.[36]

But whatever Pigott thought of the Duke of Dorset (not much), he was a great patron, much admired for his sporting prowess and, as we have seen in the Hambledon idyll, for his condescension in playing with his tenants and employees. In cricket, as in racing, gambling brought the classes together; but cricket had the added advantage of manliness the French could not hope to match.

The virtues of cricket began to attract greater notice as the younger generation of patrons found it more convenient to hold their 'great matches' in London. *The Times*[37] had been scornful at first at the antics of 'the Lordling Cricketers who amuse themselves in White Conduit Fields' and supportive of the reaction of 'spirited citizens' to being driven off the public footpath which crossed the field of play.[38] But within a fortnight it was recording the scores of the first of a series of games between Lord Winchilsea's XI and the gentlemen of Kent. The Duke of Dorset had been appointed ambassador in Paris in 1784 and George Finch, Earl of Winchilsea, succeeded him as the leading figure in cricket. Winchilsea was still prominent at Hambledon, becoming its president in 1787, but he tended to look on it as a nursery producing promising players for White Conduit.

In Paris, meanwhile, the Duke of Dorset found time for a cricket match in the Champs-Elysées, which no doubt excited French admiration. As *The Times* put it, however, 'The French . . . cannot imitate us in such vigorous exertions of the body, so that we seldom see them enter the lists.'[39] By 1787, no doubt blinded by wishful thinking, it recorded 'Horse-racing is already on the wane in France, as it is in England. Cricket, on the recommendation of the Duke of Dorset, is taking its place, and making a far better use of the turf.'[40] The French proved a disappointment in this as in graver matters.

For aspirant professional cricketers the rising popularity of White Conduit was a mixed blessing. It brought greater opportunities but also great dangers. Better roads and cheaper transport had made the trip to London easier but also greased the downward path to vice. Revd James Pycroft, looking back from Victorian times, described how Winchilsea had plucked an eighteen year old rustic lad from the harvest fields to play at White Conduit. Having gone up to London 'by the waggon' the lad had been caught up in the fast life of the Green Man and Still, Oxford Street, the favourite haunt of professional cricketers. 'You know what young folk are, Sir,' he told Pycroft, '. . . so many spent all their earnings and were soon glad to make money some other way.' Those reluctant to take bribes were reminded by the 'Sharps' that their noble backers – 'Lord this and the Duke of that' – were themselves selling matches.[41]

On the other hand there were more sophisticated provincials who cashed in on the metropolitan vogue. Thomas Lord, a young Yorkshire man, who had come to London by way of Norfolk to try to repair the family fortunes, sought work as an attendant at White Conduit as a stepping stone to higher things. He saw an opportunity for profit in the Lordling cricketers' needs for an enclosed ground. Encouraged by Winchilsea and Colonel Charles Lennox, soon to be fourth Duke of Richmond, Thomas Lord leased a plot of land at Marylebone. The first match at Lord's ground in May 1787 was a low-key affair between 'Essex' and 'Middlesex' for one hundred guineas, but a month later Winchilsea led White Conduit against All-England for a thousand guineas. According to *The Times* 'upwards of 2,000 persons attended, conducting themselves with the utmost decorum'. The ground was 'somewhat rough' but a 'very good cold collation was spread under a covered recess for the accommodation of the cricketers and subscribers. Amongst the many persons of first fashion who watched were the Duke of Bedford, Lord Derby, Lord Gallway, Mr Fitzroy and Mr Onslow.'[42]

Lord's private ground was so congenial to the gentlemen that during the winter they formed Marylebone Cricket Club. The foundation of MCC, whose members included not only Winchilsea and Lennox but the older generation like Dorset, Tankerville and Mann, marked the end of Hambledon's supremacy. MCC ventured north the following year, to Nottingham where Winchilsea's friend, Colonel Churchill, was commander of the local garrison. There had been cricket in Nottingham for some years: in 1771 they played two games against Sheffield, the second of which they lost when their opponents put coal-slack on the wicket after a downpour. But the town had experienced nothing like MCC whose visit was talked about for fifty years not just for their cricket but for their resplendent fashions, servants and carriages and their cocking matches, milling and other fashionable sports.[43]

But the London club soon built up a reputation for sharp practice as well as skill. A contemporary rhymester, Baxter, summed them up: 'Though their playing is fine, yet their tricks are so glaring / That before you've been long they will set you a-swearing'. The chief contributor to this reputation was a young clergyman and nobleman, Lord Frederick Beauclerk. A product of Eton and Cambridge, Beauclerk was the fourth son of the fifth Duke of St Albans and later became Rector of St Albans. A tougher, more austere version of Powlett, he was a gifted cricketer and an all-round sportsman, a noted runner and a first-class shot. His performance was always sharpened by the amount of money at stake. As the rhymester put it, reviewing MCC players: 'My Lord he comes next, and will make you all swear / With his little tricks he's a long way from fair.'[44] In later years Beauclerk would openly boast that he expected to make £600 a year from cricket. He was a renowned captain, both for his mastery of tactics and his dominating style and bad temper. Beauclerk was an unlikely deterrent to revolution, but perhaps the French alternative was worse.

Notes

1 For the background, political and economic, see J.S. Watson, *The Reign of George III*, Oxford, 1960.
2 *The Theory of Moral Sentiments*, 1759.
3 *The Diary of a Country Parson 1758–1802*, ed. John Beresford, Oxford, 1927–31. 21 September 1777.
4 White, *Natural History of Selbourne*, 1789, Letter VI, 21 September 1777, to Thomas Pennant.
5 E.H. Bovill, *English Country Life 1780–1830*, Oxford, 1962, p. 200, suggests that but for enclosure fox-hunting would never have become a popular sport. For the gradual change to fox-hunting and the new vogue for shooting see his Chapter XIII.
6 A.H. Higginson, *Peter Beckford*, London, 1937, p. 153.
7 *Retrospective Review*, 1825, quoted in full in Higginson, *Peter Beckford*, pp. 178–85.
8 *Rural Sports*, 1713.
9 Woodforde, *Diary*, 16 May 1781.
10 Ibid., 5 September 1759.
11 D. Jarrett, *England in the Age of Hogarth*, London, 1974.
12 For the genre see William Gaunt, *The Great Century of British Painting*, London, 1971.
13 For early forms of racing and gambling see W. Vamplew, *The Turf*, London, 1976.
14 For Epsom before the Derby and the 'roystering party' that created it, see Lord Rosebery, 'Epsom' in *Selected Modern English Essays*, ed. 'H.S.M.', Oxford, 1925. For the Derby itself see R. Mortimer, *The History of the Derby Stakes*, London, 1973.
15 *Memoirs of William Hickey*, ed. A. Spencer, London, 4 vols., 1913–25, vol. 1, p. 98. Dr Johnson, expressing disappointment that he could not be there to savour the new experience, playfully warned his friend, Mrs Thrale, not to become too excited at the prospect of 'floating down the Thames in a Fancied Dress', 21 June 1775.
16 J.A. Cuddon, *MacMillan Dictionary of Sport and Games*, London, 1980, p. 848.
17 J. Strutt, *Glig-gamena angel deod: or The Sports and Pastimes of the People of England*, London, 1801; new edition 1903, reprinted Bath, 1969, p. 89.

CHAPTER SEVEN

Watershed
1793–1815

The attraction of Adam Smith's philosophy was that it offered a cloak of rationality for whatever people with money chose to do. Its social value was that it allowed people who could acquire money to buy their way past barriers without having to break them down. Yet in the more open society that was starting to appear a few at least were willing to question the assumptions behind the existing order. One of the most radical ideas was Jeremy Bentham's notion that the law should be used to achieve the greatest good of the greatest number. Bentham's *Introduction to the Principles of Morals and Legislation*, published in the same year as revolution broke out in France, earned him international recognition and some influential support at home. Bentham's utilitarian philosophy also chimed with the pragmatism of the rising industrialists and entrepreneurial middle classes.

The climate for new ideas was greatly improved by the insistent spread of literacy. Printing, publishing and bookselling were flourishing. Education was narrowly conceived and randomly available, and for the poor it usually depended on the charitable ministrations of one or other of the churches, but nevertheless it had a profound effect. It was significant that two of the greatest poets of the era, Blake and Burns, came from poor homes. They were precursors of the Romantic poets – Wordsworth, Coleridge, Shelley, Byron, men who challenged convention from within the circle of privilege. But most intellectuals stayed well within the circle. Duty to the underprivileged was best served by offering them the consolations of religion which, as it happened, were the best safeguard against the temptation to rebellion, the scourge of the age.

Thus Bishop Barrington's Society for Bettering the Conditions of the poor; thus William Wilberforce and Dr Bowdler's Society for the Suppression of Vice and Encouragement of Religion; and thus Hannah More, the Blue Stocking, who gave her time freely to teach poor children to read but declined to teach them to write, an activity she felt should be reserved for those whom God had called to a higher station in life. And thus Blake's explosion of anger at the 'Oppressors of Albion' who 'compel the poor to live upon a crust of bread by soft mild arts'.[1]

One war for the rich . . .

By the same token, when the French revolutionary forces declared war on Britain, the nation sprang to arms in defence of the existing order. The Prince of Wales was particularly keen to combat the evil Jacobins, seeking a military role worthy of his rank. Against his better judgement the King eventually agreed to his appointment as Colonel of the 10th Light Dragoons, encamped near Brighton. The Prince spent a month with them, in a magnificent tent with a huge bed bearing fringed and tasselled hangings of 'a very delicate chintz', emerging from time to time for social and sporting purposes, often accompanied by Mrs Fitzherbert. Then the novelty palled and he went back to Carlton House, counting his debts and incurring new ones, before making the supreme sacrifice – agreeing to marry Princess Caroline of Brunswick in return for financial rescue.[2]

As Conservative fears of the spread of contagion from Paris were built up into a patriotic crusade, British radicals were isolated. The Birmingham riots of 1791 had shown how the mob could turn on rich Dissenters and much of the opposition to Pitt, who had reluctantly entered the war, was equally mindless, which, of course, played into the hands of the reactionaries. As the government sought to root out the Jacobins in their midst, Habeas Corpus was suspended and a host of radical groups were outlawed. There was a bad harvest in 1793 and the price of bread shot up. Food riots erupted spasmodically. Pitt's house was surrounded by the mob, and when the King drove to open Parliament sections of the crowd yelled 'No Pitt, no war – bread, bread, peace, peace' and 'Down with George'.

In fact the war helped agricultural production, giving fresh impetus to the enclosure movement and increasing the demand for labour. Wages went up everywhere, and especially in the north of England where farmers faced industrial competition. In the south the increases failed to keep up with prices and farm labourers had to turn to parish relief. Pressure for higher wages, as food prices soared, spurred textile manufacturers to greater efficiency, especially in the newer cotton industry, which sought new markets, and soon power-looms were operating full-blast in Lancashire and on Clydeside. In the bigger, older woollen industry Yorkshire began to supplant southern centres and start its own urban conglomerations. Ship-building, for war and trade, was hampered by shortage of timber, but nevertheless increased by a third and the ports were never busier. Above all, the demand for munitions and the consequent growth of the iron, steel and coal industries restated the 'north–south' divide. Wales and its southern coalfields became especially important to the war economy and the Glasgow region grew apace. Ireland, however, with next to no coal and a legacy of trade restrictions, was in no position to benefit.

She was also the part of the realm most vulnerable to invasion and most susceptible to seduction by the French. Pitt persuaded the Irish Parliament to give the Catholics voting rights in 1793 to win their support against the godless enemy, but the nationalist cause was taken up by Wolfe Tone's non-sectarian United Irishmen. They were implacably opposed by Dublin Castle, possibly the most reactionary institution in the British Isles, and by what Tone called the 'common prostitutes of the Treasury Bench', a group including Captain the Hon. Arthur Wesley, or Wellesley, the future Duke of Wellington, who at the outbreak of war was aide-de-camp to the Viceroy and member for the family seat of Trim. They were also opposed by the ultra-Protestant Orange Lodges in Ulster and outdone by Catholic peasants often encouraged to violence by French-trained priests. Rebellion flared up in 1798 in support of a French landing in Mayo, provoking stern government reaction and leading to Act of Union with Britain, another attempt at Catholic appeasement in which the Irish Parliament was persuaded to dissolve itself for the sake of greater trading privileges.

The ascendancy suffered some inconvenience from the troubles – in 1798 the *Irish Racing Calendar* was obliged to record that 'On account of the Disturbed State of the Country there was no June meeting at the Curragh' – but elsewhere in Britain the conflict with the French had little impact on persons of consequence. As Trevelyan put it 'The war was in the newspapers, but it scarcely entered the lives of the enjoying classes . . . For in those happy days the navy was a perfect shield to the safety and to the amenities of island life.'[3] This was certainly Pitt's plan. He hoped for a quick end to the war through direct action on the high seas and in the colonies, whilst funding allies to fight the French on land. Dutch withdrawal, financial depression at home and Austria's collapse obliged him to make peace overtures. These were contemptuously rejected, the French Directory began to make arrangements for a London branch, and invasion seemed imminent. Yet despite mutinies against appalling material conditions, naval victories at St Vincent and Camperdown bought time, and in 1798, when Napoleon was looking to the conquest of Egypt as the key to the east, Admiral Nelson won a stunning victory at the Nile.[4]

For career officers like Nelson and Wellington the war was most welcome. For others it was an escape from domestic problems. The young Harry Mellish, godson of the Prince of Wales, absconded from Eton in 1797 to join the 18th Light Dragoons, later transferring to a more fashionable regiment. When he came into his inheritance in 1801 Mellish was given permanent leave to look after his estates. He set up a lavish hunting establishment and became one of the new Leicestershire thrusting school of riders. With a stable of some forty horses, Mellish was also a prominent member of the Jockey Club and he achieved some success as an owner. But his irresistible urge to gamble overcame his judgement: he was said to have once ventured £40,000 on a single throw of the dice – and lost – a recklessness which meant that he was eventually obliged to rejoin the colours.

Meanwhile Napoleon returned from Egypt, Pitt's second coalition government started to crumble, the national debt soared, the price of wheat reached nearly three times the pre-war level and the Prince of Wales began to spend his new-found wealth. The Royal Crescent at Brighton, constructed between 1798 and 1807, was completed by a statue of the Prince in military uniform. In 1800 he began racing again, though not at Newmarket. Under his patronage Brighton and Lewes races became the most splendid social event of the year. Newmarket thrived without him, as did Ascot, which had a new attraction, an early form of roulette known as 'EO'. Epsom was handy for Londoners and the whole town became a seething mass on race days. Fear of disorder meant that both the Oaks and the Derby were run at Newmarket in 1801. Otherwise Napoleon had little effect: the Derby never had less than thirty entries during the war years. Many of the other great races were actually started at this time: the Jockey Club Stakes and Doncaster Cup in 1801, Ascot Gold Cup 1807, Two Thousand Guineas 1809, Goodwood Cup 1812 and the One Thousand Guineas 1814.

Pugilism also flourished. At the outbreak of war Big Ben Brain of Bristol held the title, having finished off Tom Johnson's career in 1791. Brain was celebrated as the conqueror of Tom Tring (a porter at Carlton House, dismissed by the Prince of Wales after his defeat) and of 'Bully' Hooper, 'the Tinman', bodyguard to Lord Barrymore. Brain died of a liver complaint in 1794. His successor, the charismatic, flamboyant, entrepreneurial, mercurial Daniel Mendoza was destined throughout his career to veer erratically between the roles of victim and exploiter. He was in and out of the debtors' prison, always getting and losing jobs (including touring Britain and Ireland with Philip Astley's amphitheatre, and serving as a recruiting sergeant for the Fifeshire Regiment). In the ring he used methods that were 'scientific', i.e. he preferred to use footwork and retreat in order to avoid punishment, but were regarded by traditionalists as un-British.

Essentially the sporting world required Mendoza to play the part of crafty Jew, and he accepted it readily and used it to advantage. Lord Althorp, former Chancellor of the Exchequer and a firm supporter of the old prize-ring, looking back in old age recalled how, in the third of his celebrated encounters with Humphries, Mendoza was 'knocked down for the first five or six rounds and seeming almost beat, till the Jews got their money on, when a hint being given him, he began in earnest and soon turned the tables'.[5] That this was probably hearsay – his Lordship was only eight at the time – merely sharpens the point. Mendoza was altogether too crafty, and flamboyant – and, well, foreign. He might have held the title for years, however, but for the return to the ring of an utterly English Gentile, John Jackson, in 1795. Jackson had not fought for six years after falling on wet boards, damaging his leg and losing to the obscure George Inglestone, 'the Brewer'. His sporting reputation had however been greatly enhanced by his offer to continue the fight in a chair, and his prowess as an all-round athlete and his pleasing manner won him many friends.

There was therefore much rejoicing when Jackson, making his third and last appearance in the ring, relieved Mendoza of the title. The contest lasted only eleven minutes. It was by some accounts an electrifying display of ring craft and if Jackson's repertoire included grabbing Mendoza by his long hair to pull him on to the punch, surely that served the Jew right. *The Times* was not impressed.

> Yesterday a Prize Battle was fought at Hornchurch in Essex between Mendoza the Jew and one Jackson, a publican of Gray's Inn Lane, when, as had no doubt been previously settled, the Jew appeared overpowered by the Christian . . . We think it worthy of the notice of the magistracy to consider whether a man who breaks the peace should be a fit person to have a licence as a publican.[6]

But 'Gentlemen' John had his sights on higher things. Whether the fight had been fixed or not, his future was assured. Mendoza had to go on fighting for a quarter of a century – in 1820, aged fifty-six, he fought 12 rounds with another veteran, Tom Owens – whilst Jackson retired at once and set up a boxing school in Bond Street.

'Jackson's Rooms' far surpassed anything previously seen, quickly attracting the patronage of the nobility and gentry. Windham was a great admirer of Jackson, as was Lord Byron, one of his pupils. Jackson also arranged glove fights at the Fives Courts in St Martin's Lane. (Fives was one of several names given to simplified versions of tennis that were played in inn-yards, and – increasingly – in the debtors' prisons. Fives itself was played like old-style *jeu de paume*, whilst 'bat-fives' was played with racquets. Their popularity had, in the new commercial age, led to purpose-built rackets courts.) For pugilistic enthusiasts, the Fives Court was, as boxing's first chronicler recorded, 'an animated inspiring lounge for the nobility and the heavy swells and . . . an attraction in general to the public'.[7]

Gloved contests were an attractive notion – an audience of up to 1,000 paying between two shillings and three shillings and sixpence (a guinea for the élite), at a convenient and pleasant location safe from prosecution: and legal tickets could be sold in advance for these 'benefits'. Yet somehow they did not satisfy true enthusiasts, and whilst magistrates throughout the land deplored and denounced bare-knuckle fights they went on under the protection of the great. The Duke of Clarence, the future William IV, was perhaps the most influential patron. Polite public opinion, following a spate of fatal accidents and growing anxieties about mob violence after the outbreak of war, turned strongly against pugilism, but the Duke more than once offered his protection to it.

The British way of life

In this war to preserve the British heritage the pressures mounted for even more severe Game Laws. An 1800 Act declared two or more poachers operating together to be rogues and vagabonds liable for hard labour and on a second offence incorrigible rogues eligible for whipping and imprisonment or service in the armed forces. That same year a Bill to abolish bull-baiting was narrowly lost. It was opposed by William Windham, now Minister of War, arguing that as there were Game Laws to protect the rich, the poor should have their own pleasures. He had himself attended baits at Eton and had come to no harm: nor had the fashionable gentleman who took up shooting.[8]

The various ingenious advances made by the gunsmith Joseph Manton, notably the breech-loader, had made the prospect of swift and safe destruction of game birds a reality for many more of the well-to-do. So far from inducing sympathy for the sports of the lower orders, however, this seemed to have the opposite effect. Joseph Strutt in 1801 asserted confidently, 'Bull and bear baiting is not encouraged by persons of rank and opulence in the present day, and when practised, which rarely happens, it is attended only by the lowest and most despicable part of the people.' Strutt also ventured to criticise cock-fighting: even 'the sanction of high antiquity' could not excuse such 'a barbarous pastime'.[9] Though such middle class morality was gaining ground, however, Parliament was not yet ready for reform. When the abolitionists tried again in 1802, they lost by 64 votes to 51. Windham, implying that bulls enjoyed being baited, went on to argue that the Jacobins and the Methodists (by teaching the lower orders to read) were encouraging much less socially acceptable habits than baiting.

Strutt had a paternalistic regard for more harmless popular recreations. There is a note of regret in his comment that football 'was formerly much in vogue amongst the common people of England though of late it seems to have fallen into disrepute and is little practised.'[10] And, though the English ruralist Arthur Young had described Irish hurling as 'the cricket of savages' in 1780,[11] Strutt referred approvingly to the games he recalled seeing twenty-five years earlier played by parties of Irishmen in the fields behind the British Museum. They used 'a kind of bat to take up the ball and strike it from them . . . I have been greatly amused to see with what facility those who were skilful in the pastime would catch up the ball on the bat and often ran with it for a considerable time.'[12] Young's remark was neatly matched when, in 1792, the

Dublin *Freeman's Journal* describing a cricket match at Phoenix Park between the Viceroy's XI and the Garrison, in which the viceroy's aide-de-camp, Arthur Wesley, took part, explained to its readers that 'the standing of the Game of Cricket is in England what that of Hurling is in Ireland'. And though Strutt was vague about cricket's origins – 'From the club-ball originated, I doubt not, that pleasant and manly exercise' – he did not doubt its social status: of late years it had been 'exceedingly fashionable, being much countenanced by the nobility and gentlemen of fortune'.[13]

Golf (spelled goff) got brief but kindly notice. It was played, he noted, with a 'bat not much unlike the bandy' and was much practised in northern parts. But it needed a great deal of room to perform it 'with propriety' and, for that reason he presumed, it was 'rarely seen at present in the vicinity of the metropolis.'[14] In fact it was rarely seen anywhere except the eastern coastal strip of Scotland and developments there were of domestic interest. In 1800 the Gentlemen Golfers of Leith successfully petitioned the Town Council for the Charter that gave them the style 'The Honourable the Edinburgh Company of Golfers' and a group of Bruntsfield players became 'The Edinburgh Burgess Golfing Society'. Times were hard: the worthies of Musselburgh resolved that 'as the price of provisions is very high Mr Moir should be allowed 1s 6d for each dinner'.[15]

No doubt the members complained bitterly but hardship is relative. The highly influential economist, Revd Thomas Malthus, whose *Essay on the Principle of Population* first appeared in 1798, saw worse times ahead for the poor unless their numbers were reduced by cataclysm or constraint. A Cambridge mathematician, he took the view that the quest for perfection of the human condition was doomed to failure since population increased geometrically and food production, at best, arithmetically. The first official census in 1801 sounded more alarm bells, for the population of the United Kingdom now exceeded 15 million including an alarming 5.22 million in Ireland: England had 8.3 million, Scotland 1.63 million and Wales 0.59 million. About 3 million in mainland Britain now lived in towns with Greater London accounting for over one million. Manchester (with Salford) was now bigger than Edinburgh (83,000) which was closely followed by Glasgow (77,000) about the size of Liverpool and slightly bigger than Birmingham, Bristol and Leeds. In Ireland, Dublin (165,000) dwarfed Cork, Limerick and Belfast.

Religion was everywhere the great divisive issue. Since 1793 Dissenters and Catholics had been able to vote but not to sit in Parliament. The emancipation of Catholics, most of whom were in Ireland, was so obnoxious to the King that Pitt felt obliged to resign. Dissent and political opposition were closely related and it took hold particularly in the new industrial towns which were greatly under-represented. Methodism began as a movement within the established church but with the evangelical upsurge that swept the country became a separate sect. Wales in particular found expression in Calvinistic Methodism and other non-conformist enthusiasms. The Baptists and Congregationalists were strong in most industrial towns, where the intelligentsia were often Quaker or Unitarian.

Pitt's successor, Addington, responding to widespread war-weariness, concluded a truce. He attended to peace-time requirements well enough. The Ellenborough Act of 1803, which introduced hanging for poachers who offered armed resistance to gamekeepers, was widely welcomed. But the war began again and the nation responded patriotically to the threat of invasion – when the French massed a fleet of flat-bottomed boats at Boulogne 3,000 men came forward as volunteers – and Addington was out of his depth. Pitt returned but his Cabinet was weak, divided and riven by scandal. Fortunately the French hesitated and chopped and changed their plans. Propaganda reminded workers that under Napoleon they would have to work in slave-gangs, eating horse-beans, drinking only water and watching their wives and daughters being raped, and the nation held its nerve.

When the threatened invasion did not come the assembled regiments looked for ways of letting off steam. Many spirited young cavalry officers, for instance, took up the cross-country horse-racing favoured by the Meltonians. In 1804 the *Sporting Magazine* reported that in Newcastle 'a wager betwixt Captains Prescott and Tucker of the 5th Light Dragoons was determined . . . by a single horse race which we learn is denominated steeple-hunting'. Flat-racing was a different world, though the prospect of a flutter was always welcome to the regiments. In 1805, the year of Allied defeat at Austerlitz, the Jockey Club offered the olive branch to the Prince of Wales. Still sulking, he occupied himself with affairs in Brighton, extending the stables and riding house of his Marine Pavilion at a cost of £55,000. The improvements took three years, partly because of a shortage of timber due to the French blockade and partly because the Prince's debts were mounting again.

Nelson's great victory at Trafalgar was a relief from depressing war news but it was achieved at the cost of his life, and the nation mourned a lost hero. Sport was a consolation, and there was great excitement when another hero, the gallant Jem Belcher came out of retirement to face his fellow-Bristolian and friend Hen Pearce, 'the Game Chicken'. Pearce was a veteran, but he had a sentimental streak, and his reluctance to damage Belcher's good eye delayed his victory. These images of gallantry – which continued when Pearce rescued a girl from a fire and later shortened his own life by driving in freezing conditions to see 'Old Jem' in his last fight – were as potent as those of war, and perhaps more real to many. Certainly Pitt's death in 1806, hastened by Napoleon's continued success, evoked little comparable sentiment, and

ed delighted the United Irishmen and other dissidents who rightly saw
his demise as a chance for them to get out of jail.

The new administration, euphemistically known as the Ministry of All the
Talents, aroused much satirical comment. Though unsuccessful in waging
war they were deeply interested in pugilism. Hen Pearce added to his popular
image as a generous winner by taking pity on a young rival, John Gully,
temporarily inconvenienced by being in the debtors' prison, and securing his
release through the good offices of Harry Mellish and the Duke of Clarence.
The political diarist, Thomas Creevey, recalled the occasion. The Duke had
been expected at a dinner, but 'as the battle, from the interference of Magistrates, was fought at a greater distance from Brighton than was intended, the
Duke was very late'.[16] Gully lost the fight after 64 rounds, but won golden
opinions ensuring aristocratic support after poor Pearce's demise the following year. Gully established his right to succeed by beating 'the Lancashire
giant', Bob Gregson, in a contest which greatly excited the aristocracy. Lord
Grey, the Foreign Secretary, and Windham, the War Minister, were amongst
Gully's admirers, reputedly using official channels to spread the word about
the return. It was an anti-climax. Gully won easily and then like Jackson
retired to lusher pastures.

The respectable middle classes thought Gully pushy. His appearance in the
lower circle at Drury Lane in 1807 drew indignant comment. They might
sneer, but as Creevey remarked: 'Since that time the Duke of Clarence has
become the Sovereign of his country, and Gully has become one of its representatives in Parliament.' Gully's chosen route led him first to service as a
commission agent for 'Old Q', Lord Foley, Colonel Harry Mellish and the like,
making sure that when they won bets the loser paid up. He progressed
through bookmaking and the Turf, investment in public houses and a coal
merchant business to earn enough in twenty-five years to buy Ackworth Hall,
near Pontefract, and become the town's MP. When he lost his seat he became a
mine-owner and founder of a racing syndicate. Gully was social mobility
incarnate.

The 'Squire of England'

Little remained of the chivalric ideal by this time except its capacity for
self-deception and a certain spurious glamour, especially in connection with
sport. One of the best known inheritors of the tradition in its modern guise,
that is flawed by self-indulgence, was George Osbaldeston, universally
known as the Squire. As an infant Osbaldeston (b.1787) inherited an estate of
some 10,000 acres in North Yorkshire. Brought up in Bath by an indulgent
mother, he was taught to ride by the celebrated Dash. At Eton he overcame his

small size by great pugnacity, afterwards claiming 'I could beat any boy at single-handed cricket, and any boy of my age at fisticuffs.'[17] Such activities were not, of course, school games in the modern sense but improvised affairs got up by the boys. Eton did, however, hold traditional events such as cock-fighting and bull-running, and more recently a rowing contest had been inaugurated to celebrate the King's birthday. In 1803 Osbaldeston recalled being in 'the first rowing boat of the school' which could 'beat any other from Windsor Bridge to Smiley Hall'. ('Bumping one another's boats was the fashion then, but now it is called fouling', he commented.) His other interests – illicit shooting and fishing, making squibs and terrorising servant-girls, visiting Ascot races, and hiring horses in Windsor for riding or furious driving of gigs – did not endear him to the authorities.

Required to leave Eton in 1803 Osbaldeston went to a crammer near Brighton to prepare for Oxford. There he acquired his first pack of hounds, engaged in horse-racing of various kinds and leapt sheep-pens on horseback to the irritation of local shepherds. At Oxford he hunted, rowed – enjoying convivial evenings at riverside hostelries and fighting with townies – and earned the dislike of the head of his college. 'I can't bear a Yorkshireman because he always offers to back his opinion by a bet', he told Osbaldeston. 'Vulgar as such a proceeding may be', Osbaldeston afterwards commented, 'and perhaps not at all convincing to your adversary, yet if it comes off you have the satisfaction of winning his money, which nine times out of ten annoys him more than being beaten in an argument.'[18]

For Osbaldeston, indeed, gambling was part of his aggression, his dis-satisfaction with a society in which there were people of higher rank than himself. He felt his lack of a title keenly, and conversely he could only tolerate the lower orders if they knew their place. Sporting parsons, especially of the 'tuft-hunting' kind, had infuriated him from his youth at his Hutton Bushell estate when the incumbent had once refused to give up a strategically-placed covert. He loathed Lord Frederick Beauclerk, who had a title as well as a clerical collar, and this led to serious trouble in 1806 when Beauclerk was a lean, hard veteran of thirty-three and Osbaldeston a tearaway fast bowler of nineteen, still at Oxford. They quarrelled over a fifty guinea two-a-side match which Beauclerk, within the letter but not the spirit of the law, refused to postpone when Osbaldeston fell ill. Osbaldeston still won because his part-ner, the professional William Lambert, outwitted and out-played Beauclerk but it was a Pyrrhic victory. Beauclerk was later to have ample revenge by provoking Osbaldeston into resigning from MCC and then refusing to have him back.

Social amenities apart, this denied Osbaldeston access to the inner circles of wagering and rule-making. The two were closely connected. For example there was a great furore in 1807 when one John Willes tried a new bowling action, swinging his arm round just below the shoulder. 'Mr Willes and his bowling were frequently barred in making a match,' wrote Pycroft, 'and he played sometimes amidst much uproar and confusion. Still he would persevere until "the ring" closed in on the players, the stumps were lawlessly pulled up and all came to a standstill.'[19] 'Crossed' matches were all too common and even more commonly rumoured. John Gully was attracted by the prospects and took to frequenting Lord's for a time, but fortunately, as Pycroft records, he lacked the patience to master the intricacies of the game.

Osbaldeston came of age in 1808, and gave a feast for his tenants and servants at Hutton Bushell. The occasion evoked a set of laudatory verses:

> The music sweetly played, and the bells did merrily ring
> Full bumpers overflowed to great George our King
> And to this noble squire and the lady they thought best on
> Unto this great lady Mrs Osbaldeston.

There was no cricket match. The young squire's attempts to teach the game to his servants had been markedly unsuccessful. One over-enthusiastic novice had hit Osbaldeston in the eye with the ball, putting him in bed for a fortnight. But there were older sports:

> Smocks waistcoats and antkerchevs was run for on the flat
> George Knaggs from Sherburn came and took away the hat.[20]

And Osbaldeston contemptuously recalled, 'Our guests partook so copiously of the ale provided that more than half of them were beastly drunk.' Such largesse no doubt helped to stave off social revolution, encouraging ordinary folk to prefer the devil they knew, the local squire, to the French devil they were told about in propaganda.

This particular squire did nothing for the war effort. During two years in the local militia, as second in command to a bigger landowner, he attended for training only twice before resigning when rebuked for getting up games for the men, and his six years in Parliament resulted in very few appearances. Electioneering brought out more of his snobberies – fellows who claimed acquaintance through joint sporting interests, thrusting out dirty paws, saying 'Give us your manus' and the like, earned a place in his memoirs. Osbaldeston was not even, literally, a squire for long, for he soon lost his estate, through gambling and living beyond his means. Yet one of the enduring stories about him concerned a man pointing him out to a friend, saying 'Look – there's the Squire.' 'Squire of where?' asked the friend. 'Squire of where? Why he's the Squire of England.'[21]

The basis of this fame and admiration was that Osbaldeston was at the forefront of every sporting activity that took his fancy and a considerable trend-setter. He was, for instance, prominent in the vogue for coaching. The war years brought a great improvement in road transport. The new roads helped trade and industry, and indirectly the war effort, but for the smart set competition between coaching companies to reach higher speeds (in the interests of securing passengers) led to road-racing. This was usually in the form of time-trials, but when rival companies' coaches found themselves on the same road they would race each other spontaneously. As early as 1802 *The Sporting Magazine* carried a vivid description of a race between the four greys of the London mail-coach and four blacks of the Plymouth.

The élite coaching clubs that appeared at this critical time in the war were, in theory at least, more concerned with fashion and with driving correctly than with racing. The Benson (1807), led by Sir Henry Payton, took its name from the village near Oxford where the inn was the club's headquarters. The Oxford road would be lined on meeting days with elegant versions of mailcoaches driven by bucks dressed in expensive and elaborate versions of coachmen's outfits – even gaudier than the swell dragsmen. The rival Whip (1808) led by Mr Charles Buxton, met at his house in Cavendish Square, London. Of a typical meeting in 1810 the *Sporting Magazine* commented, 'Every dashing pupil of the new school appeared anxious to be seen – tandems, barouches, landaus, and, in short, every tasteful vehicle in London was driven to the scene.' The Corinthians, as fashionable young bloods were currently called, continued the traditions of the dragsmen in braving the weather outside whilst the servants rode inside, and some went so far as actually to deliver the mail, especially on the London to Brighton run. But racing, to such as Osbaldeston and Harry Mellish, was much more fun, especially when there was a bet on it. The magistrates did not like racing on the public highway, but it was hard to stop, considering the eminence of the law-breakers.[22]

Touch and go

Napoleon's imperial urges gradually began to prove counter-productive. His invasion of Spain and Portugal aroused stirring resistance that was greatly admired in Britain, and the call to overthrow Bonaparte from the Foreign Minister Canning inspired people as diverse as the radical Cobbett, the romantic intellectual Coleridge and the popular poet Walter Scott. Yet Britain was scarcely a united nation. In 1808 thousand of starving weavers, ruined by the blockade that was keeping out imports of cotton from America, invaded Manchester and were only dispersed by the 4th Dragoons and the local yeomanry. These were desperate times for the poor. In industry there were years of boom as well as recession but blockades took their toll and even the coal and iron industries had their bad spells. In agriculture the weather was a worse enemy than the French. The bad harvest of 1809 threatened mass starvation, and it was averted mainly because the following year Napoleon yielded to pressure from French farmers to be allowed to sell their surplus to Britain.

A series of accidents gave command of the British army in the Peninsula to General Sir Arthur Wellesley. He was hampered by shortage of funds and, as a result, inferior troops. Poaching was the least of their villainies: they were desperate with hunger. For the officers life was more agreeable and Wellesley encouraged them to go hunting, shooting and coursing and to arrange horse-races, though he drew the line at allowing them to go home during the winter to look after their estates. On the other hand he was ready to dispense with the wilder elements who indulged in 'deep play', such as Harry Mellish, who had been obliged by a disastrous St Leger in 1806 to sell up and go to war again. Mellish did well enough until the old passion overcame him and Wellesley sent him home. Celebrating victory and elevation to the peerage Wellington enjoyed a hunt at Villa Vigosa.[23]

At home good hunting was harder and harder to come by. The countryside was now threatened not only by enclosures but by urbanisation. In 1808 a meeting of 'Noblemen, Gentlemen and Farmers' met under the chairmanship of Lord Essex at the Abercorn Arms, Stanmore, to discuss Berkeley hounds in the vicinity of the metropolis. Personal issues clouded the conflict. The Master of the Old Berkeley Hunt was the vicar of Watford, Revd William Capel, Lord Essex's half-brother and sworn enemy. The following year when the Old Berkeley Hunt chased a fox into his estate, Essex sued them for trespass and won. The judgement amazed the hunting fraternity who had taken it for granted that they had a right to cross people's property. However, though other suits followed, there were not many: most landowners hunted themselves and most tenants were either sympathetic or prudent.[24]

The gentlemen of MCC were also feeling the pinch. Players' wages were no longer left to the whim of the great aristocratic sponsors: for games at Lord's they were 'six guineas to win and four to lose . . . or five and three if they lived in town'. So, according to Pycroft 'over the fireplace at Lord's you would see a Subscription List for Surrey against England, or for England against Kent, as the case might be, and find notices at Brooke's and other clubs' to raise the guarantee.[25] Tom Lord's share of the profits obviously came to him whoever won, big matches drew crowds of four to five thousand at sixpence a time resulting in gates of £200 or £250, but he was considerably chagrined in 1809 when the rocketing price of land for housing development forced up the cost of rer ?wing his lease to an uneconomic level. He got a new ground ('which for size and beauty of situation cannot be excelled') not far away, at Lisson Grove and transferred his original turf there. But MCC were not convinced, and declined to move, and for the next few years the future of Lord's and of MCC hung in the balance.[26]

Nor were these good years for the Turf. Gully's translation to 'the black-legged tribe' had not helped. According to Charles Greville, a Corinthian with a better than average knowledge of the seamy side, it was Gully who began the 'system of corruption of trainers, jockeys and boys, which put the secrets of Newmarket at his disposal and in a few years made him rich'.[27] The oiliest specimen was William Crockford, a former fishmonger, who made a fortune out of meeting the gambling tastes of the rich and famous. At the rougher end of the trade were Jim and Joe Bland, strongly suspected of being behind the outbreaks of poisoning that had began to afflict racing stables in 1809.

So it fell to pugilism to lift the nation's spirits, home and abroad. John Gully had been something of a cult figure amongst the Corinthians, though he was scarcely a national hero. But after him there came a truly popular champion, Tom Cribb – he of the leonine features later described by George Borrow as 'perhaps the best man in England'.[28] He stirred British emotions more than Wellington himself. Cribb, not a fervent devotee of training, was fortunate to have the backing of one who was. Barclay Allardyce, known as Captain Barclay, a Scottish gentleman farmer and fitness fanatic, had started a fashion for freakish feats of athletic endurance, at suitable odds, such as walking a thousand miles in a thousand hours at Newmarket. His training regime, based on road-running, also prescribed abstinence from alcohol and sex, unusual measures for pugilists at the time.

Meanwhile, with Wellington entrenched at Torres Vedras, there were fears that politics at home would undermine his efforts. Two Cabinet ministers, Canning and Castlereagh, were so hell-bent on personal ambition that they fought a duel. Canning was wounded, both resigned and the unassuming Spencer Perceval became Chief Minister. The King went mad again, imagining himself hunting and hallooing with the hounds, and a Regency was inevitable. To everyone's surprise the Prince Regent did not bring in his Whig friends but stood by Perceval and the Iberian campaign. In such uncertain times the nation's morale depended heavily on the outcome of the contest between Tom Cribb and the American Negro, Tom Molineaux, in December 1810, as much a test of British character, many felt, as that which faced the nation in Spain.

Cribb had been resting on his laurels and living it up in London. Molyneaux, born a slave in Virginia, had won his freedom by boxing and he had been groomed for the championship in England by Bill Richmond, a freed slave from earlier times. When he met Cribb at Copthall Common, near East Grinstead, Molyneaux faced a hostile crowd, urging the champion not to let the nigger beat him for old England's sake, and a partisan referee, Sir Thomas Ap Rhys. After twenty-eight rounds of dominance the black put Cribb down. When his man failed to come up to scratch in the specified half-minute Cribb's second, Joe Ward, a wily old campaigner, engaged Sir Thomas in debate, alleging foul play. By the time the adjudication was complete Molyneaux was shivering with cold. When they resumed a blow to the throat soon finished him off and sent the crowd home happy.

The year 1811 also brought good war news early on as Wellington began to gain ground after long stalemate. The government was, however, greatly concerned about espionage though of an industrial and social as much as a military nature. Industry was in turmoil in many places, and Luddite riots, violent reaction by textile workers to the prospect of being replaced by machines, were seen by many magistrates as part of Jacobin conspiracy and drew sentences of death or transportation. There was trouble, too, in rural areas where the Game Laws were an abiding source of resentment – and of sympathy for poachers. The Turf was troubled that summer by a further outbreak of poisoning in racing stables. The Jockey Club's reward, now 500 guineas, did not bring the Blands to book, but a tout, Daniel Dawson, convicted and duly hanged at Cambridge before ten thousand spectators, served as a scapegoat. So once more the focus of attention was pugilism.

In practice pugilism, too, fell some way short of expectations, but just as Geoffrey of Monmouth had glamourised the tournament there now arose a chronicler of the Ring who made up for any deficiencies in the sport itself by his highly coloured descriptions of it. It was better than being there to read Pierce Egan's accounts, sometimes illustrated vividly by a brilliant young caricaturist, George Cruikshank. Changing social conditions had created a demand for popular literature and new technology responded with illustrated broadsheets and periodicals. Egan was able to exploit the medium to the full both by his idiosyncratic style and by his early training as a printer.

The style itself – an amalgam of the playfully high-falutin', the shrewdly knowing and the up-to-date – was exactly calculated to enliven dull lives and liberate captive imaginations, and it was embellished by printers' tricks – italicised words, capital letters and exclamation marks – to produce an effect that was vulgar, perhaps, but exhilarating. In Egan's first book on pugilism, *Boxiana*, he called himself 'One of the Fancy'. The word fancy had long been used to mean, as Egan put it 'any person who is fond of a particular amusement, or closely attached to some subject', but as 'the Fancy', it was to become an 'in'-word of powerful attraction to signify the 'in'-set.[29]

Egan began his book with a defence of pugilism against the moralists: 'Boxing came from *Nature*! wounded feelings brought manly *resentment* to its aid – and *coolness*, checking fiery passion and rage, reduced to a perfect science!' It had 'raised the valour and manly intrepidity of the English nation eminently conspicuous above all others!' Without it the English character might 'act too *refined* and the thoroughbred bull-dog degenerate into the *whining* puppy! Not for the British the long knives of the Dutch, Italian stilettos or French or German sticks and stones – in England the FIST only is used . . . The fight done the hand is given in token of peace . . . As a national trait we feel no hesitation in declaring that it is wholly – *British*!'[30]

These sentiments, and indeed echoes of the phraseology and imagery, were to be found in writers on sports of all kinds for decades to come. Meanwhile Cribb's defeat of Molyneaux – 'the Moor' as Egan called him – helped to lighten the dark days of September 1811. There was another bad harvest, and Spencer Perceval's worries were increased by a sudden drop in exports, Irish troubles and a business crisis following the loss of American markets in retaliation for belligerent British protective measures. The Prince Regent, who contracted a mysterious illness that winter, also contracted debts amounting to half a million pounds and he was universally reviled for his treatment of his consort, Princess Caroline. Fortunately Wellington at last seemed on the verge of a break through.

Then in May 1812 Spencer Perceval, who had stood his ground and seemed to be making progress, was assassinated by a fanatic. His death was greeted with joy by mobs in London and the north and it was felt unwise to give him a public funeral. In June the Americans declared war on Britain and began to threaten Canada. Napoleon crossed the Niemen and headed for Moscow, confidently expecting the Tsar to sue for peace. The Russian armies fell back, devastating the countryside and reducing Moscow itself to a shell but forcing an ignominious retreat by Napoleon's starving troops through the snow, mercilessly satirised by Cruikshank.

United Kingdom

Whilst these great events were unfolding in Europe the young Shelley, a sprig of minor aristocracy, paid a visit to Ireland to add his voice to Daniel O'Connell's nationalist cause. English missionaries were by no means rare – indeed anyone who wanted to cut a bit of a literary or political dash made a quick trip to Ireland – but their objective was rarely to assist rebellion. The English perception was still, as it had been for centuries, that the Celts were barbaric, slothful and refractory, though recent visitors had been inclined to evince a paternalistic concern to elevate the standards of their new fellow countrymen. One such had been a young lawyer, George Cooper, whose learned analysis blamed the gentry, expatiating on the decay of the chivalric ideal and supporting Paley's thesis that the code of honour was no more than a mutual benefit society for the inner circle. Cooper thought it essential that the *honnête homme* should bestow enlightenment on the Irish boors (as foreign peasants were called) whom he likened to the Germans of Tacitus' time and other primitive societies.[31]

Shelley, who had seen the end of the Union as an obvious solution, quickly fell into despair and disillusion on seeing the depths of human misery in the Dublin streets on the one hand and the bigotry of the Irish reformers on the other, and shifted his attention to rural Wales. When his attempts to form a radical commune failed he lent his aid to the scheme of an enlightened speculator to build the new Jerusalem on the Caernarvon peninsula. This worthy cause, which included a model village, depended on containing the waves. It had opened in a flourish in September 1811, with an Embankment Jubilee, complete with ox-roasting, Eisteddfod and horse-races, but it had since been foundering on the hostility of wind and weather, the reluctance of the farmers to keep up payments and the disaffection of a hungry work-force. The climax came in the spring gales of 1812 when Shelley, who had outworn his welcome amongst the local *honnêtes hommes* and their fair ladies by failing to share their satisfaction at the execution of fourteen Luddites in York and the two less publicised hangings on the nearby Lleyn peninsula, was fired upon in a mysterious nocturnal attack on his house. He departed post-haste for a secluded cottage in Killarney.[32]

The tide in Europe began to turn when, after a winter hunting behind the lines at Torres Vedras and negotiating for a pack of hounds in Buckinghamshire, Wellington invaded France in the spring of 1814. The Allied armies led by the German veteran General Blucher entered Paris, and Napoleon, deserted by his ministers, abdicated. The peace-makers reinstated the Bourbons on the French throne. The Americans were also sorted out and, after over-zealous British troops had burnt down the White House, peace was concluded. Wellington, now a duke, became ambassador to the court of the Tuileries, a job which involved taking part in the royal family's hunting expeditions, stately affairs that Gaston Phoebus would have thought lacking in vivacity.

At home the defeat of Napoleon gave a fillip to the sporting season. The Derby, attracting a record entry of 51, was attended by the King of Prussia, the Tsar and General Blucher, after whom the winning horse was named. Blucher also attended Ascot for the Gold Cup, and the rapturous crowds even included the Prince Regent in their cheers. He was less kindly treated in a skit written and printed by Egan and illustrated by Cruikshank entitled *The Mistress of Royalty* which described the Regent's lurid association with an actress. Another victory event was an exhibition of pugilism at Lord Lowther's residence in Pall Mall, with John Jackson as master of ceremonies. The Emperor of Russia, the King of Prussia and three of his sons, as well as the top military brass, were amongst those who witnessed what Egan called 'the national sport'.

Jackson's enterprises that year also included the foundation of the Pugilistic Club, which numbered amongst its members the Royal Dukes of York and Clarence, the Duke of Queensberry, and the fabulously rich Welsh landowner Sir Watkin Williams Wynn. Club members, limited to 120, subscribed an annual sum to provide guaranteed if relatively modest purses of ten to fifty guineas, and its articles recorded the expressed determination of the members to see fair play and expose all crosses. Sir Henry Smith took the chair at the first meeting and Lord Yarmouth was the main speaker: they wore blue and buff uniform coats (with lapel buttons engraved PC) over yellow kerseymere waistcoats, and, of course, top hats. Indeed the Fives Court itself became almost decorous, with a roped square for a ring to keep out over-enthusiastic or spoiling spectators, and official 'bouncers' with distinctive ribbons in their hats. Egan was a keen supporter, dedicating his next work – a panoramic strip drawn by George Cruikshank's brother Robert, with a commentary – to 'Mr Jackson and the Noblemen and Gentleman comprising the Pugilistic Club'.[33]

Another cause for celebration was the resolution of the long-standing argument between Tom Lord and MCC. His obstinate adherence to the Lisson Grove ground was set at naught when it was revealed that the proposed new Regent's Canal was to go right through the middle of it. Cutting his losses, Lord took a new site in St. John's Wood, lifted and re-laid the turf once again, built a tavern and various other amenities and won back the good opinion and patronage of MCC who resumed their annual dinners in the 1814 season and stayed happily in their new home ever after.

The war still held a surprise or two, though. Napoleon's escape from Elba and subsequent march on Paris showed the Allied junketings to have been premature and sent tremors down many English spines. Not that of Wellington, of course. His officers, led by Lord Uxbridge and Sir Hussey Vyvian, got up a series of race-meetings at Grammont, properly conducted affairs with young cavalry officer acting as Clerk to the Course, to while away the waiting time. As the tension mounted Wellington himself set a good example by escorting one of the Duchess of Richmond's daughters to a cricket match and, on the eve of Waterloo, relaxing at the Duchess's ball.

The same sang-froid was displayed by the sporting set at home. Dubliners diverted themselves with a return match between their pugilistic hero, Dan Donnelly, and the English champion, a less erudite George Cooper, who had won a disputed decision the year before. Donnelly, widely known as 'Sir Dan' because the Prince Regent had reputedly once clapped him on the shoulder, was universally popular – except with the moralists. No follower of Captain

Allardyce's training methods, Dan liked to take a bottle to bed to help him sleep and he did not care whose bed it was. Trained or not, he delighted the thousands who flocked to a natural amphitheatre outside the city, by taking a terrible revenge on Cooper.[34]

The victory was commemorated in triumphant verses, circulated in broadsheet:

> You sons of proud Britannia your boasting now recall
> Since Cooper by Donnelly has met his sad downfall,
> Out of eleven rounds he got nine knockdowns,
> beside a broken jawbone:
> Says Miss Kelly, 'Shake hands, brave Donnelly,
> the victory's all your own[35]

It was a sad downfall indeed. In December 1815 the *Sporting Magazine* reported that 'Cooper the pugilist who was vanquished by Donnelly . . . died a few weeks since, supposed from the tremendous blows he received in that occasion.' Like Napoleon he had met his Waterloo.

Notes

1 'Jerusalem', 1814, Chapter 2, xiv, lines 26–31.
2 C. Hibbert, *George IV: Prince of Wales 1762–1811*, p. 122.
3 *English Social History*, London 1944, p. 466.
4 For a balanced view of the Napoleonic era see *Larousse Encyclopedia of Modern History*, ed. M. Renan, English edition, London, 1964, pp. 238–78.
5 G.M. Trevelyan, *English Social History*, London, 1944, p. 504.
6 16 April 1795.
7 P. Egan, *Boxiana*, New Series, London, 1825, vol. 1. For Egan see J.C. Reid, *Bucks and Bruisers*, London 1971, pp. 12–40.
8 For the long history of blood sports legislation see E.S. Turner, *All Heaven in a Rage*, London, 1972.
9 J. Strutt, *Glig-gamena angel deod: or The Sports and Pastimes of the People of England*, London 1801; new edition 1903, reprinted Bath, 1969, p. 205.
10 Ibid., pp. 93–4.
11 'A Tour in Ireland' in J.P. Harrington (ed.), *The English Traveller in Ireland*, Dublin, 1991, p. 187.
12 *Sports and Pastimes*, p. 92.
13 Strutt, *Sports and Pastimes*, p. 100–4. Strutt's original brief comments were largely stricken from the 1903 and subsequent editions, being replaced by four pages of more high-flown matter in keeping with game's later dignity.
14 Ibid., pp. 97–8.
15 The price had been eight pence. See R. Browning, *A History of Golf*, London, 1955, p. 46.
16 J. Gore (ed.) *The Creevey Papers*, London, 1963, p. 54.
17 E.D. Cuming (ed.), *Squire Osbaldeston: His Autobiography*. London, 1926, p. 5.
18 Ibid., p. 13.
19 *The Cricket Field*, 1851, ed. F.S. Ashley-Cooper, London, 1922, p. 124.
20 Cuming, *Squire Osbaldeston*, pp. 212–13. A new hat sometimes with silver hat band,

was a customary prize: hence 'hat-trick' in cricket.

21 Ibid., Introduction by T. Cook, p.v.

22 See E.H. Bovill, *English Country Life*, Oxford, 1962, Chapter XI 'Swell dragsmen', pp. 140–57.

23 For the social side of the war see E. Longford, *Wellington: The Years of the Sword*, 1975, passim.

24 Bovill, *English Country Life*, pp. 214–32.

25 Pycroft, *The Cricket Field*, p. 111.

26 F.S. Ashley-Cooper and Lord Harris, *Lord's and MCC*, London, 1914, p. 55.

27 *The Greville Memoirs*, ed. L. Strachey and R. Fulford, London, 1938 (8 vols.) quoted in R. Mortimer, *The Jockey Club*, London, 1958, p. 77.

28 *Lavengro*, London, 1851, 1906 edn, p. 162.

29 J. Moore, *Columbarium or the Pigeon-house*, 1735, had spoken of 'Gentlemen of the Fancy' who had to attend the birds, and its later use was chiefly in expressions like 'pigeon-fancier' or 'dog-fancier' (*OED*) There was also much literary debate about the distinction between fancy and imagination, the first usually being thought more superficial.

30 *Boxiana*, London, 1813, p. 2.

31 *Letters on the Irish Nation*, 1799 in Harrington, *English Traveller in Ireland*, pp. 185–95.

32 R. Holmes, *Shelley: the Pursuit*, London, 1974, pp. 117–94.

33 'A Picture of the Fancy', commentary on panoramic strip 7 September 1814.

34 S.J. Watson, *Between the Flags*, Dublin, 1969.

35 Miss Kelly was the daughter of Donnelly's landlady.

CHAPTER EIGHT

'Sporting personal'
1815–37

Though the Restoration of the Bourbons doubtless enabled the gentlemen of England to sleep easier in their beds, the war had solved nothing for their inferiors. The mob left a blood-stained loaf on the balcony of Carlton House, the grandiose London residence of the Prince Regent, in protest at the passing of the Corn Laws of 1815. The new law, which banned imported corn when the home price fell below 80s a quarter, was good protection for the farmers but disastrous for the poor. After the bad harvest of 1816 there were riots in the rural south, and barns, stacks and even houses were burned in East Anglia. In the industrial north, where thousands were driven to poor relief by post-war recession, Luddism broke out again. For a time trade recovered and radical fervour declined, but then in 1819, after another slump, troops were sent in to control a crowd at St Peter's Field, Manchester, leaving several dead and many injured. 'Peterloo' polarised opinion. Liberals were outraged, but the government reacted sternly.

The accession to the throne of the Prince Regent added to Parliamentary strife. As a monarch he was an anachronism, still trying to manipulate the machinery of government for his own ends, at a time when people wanted to be rid of what Cobbett called the 'Dead Weight' of pensions and patronage. A new spirit was arising – stimulated by the promptings of the Clapham Sect and the Methodists – in public affairs. It was not quite morality, but it included a sense of shame, a quality George IV conspicuously lacked. Other influences encouraged collective prudence. The adoption of the Gold Standard in 1821 not only stabilised the currency but helped to establish communal integrity. The notion of free trade showed that self-interest could be enlightened, and even the protectionists saw the dangers of volatile wheat prices and agreed to modification of the Corn Laws. In the atmosphere of free trade the new inventions began to make an even greater impact on people's lives, offering opportunity, but erratically and chiefly to the skilled, and always at the cost of unsettling change. Lower death rates contributed to the continuing population growth. By 1831 the numbers had reached over 13 million in England, 900,000 in Wales, 2,300,000 in Scotland, and, ominously, 7,750,000 in Ireland and there was further growth in all the industrial towns and cities. The long hours of work, for children as well as adults, were seen not as an encroachment on leisure but as a deterrent to vice.

Mobility in search of work added to ethnic tensions. Irishmen in particular flooded into mainland cities and country areas, into London and Lancashire, Glasgow and Edinburgh, competing with more local immigrants for work.

Only Ulster, where Belfast was the magnet, benefited from the Act of Union: the south found it impossible to cope with the rush of cheap manufactured goods from England and its emergent industries were nipped in the bud. Both Irish and English workers flocked to Cardiff whilst north Walians joined the influx of Irish to Liverpool. The coalfields of Durham attracted workers from all over Britain. The cultural mix in the big towns brought racial tensions that were to give a sharper edge to sporting rivalries. The demand for skills also brought social tensions.

Popular education, albeit still charitably oriented, was beginning to gather momentum. The Yorkshire physician George Birkbeck brought his Mechanics' Institute idea from Glasgow to London in 1823, and four years later the Society for the Diffusion of Useful Knowledge was formed. Everywhere there was a great efflorescence of pamphlets and tracts from sects and societies and a proliferation of treaties of an uplifting kind in periodical parts. The 'march of mind' was the subject of endless discussion and much mockery by superior folk. Traditionalist gentlemen cricketers were inclined to dub the new rule-testing bowling 'march of intellect' stuff.

But the lower orders were restive. In a period of relative calm trades unions were legalised, with the predictable result that recessions and booms brought strikes or lock-outs. Political agitation also increased. When the Duke of Wellington became Prime Minister his aim was to preserve existing institutions as a bulwark against chaos. The Metropolitan Police Force was set up in 1829 not just to fight crime but to quell disorder. Even Wellington had to support Catholic emancipation in order to avoid Irish rebellion and though he steadfastly declined to have anything to do with Parliamentary reform, there was no doubt that change had to come. John Bull was at bay.[1]

Squires and parsons

John Bull, as a national emblem, was in fact already much changed. Since he had first appeared in the political prints in 1712 exemplifying short-sighted government policies, as an irascible, blundering, hen-pecked clothmerchant, he had adapted to the increasingly self-indulgent national self-image and become a stubborn, plodding, honest, dependable, strong and virile fellow. This last quality was criticised even by the Anglophile American Washington Irving:

> [John Bull] unluckily took lessons in his youth in the noble science of defence; and having . . . become a perfect master at boxing and cudgel-play, he has had a troublesome life of it ever since . . . He is a little fond of playing the magnifico abroad . . . flinging his money bravely about at boxing matches, horse races, cockfights, and carrying a high head among 'gentlemen of the fancy'.[2]

The English essayist Hazlitt was more trenchant. John Bull's pleasures were sad ones because he had no taste for amusement, preferring working six days a week to being idle on one with nothing better to do to kill time than get drunk. 'An idiot in a country town, a Presbyterian parson, a dog with a canister tied to its tail, a bull-bait and a fox-hunt are irresistible attractions to him.'[3] This deep-died love of blood sports was shared even by Radicals. William Cobbett's nostalgia for pleasant days spent on Squire Tom Assheton Smith's estate was soured by his recollection of 'the hanging of the men at Winchester last Spring for resisting some of this Smith's gamekeepers', but it was not destroyed. For Cobbett, indeed, 'the game' kept 'all in life and motion from the lord to the hedger'.[4]

He preferred hunters to shooters – 'a disagreeable class', immodest and inclined to lie about their exploits. He cited as an example a Philadelphia lawyer that he knew, but he could have found one nearer home. Colonel Peter Hawker, the foremost pundit of the age, whose *Instructions to Young Sportsmen* (1814) had achieved near-biblical status in shooting circles, went beyond the usual hypocrisy of 'shooting flying' to sanctimonious disapproval of any element of competition: he even thought shooting parties likely to encourage an unhealthy spirit of emulation. But his private diaries show the truth beneath the snobbery. For example, 'I had some very fine grouse shooting, though with parties (as is the unpleasant custom of this county [Norfolk] and Suffolk)', 'I kept no account of what I killed' and 'this kind of shooting leads to jealousy that I detest'. However, he could not forbear to add 'though I have never yet been beaten by anyone in any county that I have ever yet seen'. Furthermore this stern critic of 'long shots' (which might wing birds rather than kill them outright) confided to his diary the secret joy of an occasion when 'The constant succession of long shots that my favourite Joe Manton barrels continued bringing down surpassed anything I had before done, or seen, in my whole career of shootings.'[5]

Not everyone was quite so hypocritical. A less solemn treatise by the impoverished but unregenerate George Hanger, following advice on rat-catching and teaching dogs to course hares without 'fair law', announced 'I solemnly declare that I have shot numbers of hares above seventy yards.'[6] Most sportsmen, however, went in for sanctimony rather than satire. Revd W. B. Daniels, a leading authority on field sports, denounced Thomas Coke, Earl of Leicester of Holkham as the most lethal shot in England, earning a rebuke in turn from the *Gentleman's Magazine* because of his own notoriety as a 'sportsman' in the traditional mode. Another sporting characteristic was the mock-modesty of Squire Osbaldeston whose memoirs recalled: 'I shot 100 pheasants one day during one of [Sir Richard Sutton's] battues at Lynford . . . a performance which he always cracked up as the best he had ever witnessed, and I dare say few have done as much when five or six men are shooting together.'[7]

Daniels was particularly severe on the 'wanton barbarism' of competitive shooting with live birds.[8] The Squire was immensely proud of his gun 'a flint and steel of 18 bore, made by the celebrated Joe Manton' which he used to great effect in the trap-shooting matches with live pigeons. He was taken to task by a member of the Burton Hunt in the *Sporting Magazine* not only for taking part in such exercises but for his excessive fire power: 'Mr Osbaldeston will excuse me when I say that he may as well carry a field-piece as the gun with which he usually shoots his pigeon matches. Surely this cannot be called fair work.[9]

Such nuances of morality were lost on the pigeon shooters who foregathered at the Old Hat public house in Ealing High Street. The Old Hat Club had as members such notabilities as Colonel (later General) Anson, Lord Foley, the Hon. Charles Greville, and two renowned sporting Scots, Lord Kennedy and Captain Ross. Kennedy was wild and usually to be found at the losing end of extravagant bets. Ross was a very different proposition: the son of a laird and a hard physical and mental specimen, he lost few bets, even to Osbaldeston, and was probably the best all-round shooter of the day. The Squire recounted racist jokes about Ross, reflecting on his sportsmanship, but was manifestly envious of him.

As we have seen Osbaldeston's fervour for sportsmanship did not preclude his using winning as a social and economic weapon: indeed he took a perverse pleasure in parading it. Yet oddly enough (or perhaps in consequence), when it came to hunting he was sternly and sincerely opposed to excessive competition and paranoid on what he called 'jealousy'. He faced relatively few challenges when leading the Burton from 1810–1815, earning a reputation as a fine rider and a stickler for etiquette. His troubles began in 1817 when despite the grave handicap of diminishing funds he took over the prestigious Quorn only to find his martinet style not only resented but laughed at by the thrusting Meltonians. His autobiography reveals how deeply he felt the slights he had suffered. Some were dismissed with mild irony: Sir James Musgrave who rode into Osbaldeston from behind, broke his leg and galloped on regardless as soon as his own horse was free, is described as 'rather a jealous rider'. But the hare-hunter Sir Henry Every, who insisted on beating his own osier beds, the Squire felt had perpetrated 'an insult to me as master'. And he excoriated the wretched 'Boniface', an inn-keeper who so far forgot his station as to ride his horse into the pack and then appeal to the Duke of Beaufort for protection against the Squire and his wrath. Equally abhorrent, the Duke's placatory intervention was an insult arising from 'sheer jealousy'.[10]

Osbaldston's own jealousies were, of course, rancorous. His envy of

Captain Ross spilled over into scorn for all Scottish pursuits including the newly-fashionable sport of deer-stalking in the Highlands. One of his favourite stories was that the leading English devotee William Coke, nephew of old Thomas, was so keen that on his first trip he never took off his breeches for a fortnight. Yet he could not easily shrug off Ross's achievements. In deer-stalking he was supreme, killing 87 stags in 1827 and no fewer than 118 in 1851, 'I was always up at 3 a.m.', he wrote, 'and seldom back to the lodge before 7 or 8 p.m., walking, running or crawling the whole time'.[11]

The Squire had a great dislike of sporting parsons, notably but by no means exclusively Lord Frederick Beauclerk, and indeed there was little to admire in the stereotype of the younger son stricken by primogeniture and seeking to cash in on his sporting skills. Another source of irritation was that many rose above temporary disadvantage to rival the squires themselves: one such was Revd Ellis St John, originally a hare- and buck-hunter, who led the South Berkshire for years, whilst a northern neighbour, Revd John Loder founded a great pack and through marriage joined his territory with that of Revd Robert Symonds in Hertfordshire. Judicious marriage was undoubtedly the most convenient way for a parson with a taste for hunting to set himself up in the sport. A good example was Revd Jack Russell, breeder of the terrier that bore his name, and a consummate master of foxhounds. Russell was a sore trial to the Bishop of Exeter (whose diocese was knee-deep in hunting clergy), but his wife's income of £50,000 a year gave him an independent outlook, and he conscientiously did his duty on Sundays, attracting folk from miles around to hear him dilate on the evils of drink, strong language and the 'filthy habit' of smoking.

Those without suitably endowed wives tended to resort to gambling. Powlett was a good example and the torch was effectively borne by Beauclerk, whose grip on cricket grew tighter as he grew older. The game was now spreading north, adding to its commercial possibilities and its dubious reputation. An old professional, John Bowyer, recalled an early game in Sheffield for which he got a handsome fee of £10 and all expenses out and home when the sponsors took £1,200 at the gate, but the game lasted four days because stumps had to be 'drawn each day at a quarter to six, before the factories closed, as they were afraid of the roughs'.[12] Nottingham drew even bigger crowds, and was even rougher. It was there that Osbaldeston, seeking revenge on Beauclerk, made a match against MCC. The game became notorious as one in which both teams sold out. The Squire did not appear himself but his professional front-man Lambert, who did, was forbidden to play at Lord's in future.

Double standards were nothing to these tyrannical exponents of sporting values. Beauclerk was an unlikely legislator, but his word was law at Lord's.

Take the case of Mr John Willes with his controversial new style of bowling. As a later cricketing autocrat, Lord Harris, put it: 'When he played on the side of Lord Frederick his bowling was fair, when against him the contrary.'[13] In 1822 – on the wrong side – Willes was no-balled and felt so disgusted that he flung down the ball and gave up cricket altogether:

The age of Nimrod

The twenties introduced a new and highly influential type of penurious gentry, the sporting journalist. The prototype was the celebrated Nimrod who perfected the art of 'puffing' as applied to field sports. Charles Apperley, second son of the travelling tutor to Sir Watkin Williams Wynn, had been brought up to hunt with the sons of the family and sent to Rugby School, which was popular with the new thrusting classes, a place where it was easy to cultivate rich friends and expensive habits. After a spell in the Wynn family yeomanry, a judicious marriage with one of the Wynn girls allowed Apperley to settle in the Shires and hunt with the Quorn until his taste for experimental farming and his losses in horse-breeding brought him to the verge of bank-ruptcy. He turned to journalism in 1821 when the *Sporting Magazine* sought to improve its flagging circulation by a series of articles on hunting 'from the inside'. Apperley at first declined the invitation – the *Sporting Magazine* was a mere cockney concern to which no gentleman contributed – but eventually consented on condition that he could use a *nom de plume*.

Apperley's eight years touring the country, all expenses paid and with horses and a manservant provided, visiting the leading hunts, made anonymity an irrelevance. His highly-coloured accounts of the sporting and social prowess of the rich, sprinkled with Latin tags and classical allusions, soon made him an honoured guest who might be induced to write a favour-able report by lavish hospitality or discreet presents. Typical of the Nimrod approach was his comment after a month-long visit to Duns in Berwickshire, which he called 'the Melton Mowbray of the North', that he could not speak of the virtues of a neighbouring spa because he 'never once drank aqua pura, much less aqua medicata'.[14]

Scotland was much less universally given to fox-hunting than England, not from shortage of quarry – there were areas like Wigtownshire where they were treated like vermin and there was a premium on shooting them – but because tradition and terrain restricted the necessary patronage. However, the early years of the century saw the revival or take-over of earlier packs, notably by the fifth Duke of Buccleuch in Roxburghshire and Lord Kelburne (said by Nimrod to be 'as regular in his kennel-hours as an old maid at her tea-time') in Lanarkshire and Renfrewshire serving the better sort around Glasgow. Similarly, Wales, whose hounds had been highly praised by Gervase Markham, but where hare-hunting was more popular, mainly relied for fox-hunting excellence on the old Tudor family settlers – notably the Pryse family with a famous pack at the Gogerddan, the Joneses at Ynysfor and later the Wynns at Wynnstay. And in Ireland, where foxes were scarce and harrier packs abounded, the celebrated Duhallow in Cork was followed by Sir Fenton Aylmer's Kildare, Colonel Pigott's Wexford and Sir Walter Burrowes' Laraugh (with hounds mostly from the Belvoir), and several others began in the early nineteenth century to imitate the Quorn as best they could.

In England meanwhile foxes were so scarce that even Osbaldeston had to resort to buying them from Hopkins, the dealer in Tottenham Court Road, though he drew the line at imported French 'dunghills'. Bagging foxes for release at strategic moments was common and sometimes they were captured for re-use. Even Nimrod's glory days were numbered. Soon the *Sporting Magazine*, under a new editor, decided it could no longer afford the £1,500 a year Apperley was costing. He was obliged to move to Calais, out of range of his creditors, to write nostalgic reminiscences and pot-boiling efforts, such as a scandalous biography of an erstwhile neighbour, Jack Mytton, a modern version of Mellish and Barrymore. But he had set the style and the standard for a generation. Nimrod's achievement was to modernise and reinvigorate the pretentious snobberies of Beckford, and he did much to establish the notion of lavish expenditure as a mark of superior sportsmanship.

Apperley shared the view of the fox-hunting establishment, that the growing enthusiasm for steeple-chasing was a debasement of their sport. People like Tom Assheton Smith called it rough-riding. The *Sporting Magazine* in 1819, describing it as the sort of racing for which the Paddies were particularly famous, gave an account of a race at Lismore, a 'complete tumbledown' affair in which the winner got up after four falls to win. Nevertheless the betting potential had a great appeal to such as Osbaldeston, who had good success in early head-to-head matches even against the professional riders, like the famous Dick Christian. When he rode his own Clasher to victory over Colonel Peel's Clinker, heavily backed by Captain Ross and ridden by Christian, the Squire composed a celebratory verse:

> Why Clinker with Clasher can ne'er go the pace;
> Then the Captain's outwitted, and I'm sure it's no sin
> For the many good Christians he's oft taken in.[15]

But Clinker was on the winning side in 1825. Ross, having infuriated his volatile fellow-Scot Kennedy by beating him in a pigeon-shooting contest, found himself landed with a challenge to ride against Kennedy's man Captain Douglas in a four mile steeple chase for £1,000. Kennedy spared no expense to secure a horse for Douglas, acquiring several before buying Radical from Assheton Smith for 400 guineas. Ross was able to borrow Clinker for nothing. The excitement that built up in Leicestershire over the race was distasteful to conventional hunting men but greatly to the liking of the Meltonians. Nimrod, though disapproving of such manifest vulgarity, was nevertheless there to record the occasion for posterity.

It fell below expectations: because, according to Ross, of Kennedy's insistence that it was to be a free-for-all contest. So, at the first obstacle, a five-barred gate, Ross, sensing that Radical was going to refuse, held back until it swerved across him, dug his spurs in and knocked Douglas over the gate, going on to win easily. An objective observer commented, 'To use the language of the ring it was but a hawly mawly sort of scrambling fight, though so highly embellished by the pen of Nimrod.'[16] Osbaldeston was scathing: 'Two greater tailors never exhibited a steeplechase. By my troth they both rode like hackney coachmen.[17]

Gentleman riders were less frequently to be found on the flat where the combination of handicapping by weight and the sweepstake meant that the leading professional jockeys like Clift, Goodison, Buckle, Arnull, Sam Chifney junior and the new star, Jem Robinson, could make a difference to a horse's starting price. A cynical article in *Brown's Turf Expositor* in 1829 put modern professional riders into three categories, Southern, Northern and Dirty. Of the first two Northern jockeys were preferable because they didn't put on airs. The Southerners rode better, but, though usually 'illiterate, ignorant men', affected 'a mysterious but plebeian importance and would willingly be thought a sort of semi-gentleman'. The third category were men from Westmorland and Cumberland 'remarkable for their slovenly, dirty and unworkmanlike appearance'.

Trainers came in for even more sarcasm. 'A modern trainer is a personage of the most mysterious and the utmost importance. His appearance is vulgar but he makes up for his vulgarity in affecting a sort of semi-solemnity of aspect.' Most trainers were 'men with scarcely pretentions to a common village education', though there were exceptions: Pierce of Richmond, Yorkshire, had 'much sound sterling sense' and could convey his ideas 'in correct and expressive language' and Edwards had been at veterinary college for a while. The article went on: 'Jockeys I regard in the aggregate as honester men than Trainers, unless indeed the two professions are united, and when I behold a man thus circumstanced I cannot help viewing him as a Janus of mischief.' The mischief was becoming dynastic. One of Sam Chifney's sons was a jockey, the other a trainer. John Scott, the leading trainer of the next age, and his brother Bill, one of the few gentlemen riders who could hold his own with professionals, were the sons of a jockey who had turned trainer and publican.

In 1816 a remarkable notice had appeared in the *Racing Calendar* stating that 'persons who may be inclined to submit any matters in dispute to the decisions of the Jockey Club are at liberty to do so on observing certain conditions'.[18] The voluntary nature of subsequent transactions was to prove an invaluable defence against unwelcome legal and Parliamentary intervention and the onset of democracy. However, the legal protection afforded to the honour code also made it something of a bookmakers' charter, thus further confusing a situation in which the likes of Gully and Crockford had become important racehorse owners. Both were involved in peculiar goings-on in the 1827 St Leger, beginning when Gully's horse Mameluke was seriously hampered at the start. Gully had brought the horse from George Villiers, fifth Earl of Jersey, under whose ownership it had won the Derby in suspicious circumstances. Lord Jersey, a pillar of the Jockey Club, was given the benefit of the honour code and was generally thought fortunate to escape censure. Crockford had aspirations to rise above mere bookmaking. That same year he acquired two adjoining houses in St James's Street and turned them into a gambling club that put White's and Brook's into the shade.

Gully, for all his guile and outward success, was accident-prone socially. George IV had been a regular visitor to Ascot since his accession, having a new stand designed by his architect Nash and initiating the custom of a Royal Drive along the course, and though he sat immobile for most of the time, deep in contemplation or laudanum, he was thought to enjoy the occasion. He had been graciously pleased to forgive the Jockey Club for their affront in his Regency days and as a mark of favour gave a lavish dinner to them in 1828. It was Gully's misfortune the following year at Ascot to walk in front of the Royal Box without raising his hat. His apology was deemed insufficient and he was cast into outer darkness as an expression of the Jockey Club's respect for the sovereign.

The age of Jorrocks

They soon had to cultivate a new one. Wellington was surprised when William IV invited him to carry on as Prime Minister for he was an adversary of the former Duke of Clarence, but they were at one in opposition to Parliamentary reform. Wellington did not last long, however, and by the end of the year the Whigs were in office. They faced growing disorder in agricultural districts. In Kent threshing machines were being smashed, ricks were burned and notes were left by a mysterious Captain Swing. The workers' demands were moderate and many farmers sympathised with their plight but the new Home Secretary Lord Melbourne came down hard, hanging the ring-leaders – and awarding an extra shilling a week to the law-abiding. Over four hundred were transported. Emigration reached 60,000, more than double that of any previous year.

The Whig leader, Earl Grey, was no radical but he favoured giving more power to the rising middle classes in order to stave off the mob rule that was sweeping much of Europe. Parliamentary reform had to wait two more years – years of royal opposition, Commons' rejection, general elections and Lords' resistance, provoking riots, radical agitation and plans for politically-motivated strikes. The Reform Act of 1832 did not satisfy the radicals but it took some of the steam out of the situation: only one in six men (fewer in Scotland and Ireland) got the vote, but the redistribution of seats and the end of rotten boroughs shifted power away from the old landed gentry towards the middle classes. The Municipal Reform Act of 1835 continued the process.

The pace of the industrial revolution accelerated as railways developed. George Stephenson's Stockton and Darlington in 1825 and the Liverpool and Manchester in 1830 were highly successful and no less than 54 Acts authorising new lines were passed by 1835. Industrialisation helped bring about a realignment of the old party groupings. There gradually emerged a modern Conservative Party under Sir Robert Peel, steadfast against radicalism but efficient in administration and relatively enlightened in trade and industry. The old Whigs were still very far from modern Liberals but they enjoyed enough middle class support to survive with the assistance of Daniel O'Connell's Irish Catholic votes.

Their new leader, Melbourne, was no enthusiast for progress, but he brought an eighteenth century suavity to the stresses of nineteenth century life, and he presided over some important advances – the abolition of slavery; the first substantial Factory Act (forbidding the employment of children under nine, and restricting the hours of the under-thirteens to 8 and of women to 10); a government grant (£20,000) in support of elementary education in non-conformist and Church of England schools; and the reorganisation of local government. The Whigs also did well in foreign affairs. Lord Palmerston, given a free hand as Foreign Secretary, combined staunch defence of British interests with support for liberal movements abroad. On the looming question of industrial relations, however, the Whig touch was less sure. The philanthropic manufacturer Robert Owen's Grand Consolidated Union collapsed under the weight of its own idealism, but not before the six Tolpuddle labourers who were deported in 1834 for resolving to join it had become martyrs.

For sportsmen the most significant Whig measure was the reform of the Game Acts in 1831, replacing the established system of property qualifications by licensing. This concession to the bourgeoisie greatly encouraged the taste for shooting. By the same token it was a blow to the fox-hunters, adding to their bitterness against the railway networks which brought the countryside within range of prosperous but ill-bred townees. The die-hards found a spokesman in Robert Smith Surtees, second son of a minor Durham squire who used his modest legacy to go into publishing founding the *New Sporting Magazine*. Surtees himself contributed between 1831 and 1834 a series of sketches that were to make his magazine popular and himself famous. These were sharply satirical stories about a Mr Jorrocks, a London grocer of riveting vulgarity, supposedly a typical product of the new Game Laws. Surtees' broadsides were also directed, for professional and social reasons, at the pomposities of Nimrod and his gullible circle. With this in mind he made Jorrocks an enthusiastic but semi-literate admirer of Apperley's style – 'sporting personal' as Surtees called it – who was eventually disillusioned by the poor return he got for the lavish entertainment and personal flattery he showered on Nimrod in order to have his accomplishments lauded in print. To the modern reader Jorrocks may seem no more vulgar than Barrymore, Osbaldeston or Mytton and a good deal better-natured and unpretentious than his creator. But Surtees went on in a series of successful novels to excoriate everyone connected with unfashionable hunts, steeplechases and what he called 'that still smaller grade of gambling, coursing.'[19]

It was the railways, Surtees reckoned, by marooning the old coaching inns, that had forced their landlords to think up low-grade sporting activities of this kind to win back customers. Yet they could scarcely have done it without the patronage of the great and their enthusiasm for sweepstakes. When Henry Coleman, horse-breeder and proprietor of the Turf Hotel, St Albans, organised the first successful modern steeplechase in 1830 it was for the delectation of the officers of the 1st Life Guards who dined there: the race was won by Captain McDowell on Lord Ranelagh's Wonder from Lord Clanricarde's Nailer, owner up. Similarly it was for the élite Altcar Club, set up in 1825 by Lord Sefton on his estate near Liverpool, that the landlord of the Waterloo Hotel, where the Club dined, organised the sweepstake for eight coursing dogs from any recognised club which became known as the Waterloo Cup: its first winner, in 1836, was Lord Molyneux. And conversely when that same year at nearby Maghull a Mr Lynn advertised a 'sweepstake of £10 each with £80 added, for horses of all denominations, twelve stones each, gentlemen riders. Twenty fences in each of two circuits' the race had to struggle for survival until it secured aristocratic patronage.

The organisers of the first steeplechase sweepstakes tried hard to restrict the ventures to gentleman riders, but they were fighting a losing battle. Decisions about eligibility were, in any event, left to local stewards who varied greatly in attitude: Lord Derby was said on one occasion to have given the benefit of the doubt to a rider because he spoke French and wore a gold ring. Subsequent steeplechases, like the Grand Northampton in 1833 and the Cheltenham Grand Annual in 1834, seem to have made little attempt to discriminate and before long the pace was being set by professionals or by those who spent most of their lives riding. The most famous of these 'gentlemen' riders over the sticks was Captain Becher, a farmer's son who owed his rank to service in the Buckinghamshire Yeomanry, and an habitué of the Turf Hotel who did most of his riding for the entrepreneurial Coleman. But it was the professional Jem Mason, from a plebeian horse-breeding background but noted for his flamboyant style of dress, who won the St Albans in 1834 and Tom Oliver, an engaging gypsy-type from Cheltenham, who won the Liverpool in 1837.[20]

'Cheat, flatter, humbug – anything for gain'

Such incursions provoked even stronger élitist urges in the inner circles of sport. Thus the Jockey Club's reaction to Gully's offence was to limit the 1830 Ascot Gold Cup to Jockey Club members, in the hope of leaving him and other low-bred types like Crockford in the cold. The result was that in 1831 entries were down to two. Nevertheless William IV thought the idea sound and in 1832 presented a trophy for competition by Jockey Club members only. The artefact – a hoof of Eclipse mounted on a gold salver – was suitably grotesque and carried ironic overtones of an earlier social outcast, Dennis O'Kelly. *The Times* roundly condemned this mispaced élitism. Internal critics also began to ask awkward questions – why did Lord Jersey's horses always get such favourable handicaps, for instance? At this hour of need there came a zealous young reformer, Lord George Bentinck.

Second son of the Duke of Portland, nephew and protégé of George Canning, the Foreign Secretary, Bentinck had, in his brief military career, narrowly escaped having to fight a duel with his Commanding Officer who resented Bentinck's attempts to use his wealth and power to undermine him. Entering politics as a reforming Whig in 1828, aged twenty-six, he soon narrowed his range to opposing free trade. He found more scope on the Turf for his talents, temperament and money. In his early days Bentinck had gambled and lost heavily and – perhaps for no more sinister purpose than to conceal this from his father – had often raced under the colours of front-men. His overbearing manner had led him into difficulties with partners such as the Duke of Richmond with whom he shared stables, with John Day, his skilful but dodgy trainer, and with his cousin, Charles Greville.

In 1831 Bentinck fought a duel with Osbaldeston over a bet, a battle of moral pygmies about which accounts differ but which reflect no great credit on either. The Squire's fury at the establishment was subsequently redoubled and he took pleasure in getting revenge on Bentinck's crony, Lord Wilton –

another beneficiary of favourable handicaps – at his home course Heaton Park, Manchester, in 1835. But Osbaldeston was beating the air. Bentinck, although capable of pulling a swift trick to get a good price for his horse Elis in the following year's St Leger, was taken seriously as a great reformer in his self-appointed role as saviour of the Turf.

For true exclusiveness the summer sport to choose was yachting. In Regency days there had been only some fifty yachts in the whole country and the groups who met at the Thatched House, St James's in 1815 to found the Yacht Club (including two marquesses, three earls, four viscounts, four barons and five baronets) fixed the lower limit of members' boat size at 10 tons. The Prince Regent, who had recently laid down the Royal George of 330 tons, joined in 1817 and the Royal Dukes of Clarence and Gloucester a year later. When the club became Royal on George IV's accession in 1820 the minimum was raised to 30 tons. Its aimless ostentation aroused criticism in the press. What was the point of such lavish expenditure if it did not seek to improve performance through competition? Lord Belfast, a virtuous exception, commissioned Samuel White of Cowes to design a faster, more weatherly and safer boat than the navy's 'coffin brigs' and eventually convinced the Admiralty of the need to change. But Tom Assheton Smith, who had bought five new boats in the years up to 1830, resigned over the club's refusal to allow steam yachts and went on independently to commission Robert Napier to design the *Menai* of 400 tons, the first of his nine steam vessels. The prejudice against steam was not easy to understand since gentlemen yachtsmen were totally reliant on professional crews to propel them even under sail.

The club also maintained a supercilious attitude towards racing. Some suspected that whilst noble owners professed to find the idea rather vulgar they were actually afraid of challenges to the notion that biggest is best. Whatever their motives the purists missed the tide of public opinion. The Cumberland Fleet, despite sycophantically changing its name to His Majesty's Coronation Sailing Society in 1820, managed to achieve the worst of both worlds. In 1823, when the Thames Yacht Club was founded on more progressive lines, many members seceded. It was salt in the loyalists' wounds when the upstarts became Royal Thames in 1830 under William IV, and magnanimously agreed to allow the old Coronation Society to break up and rejoin them.

The new king freely bestowed the appellation Royal on provincial clubs like the Northern, the Western, the Southern and the Cork, the Irish and St George. This scarcely opened the door to bare-footed hordes, but it did create more interest in competitive racing, which some thought anarchical enough. Fortunately by and large the bigger boats did best except in freak weather conditions. Primitive attempts at handicapping by weight, as at the Solent in

1820, and Cowes in 1829, were bedeviled by the unresolved problem of how to measure size and by the rich men's determination and ability to buy success.[21]

In Scotland the national sport was less susceptible to purchase. Nevertheless when a group of new and wealthy players took up golf it helped the game over a difficult hurdle. At St Andrews in 1827 funds had got so low that it was decided to discontinue the allowance of two guineas paid to 'the Leith Clubmaker' for attending the Annual General Meeting. Yet within no time the financial situation was transformed. The new recruits were mostly from the field sports set and they brought the fervour of all converts. Sir David Baird of Newbyth put golf before all his other sporting interests, Captain Campbell of Glensaddell gave up hunting for it, and George Fullerton Carnegie of Pitarrow found it a useful supplementary way of disposing of his lavish inheritance. By contrast, at Edinburgh the Honourable Company, dissatisfied with encroachment by buildings and the vulgar throng on the Leith links, actually went out of existence in 1830, only emerging six years later at Musselburgh, already used by the Musselburgh Club (formed 1774), but further out of town and so less crowded. Many of the notables preferred to make the journey to St Andrews, on which in 1834 William IV bestowed the title of Royal and Ancient Golf Club. Carnegie added to St Andrews lore by a series of verses, published in the celebrated Edinburgh magazine, *Blackwood's* (Blackwood and his son were St Andrews members). In one, Carnegie poked more or less affectionate fun at such worthies as David Baird, Campbell, Captain Moncrieffe, Colonel Playfair, the Laird of Clanronald, Sir Ralph Anstruther and the Laird of Lingo whose golf got worse as the round wore on and he increased his alcoholic intake. Another effort poked sharper fun at the professional, David Robertson, the celebrated ball-maker and caddie master:

> Davie, oldest of the cads,
> Who gives half-one to unsupicious lads,
> When he might give them two or even more
> And win, perhaps, three matches out of four,
> Is just as politic in his affairs
> As Talleyrand or Metternich in theirs.
> He has the statesmen's elements, 'tis plain,
> Cheat, flatter, humbug – anything for gain.[22]

Today's top professional golfers, closely scrutinised by crowds and television cameras, have considerably higher ethical standards than the average club member – but perhaps it was different then.

Public school games

The age of reform inevitably left its mark even in the reactionary world of sport. The change began in England in the new educational establishments known as public schools. These schools were not state ventures aimed at widening access but private boarding schools for the sons of the well-to-do. They were public only in the sense that their headmasters, instead of owning the schools, were employed by trustees at a salary. This tended to weaken the masters' authority over pupils, not all of whom appreciated the privilege of being educated. Though middle class parents might support the public schools' emphasis on character-building the youths whose characters were being built could make or break a headmaster. They expected to be consulted about the appointment and subsequent conduct of their teachers and insisted on the fagging system in which small boys served an apprenticeship as slaves to bigger ones. The resulting hierarchy of discipline based on flogging, together with communal prayers and systematic study of the classics, was the principal ingredient of the public schools' offerings.

Games in such a context were not a planned part of headmasterly policy but an incidental aspect of pupil power: football in particular was the emblem of a rising generation of frustrated pent up young men. Why football? The old Shrovetide folk contests were no longer of much significance. In 1815 the antiquary William Hone had been surprised to find one surviving so close to London as Kingston upon Thames.[23] In 1825 at Beverley, when constables had been roughly treated for trying to stop a game, the magistrates handed out stiff sentences including hard labour and another local tradition ceased. two years later at Alnwick the Duke of Northumberland struck a blow for modernity by withdrawing his patronage from the annual street game and allowing the use of a field instead.[24] Over the next decades the magistrates, aided by the Peelers and their local equivalents, were to stamp out the old anarchical encounters.

But the game enjoyed powerful support in Scotland. Sir Walter Scott in 1815 helped to sponsor a match between Selkirk and Yarrow in Ettrick Forest. Broadsheets commemorating the occasion included poems by James Hogg, 'the Ettrick Shepherd', and by Scott himself:

> Then strip lads and to it, though sharp be the weather
> And if by mischance you should happen to fall
> There are worse things in life than a tumble on heather
> And life is itself but a game of football

The Duke of Buccleuch graced the occasion and Scott's fifteen year old son carried the Buccleuch flag in the ceremonial parade, prompting his biographer to comment that the great poet 'would rather have seen his heir carry the banner of Bellenden gallantly at a football match on Carterhaugh than he would have heard that the boy had attained the highest honours of the first university in Europe'.[25]

Another more prosaic reason for football's recrudescence was, however, its primitive appeal to the well-fed, high-spirited sprigs of good families, despatched to live in herds at boarding schools. Public school football was organised by senior boys as a hierarchical virility contest and played according to rules heavily influenced by the idiosyncrasies of the environment. Hence the Wall Game at Eton, whereby the early nineteenth century annual matches were being played between fee-payers and scholars on a long thin strip of turf adjoining a high wall, continued after the acquisition of a much wider, unwalled pitch on which the field game developed. (Both, it seems, were eleven-a-side, presumably on the analogy of cricket; and the newer field game used small goals, like those in hockey, another game apparently played at Eton at this time.) At Charterhouse and Westminster football was played in the cloisters which meant that buttresses were part of the pitch, and in another Westminster game two pairs of trees were used for goals. At Harrow they played in the old muddy schoolyard until a new wing was added in 1823, at which time the yard was levelled and gravelled and big games moved out into a field, very muddy but with plenty of space.

More space did not always mean more open play. Big games were about power, not style. A Carthusian recalled:

> When the game was played by a limited number it was a really fine game. But when a big game was ordered, such as Gownboys versus School, in which all the boys used to block the respective goals, it was in my opinion a very poor game indeed, consisting of a series of 'squashes' or dead blocks, in which the ball was entirely lost to sight, and a mass of humanity surged and heaved senselessly, often for as much as half an hour at a time'.[26]

The fact that the extra players brought in included the smaller fry emphasised the relationship of school football to the fagging system. At Shrewsbury footballing was known as 'douling', the same word, based on the Greek for slave, as was used for fagging.

Headmasters and many Old Boys did not like the new trend. Samuel Butler, headmaster of Shrewsbury School from 1798 to 1836 thought football 'more fit for farm boys than young gentlemen'.[27] An old Etonian wrote in 1831: 'I cannot consider the game of football as being at all gentlemanly. It is a game which the common people of Yorkshire are particularly partial to, the tips of their shoes being heavily shod with iron, and frequently death has been known to ensue.'[28] This was perhaps an exaggeration, but a more sober Carthusian account rings true: 'there were a good many broken shins, for most of the fellows had iron tips to their very strong shoes'.[29] Yet they were as powerless to stop the new games as Cnut to turn back the waves.

Within half a century football had become important enough for the products of the greatest schools in the land to squabble over its origins. Rugby even set up a committee of Old Boys whose solemn but not very objective enquiries led to the construction of a plaque commemorating one William Webb Ellis who as early as 1823 'with a fine disregard for the rules of Football as played in his time, first took the ball in his arms and ran with it'. This illicit action, it might be thought, would be a puny enough excuse for a plaque implying that this was the origin of Rugby football, even if Ellis actually carried it out. There is no evidence that he did.

The best account of early public school games is in a work of fiction, *Tom Brown's Schooldays* by an earnest, wholehearted Christian Socialist, Thomas Hughes, based on his own days at Rugby School, beginning in 1834.[30] In his detailed description of football there is no mention of running with the ball. Indeed Hughes, when called upon to give evidence to the Old Boys' Committee, stated that in his day, though stopping the ball with the hand was allowed, running with it to score was unknown. He recalled that a big fellow called Mackie had begun to test the possibilities of carrying the ball in 1838–9 and that it finally became legal, under certain circumstances, during his own captaincy of 'Big Side' (the assembly of older boys who controlled football) in 1841–2. The Old Boys' Committee preferred the account of one Matthew Bloxam in an article in the school magazine in 1880, even though Bloxam had left the school four or five years before the alleged Ellis incident.[31] The intrinsic improbability of the Ellis myth appears in fact from Bloxam's own article, which emphasises the dependence of the game on fagging and its control by prefects or other senior boys. This control was a very serious issue in the schools. At Winchester in 1828 the commoners rebelled because the head-master appointed unacceptable prefects.[32] Rule-making and the observance of the code were just as important to Rugby's Big Side levee as to the nobility and gentry of the Star and Garter. Indeed like 'fair law' or 'shooting a sitting bird' the early rules of football begged a few questions in the interests of conformity. Tom Brown, on his first day at school, was drafted into a football match. Trampled underfoot in a scrummage and discovered afterwards 'a motionless body', Tom eventually recovered, made no complaint and earned the reputa-tion of a 'good pluckt 'un'.[33]

'Wet bobs' and 'dry bobs'

Neither the game nor Rugby School, were, however, thought of any great importance at first. It was Eton and its metropolitan rival Westminster that supplied the Old Boys who ran the country. And the sport held in highest social regard by masters as well as boys was rowing. Both schools had easy access to the river and though inter-school games of all kinds were regarded with suspicion by the authorities for fear of unruly behaviour, the two schools competed on the river whenever they got the chance. Indeed the event attracted the interest of parents and Old Boys as a suitably élitist, virile yet not violent pursuit.

The social standing of rowing on the Thames established by the Regatta had been maintained during the war years, in which three clubs, called after their boats The Star, The Arrow and The Shark, came to the fore. The Star and The Arrow amalgamated and in 1881 became part of a club called Leander which unashamedly aimed at exclusivity. The sport also attracted the attention of members of fashionable regiments who now had more time on their hands. Time trials were the first form of competition: in 1825 a Westminster School crew rowed from London to Windsor and back in 21 hours to beat the time of six gallant Guards captains the year before. Team rowing was considered superior to sculling for the schools. In wider sporting circles, however, there was more scope for individualism. When Henry C. Wingfield presented a prize in 1828 for a sculling race 'for gentlemen' it was augmented by a sweepstake of the entry fees, a happy arrangement which lasted until 1861 when the sterner concept of amateurism was introduced. In 1829 the indefatigable George Osbaldeston, no amateur and not much of a gentleman, was at the age of forty-two waggishly described by the *Sporting Magazine* as 'one of the young hands who have come into aquatic life'. His first public outing was a disaster – he lost heavily in a sculling match with a Captain Bentinck – but he took his revenge in the way he liked best in a match for 1,000 guineas. This was a four-oar challenge in which Bentinck, Lords Chetwynd and Douglas and Colonel Hobhouse of the Guards were beaten by the Squire assisted by 'three friends from offices in the city, little if at all inferior to the professionals or myself' as he modestly put it.[34]

Rowing was still a casual affair at both universities, though it was further advanced at Oxford largely because the river was in a better state. Since the river was the Thames, the Eton connection was an easy and obvious one, and Christ Church in particular benefited from an influx of Etonian 'wet bobs'. An Etonian of the 1830s later recalled the grip rowing had on the school: there were 'dry-bobs' but 'to them the real glories of Eton were never revealed'.[35] Westminster, who had acquired a new boat with sheepskin seats in 1817, were always keen to challenge Eton, but it was not until 1827 that official permission was given, after which there were regular encounters which were taken very seriously indeed. This rivalry also had an impact on Oxford: by 1822 Oxford colleges were taking part in organised bumping races in which, to compensate for the narrowness of the river, crews started off at intervals and tried to catch the boat ahead.

Cambridge was not so advanced. In 1825 St John's College students formed the Lady Margaret Boat Club, but by 1827, a contemporary recalled, Trinity was the only other college to have acquired an eight, and the only races were quasi-impromptu encounters. However, that summer a group of Cambridge students, led by Charles Wordsworth, nephew of the poet and a future public school master and bishop, challenged Oxford to a cricket match and two years later the return match was preceded by a boat race. (Wordsworth blistered his hands so badly at rowing that he could hardly hold the bat the next day.) The race aroused great interest amongst the general public, perhaps attracted by the story in the *Sporting Magazine* that £500 was at stake (Charles Merivale, future Dean of Ely Cathedral, felt it necessary to assure his mother that he was not involved in any bets.)[36]

The highlight of the 1830 season was a randan match in which Osbaldeston and Ross competed, each supported by a pair of professionals. The following year a grandly named World Sculling Championship was launched (the finalists were both London Watermen) but generally speaking the professionals served the gentlemen either as junior partners or as coaches. The job of coach usually included participating in eight-oared races as coxswain, a function of particular importance when bumping and boring were allowed. When Eton and Westminster met in 1831 both crews had professional watermen as coxes. Westminster's Paddy Noulton, renowned for his crafty tactics and ability to spoil, was also employed by Leander for important races, such as when, that same year (calling themselves London), they took on Oxford in a match for £200 when Oxford's projected race against Cambridge had fallen through.

Both coaching and coxing were soon hotly disputed aspects of the honour code. For the second Oxford and Cambridge Boat Race in 1836 both crews used amateur coxes, but whereas Oxford retained their professional coach Cambridge were coached by their cox Mr T. S. Egan who believed professional coaches too 'limited'. Both Eton and Westminster kept professional coxes and Paddy Noulton was at the centre of a heated debate after a bruising and bad-tempered encounter in 1836. The circle of public school rowing was increased in 1835 when Charles Wordsworth, now a master at Winchester, imported a boat and began to teach the boys on half holidays. But Eton versus Westminster was *the* race. The following year the two schools were honoured by the presence of the King, an avowed Eton partisan. It was an anti-climax. Westminster established a commanding lead and William pulled down the blinds of his carriage and went home. This turned out to be his last public appearance, a suitably muted end to his bewildered reign, but confirmation of the advance of the 'wet bobs'.

The range of sports available to the leisured classes was widening even as the circle of privilege widened with the country's growing prosperity. Rowing offered the opportunity for regular but relatively brief periods of strenuous exercise combined with congenial social activities. Soon 'wet bobs' were organising clubs and regattas all over the country. Chester was one of the first to achieve prominence, in 1832, and two years later the new Durham University staged the first of its annual regattas: both the Wear and the neighbouring Tyne were to be important rowing centres.[37]

By contrast cricket was undergoing one of its periodic crises, this time centring on Lord's ground. It needed a rescue act from Mr William Ward, Wykehamist Member of Parliament and fanatical cricketer, who bought Tom Lord's interest in the ground in 1825 to prevent his selling the ground for housing development as a preliminary to retirement. Thus the game was assured of a gracious setting for prestigious encounters such as Eton versus Harrow, introduced almost incidentally but with lasting impact in 1833. As *The Times* put it

> On the morning of Friday, after winning the match with Winchester, the gentlemen of Eton entered the field at Lord's with eleven gentlemen of Harrow School, and a similar assemblage of spectators as honoured the contending parties with their presence on the previous day congregated on this occasion. We noticed upwards of thirty carriages containing ladies, cn the ground alongside the pavilion.[38]

William Ward was also influential in resolving a crisis concerning the development of the game itself. Ward had been a big hitter of underarm bowling and had shared Beauclerk's reservations about the new style, but he was a much more open-minded character and, with Beauclerk retiring from active cricket in 1826, when Ward made runs against the new style the following year he supported its legalisation. This, in 1828, saved cricket from the antiquarian fate of stool-ball and the like.

One of the great exponents of the new style, Alfred Mynn, was cricket's equivalent of Captain Becher, technically a gentleman but not quite from the top drawer. Mynn, from a farming family and with vague commercial interests in the hop-trade, was more than once imprisoned for debt. He spent most of his early summers doing what he was best at – playing cricket – getting a share in gate-money and receiving the proceeds of testimonial matches. This certainly brought him more income than the out-and-out professionals. But there were changes for them, too. In 1833 Fuller Pilch of Norfolk had taken on and beaten the Northern champion, Thomas Marsden of Sheffield, at single-wicket in two matches home and away before big crowds. Several Kent clubs were at once ready with lucrative offers for Pilch with ground-keeping, public houses and so forth to augment his cricketing earnings.[39]

The game's advance helped to reinforce the chauvinistic tendency of cricket lovers, well exemplified by Revd John Mitford's review of Nyren's account of Hambledon 'Cricket is the pride and privilege of the Englishman alone – into this, his noble and favourite amusement, no other people have ever pretended to penetrate; a Frenchman or a German would not know which end of a bat they were to hold.' But Mitford's England was little England indeed: he went on to declare that 'so fine, so scientific and so elaborate is the skill regarding it that only a small part of England has yet acquired a knowledge of it . . . In this Kent has always been pre-eminent.[40] In fact in the first North versus South encounter at Lord's in 1836 the North won, another signal of impending social change.

'Where were you, Mr Hazlitt?'

The new bowling, though dubbed 'march of intellect' by the conventional, was manifestly more physically testing than the old. And virility was John Bull's greatest pride. Hence for all the reforming influences and new sporting fashions that were in the air it was the style and ethos of the prize-ring, shaped by earlier generations, that governed the manly clashes central to the honour code of public schoolboys. The youngest son of the future Earl of Shaftesbury, who was killed in a fist-fight at Eton in 1825, might have survived a simple schoolboy scrap but the affair was conducted like a professional prize-fight. So when Ashley minimus flagged, taking a thrashing from a much bigger boy, his seconds, who included his older brother, used the respite to pour half a pint of brandy into him. Fortified but bemused he was so battered around the temples that he died.

Significantly Pierce Egan by this time was proclaiming the decline of the Ring, not for excessive violence but for want of it. Describing a bout in 1824 between Bishop Sharp, 'the rope-spinner', and Alick Reid, 'the Chelsea snob' Egan complained 'The fight, if it could be so termed, did not occupy more than three minutes, and to be dragged sixteen miles from the metropolis to witness such a representation of fighting was truly disgusting. But *Milling* may be said to be at an end: the *Beaks* will have little if any more trouble to interrupt it.'[41] Such rhetorical flourishes served to emphasise the absurdly high expectations built up by the modern troubadours. Apart from Egan himself and his journalistic imitators like Vincent Dowling there had been plenty of dilettante support from highbrow writers. In 1816 *Blackwood*'s satirical commemoration of the demise of the rumbustious Irish pugilist by a 'Luctus to Dan Donnelly' in the manner of various classical authors indicated the seriousness with which intellectuals and creative writers were treating this basic sport. Byron immortalised John Jackson in a fulsome footnote to *Don Juan*.[42] Both Thomas Moore (whose works included *Tom Cribb's Memorial to Congress*) and John Keats were enthusiastic spectators at the last fight of the lightweight champion, Jack Randall.

Some semblance of balance was restored by a sympathetic but more astringent writer, William Hazlitt, who put Randall's reputation for chivalry in the ring into perspective. Hazlitt, who had visited Randall's hostelry to find out where the forthcoming fight between Bill Neate and Tom Hickman was to be held, made the mistake of asking for a mutton chop 'when the conqueror in thirteen battles was more full of blue ruin than good manners' and concluded that, whatever his prowess in the ring, Randall was no gentleman. This astringency is part of the attraction of Hazlitt's essay *The Fight*. His description of the fight itself, between Neate, yet another Bristol butcher, and Hickman, called 'the Gasman' after the new incandescent style of lighting, occupies only two pages out of sixteen. And his account is vivid rather than technically illuminating. The context is all – the visit to Randall's, the two-day journey to the venue only to find all the inns full; the setting up of the ring 'on a gentle eminence . . . shrouded by covered carts, gigs and carriages'; the huge crowds, the flags, streamers and music; and the laconic summary 'Gully had been down to see Neate and backed him considerably . . . About two hundred thousand pounds were pending.'[43]

Egan's disregard for mere reality was reflected in the increasing flamboyance of his style, which incorporated bizarre juxtapositions of the stately and the slangy, circumlocutions and weird parodies of the Augustan poetic diction that highbrow radicals like Wordsworth and Coleridge were now beginning to question. When much was spent on food and drink Egan wrote 'a dollop of blunt was got rid of in the peck and booze way'. When it suddenly came on to rain as the crowd walked to the Painter versus Oliver fight in 1820 'The hedges were now resorted to, and hundreds sought for shelter' and the 'daffy and eaudevie were tossed off like milk to put the toddlers in spirits'.[44] It is a kind of wild poetry. 'Here were the NIB SPRINGS in their gigs, buggies and dog carts, and the TIDY ONES on their trotters, all alive and leaping.'[45]

The verbal fireworks disguise the actual state of the pugilistic art. Boxing had experienced a resurgence in style and sportsmanship when Tom Spring, Cribb's protégé and adopted son, took the championship in 1823. Yet the following year Egan was predicting its demise. As his friend and rival Vincent Dowling put it: 'The Corinthians . . . have ceased to grant either the light of their countenances or the aid of their purses towards the encouragement of the Ring.'[46] Happily the Pugilistic Club, though somewhat faded in glory, still gave the aid of their purses to the two contests in 1824 in which Spring faced Irish champion Jack Langan. The first bout, at Worcester racecourse in January, showed that there was no lack of public interest. All seats, including the ten shilling grandstand ones extended by two sets of scaffolding, were filled, according to Egan, three hours beforehand, and the lower orders had to stand up to their knees in mud. Spring, dressed 'remarkably genteel', threw

his hat into the ring and waited for his opponent. There were moments of unexpected drama, in the tension of waiting, when one of the scaffolds suddenly collapsed, but order was restored and battle commenced.

It was, however, so frequently interrupted by invasions of roughs from the outer rings despite the ministrations of ex-pugilists and 'constables' with long poles, that the referee, Colonel Berkeley, kept threatening to stop the fight, before Langan succumbed in the seventy-seventh round. Making bricks without straw, Egan resorted to playful hyperbole – 'Where were you, Mr Hazlitt? . . . Even the celebrated pencil of a George Cruikshank would be at fault to give the richness of its effect' – before getting down to describing the fight.[47] The return contest required even more descriptive skill. Egan had been deputed by the Pugilistic Club to make the match, and after some difficulty it was staged in a ploughed field near Chichester. It was quite well-attended but, though Langan did his best, his resistance merely delayed the inevitable and reduced the excitement, making the fight long (seventy-six rounds) and, one suspects, more than a little boring.

Spring's knuckles gave way under the strain and his successor, Jem Ward, did nothing to reinstate chivalry. He was a coal-heaver, rejoicing thereby in the soubriquet 'the Black Diamond', a talented painter, violinist and singer with more interest in entertaining than in the purity of the pugilistic art. The champion's form could be in-and-out. Peter Crawley, who beat Ward on an occasion when the odds were right, reputedly gave up the Ring for the purer air of cock-fighting. Ward himself was obliged to retire through the stresses of defeating an Irishman, Simon Byrne, who afterwards fatally injured a Scot, Sandy McKay, in a bout refereed by Squire Osbaldeston. When Byrne was prosecuted for manslaughter the magistrate, acquitting him, made scathing comments about those of higher station who ought to have been in court and it cost Osbaldeston several hundred pounds to escape arraignment.[48] Byrne himself died as a result of a gruelling contest with James 'Deaf' Burke in 1833 after which the new champion skipped off to America until the dust settled.

It was the end of an era. Jackson closed his rooms and the Pugilistic Club dissolved. Egan, ever the optimist, became a fervent supporter of its infinitely less socially-distinguished successor, the Daffy Club. Its very name, over-elaborately explained by Egan, indicated its raffish nature – it was one of the many names for gin, which as Egan authoritatively explained was called white wine by the squeamish fair one, blue ruin by the swell chaffs, Ould Tom by the laundress, max by the drug fiddler, flash of lightning by the costermonger, jacky by the hoarse cyprian, stark naked by the link-boy and mudlarks, and fuller's earth by the out-and-outers but Daffy by the Fancy.[49]

The president was Jemmy Soames, a bum-bailiff described by an Egan imitator as 'as good a fellow in his ways as ever *tapped a sly one* on the *shoulder-joint* or let fly a *ca-sa* at your goods and chattels'. Amongst the leading members were Lucky Bob, 'a fellow of another stamp', Lawyer L—E 'a true sportsman whether for the turf or for the chase', betting the odds with his brother Adey, Tom Spring (carrying a fighting cock in a bag) and Scroggins and Turner, heroes of a great battle in 1817.[50] But its main stay was Egan, who gave it a kind of gas-lit glory.

The Daffy Club met in the upper rooms of various public houses, but most notably at the castle Tavern in Holborn, kept first by Bob Gregson and then by Tom Belcher. The landlords of metropolitan taverns had to be just as sensitive to new sporting fashions as their counterparts in the country cut off by the railway. To the old Cock, Bull and Bear signboards were now added novelties like the Dog and Duck. To such outposts Londoners could take their dogs to compete for a pinioned duck in a pond. Nearer the city centre there was more attention to the new racquet games, spin-offs from the revival of tennis stimulated when Philip Cox of the St James' Club beat the seemingly per-manent French champion Barcellon. These derivative games, much enjoyed by patrons of city public houses, were also boosted by the interest of three captive groups who, like the monastic clergy and soldiery of the middle ages, found themselves with time and energy on their hands and with walls and yards to play in.

The first of these was in the public schools, where fives and rackets, adapted to the accident of physical environment, such as the chapel steps at Eton, became a consuming passion and a basis for organised competition. Thus a new wing at Harrow, putting a stop to yard football, offered a gable-end against which racket players developed such skills in what became known as 'open-court' play that the school tennis professional and national champion, Pitman, found it worth his while to produce special equipment. Other schools developed their own variants. Fives, for instance, a name applied at first somewhat loosely to all kinds of handball, with or without rackets (perhaps by association with the slang phrase fives, as in bunch of fives, a fist) came to have three different codes Eton, Rugby and Winchester.[51] A second important influence was that of the armed services: both the navy, at Dartmouth and the army at Woolwich had special racket courts built and were later responsible for spreading the game to the far corners of the earth. However, the foremost breeding grounds were undoubtedly the debtor's prisons. In the famous account of these remarkable institutions in Dickens' *The Pickwick Papers* there are references to the racket court in the Fleet, formed, as at Harrow, by the disposition of the walls. *Pickwick* was written in 1837 but the game was well established long before then. A painting by Rowlandson in 1807 shows prisoners playing and a piece by Hazlitt, himself an addict, suggests a flourishing competitive scene in 1820 by which time one Robert MacKay claimed the world rackets championship.

Hazlitt does not mention MacKay but recalls an earlier era in which John Davies was supreme. 'He was also', writes Hazlitt, 'a first-rate tennis player and an excellent fives-player. In the Fleet or King's Bench he would have stood against Powell, who was reckoned the best open-ground player of his time.' Powell, the keeper of the Fives Court in St Martin's Lane, could always 'fill his gallery at half-a-crown a head'. The character with whom Hazlitt concluded his essay, however, was John Cavanagh, 'the famous hand-fives player'. Cavanagh, a debonair Irish house-painter who played for wagers and dinners was not an habitué of the Fleet: he would perform at the Fives Court or in casual encounters at the Rosemary Branch, Copenhagen House or one of the numerous public houses with courts, often in the vicinity of the prisons.

Cavanagh's death, after a three-year illness, prompted Hazlitt to philosophical speculation:

> When a person dies, who does anything better than anyone else in the world, it leaves a gap in society . . . It may be said that there are things of more importance than striking a ball against a wall – there are things, indeed, that make more noise and do as little good, such as making war and peace, making speeches and answering them, making verses and blotting them, making money and throwing it away.[52]

The thought was very much of its time not merely as an apologia for sport and its values but as a harbinger of the slow but relentless advance of democracy.

Notes

1 For the background see E. L. Woodward, *The Age of Reform*, (2nd edn), Oxford, 1962.
2 'John Bull' in *The Sketch Book of Geoffrey Crayon. Gent* 1819. (1843 edn.) p. 366.
3 *The Round Table*, 1817, Everyman edition, London, 1936, p. 99.
4 *Rural Rides*, 1830, ed. G. Woodcock, Harmondsworth, 1967, p. 243.
5 'Colonel Peter Hawker' in E. Parker (ed.), *The Shooting Week-end Book*, London, 1934, pp. 215–24.
6 *Colonel George Hanger to all Sportsmen*, London, 1814, in Parker *Shooting Week-end Book*, p. 246.
7 E. D. Cuming (ed.), *Squire Osbaldeston: His Autobiography*, London, 1926, p. 232.
8 In *Rural Sports* (2nd edn), 1812.
9 Cuming, p. 323.
10 Ibid., pp. 48–50, 55, 154.
11 C. A. Wheeler (ed.), *Sportscrapiana* (2nd edn), 1868, p. 72.
12 F. Gale, *Echoes from Old Cricket Fields*, London, 1871, p. 55.
13 F. S. Ashley-Cooper and Lord Harris, *Lord's and MCC*, London, 1914, p. 80.
14 H. Hutchinson-Bradburne in M. Seth Smith (ed.), *The Horse*, London, 1979, p. 85.
15 Cuming, *Squire Osbaldeston*, p. 77.
16 'Sir Mark Chase', quoted by Cuming, *Squire Osbaldeston*, p. 230.
17 Cuming, *Squire Osbaldeston*, p. 77.
18 J. Mortimer *The Jockey Club*, London, 1958, p. 59–60. The facility was extended beyond Newmarket in 1832.

19 Mr Sponge's *Sporting Tour*, London, 1853, Chapter LXVII, p. 525.
20 For early steeplechasing see M. Seth-Smith, P. Willet, R. Mortimer, J. Lawrence, *The History of Steeplechasing*, London, 1966; V. Smith, *The Grand National*, London, 1969.
21 For sailling see D. Phillips-Birt *The History of Yachting*, London, 1974.
22 'The First Hole at St Andrew's on a Crowded Day', first published in *Blackwood's Magazine*, 1833, and 'Another Peep at the Links; both published in *Golfiana*, Edinburgh, 1842, quoted and discussed in R. Browning, *A History of Golf*, London, 1955, pp. 53–8.
23 *The Everyday Book*, London, 1827–32, quoted in P. M. Young, *The History of British Football*, London 1973 edn., p. 24.
24 M. Marples *A History of Football*, London, 1954, pp. 101–2.
25 J. G. Lockhart, *Memoirs of Sir Walter Scott*, Edinburgh, 1900. vol. V, p. 453 (Magoun).
26 G. S. Davies, *Charterhouse in London*, London, 1922, p. 295, quoted in E. Dunning and K. Sheard, *Barbarians, Gentlemen and Players*, Oxford, 1979.
27 J. B. Oldham, *History of Shrewsbury School*, Shrewsbury, 1852, p. 231, quoted in Dunning and Sheard, *Barbarians*, p. 47.
28 Anon., *Reminiscences of Eton*, Chichester, 1831, p. 47, quoted in Marples, *History of Football*, p. 96.
29 Revd T. Mozley in A. H. Tod (ed.) *Charterhouse* London, 1900, p. 124, quoted in Dunning and Sheard, *Barbarians* p. 57.
30 London, 1851, Chapter 5, pp. 61–78.
31 'Meteor' no. 157, 1880 quoted in Dunning and Sheard, *Barbarians*, p. 55.
32 E. C. Mack, *Public Schools and British Opinion*, London, 1938, p. 80 quoted in Dunning and Sheard, *Barbarians*, p. 52.
33 Hughes, *Tom Brown's Schooldays*, p. 78.
34 Cuming, *Squire Osbaldeston*, p. 11.
35 J. A. Bridges, *A Sportsman of Limited Income*, London, 1910, p. 22.
36 H. Cleaver, *A History of Rowing*, London, 1954, p. 95. See also R. D. Burnell *The Oxford and Cambridge Boat Race*, Oxford, 1954. C. Dodd, *The Oxford and Cambridge Boat Race*, London 1983 updates the story.
37 Cleaver, *History of Rowing*, pp. 52–68.
38 30 August 1833.
39 For the cricketing significance and social status of Mynn, Pilch and Ward see the respective articles in *Dictionary of National Biography*.
40 *Gentleman's Magazine*, 1833. The Belief in Kent's supremacy was of long standing; cf. Lord Harley, describing a journey through Kent in 1723:' the men in Tunbridge and the Dartford men were warmly engaged at the sport of cricket, which of all the people of England the Kentish fold are most renowned for.' Historical Manuscripts Commission, vol. VI (1901).
41 *Boxiana*, new series, vol. III, 1825. Snob = shoemaker.
42 'To my old friend and corporeal pastor and master, John Jackson Esq., Professor of Pugilism', *Don Juan*, Book IX, 1819–24.
43 First appeared in *New Monthly* Magazine, January 1822. Blue ruin = gin.
44 *Boxiana*, vol. III, 1821.
45 *A Picture of the Fancy*, see note 31, Chapter 7 above.
46 Supplement to *Bell's Weekly Dispatch*, 11 January 1824.
47 *Boxiana*, new series, 1825. Tom Spring was eulogised by Borrow (*Lavengro*, p. 163) 'six-foot Englishman of the brown eye, worthy to have carried a six-foot bow at Flodden, where England's Yeomen triumphed over Scotland's king, his clans and chivalry'.
48 Cuming, *Squire Osbaldeston*, p. 262.

49 *Sporting Anecdotes, Original and Selected*, London, 1825. p. 351, quoted in full in J. C. Reid, *Bucks and Bruisers*, London, 1971, pp. 44–6. For surviving slang coined by Egan see Reid, pp. 69–70.
50 B. Blackmantle, *The English Spy*, London, 1825–6, pp. 325–9.
51 See article by J. Arnan Tait in E. Bell (ed.), *Handbook of Athletic Sports*, London, 1890, vol. I.
52 'The Indian Jugglers' in *Table Talk*, 1821–2, ed. W. C. Hazlitt 1870, pp. 103–21. Hazlitt was a fanatical rackets player, lying awake at night worrying over missed shots: see A. Birrell, *William Hazlitt*, London, 1902, p. 150.

CHAPTER NINE

Victorian dawn

1837–1851

There was excitement in the air when the young Princess Victoria succeeded the old sailor king, William IV. Tennyson greeted the new dawn with rapture:

> When I dipt into the future far as human eye could see
> Saw the vision of the world, and all the wonder that would be.[1]

Lord Melbourne was not given to visionary wonder but, charmed by the young Queen, he took on a new lease of Prime Ministerial life. Victoria shared his pleasure in riding: though tiny, she looked good on a horse, and knew it. Melbourne rode proudly by her side in great cavalcades along the Berkshire lanes. Their innocent pleasure in visits to the races was, however, marred in 1839, when, after blunders over court appointments, Victoria was hissed by Tory ladies at Ascot and someone called out 'Mrs Melbourne'. The Prime Minister remained the dominant influence in her life for two more years, but after her marriage to Prince Albert of Saxe-Gotha, though she retained an affectionate regard for Melbourne, she began to consider him superficial.

Progress

He was certainly obsolescent. After centuries of domination by landed interests the country now had to try to cope with industrial change. Tinkering with the Corn Laws was no longer enough; it merely restricted foreign trade and brought recession in the cotton industry. Fortunately expansion of the railways, linking the ports with the factories and the coal and iron fields, helped regain momentum in industrial production and revitalise the economy. Exports virtually doubled between 1830 and 1850, two-thirds of the expansion being in cotton goods, dramatically increasing profits and investments. The workers did less well and the new Poor Law of 1834 which put its trust in workhouses kept paupers alive but at the cost of human dignity.[2]

The political pendulum swung erratically. After five challenging years in office Peel's Conservatives, who had felt obliged to re-introduce income tax (seven pence in the pound, old money, approximately 3% for the upper tenth of the population with income over £100) were given a sharp reminder of electoral realities and Lord John Russell's conversion to repeal of the Corn Laws helped bring the Whigs to power in 1846. This was the time of the potato blight in Ireland whose eighteen million population, totally dependent on agriculture, fell by a million through starvation and by a million-and-a-half through emigration in the next four years. Ireland's deep and lasting

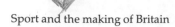

resentment was intensified when after the 'hungry forties' England reached new levels of prosperity.

They were good years for the rich. The average annual income of the richest 1% in 1800, £130, had by 1850 become £200, and the cost of living, furthermore, had also fallen by almost a third. But many ordinary folk also did well, at least maintaining average earning level, despite increased numbers as well as feeling the benefit of lower prices. The young German radical Engels, currently managing his father's factory in Manchester, in 1844 confidently predicted revolution.[3] The following year Disraeli, on his way to the top of the Conservative party, gave the sub-title 'Two Nations' to his cautionary tale *Sybil*. But in 1848, as the rest of Europe was swept by revolution, Dickens' latest novel *Dombey and Son* offered a vivid sketch of the reasons for England's escape. As the industrialist Dombey ceremoniously begins his first railway journey Mr Toodle, dressed in a canvas suit abundantly smeared with coal and oil, ducks his head at the great mogul and says 'I shall have the honour of stokin' of you down, Sir.'[4]

To such pragmatic working classes having a job and trying to secure a good wage were more important than improvement of working conditions – shorter hours meant less money if you were not on piece work. Consequently industrial reform and the extension of working class leisure owed less to Marxism than to old-fashioned philanthropy. The Ten Hour Act of 1847, proposing a reduced daily stint for juvenile and female textile workers, was sponsored by Lord Shaftesbury who called Socialism and Chartism 'the two great demons in morals and politics' and regarded State-sponsored elementary education as 'a water rate to extinguish religious fire among young people'. Trade unions, whose male members in the cotton mills were threatened with reduction of hours, supported the measure not as a great step towards liberation but as a work-sharing gesture in the battle against the encroachment of machines.[5]

Nevertheless their members took full advantage of the increased leisure the law now thrust on them. In 1850 the mills were ordered to close before two o'clock on Saturdays, and in the prevailing atmosphere of prosperity market forces soon led individual employers to improve even on this, without loss of pay. The process began with specialised workers in the most prosperous trades and localities and worked its way down to the unskilled.

Science promised progress without pain. Lofty-minded thinkers like Prince Albert, inspired by the promise of Bentham and the Utilitarians, thought the greatest good of the greatest number could be achieved through a scientific approach. Unfortunately the woolly-minded British were quite unable to grasp this or to visualise a world conducted on rational principles. The Prince Consort was particularly dismayed by Lord Palmerston, Russell's Foreign Secretary, who thought the British way of life and liberty so manifestly superior that he took every opportunity, by brinkmanship, gun-boat diplomacy or whatever, to put things over on potential enemies. So when the exasperated Russell replaced Palmerston by young Lord Granville in the interests of free trade, Albert seized his opportunity to demonstrate its possibilities.

The Great Exhibition of 1851 was an outward and visible sign of the confluence of industrial, intellectual, artistic and political ideas that underlay the notion of progress in which he so fervently believed. The government declined to pay for it but Albert raised the money himself, and as chairman of the organising committee supervised the enterprise in meticulous detail: 'I do feel proud at the thought of what my beloved Albert's great mind has conceived', Victoria confided to her diary.[6] And she was most indignant when the fashionable set objected to Paxton's Crystal Palace for the Exhibition being built in Hyde Park because it impinged on their fashionable riding track in Rotten Row.

Victoria had come a long way since her cavalcades with Melbourne. Albert himself greatly enjoyed riding and was proud of his 'beautiful seat', but sternly disapproved of the horsey set. When he made his first and last appearance in Parliament in 1846 (to speak in favour of free trade) the Queen was furious at his hostile reception by the Protectionists, 'gentlemen who did nothing but hunt all day, drank Claret or Port Wine in the evening and never studied or read about any of these questions'.[7] As for the Turf, the royal couple had attended the Derby in 1840 and had been received very civilly by the crowds but never went again. It was just not their kind of scene.

Horses in the railway age

They can scarcely be blamed. The Turf was both dissolute and corrupt and the Jockey Club's reforming Steward Lord George Bentinck was a hypocrite. In 1838 the Jockey Club expressed 'extreme disapprobation of horses being entered for races without . . . owners . . . trying to win with them'. There was serious doubt about the identity of the Derby winner in 1839, and the next year it was won by a four year old impersonating the 50-to-1 Little Wonder. The trainer won £18,000 but nothing could be proved. Racing, according to Charles Greville, who was in a good position to know, was a 'system of plunder', an addiction like 'dram-drinking'. Greville himself was involved in scandals in 1842 and 1843. He noted in his diary, 'I grow more and more disgusted with the atmosphere of villainy I am forced to breathe – it is not easy to keep oneself undefiled.' And when Bentinck produced evidence of swindling and became the hero of the hour Greville wrote bitterly, 'What a humbug it all is . . . if everybody knew all that I knew of his tricks and artifices, what a rogue he would be thought.'[8]

In 1842 the 1710 Qui Tam Act was invoked against a gaming-house owner who had to flee the country to avoid a £3,500 fine. But when the following year it was invoked against Bentinck, General Peel and other members of the Jockey Club the ranks closed. The Duke of Richmond introduced a Manly Sports Bill in the House of Lords, and secured suspension of the Qui Tam Act until a Parliamentary Select Committee – which he was to chair – reported. Meanwhile, though Bentinck exposed the false claims of a Mr Wood, the owner of the four year old Maccabeus, who was accused of switching it with a three year old, Running Rein, in the 1844 Derby, by the time the case came to court Running Rein had disappeared along with the bookmaker Goodman Levy.

The Jockey Club made a rod for their own backs: as the judge put it, 'If gentlemen condescend to race with blackguards they must condescend to expect to be cheated.'[9] They were safer in Crockford's exclusive St James' Street Club. This discreet haven for the great went undisturbed though strenuous efforts were made to curb the activities of back-street gambling dens. Restrictive legislation in 1839 was ineffective because the new police force could not cope with the touts and bruisers and this was the main preoccupation of the Select Committee. Crockford, though obliged to appear before it, refused to 'divulge the pursuits of private gentlemen'. Crockford himself joined his maker in 1844 following heavy losses in the Running Rein affair – dead of a Derby Winner, the wits said – but his soul went marching on.

The Gaming Act of 1845 made life easier for the police by authorising them to enter suspected premises following a complaint by two householders. But during the debate preceding the Act Lord Brougham warned Parliament that 'gambling had far more fatal consequences and was far more injurious to morals among the inferior classes than among the superior classes'[10] and this remained the philosophy behind the administration of the law. The Duke of Richmond did his duty, the Qui Tam Act was abolished and the new Gaming Act made gambling debts no longer recoverable at law but left the control of betting on sport in the hands of the sporting authorities.

As long as Bentinck was in charge there was little hope of the Turf putting its house in order, for there were blackguards inside the Jockey club as well as out. For the lower orders the 1845 Act spawned a great number of off-course betting shops – known as listers from the lists of runners they posted up. Tobacconists' shops, now proliferating after some years of declining interest in smoking, often began taking bets as a sideline to oblige customers. Listers like Dwyer's of St Martin's Lane offered better odds and took smaller stakes than Tattersalls, and many were entirely reliable and paid up promptly. Others might not be there when you went to pick up your winnings, and

Dwyer's itself folded after a ruinous 1851 Chester Cup.

The dominance of gambling interests did nothing for the quality of the racing and even Newmarket and Ascot found it hard to attract good, or even big fields. Increased prize-money was needed: the total, which had slowly gone up from £115,950 in 1807 to £143,204 in 1839, shot up to £198,990 in the next four years and helped increase income from entry fees. Proprietors of less fashionable courses also needed big crowds of spectators. Rents from caterers and other stall-holders, increased according to attendance, were the main source of income. It was usual to charge for admission to grandstands or for viewing from private carriages but early attempts to impose a general admission charge failed miserably, as when John Whyte, owner of the Bayswater Hippodrome, enclosed it and asked one shilling to go in.

The railways brought new opportunities but also new social challenges. The enterprising London and Southampton Railway Company put on eight special trains for the 1838 Derby but even this was not enough and the frustrated 5,000 waiting at Nine Elms Station with only one train left stormed the gates, requiring police intervention. Newmarket, which, like Ascot, did not want or need paying spectators, resisted proposals to build a branch line until 1847. By this time, however, lack of railway access was putting Newmarket at a disadvantage as a training centre and diminishing the attractions of the racing itself to owners. Bentinck himself had demonstrated – sneakily – the advantages of horse-vans over making racehorses walk to meetings, and rail cars were even better. Trainers could send horses further and faster, choose their races more carefully and reduce the risk of nobbling. Owners need no longer select trainers whose stables happened to be near fashionable courses. So Newmarket got a branch line, though excursion passengers found that since the stewards arranged the finishes of their races in considerately scattered fashion they still had vast distances to walk once they got there.

Bigger prize-money and the mobility offered by the railway increased the gap between the leading group of jockeys and the rest because the top men could fulfil many more engagements. Increased competition amongst these go-getters did little to improve the ethical standards of either the professionals or the few surviving gentlemen.

The average level of gentlemanly riding was now derisory and in 1845 the Jockey Club prohibited races for gentlemen riders during the regular season without express permission. The more enthusiastic, particularly hunting men or cavalry officers, turned to the less sophisticated and more rugged sport of steeplechasing in which weight was less of a problem. Many hunts and good regiments had their own private race meetings. Public steeplechases were more socially suspect but one at least, in Liverpool, secured patronage from some of the highest in the land – the Earls of Derby, Sefton, Eglinton and Wilton, Lords Stanley and Grosvenor and Bentinck himself.

It was an immediate success. 'As early as nine o'clock,' *Bell's Life* wrote of the 1839 occasion,

> the road leading to Aintree was crowded with pedestrians of the usual class, including piemen, chimney sweeps, cigar sellers, thimble-riggers and all the small fry of gaming-table keepers . . . Not a vehicle of any description that could be by any means made to go was left in town . . . For places in the omnibus, the original price of which was 2s 6d, half-a-guinea was offered and refused. The Grandstand was 7s for a single ticket and 10s for two days.[11]

The prize-money for the main race was good (53 entries, 17 runners at £20 (£5 forfeit) gave a sweepstake of £520 with £100 added) but it was unpredictable and the thrills and spills attracted the crowds more than high quality racing. Captain Becher had been expected to win but he fell at a post-and-rail fence and took refuge in a ditch that was ever after known as Becher's Brook, and the winner was the flamboyant Jem Mason.

Respectable opinion was against the very idea: 'It was no doubt a very exciting spectacle', commented the *Liverpool Mercury*, 'but we can be no more reconciled to it on that ground than we are to cock-fighting, bull-baiting or any other popular pastime which is attended by the infliction of wanton torture on any living being.'[12] The following year *The Times*, commending rowing, found it 'not a little refreshing to the lovers of old English sports to find these sorts of amusements beginning to supersede the swindling, dangerous and unsound practices of steeple-chasing, things merely set up by publicans and horse-dealers to pillage the unwary and enrich themselves'.[13] Traditional hunting men also disapproved. Nimrod predicted its early demise.[14] But by the early forties there were already sixty-six steeplechases a year and enthusiasm was mounting, not least in Ireland.

The Irish horsey set had expected to dominate the new Liverpool event – renamed the Liverpool and National in 1843 – and at first blamed their failure on the 'made up, unnatural' course, which lacked, for instance, the five foot stone walls common in Galway and Mayo. But an experiment with a wall was as disastrous for the Irish as for the English favourite, Lottery, so the stewards put in a water jump instead. It was not until 1847 that an Irish owner won what was now called the Grand National. With the great famine at its height *Bell's Life* fatuously commented, 'Though a considerable amount of cash has been carried off to the sister island, everyone is satisfied that it should find its way to places where all classes cry out that they so very much want it.'[15] It seems unlikely that a great deal found its way to the starving masses.

Surtees' verdict on the new sport was predictably harsh. Steeplechasing, he reckoned, combined the worst features of hunting and of flat-racing 'having neither the wild excitement of the one, nor the accurate calculating qualities of the other'. They were generally 'ill-arranged things': few gentlemen would ever act as stewards a second time. He reckoned that the publicans, deprived of the carriage trade by the railways, were chiefly to blame. If coursing was out – because landowners shot hares nowadays – they put on a Grand Aristocratic Stakes:

> The more snobbish a thing is the more certain they are to call it aristocratic. When it is too bad for anything they call it a 'Grand'. A few friends or farmers might have got up a quiet thing amongst themselves, but it would never seem a regular trade transaction, with its swell mob, sham captains, and all the paraphernalia of odd-laying, 'secret tips' and market rigging.[16]

Fox-hunting men in this new era saw themselves as defenders of the environment. The new 'railroads' were particularly obnoxious to F. P. Delme Radcliffe, landowner, brilliant gentleman rider and MFH, who thought they must become the most oppressive monopoly ever inflicted upon a free country. He foresaw tenantless inns, unemployment and a vast reduction in the number of horses.[17] What irked these conservationists most, however, was the influx of townsfolk, vulgarians with more money than manners. Nevertheless their money was very attractive and much needed. Even the most modest hunt nowadays cost masters two or three thousand a year which added the nuisance of seeking subscriptions to keeping the farming community sweet. To the lesser hunts the rail-borne vulgarians were a god-send. According to Surtees, Jorrocks, the London grocer whom the railway allowed to tour the country, Beckford in one pocket, order-book in the other, became the Master of the ailing Handley Cross solely because he was 'as rich as Croesus'.[18]

Violence old and new

It is a nice point whether the fox-hunting upstart Jorrocks was as bad as what old Parson Jack Russell called the 'gormandising battue-shooter' who often enough came from aristocratic circles. The combined effects of the railways, the 1831 Game Act and the Purday breech-loader were certainly devastating. The Game Book of Colonel Rawsthorne's Penwortham estate in the early Victorian years tells its own story (see Table 9.1).[19]

Prodigious bags of game were an accepted feature of shooting-weekend hospitality; but they could also be a source of profit. The new satirical magazine *Punch* suggested that the Duke of Marlborough should add 'licensed to sell game' to his crest. Nor did it escape notice that the high-minded Prince Albert was a fervent shooter.

Table 9.1

Year	Partridges	Pheasants	Woodcock	Snipe	Wildfowl	Hares	Rabbits
1837	76	356	22	201	32	236	1225
1838	188	636	16	73	20	245	1999
1839	104	230	18	45	23	145	1647

When Victoria acquired Balmoral in 1848 this 'pretty little Castle in the old Scotch style' was used for family holidays, the royal couple idyllically fishing for trout from a boat, with Albert taking over the rowing to allow one of the ghillies to play the bagpipes. But the Queen's diaries also record '½ shooting expeditions', beginning with pony-rides when Albert would go off in search of deer or ptarmigan while Victoria sketched. The Prince Consort took his shooting very seriously indeed, and his 'angelic good humour' could fade if he did badly, so that Victoria sometimes dare not ask how he had fared.[20]

Other cruel sports persisted. Cock-fighting became illegal in 1849, but it continued nevertheless, especially outside the range of the metropolitan police. In the capital there were two compensatory vogues in the sporting inns. One was ratting. Perhaps the most famous rat-pit was that of Jeremy Shaw, an expugilist, where the turnover was between 300 and 700 rats a week, and where handling rats dead and alive was a mark of virility.[21]. The dogs pitted against them were often little bigger than the rats: Henry Mayhew, the journalist, described the 5½ lb wonder, Tiny, who wore a lady's bracelet as a collar and had killed two hundred rats.[22] Another London attraction was dog-fighting; in some hostelries there were contests every night and for some it was the sole topic of conversation. George Borrow recalled the scorn of a dog-fancier when the topic of religion came up. 'Religion, indeed! If it were not for the rascally law my pit would fill better on Sundays than any other time. Who would go to church when they could come to my pit? Religion! why the parsons themselves come to my pit.'[23]

The pugilists who kept the pubs were themselves a major attraction. There had been a revival of interest, beginning in Nottingham. The best of the new school was a streetwise eighteen year old, William Thompson, known as Bendigo (because, apparently, two of his brothers were called Shadrach and Meshach), who was trying to keep his pipe-smoking old mother out of the workhouse. Bendigo had the knack of infuriating opponents by evasive tactics, particularly the huge Ben Caunt, a Nottingham rival, whom he tempted into a disqualification, and when Caunt, after winning the return by bear-hugging and other rough behaviour, went off to America in search of easier pickings Bendigo beat the former champion Deaf Burke, newly-returned, in ten rounds.

So when Caunt himself came back to keep the Coach and Horses in St Martin's Lane, the inevitable decider was keenly anticipated. It was not so easily arranged. After various abortive efforts with the two principals and half the crowd going to different venues on two occasions they finally got together in the depths of Oxfordshire. The referee, Squire Osbaldeston, no guarantee of moral probity, seemed more conscious of the menacing presence of Bendy's Nottingham 'lambs', than of Broughton's rules and brought the long-drawn out affair to an end in doubtful circumstances. *Bell's Life* reckoned it 'a disgraceful and disgusting exhibition' that had given a blow to 'the boxing school' from which it could never recover.[24]

Yet when Bendigo retired he had a town in Australia named after him and was eulogised in a poem by Adam Lindsay Gordon. At home Lord Palmerston was a staunch supporter of pugilism and Borrow warned of its neglect:

> Let no-one sneer at the bruisers of England . . . all I have to say is that the French still live on the other side of the water and are still casting their eyes hitherward – and that in the days of pugilism it was no vain boast to say that one Englishman was a match for two of t'other race.[25]

Thomas Hughes included a chapter in *Tom Brown's Schooldays* about it, in reaction to 'the cant and twaddle that's talked of fighting with the fists nowadays.'[26]

Hughes, a Christian Socialist who saw fist-fighting as an upright, manly British way of settling quarrels, implied that it was part of a code his old Rugby School headmaster, Thomas Arnold, was trying to introduce in place of the barbarism, field sports and 'vice' of earlier public school life. He portrayed 'the Doctor' as a positive supporter of team-games like football and cricket. Arnold was not, in fact, greatly interested in physical activities except insofar as they helped or hindered him in turning out Christian gentlemen. Work was the first sacred duty, with academic brilliance less important than honest endeavour. He would have been just as interested in seeing swimming, gymnastics or javelin-throwing replace poaching and idleness, but the senior boys had other interests and he found it expedient to go along with them, much as Bishop Mellitus had been advised by Augustine to do. So he used team-games, the instrument of fagging, to canalise bullying in an attempt to subordinate it to his own prefectorial system and thereby managed to introduce, with remarkable success, his own brand of Christianity.

Thomas Hughes, less ascetic or intellectual, memory made rosy by nostalgia, not only humanised and jollified the image of Arnold's regime but implied that team-games were at the centre of the educational process. In *Tom Brown's Schooldays* old Brooke, the school captain, publicly defends the headmaster against those who think him an authoritarian kill-joy: putting down 'six or seven mangy harriers and beagles' was no great crime, whereas 'If I saw him stopping football or cricket, or bathing or sparring I'd be as ready as any fellow to stand up about it. But he don't: he encourages them.'[27] The central theme of the book – the conflict in the minds of Tom Brown and his friend Harry East between the pagan attractions of the old style and the Doctor's Christian message – is authentic enough but Hughes invests cricket and football with values Arnold would not have claimed for them. Arnold's first disciples within the public school system, such as C.J. Vaughan who took over Harrow in 1844, were Christian educators first and foremost. Yet within a decade men like G.E.F. Cotton, who became head of the new but already ailing Marlborough, gave games a special place in their Christian and educational mission. It was a recipe for success, not least for its chauvinistic overtones – Hughes used 'British', 'sporting', 'courageous', 'manly', 'Christian' and 'gentlemanly' as if they were synonymous, or at least aspects of the same basic virtue.

The games cult was slower to hit the universities. J. A. Bridges, who went to Christ Church, Oxford, in the forties was shocked to find that at this mecca of Etonian 'wet bobs' the popular sport was riding – even the scholarship boys hired cheap nags from a dealer in Bear Lane. Football enthusiasts were thought outlandish, as Albert Pell found when he tried to form a club at Cambridge in 1839: spectators of early games on Parker's Piece thought the players slightly deranged.[28] One report told of 'a number of Rugby men, mostly freshmen, playing a new game' in which they 'made a circle round a ball and butted each other'.[29] Yet by 1848 serious efforts were being made to establish a set of rules acceptable to partisans from the various schools.

The Rugby men were the most fervent, although at Rugby School itself the rules were still in dispute until 1845 when Sixth form levee set up a committee to iron out contentious matters. Their first recommendation concerned the right of prefects to punish absentees. This priority settled, they proposed two distinctive rules: (a) allowing players who caught the ball to run with it, and (b) permitting 'hacking'. Both were adopted in 1846, and the second in particular proved divisive, for whereas limited handling of the ball was allowed in most schools, there was growing concern about the damage that could be done by unrestricted use of the feet: for example the Harrow rules did not allow 'tripping, pushing with the hands, shinning or back-shinning'.[30]

There was no pressure within the schools themselves to agree rules with other establishments. Indeed at the most exclusive schools the authorities' ancient fears that violence and disorder would be incited by inter-school sport and the boys' own inordinate pride in their own idiosyncratic versions of football meant that internal competitions – between houses, or different categories of pupils – offered excitement enough. And, of course, both boys and masters were acutely conscious of the social gradations of the various schools. There were several instances of socially superior schools rejecting sporting challenges from lesser outfits. In 1818 Westminster spurned Charterhouse as a mere private school: in the 1840s Harrow boys were said to recognise only Eton, Winchester, Westminster and Charterhouse. In 1846 Old Etonians up at Cambridge rejected the overtures of a group of Salopians who were trying to start a football club. Twenty years later, Westminster, whilst by then acknowledging Rugby, still rudely put down Shrewsbury when they asked for a fixture.[31]

Nevertheless Old Boys had to swallow some of their pride if they wanted football to achieve the same standing as cricket and rowing. At Cambridge they seem to have been spurred into action by another threat. When Henry C. Malden was asked to chair a meeting of public school men in 1848 the idea was 'to get up some football in preference to the hockey then in vogue'.[32] Malden, though only a private school man himself, was called in as a neutral. The meeting, attended by representatives of Eton, Harrow, Winchester, Rugby and Shrewsbury, during which 'the Eton men howled at the Rugby men for handling the ball' lasted seven hours and even then agreement was only reached through Malden's casting vote. The result was an amalgam, largely based on Harrow style (which allowed very little handling and discouraged hacking.) According to Malden the new rules were posted up and 'loyally observed'. His view may have been coloured by parental pride, and the controversy was by no means over, but the truce seems to have been long enough and firm enough to fend off the threat from hockey even if it did not yet confer on football the social status of rowing and cricket.[33]

Social tensions in rowing and cricket

Ironically, however, both these recreations were having difficulty in shedding undesirable legacies from the past. In rowing the great Leander club, which was supposed to exemplify all the virtues, social as well as sporting, slipped a little from its pedestal. Strained relations, exacerbated by the controversy over professional coaching and coxing, meant that university crews did not compete against each other in 1837. The Cambridge Subscription Rooms, however, issued a challenge to Leander, dominated by Eton and Oxford men, and to everyone's surprise beat them: 'The Pride of the Thames, the beautiful, the brilliant Leander, which has stood alone, the foremost for years, yesterday sustained a defeat', wailed the *Morning Post* on 10 June.

The writer was reconciled to this catastrophe by the noble way in which Leander accepted defeat: 'Their gallant conduct deserves the highest compliment.' Alas, gallantry evaporated somewhat in the return match the following year. Both crews had been steered by professionals on each occasion – Cambridge by Paddy Noulton – but this time the race was declared null and void because of fouling, and Leander, huffily rejecting Cambridge's offer of a re-run, sought to blame Noulton. This drew a long, pained letter from the Cambridge president, complaining of Leander's off-hand attitude – the match had had to be postponed to allow them to go to Ascot – and alleging that the fouling had been started by Leander's own cox, Parish. Noulton had wanted to retaliate at once but his gentlemanly crew had dissuaded him only to find that their use of sporting tactics, such as giving ground to avoid collision, was not reciprocated: only then did they allow Noulton to resort to 'Waterman's practice'.[34]

In the absence of any law-making body it was for the clubs themselves and the organisers of regattas to decide on such matters. Challenge matches would specify whether the bouts were to be 'steered by gentlemen' or otherwise. Chester Regatta, the first such annual event, included separate races rowed consecutively over the same course for skiffs rowed first by gentlemen amateurs and then by mechanics, as well as a £20 prize race for mechanics only.[35] The stewards of the Henley-on-Thames Regatta, founded in 1839, followed an even more exclusive policy. Though the intentions of the prominent townsfolk and county worthies who sponsored it were to some extent commercial – they believed it would produce 'beneficial results to the town of Henley' whilst providing a source of amusement and gratification to the neighbourhood and public in general – the idea had arisen because the first university Boat Race, rowed at Henley, had aroused much interest. The principal event, a Grand Challenge Cup for eights, was restricted to the universities, Eton and Westminster Schools, officers of the Household Brigade and recognised boat clubs established for over a year. Like Chester, Henley did not allow fouling and specified that 'every boat shall be steered by an amateur member of the club or clubs entering'.[36]

In the universities, though the Boat Race – moving to the tideway from Westminster to Putney – resumed in 1839 it continued only fitfully as the argument over waterman's practice continued. Cambridge, led by the energetic T.S. 'Tom' Egan as coxswain and coach, seemed at first to have clinched the argument, beating Oxford, who persisted with professional coaching, three times running. And the point was reinforced in 1842 when, after a palace revolution, Fletcher Menzies, a dedicated amateur, took over at Oxford and won. But Cambridge reverted to professional coaching and after a three year interval between races, won twice in a row, and then it was Oxford who wanted to make amateur coaching a condition and Cambridge who declined. Diplomatic relations were not resumed until 1849.

On several occasions when arrangements for an official Boat Race fell through the two crews went to Henley to fight it out there, and the colleges also found the Regatta a convenient place to pursue challenges. Pseudonymity was sometimes needed: at one point, for instance, the Oxford authorities refused to allow college names to be used and the entrants used the names of their boats instead. The first Regatta had attracted nine thousand spectators who admiringly watched as the great Leander gave an exhibition of rowing and staged a special waterman's race, and in the second year Leander actually entered the Grand (winning of course). Greatly encouraged, the stewards expanded their programme on similar lines (though without the watermen), introducing the Stewards' Cup for fours in 1841, the Diamond Sculls in 1844, the Silver Goblets for pairs and the Ladies' Plate for school and college eights in 1845, and the Visitors' Cup for fours in 1847. Throughout the decade the event was dominated by university crews in various guises.

But this dependence had its negative side and the Regatta had a precarious existence with the number and quality of entries fluctuating wildly. The low point was reached in 1850. The previous year's *Laws of Boat Racing*, approved by a meeting of the Oxford and Cambridge and leading London clubs and adopted by Henley, ought to have inaugurated a harmonious era but there was no Boat Race that year nor did the two crews meet at Henley. Indeed there were only 15 entries for all competitions, Oxford crews rowed over in the Grand and the Stewards' and there were no entries at all from Cambridge.

This gentlemanly pettifoggery at the top had its effect on rowing generally. In the early forties the Thames had had a score of clubs but they were now reduced to a handful. Ironically it was professional ingenuity and skill that saved the sport for the gentlemen. The great technological advance of the keel-less boat, made by Harry Clasper, a Derwenthaugh boat-builder, was used by its designer in innumerable races on the Tyne, notably in 1844 against his great rival Coombes, bringing him considerable sums in prizes and wagers. Clasper also solved the problem of getting adequate leverage for the oars in the new narrow-beamed boats, a problem that had vexed designers for some years, by an iron outrigger, which he successfully tried out on a four-oared boat in 1845. These devices did not come into commission in the best circles until the fifties, when an Ouseburn ship's carpenter and sculler, Matt Taylor, was to make his mark, and they brought no change of heart amongst the gentlemen on whose patronage this expensive sport depended.

Rowing required not only money but also day-time leisure in which to practise. It was thus an ideal pastime for university men and for professions such as the church. But muscular Christians also saw something spiritual in it, as they also did in cricket. Rowing inspired less rhetoric, at least in print, which was a medium in which cricket-lovers excelled. For Revd Mr Pycroft *The*

Cricket Field offered an opportunity to moralise. Cricket, he declared, was 'a standing panegyric on the English character: none but an orderly and sensible people would so amuse themselves'. Its effect was to 'both humanise and harmonise our people'. Indeed there was nothing to equal it for moral uplift: 'Drinking, gambling and cudgel-playing insensibly disappear before a manly recreation which draws the labourer from the dark haunts of vice and misery to the open common.' Clerical oarsmen could certainly make no such claim for the welfare of labourers but cricket retained its feudal relationships.

Indeed gentlemen and players were drawn closer together as first-class cricket became increasingly a three-day affair: as William Ward reminded Pycroft, three consecutive days was more than was required by hunting, shooting, fishing or even yachting, and few gentlemen were willing to invest so much time in it. MCC itself scarcely changed its character, however. Its membership was no more than 562 in 1850 and proficiency at the game was not a requirement. Nor did the members concern themselves with the vulgar business of owning and maintaining the ground. The unexpired portion of the lease was purchased from William Ward in 1836 (for £2,000 down and £425 a year) not by the club or one of its members but by James Henry Dark. James Henry was the son of Ben Dark, cricket-batmaker, and of Mrs Matilda Dark who took over the business from Ben in 1840, and older brother of Robert, who having been apprenticed to the great John Small, specialised in ball-making.[37]

James Dark had joined Tom Lord's ground staff as a boy in 1804, and had been a professional cricketer and umpire. On taking over the lease he spent £4,000 on extensions and improvements to the pavilion, installing gaslight and adding a billiard room, a tennis court and a running track. Dark, though not a member of MCC, was more than a mere inn-keeper for it. He ran Lord's ground, hired and fired staff and was influential enough to ensure that only brother Robert's balls were used in great matches. The scope of equipment-making was extending. For one thing the new 'march of intellect' bowling was making cricket a dangerous game, creating a demand for protective clothing. Alfred Mynn inflicted and received terrible injuries. Eton produced a stream of very fast bowlers, one of whom, Marcom, an intending clergyman, actually broke a batsman's leg. Hitherto no gentleman had deigned to wear pads in public. Beauclerk, now retired but still a magisterial influence on the game, had declared that leggings were acceptable for practice but unfair to bowlers if worn in a match. This set the tone for everyone. Professionals, with their livelihood to think of, might have been forgiven for taking a different view but when 'Long Bob' Robinson devised a primitive pair of pads he had been laughed out of court. Now, however, new clothing fashions came to the rescue: when trousers replaced knee breeches in the 1820s padding could be pushed inside stockings or strapped to the legs without anybody knowing. A

Nottinghamshire professional, Thomas Nixon, patented cork pads in 1841 and two years later the London Toy Repository were also offering 'knee-pads'.

In America, meanwhile, Goodyear's invention of the vulcanisation of rubber in 1839, which had profound effects on sporting equipment generally, directly impinged on cricket. The possibilities were quickly grasped by one of the more enterprising gentlemen cricketers. The debonair Nicholas Wanostracht had inherited a private school and augmented his income – under the name of Felix – by playing cricket for Kent and for representative sides, by writing books about the game, and also by inventions such as the 'catapulta' or bowling machine. Felix firmly advocated 'paddings' for batsmen, including 'longitudinal socks' of linen, worn under the trousers and filled with strips of rubber. Felix also invented one of the first practical types of batting glove, using tubular strips of rubber, selling his patent in 1848 to Duke and Sons, ball and equipment makers.[38] That same year, however, Dark was offering 'TUBULAR and other INDIA-RUBBER GLOVES' as well as 'newly-invented leg-guards'. There were batsmen of the old school who scorned such namby-pamby aids, but they were soon the exception.[39]

By contrast there was fierce controversy about whether wicket-keepers and long-stops ought to wear pads and gloves for fielding. There were practical as well as ethical considerations. In the early days of 'march of intellect' bowling as many as three long-stops might be required for the likes of Marcom. (Wicket-keepers, though on the alert for chances of stumping and other attacking moves, did not attempt to stop every ball.) Pycroft's friend, John Marshall, a specialist long-stop, wore thick 'leggings'. A social complication supporting the use of gloves was that gentleman wore them in ordinary life and were not expected to have hands calloused by toil. Pycroft thought this meant that wicket-keepers must all be professionals, but others reckoned that rowing was the answer for the gentlemen.

The changes in the game brought bigger rewards for the professionals. Fuller Pilch left his £100 a year job at Town Malling in 1842 for better opportunities in Canterbury. Match fees were not the only consideration: there were good wages for other services like ground-keeping or coaching and, even better, the chance of year-round income from catering, inn-keeping and the like. Private enterprise was lucrative but risky. For instance, Daniel Day of Southampton, appointed by the gentlemen of the South Hampshire Club as ground professional, also held the tenancy of the Antelope but when he moved to Itchen to set up his own ground the venture failed.

It was not a question of cricketing skill alone. William Lillywhite, known as 'the Nonpareil', was unsuccessful with his ground and associated public house in Brighton. On the other hand the unknown Tom Adams of Gravesend, who left a twelve shilling a week job as a factory hand to keep the

Bat and Ball and ground, did well out of cricket. For a while a Town Malling member sponsored him to the tune of £5 a match, and then he gradually levelled and fenced his own ground, and arranged fairs after cricket matches whilst his wife ran the refreshment tent. Old-style patronage arrangements were rare (though Mr Alfred Smith of Henfield employed Edward Bushby, a noted long-stop, as a gardener). On the other hand schools and colleges were beginning to hire coaches: Eton set on their first, Samuel Redgate of Nottingham, in 1840.[40]

The counties offered very little employment. Indeed there were no county clubs until Sussex made a diffident debut in 1839, and for years, though teams bearing county names played each other, the matches were *ad hoc* casual affairs. Neither Middlesex nor Hampshire had formal organisations. In Kent Town Malling tried to grow into a County Club but failed, for lack of support, and afterwards the Beverley Club at Canterbury, which staged an annual Festival Week, stole their thunder. However, the chief patrons (the Hon. F. Ponsonby and his friends from Cambridge) were more interested in the Festival with its evenings of amateur theatricals than in competitive cricket on a systematic basis.

The two northern outposts had mixed fortunes. In Yorkshire rivalry amongst the various districts held back progress, whilst Nottinghamshire made an early start but could not sustain it. Remarkably this early venture owed nothing to the aristocratic patronage that was so influential elsewhere and much to the entrepreneurial skills of a one-eyed former bricklayer called William Clarke. In the thirties Clarke had kept the Bell in Nottingham, the meeting place of the 'Old Club' who played their matches on common land, part of the racecourse in the Forest. Then in 1837 he married the landlady of the Trent Bridge Inn, made a cricket ground alongside, enclosed it and charged sixpence admission. The ground became the venue for big matches and the inn the headquarters of Clarke's own team which became a county club in 1841.

Clarke still had unsatisfied ambitions, however, and in 1844, now aged forty-six, he left his son-in-law in charge at Trent Bridge and took a job on MCC's ground staff. MCC was at that time by far the biggest source of employment for professional cricketers: they hired '8 bowlers and 6 men as scouts' to give the gentlemen batting practice five days a week in May, June and July. The pay – which was at Dark's discretion – was not great but apart from this work the ground staff were favourably placed to be picked for representative games. (For these MCC had fixed rates in 1827 at £6 a win, £4 a loss in three-day games, £5 and £3 in shorter ones.) Clarke's bowling in big games that season was a revelation: it was old-fashioned, crafty twisty stuff, not of 'march of intellect' ferocity but highly successful.

He had greater surprises in store. At the end of MCC's season, which came early so that the gentlemen could be on the moors for the 'glorious twelfth' of August, Clarke organised a number of matches on his own account, getting together an All-England XI, which included not only leading professionals like Pilch and Hillyer of Kent but impecunious gentlemen like Alfred Mynn, to play 22 of Sheffield, 18 of Manchester and 18 of Yorkshire on their home territories. This netted him a nice profit and the following year the tour included games against local sides at Manchester, Liverpool, Leeds, York, Stockton, Sheffield, Birmingham, Newcastle and Stourbridge – unfashionable but sport-hungry places flourishing economically as a result of the industrial revolution. As Robert Dark told Pycroft, he had been amazed at the idea of touring such outlandish places but his own increased sales testified to its success. In 1846 MCC reduced their match fees and expenses to take account of the greater ease of travel in the railway age and two years later Clarke parted company with them and took his players on a summer-long 17 match tour. He did not pay generously – £4 to £6 a match – but this compared favourably with MCC's new rates, and the work was plentiful and did not stop for the grouse season. By 1851 when Clarke's XI played 34 games MCC's authority had been severely dented.

Whether or not Clarke's activities stunted the growth of county cricket is hard to say. There had been very little growth apart from Clarke's own enterprise at Nottinghamshire (which began to founder after he left). In 1844 the Cambridge Club, which had beaten MCC several times, assumed county status. The town, county and university all played on Parker's Piece, a vast, open and very public place where charging admission was impractical. The following year London acquired its first county club and ground: Surrey's foundation stemmed from the initiative of the Montpelier Club which secured a lease on the market garden in Kennington and created the Oval with the aid of 10,000 turves brought from Tooting Common. These modest efforts were nothing to compare with Clarke's missionary zeal in taking cricket to the far corners of the land. Needless to say, however, Clarke's 'travelling circus' was regarded as a mischievous intrusion by the MCC establishment and all those who shared Pycroft's view of life. When Beauclerk died in 1851 the battle for cricket's soul, and the right to impose arbitrary conditions on its professional players, was raging in earnest.

Golf: old professionals and new balls

Changes in relationships between gentlemen and players as a result of commercialism and technical advance also took place in Scotland, not only in those sports shared with the English (such as hunting, and shooting and even cricket, in which the Edinburgh club employed a professional at £30 a year), but in native idiosyncrasies like golf. The organised game was still confined to the area east of Glasgow (though Colonel Fairlie, travelling to St Andrews from Prestwick, had plans for putting his native town on the golfing map), but it was intensely popular in its heartland. In Edinburgh, with Leith submerged by the masses, the Honourable Company was re-born at Musselburgh, though it had to co-exist with the Musselburgh club and the general public until it finally (1891) bought its own land at Gullane and constructed Muirfield. Bruntsfield links, home of the Edinburgh Burgess, the Bruntsfield Links Club and several other groups, was encroached upon by building and the cause of fierce dispute over usage with the city magistrates in 1843.[41]

It was mainly from St Andrews, where the land was so spacious that the R and A was not unduly troubled by the communal nature of the links, that the advances in legislation, for inter-club competition and the like, were to come in the new, expansionist era. The spread of the game was greatly assisted by technical improvements in equipment that gradually made it easier, and more fun to play. There was great competition between the club-making firms, branching out from beginnings as wheelwrights, carpenters and cabinet-makers, notably McEwan at Leith and Philp at St Andrews. Philp was a late developer but since 1827 had ousted McEwan from the St Andrews connection. But it was a change of ball – still the old leather-covered 'feathery', difficult to use and expensive – that was to do most for the spread of the game.[42]

The son-in-law of Gourlay, the most famous ball-maker of the day, explained the problem of the feathery.

> It was considered good work if a man could turn out three feather balls in a day. The case was of cow-hide, and a high hat full of feathers in their loose and dry state was needed for the stuffing. These were damped and crammed into the three parts finished case and sewn up[43]

One cramming device was a spike attached to a leather strap worn around the chest so that risk of injury to the chest wall was added to that of pulmonary disease from the feather dust. By the same token the trade was profitable to the maker and costly to the player. The Robertsons were already famous for their skill in 1743 ('Bobson', an ancestor of Davie, the old caddie master, 'crams and swears, yet crams and urges more' in Matthewson's mock-epic) and Davie passed on the art to his son Allan, the greatest golfer of his generation, who went on to rival Gourlay. The high price was maintained despite the competition because of the increased demand. Allan Robertson's output – 1,021 in 1840 – rose by 1844 (when he was assisted by another St Andrews professional, Tom Morris, who had been apprenticed to him) to 2,456. Dr William

Graham, a scholarly but convivial member of the Innerleven (Fife) Club, put the problem neatly in an after-dinner song:

> When Gourlay's balls cost half a crown
> And Allan's no' a farthing down.[44]

The theme of his song, however, was the advent of a revolutionary new ball. In 1845 Dr Robert Patterson, a St Andrews cleric, had received from eastern parts a statue of Vishnu which seems to have interested him less than the yellow-brown substance in which it was packed. This was gutta-percha, derived from latex, resistant to water, plastic when heated but hard when cold: so it could be moulded into golf balls and reshaped when it was hacked – surface scratches in fact improved its flight and were imposed deliberately. Soon 'Patterson's patent', first introduced at Blackheath, was being acclaimed all over Scotland, not least because the new gutties cost only one shilling compared with the old featheries. Gourlay, in fact, saw an early trial at Musselburgh and got the message, reputedly disposing of most of his old stock by fulfilling a standing order from Sir David Baird of North Berwick, sending him nine dozen featheries with the result that Sir David continued to use the old type long after everyone else. Allan Robertson held out longer for the feathery and he and Tom Morris tried to demonstrate its superiority by their own skills, but these, of course, were not shared by the ordinary golfer and even Allan had to accept the inevitable by 1850.

The money to be made from actually playing golf was distinctly limited. Apart from judicious bets and occasional earnings from teaching or playing with the gentry, the professionals had to rely on club and ball-making, green-keeping, or at a pinch, caddying. St Andrews employed two 'cadies' in 1848, at £6 a year between them. Allen Robertson was in demand to play against the leading gentlemen, partly because he was adept at winning by a flatteringly narrow margin. He was shrewd enough never to play against Tom Morris, his assistant in the workshop, but played with him in an epic contest against Willie and Jamie Dunn of Musselburgh in 1849. The Dunns were somewhat restricted in scope in the limited Scottish set-up and the following year Willie took up the post of greenkeeper at Blackheath for fifteen shillings a week. The scene was to change markedly in 1851 with the founding of Prestwick, where the magnificent and munificent Earl of Eglinton was the first honorary captain, and competition became more organised. But there were still fewer than twenty golf clubs in all.

By contrast there were a dozen times as many bowling clubs in Scotland. The satisfactions of bowling, which appealed to men of judgement of all ages, were greatly enhanced by the Scottish talent for horticulture which had led to the importation of sea-washed turf to inland areas, often from the

Cumberland and Lancashire coasts. Scottish bowling greens were noted for their true and level surfaces, where such English enthusiasts as there were – not many – had to make do with rough ground. The Belfast Club, inspired by Scottish immigrants, was founded in 1842 but it was the only one in Ireland for another thirty years, and Wales had no club until Abergavenny was formed in 1860. There were a number of English clubs but they showed no interest in an organised approach until 1882 and the English game only really came to life in 1899 when the Imperial Bowling Association was formed on the initiative of Australia where the game had been popularised by Scottish immigrants.

Back in 1848, meanwhile, representatives of some 200 Scottish clubs met in Glasgow Town Hall to try to form a national association. Nothing happened for another year, but then the decision was taken to appoint a committee to draft a set of laws (like English cricketers, Scottish bowlers, unlike their golfing counterparts, were not content with mere 'rules') and the task was accomplished almost single-handed by the honorary secretary, W.W. Mitchell, a Glasgow solicitor, and the laws were immediately adopted in the west of Scotland. Mitchell was later to publish a *Manual of Bowls Playing* and slowly his laws came to be accepted and jealously guarded – by the Scottish Bowling Association. It took more than forty years but the seeds had been sown and Scotland's reputation was acknowledged by the time England, Wales and Ireland began to take the game seriously.[45]

Notes

1 'Locksley Hall', 1838.
2 For the economic and social background see C. Harvie, 'Revolution and the Rule of Law; in K.O. Morgan (ed.), *The Oxford Illustrated History of Britain*, Oxford, 1984, pp. 419–62, G.D.H. Cole and R. Postgate, *The Common People*, London, 1956, A. Briggs, *The Age of Improvement*, London, 1959, E. Longford, *Victoria R.I.*, London 1964.
3 In *The Condition of the Working Class in England*.
4 Chapter XX, 'Mr Dombey goes upon a journey'.
5 Cole and Postgate, *The Common People*, p. 314. See also S. de Grazia, 'Of Time, Work and Leisure' in M.R. Marrus (ed.), *The Emergence of Leisure*, Philadelphia, 1974.
6 22 February, 1850, quoted in Longford, *Victoria*, p. 277.
7 Ibid. p. 229 (14 March 1846).
8 R. Mortimer, *The Jockey Club*, London, 1958, p. 94, 77–8.
9 *Annual Register*, 1844, quoted in K. Chesney, *The London Underworld*, Harmondsworth, 1970, p. 352. See also W. Vamplew, *The Turf*, London 1976, pp. 89–91.
10 Quoted in Vamplew, *The Turf*, p. 203.
11 28 February 1839.
12 27 February 1839.
13 16 April 1840.
14 In *The Life of a Sportsman*, 1842.
15 7 March 1847.
16 *Mr Sponge's Sporting Tour*, p. 525.
17 *The Noble Science*, 1839.

18 *Handley Cross*, 1839. Jorrocks first appeared in *Jorrocks' Jaunts and Follities* in 1838. Both were first serialised in the *New Sporting Magazine*.

19 E. Parker (ed.), *The Shooting Week-end Book*, London, 1934, p. 267.

20 Longford, *Victoria*, pp. 266–8.

21 Chesney, *London Underworld*, p. 346.

22 *London Life and Labour*, vol. III, p. 5 et seq., quoted extensively in Chesney, *London Underworld*, pp. 347–53.

23 *Lavengro*, pp. 206–7.

24 14 September 1845.

25 *Lavengro*, p. 161.

26 Hughes, *Tom Brown's Schooldays*, Chapter V.

27 Ibid., pp. 85–6.

28 U.A. Titley and R. McWhirter, *Centenary History of the Rugby Football Union*, London, 1970, p. 39.

29 J. Venn, *Early Collegiate Life*, Cambridge, 1913, quoted in P.M. Young, *The History of British Football*, London, 1973 edn., pp. 111–12.

30 The Harrow rules were printed in Young, *History of Football*, pp. 105–9.

31 Various original sources cited in *History of Football*, E. Dunning and K. Sheard, *Barbarians, Gentlemen and Players*, Oxford, 1979, p. 102.

32 Letter from Malden 8 October 1897, quoted in J.B. Oldham, *History of Shrewsbury School*, Shrewsbury, 1852, p. 233.

33 Hockey and football were 'left to boys' according to Venn, *Early Collegiate Life*.

34 H. Cleaver, *A History of Rowing*, London, 1954, pp. 54–8.

35 Poster reproduced in *British Rowing Almanack*, 1982, p. 38.

36 C. Dodd, 'Rowing' in T. Mason (ed.), *Sport in Britain*, Cambridge, 1989, p. 251. For Henley see R.D. Burnell, *Henley Royal Regatta*, Oxford, 1957, and (revised and updated version) *A Celebration of 150 years*, London, 1989.

37 For the Darks see H. Barty-King, *Quilt-Winders and Pod-Shavers*, London, 1979, pp. 64–5.

38 N. Wanostracht, *Felix on the Bat*, London, 1845.

39 Dark's advertisements are reproduced in Barty-King, *Quilt-Winders and Pad-Shavers*.

40 For professional cricketers' pay and conditions and the impact of 'Old Clarke' see R. Sissons, *The Players*, London, 1988, esp. pp. 72–6.

41 H. Gardiner-Hill, 'The History of the Rules of Golf' in B. Darwin, et al. (eds.), *A History of Golf in Britain*, 1952, p. 20.

42 G. Campbell in Darwin, *History of Golf*, pp. 73–5, 80–1.

43 W.W. Tulloch, *The Life of Tom Morris*, Edinburgh, 1908, p. 61, quoted in W.H. Gibson, *Early Irish Golf*, Naas, 1988.

44 *In Praise of Gutta Percha*, 1848, Darwin, *History of Golf*, p. 84. In fact Gourlay charged four or even five shillings for his best balls, though they were cheaper by the dozen (Darwin, pp. 81–83). By comparison cricket balls, shared amongst 22 players could cost as little as three shillings, and seven shillings and sixpence for the best (Barty-King, pp. 64–90, *passim*).

45 P. Sullivan, *Bowls: The Records*, Enfield, 1986, pp. 17–18.

CHAPTER TEN

Judicious bottle-holding: die-hards under pressure

DRAWING THE STUMPS.

Cobden to Dizzy. "CARRIES OUT HIS BAT? OF COURSE HE DOES! YOUR UNDERHAND BOWLING 'LL
NEVER GET HIM OUT! I'LL SHOW YOU HOW TO DO IT NEXT INNINGS."

By 1851, uniquely in history, more people in mainland Britain were living in the town than in the country. The population of 21 million (England 17, Wales 1, Scotland 3) had increased significantly and was to go on increasing. Only in Ireland had it fallen – to 6.5 million – and was still falling. The main cause of the continued decline was emigration: of the 1,365,000 who emigrated in 1850 nearly a million were Irish. Irish families seeking work also helped swell the burgeoning populations of the towns as the balance between agricultural and industrial employment shifted (from 34%–28% in 1801 to 21%–40% in 1851). London, with 3.25 million, was prodigious, nearly ten times the size of Dublin, Liverpool and Glasgow. Glasgow was growing fast, having far outstripped Edinburgh, and it was the centre of a network of industrial towns, as were Birmingham, Manchester and on a smaller scale Leeds and Sheffield. Cardiff and Swansea and their satellites were transforming South Wales, whilst in Ireland the main growth point was Belfast with its linen and shipbuilding industries. Feeding and housing these urban masses, rootless and culturally mixed, and keeping them clean and in good working order were targets for social reformers and new-style politicians.

Material issues increasingly came to the fore in politics but religion was by no means a dead letter. The census startled people in England by revealing that as against 5.2 million adherents of the established church there were over 4 million dissenters, overwhelmingly Protestant. That over half did not attend church, especially the Church of England, made no difference to the sharp cultural division between the two groups: politically speaking the one was roughly aligned to the Tories, the other to the Whigs, or Liberals as they became. And it roughly coincided with the 'north–south' divide, though within the conurbations there were microcosmic divides and there was a strong conservative tendency in rural parts whatever their location. Industrial change, movement of population and the elaboration of the class structure so complicated matters that the two main parties were afflicted by splinters of varying size and sharpness, and forming a government became an exercise in coalition.

In Scotland where the divide was east–west as well as north–south, (the east with the best land, three of the four universities, not to mention the best golf-courses), the gentry and the professional classes held on to their political perch, though with increasing difficulty as the west grew stronger economically with the boom in shipbuilding on the Clyde. In the more hierarchical Highlands the crofters and the graziers were at odds and, though

was no famine, emigration was a popular option for the poor. As a final
to the tangled political story two-thirds of the Church of Scotland
seceded in 1843, forming the more nationalistic Free Church. South Wales,
saved by industrialisation from mass emigration, became a cultural melting-
pot of Welsh, Irish and English, and a gulf opened up between the east and the
intensely rural inward-looking, agricultural west. In the north the Wynn
family held on to political power but in a rising tide of anti-establishment
dissent. The 1851 census showed that Wales had some 800,000 fervently
Protestant dissenters as against 100,000 Anglicans. Ireland, too, saw the
decline of the old ascendancy, though it had a long way to fall. It persisted
longer in Ulster where it was challenged mainly by the Presbyterian middle
class; unlike the south where there was a rising Catholic middle class, the
more politically minded of which tended to line up with the dissident, radical
splinters of the Whig Party.

The aristocracy and gentry supplied most members of the government from
both parties, though they had to look more and more for support from the
middle classes. There was still in 1851 a fairly compact, identifiable middle
class of professional and business men but it was spreading and dividing. The
prevailing ethos was that of the leading professions, the law, medicine and the
church, who traditionally sent their sons to public school and university. They
were followed in this by the industrialists, however self-made they were
themselves, who tended also to veer towards the more respectable avenues of
commerce and banking. And commerce now spawned a vast army of white
collar workers who along with the shopkeepers, elementary school teachers
and supervisors in industry, made up the proliferating lower middle class. All
were conditioned to look up to the aristocracy and gentry, who commanded
the top posts in the army and colonial service as well as government.[1] Not least
were they admired and envied by the new bigger reading public (the stamp
duty on newspapers was abolished in 1855) for their conspicuous enjoyment
of leisure, racing, hunting, shooting and fishing and the fashionable urban
scene which were lovingly recorded in the popular prints.

Free trade was the philosophical lode-star of the age, the way to eliminate by
painless means the horrors of poverty and war, and the Great Exhibition was a
source of inspiration for peace-loving free traders. The Prince Consort's sense
of satisfaction was sharply reduced when a year later the Whigs lost office.
Victoria, who had greatly enjoyed the amenable Lord Glanville's despatches
from the Foreign Office, shared Albert's disappointment as the Tories formed
a minority government. The Tory Prime Minister, Lord Derby, was a fine
classical scholar but an indolent fellow who seemed too blasé even to use his
social influence for party purposes. Disraeli, somewhat bemused at being
made Chancellor of the Exchequer, was troubled that the Prime Minister was

never available because he was always at Newmarket or Doncaster. Prince Albert went further, complaining that Derby was intent on installing at court 'the Dandies and Roués of London and the Turf'.[2]

Troubled waters

Derby's first appointment was the notorious Earl of Wilton who became Master of the Horse. It was Wilton, who, as Commodore of the RYS, had betrayed the ideals of the Great Exhibition in the interests of the upper classes and their code of honour. Critics of the Exhibition had warned that it would attract not only industrial spies and continental anarchists but American republicans. James Hamilton, one of the syndicate from the New York Yacht Club taking their new boat *America* to England in search of sporting challenge, was warned by Horace Greeley, editor of the *New York Tribune*, 'You will be beaten and the country will be abused as it had been in connection with the Exhibition.'[3]

In theory the RYS, the rarefied elite of a rarefied sport, was above the stark vulgarity of open competition. Racing might suit the Royal London Yacht Club (founded 1839) whose boats averaged a mere 11 tons or so, but the RYS had one of 392 tons and were opposed to such insidious modern notions as handicapping according to size. It was in this spirit that Wilton invited the syndicate who owned the 140 ton *America* to call in at Cowes on their way to the Exhibition to give the squadron the benefit of 'any improvements in shipbuilding' their new boat might reveal. The New Yorkers duly sailed *America* across to Brest, put her in racing trim and set off for the Solent. Six miles out the English cutter *Laverock*, under the pretext of greeting the visitors, put *America* through her paces in a 'spontaneous' race.

The result was so alarming that RYS declined to respond to the Americans' formal challenge. *The Times* was scathing about the Squadron's attitude and a group of professionals offered to rig a boat themselves to defend the national honour. Cornered, the RYS eventually condescended to invite the New Yorkers to take part in one of their regular races, a mere 100 guinea Cup affair. The insulting gesture misfired, for despite the Squadron's manipulation of the rules and collusive and very rough tactics in the race itself, *America* was easily first in a field of sixteen, beating, without time allowance, much bigger yachts, including the 392 tonner.

Amongst the many excuses for the English performance was the assertion – ludicrous in view of her Atlantic crossing – that *America* was designed purely for racing, a breach of gentlemanly practice. Nearer the truth was that its design and appurtenances paid less attention to creature comforts for the owners than to the requirements of actual sailing: when *America* was sold in

England and adapted to gentlemanly standards, she was never the same. And, part of the same problem, English owners behaved like first class passengers whilst the professionals did the actual sailing, whereas rich Americans were not above manual activity and their crews were no mere hirelings.

The extent of English snobbery can be seen in a book edited by Anthony Trollope on 'those sports which are essentially dear to the English nature, and which are in the present day so strongly in vogue in England as to have a manifest effect on the lives and characters of Englishmen'.[4] His first choice was yachting, 'a tolerably select if not exclusively aristocratic sport'. The superior, bourgeois Trollope made great fun of the cockney impudence of Albert Smith, a celebrated public lecturer who dressed like a stage Admiral and handled his 'morsel of a cutter' with aplomb, but was merely masquerading as a real yachtsman. These, Trollope took for granted, were employers of labour – some 200 yachtsmen, he reckoned, hired about 5,700 crew, roughly one man to every 10 tons.

Boats, indeed, were getting bigger. The Clyde Model Yacht Club had been founded in 1856 for boats under 8 tons. By 1870 (now Royal Clyde) some were over 100 tons. This was partly from sheer ostentation, but size was also the most obvious way of ensuring victory. Buying success became somewhat more complicated when handicapping could no longer be resisted. Historically ships' tonnage had been measured according to cargo capacity and this was the basis of the Builders' Measurement used in the earliest attempts at handicapping for racing purposes. So yachts began to be designed with increased waterline length and reduced beam width and keel size – 'tonnage cheaters' with huge areas of sail. In 1854 the Royal London and Royal Mersey began to take length into account, to the great chagrin of influential owners, and the following year Royal Thames produced a formula known as Thames Measurement which allowed more scope for 'rule-cheating' designs such as yachts with thick exterior 'leadmine' keels to hold them upright.

Trollope was more concerned with cruising – and its costs, a topic which always engrossed him. You could get a suitable boat for £26 a ton completely fitted, including blankets, racing sails (£125 to £160) and iron ballast extra. The wage bill, which was being forced up by the expansion of the sport, was quite another matter. A sailing master, who also looked after his owner's boat in the winter, could command £120 a year: other crew were employed only during the summer, at weekly rates – mate 32 shillings, cook 27 shillings, able seaman 25 shillings or 26 shillings with clothing provided. A 65 ton cutter or 90 ton schooner needed seven men and a boy plus personal servants. (A few who made enough out of racing including presents and bonuses for winning could afford to remain idle in the winter but most crews took on other work – in the

Isle of Wight as fishermen, in Portsmouth as watermen, in East Anglia as oyster-dredgers or long voyage sailors.) Yacht owners, Trollope believed, took insufficient care in selecting crews. Cowesmen had a high reputation, but were inclined to be 'lazy insubordinate and insolent': they were smarter than the average but needed firm handling. This meant hiring a good sailing master who should not be from the same district as the crew lest familiarity breed contempt. Sailing masters themselves needed to be watched, lest they conspired with local tradesmen to bilk owners; they should be neither sea-lawyers nor long-shore loafers, neither too easy-going nor too fussy.

This neo-feudal relationship was even more evident in the racing end of the sport in which the least important consideration was the crew's well-being or even safety. According to the rules only fixed ballast could be stowed below decks but shifting or trimming it was commonplace. Another device was stationing crew below deck with instructions to run from side to side at strategic moments: sometimes the crew filled their life jackets with lead shot. Stewards of yacht race meetings were in a difficult position since poking around below deck was a reflection on a gentleman's honour. Yet clearly yachtsmen's honour was not always capable of sustaining the burdens placed on it. Hence in 1867 the RYS appointed a Sailing Committee with a role analogous to that of the Jockey Club, not perhaps the best of models, but at least an admission of need.

The America's Cup episode was emblematic. The Great Exhibition before many decades were out could be seen as a premature celebration of British mastery of industrial processes she had sparked off but no longer fully understood and greatly undervalued. The processes, in fact, needed to be advanced by relevant education and training of a kind that Britain, largely for reasons of social prejudice, was unable to deliver. Her deficiencies were masked by John Bullish aggression. In 1854 the nation's energies were focused not on technology but on the Crimean War. Albert's disappointment was increased by the sturdy patriotism shown by Victoria who reflected the popular view that though nobody wanted war the Russians, who had their eyes on India, had to be taught a lesson. The steam-powered ironclad ships, military reforms and improved military hospitals that resulted from the war were in sad contrast to the idealistic hopes raised by the Exhibition.

Palmerston, John Bull incarnate, was not Victoria's choice as Prime Minister in 1855, but there was no alternative, and in fact both she and Albert found him easier to deal with once he was no longer directly in charge of foreign affairs, in which they felt themselves supremely well qualified to advise on policy. The Indian Mutiny of 1857 led Victoria to the conclusion that she ought personally to be given charge of Indian affairs. Amongst her subjects there was more concern about the collapse of American banks and the repercussions in Liverpool, Glasgow and on the cotton trade, in which American raw material was now vital.

In politics style rather than coherent party politics was the greatest source of division. Palmerston, who introduced an anti-terrorist Bill after an Italian had tried to assassinate Napoleon III, lost a Parliamentary vote when the opposition accused him of truckling to the French and Lord Derby took over for a brief ineffectual spell but 'Old Pam' was back in 1859. With his old enemy Russell at the Foreign Office and his old enemy Gladstone at the Treasury, Palmerston presided benevolently over a talented, opinionated group who struck enough sparks off each other to survive. He lost another old adversary in 1861 with the demise of Prince Albert. Albert's untimely death, his last hours clouded by the discovery of the Prince of Wales's dissolute behaviour with a young actress in Dublin, was a sickening blow for the queen. Victoria never forgave her son. For years she left her cocoon of grief only to dedicate herself to performing what she thought Albert's wishes would have been.

Ironically enough, he would probably have approved of many of Palmerston's later efforts. The old warrior had learned from the disastrous and costly mistakes of the past, thereafter pursuing a policy of 'judicious bottle holding' – a metaphor from the prize-ring – that profitably kept the peace for fifty years. In home affairs Gladstone did particularly well at the Exchequer, bringing tariffs and taxes down (income tax fell to four pence in the pound) and the 1862 Companies Act extended the scope of limited liability enterprises. Industrial wages kept on increasing, but so did the cost of living, so that the real benefit to the workers was in improved conditions.

American big-scale farming was making inroads into the British market; but otherwise agriculture had survived the repeal of the Corn Laws surprisingly well: food prices fell but productivity increased through enclosure and better land use. Rural wages, though still not much more than ten shillings a week in some places, improved for the smaller numbers who remained on the land. Their conditions, of course, remained unchanged.

More fundamental, sustained advance depended on society coming to terms with technology which was a distant prospect indeed. Even pure science was looked at askance by the classical and humane scholars who ruled the roost in Oxford and Cambridge. Orthodox religion was wholly reactionary: the church's response to Darwin's *Origin of Species* in 1859 was hysterical and abusive. Meanwhile the working man was turning away from organised religion. The Christian Socialist Co-operatives of F. D. Maurice and Charles Kingsley were bedevilled by piety and soon faded away, whereas the workers' own Co-operative movement, starting in a retail shop in Rochdale in 1844, was solidly based on the profit motive and did well, especially when the government prudently gave Co-ops the status of Friendly Societies. The writing was on the wall for followers of Marx and Engels. Capitalism was tolerated by the lower orders provided it offered the chance of a little profit.

Seeking the wholesome

The capitalists themselves were often slow to grasp this, believing the rich man in his castle, the poor man at his gate a divinely ordained juxtaposition. When the off-course betting shops collapsed Sir Alexander Cockburn, introducing a new Bill to Parliament, referred to an awful possibility: 'Servants, apprentices and working men, induced by the temptation of receiving a large sum for a small one' might be 'driven into robbing their masters and employers.[5] The subsequent Act of 1853 shut down the listers but left on-course betting and private transactions untouched. This, of course, simply drove off-course betting underground and created a new growth industry, with wider opportunities in such trades as bookie's runner.

Here was Adam Smith's philosophy in action, a little benefit trickling down from the self-indulgent antics of the rich. The Turf, despite Bentinck's ministrations, was a disgrace. Regular scandals surrounded the Derby. In 1852 the second favourite was got at, and so was its jockey whose replacement 'pulled' the horse. In 1855, the favourite, Wild Deyrell, was the target of a scheme organised by the bookmaker Harry Hill. That year Lord Francis Villiers, a Jockey Club steward, fled the country owing £100,000, making a nonsense of the open letter written by Lord Derby, then leader of the Opposition, urging the Jockey Club to 'exercise a wholesome influence upon the character and respectability of the Turf'.[6] It stimulated intervention in the 1857 scandal, *Adkins* v *Sidebottom*, and in due course the Jockey Club took action also against Ignatius Coyle, a plebeian who had been involved in the Running Rein affair. But plebeians were not the problem. Despite the manifest inadequacy of the Jockey Club in 1860 Palmerston supported Lord Derby's petition on behalf of the Jockey Club deploring 'the interference of the legislature' in racing affairs.[7] The mantle of authority had by then fallen upon Admiral Rous, a typical younger son of the nobility enabled by a wealthy marriage to indulge a life-long obsession with horse-breeding and the Turf. In youth a successful racing manager for the Duke of Bedford, he had been a Jockey Club Steward since 1838, becoming an acknowledged expert on technical and legislative matters, notably handicapping.

Rous brought no great groundswell of idealism into the affairs of the Jockey Club, but at least was Victorian enough to set store by the avoidance of scandal. Both Victoria and Albert had high standards of private morality. This added to their concern about the behaviour of their impressionable son, Edward, Prince of Wales. One of his raffish friends was Henry Chaplin.

Immensely rich, Chaplin had been brought up to hunt with the Cottesmore by his clergyman father and 'finished' at the Burton by Lord Henry Bentinck whom he eventually succeeded as Master. Chaplin hunted six days a week at Oxford, keeping four horses, a style which dazzled Edward, who when sent to the university in 1859 was kept on short commons by his father. Their friendship had continued and there were soon many stories of their escapades together.

Though harum-scarum, Chaplin, who later was to become a Cabinet Minister, had some decent instincts. The same could not be said for his friend the Marquis of Hastings, spoilt, rich, vain, empty-headed and hell-bent in the Barrymore or Jack Mytton mould. As Master of the Quorn Hastings did nothing for its reputation or that of the Jockey Club which he joined on his coming of age in 1863. In 1864, largely out of mischief and the desire to show off, he eloped with Lady Florence Paget, daughter of the Marquis of Anglesey, a few days before she was due to marry Chaplin. Chaplin was made to look very foolish but he took the blow like a man, retiring to the country and his horses and dogs. This noble reaction infuriated Hastings who went off into a frenzy of gambling. He had some good horses, and in 1866 won £70,000 on the Cesarevitch alone. But his avowed object was to smash 'the ring' of bookmakers, a difficult enough task, even if it had not been complicated by his consuming hatred of Chaplin. In 1867 when Chaplin's colt Hermit was fancied for the Derby Hastings bet heavily against it, and was delighted when ten days before the race it burst a bloodvessel. When it recovered, and though starting at 66–1 and carrying a substitute jockey, came from nowhere to win by a short head, Hastings' loss of £120,000 was only part of his chagrin.

He set about recouping his losses by relentlessly over-running his two year old Lady Elizabeth, even running her against three year olds. This outraged the finer feelings of horse-lovers as well as moralists and writers of editorials. Furthermore despite his diatribes against the ring he was now financially reliant on Harry Hill and the money-lender, Padwick, to the extent that he was forced to resign from the Jockey Club. He had a good horse in the 1868 Derby, the Earl, but Hill and Padwick forced him to withdraw it. He still had Lady Elizabeth. Hastings' trainer, John Day, knew she was not up to racing but kept silent, and she gave in under the strain. As usual the racing establishment, though horrified by Hastings' behaviour, chiefly blamed Day and the bookmakers. One of the rumours flying around was that Admiral Rous had accused John Day of giving laudanum to Lady Elizabeth. Rous wrote to *The Times* denying it, but went on to state 'Lord Hastings has been shamefully deceived' and, after an account of Hastings' dealings with Hill and Padwick, concluded, 'What can the poor fly demand from the spider in whose web he is enveloped?' Day decided to sue (Hill and Padwick thought it prudent not to) but before the case could come to court Hastings was dead, physically and mentally wrecked at twenty-six. Dying, he is supposed to have said 'Hermit's Derby broke my heart – but I didn't show it did I?'[8] The honour code was satisfied.

Steeplechasing was not as corrupt or as dependent on gambling as the flat but socially it was handicapped by the 'sham captain' image, and it badly needed the support of the hunting fraternity. There were some hopeful signs. Fothergill Rowlands, a Monmouthshire doctor's son who owned and trained a few horses, got up a race in 1851 at Market Harborough, which by the following year, supported by a dozen local hunts, had grown into a Grand National Hunt Steeplechase, won by E. C. Burton, a former President of the Oxford University Boat Club no less. Dissension nipped the venture in the bud but Rowlands started afresh at Cheltenham and his enthusiasm had some reward. Meanwhile, the sport's reputation was helped by the Crimean War, when real captains took it up. 'Why do the cavalry officers of England and France encourage steeplechasing amongst their subordinates?', asked *Bell's Life*. 'Because it excites that courage, presence of mind and skill in horsemanship without which their glorious achievements at Balaclava would never have been recorded. It also checks riotous living and its worst accessory, the use of the gambling table.'[9]

But despite these moral advantages only in Ireland could steeplechasing compete socially with the flat. One of its devotees was the third Marquis of Drogheda, who spent the winters of the famine years leading the Elmo foxhounds or coursing at his estate, Moore Abbey. His summers were spent yachting (he was Commodore of the Royal St George's and a member of the RYS) and the autumns holding battues. He went racing all the year round and was senior steward of the Irish Jockey Club, but in later years he particularly enjoyed the Kildare Hunt's annual steeplechase at Punchestown. By 1854 this had attained some grandeur. Angelo Hayes was commissioned to paint the scene at the Corinthian Cup. His picture shows Henry Beresford, third Marquess of Waterford, founder of a famous sporting dynasty renowned in England as well as Ireland, along with Lord Drogheda, and Lords Conyngham, Howth, St Lawrence, Clonmel and Cloncarty together with numerous gentry. The riders included nine army captains. Punchestown was the pinnacle of Irish steeplechasing. By 1861 there were seven races, four of them sweepstakes (£5 each with some £770 prize money) and a Hunt Cup for members only. By contrast at most Irish meetings – at Cashel, Tipperary and Newcastle Co. Down, for instance – the courses were basically a set of flags marking out a series of natural obstacles. There might be a tiny grandstand but the riders usually had either to arrive in riding gear or change under a hedge. Superior spectators, of course, kept to their carriages, but for the lower orders there were tents where liquor was sold and bets transacted. As Harry R. Sargent, a gentleman rider of the time, recalled, 'a £50 plate was considered a biggish affair' and would attract 15 or 20 of the best horses in Ireland. The honour code was strong: 'Men who raced in those days, did so for sport, for honour or for glory. As a rule they were well-to-do and did not seek to supplement their incomes by either the stakes or gambling on the Turf. Indeed tradition required the leading amateurs – 'Captains Shaw, Trocke and McCraith with Sir Richard de Burgho and sporting Pat Russell' – to pay the professionals a fee to stand down, otherwise things were made hot for them. Captain Shaw, who ignored this custom, did so once too often and lost his life at Youghal.[10]

The English did things more formally. In 1862 a correspondent of *Bell's Life* proposed 41 rules to govern steeplechasing based on 'those recommended by a committee of noblemen and gentlemen in 1850' and even Admiral Rous, hitherto critical of what he called 'an extraneous branch of horse-racing', joined in the ensuing discussion with constructive suggestions. The following year three members of the Jockey Club, under the chairmanship of Mr W. G. Craven – a man of impeccable credentials: Eton, Life Guards, yachtsman and leading rider to hounds – formed a National Hunt Committee. They inevitably spent much time on trying to define gentlemen riders. Their first efforts included as well as the usual army and navy officers and members of the professions, the somewhat circular notion of 'persons generally received into Society as Gentlemen', such as members of the London leading clubs. But which were the leading clubs? It was not acceptable, an indignant correspondent told *Bell's Life*, to suggest that a member of the Reform was a gentleman and a member of the Conservative is not. Problems of a different kind arose from another stipulation, that gentlemen should not take money for riding or travelling expenses. To be both a gentleman and an amateur was frequently to prove too demanding a requirement.

Field sports – modern style

Many in the hunting circles that had bred this hybrid monster were more concerned with how the railways had debased their own sport. Trollope, introduced to hunting as Post Office official in Ireland and thereafter a life-long addict, had no time for such purists, contending indeed that the dreaded railway, despite eroding land, increasing noise and reducing the fox population, had 'created the sport anew'. The much-maligned money men from the city, he pointed out, at least paid their way, which could not be said of many country-bred hunt followers. Trollope estimated the expenses of the average MFH, hunting four days a week, at around £2,700 a year, apart from personal expenses such as servants (£250 a year for two huntsmen and two whips, £55 for a feeder, £300 for grooms, second horsemen, stable assistants, etc., and £160 for hunt uniforms and clothing). By contrast hunt followers could have the same amount of sport for about £480 a year. Of this 10% would be not unreasonable but the subscription was the element of expense most members begrudged: indeed, three-quarters of hunt followers paid nothing – farmers who lent their fields, clergymen who acted as chaplains, doctors who offered emergency services were not charged. Ladies, schoolboys home for Christmas, old gentlemen and strangers were guests. The small tradespeople and 'the ruck of horse keepers, inn keepers and of horsey men generally' were exempted as social inferiors.[11]

J. A. Bridges also pointed out some of the realities. He was not impressed by the hunt he joined as a gentleman farmer in the Midlands in the sixties: they had a 'rough and ready pack' and a membership to match, 'only on very rare occasions supplemented by an iron-master or two, or a sporting publican from the Black Country'. The railway helped them secure, for a time, a dedicated young MFH, prepared to commute from his job as agent to a big landowner in Wales at great personal sacrifice. Yet he was thought avaricious when he put up the subscription to £40, and when he left for higher things he was replaced by a local wine-merchant who looked well in the uniform but 'hadn't an idea in his head, and he never rode a yard'. The old hierarchies were no guarantee of etiquette. The farmers, decent cider-drinking fellows on their £15 cobs, 'were true sportsmen to a man', unlike the handful of small landowners who thought heavy drinking was an essential part of the sport.[12]

However, not withstanding misplaced snobberies, Trollope had no doubt of the superiority of hunting, in which 'manly and genuine sportsmen took pride', over shooting 'those deadly missiles, which the breech loaders of Purday and his multitudinous professional brethren drive with such accuracy and force through the spangled plumage of grouse, pheasant and partridge'. He was revolted by battue shooting and deplored the fact that pheasants – 'imported foreigners' – were bred like barnyard fowls and slaughtered in vast numbers. The passion for huge 'bags' was greatly endangering the supply of game, especially since Purday. There were not many coverts that Mr Thomas de Grey, MP for West Norfolk, could not make a clean sweep of in three hours, if let loose with his couple of breech-loaders. The Game Laws – 'surviving remembrances of feudal institutions' – were an incitement to violence by poachers. He took comfort that the 'responsibility of jeopardising men's lives' for the sake of 'selfish indulgence in what is, after all, a pastime' was persuading some enlightened landlords to give up their coverts.[13]

Fishing aroused less emotion in Trollope as in most of the rest of the population, though he made tart observations about the changing economics of the sport. Salmon had once been so plentiful that people even caught grilse – unspawned fish. Now it had become fashionable and expensive: 'in spring a twenty-five pound salmon on a Bond Street counter may be estimated at seven pounds ten shillings sterling'. Rivers could be profitable: the Spey made over £12,000 a year for the Duke of Richmond. It was 'rather annoying' to be required to pay a sovereign a day for the right of angling on a stretch of salmon water and have in addition to surrender your take of fish to the lessee.[14]

Indian summer of the prize-ring

Unlike Bridges, Trollope was not an admirer of pugilism which he did not admit into his select sports. By any standards the prize-ring was currently at a low ebb. In 1851 the Chief Constable of Belper, trying to stop a fight for a purse of £1,000 between Tom Paddock, a farm-worker, and Henry Paulson, a railway 'navigator', was knocked from his horse by the mob and both boxers were sentenced to ten months' hard labour. Very few of the gentry and nobility retained an interest. There was no modern equivalent of Jackson's Rooms. Harry R. Sargent, coming to London from Ireland in 1855 to serve a business apprenticeship, went to Nat Langham's to spar but found that the 'noble art' was looked at askance in the City. A few Corinthians still went to Jim Burns' Queen's Head, and other places where there were old 'pugs' willing to be knocked about for a few shillings: at the Black Lion near Drury Lane, 'Sambo' Sutton would intersperse sparring exhibitions by dancing an upside down horn-pipe.[15]

The situation was temporarily saved by the growing demand for open competition. The Fancy, who now frequented Limmer's Hotel, came up with the idea of a championship Belt, open to all, but to be contested for not less than £200 a side. Holders could keep the Belt (designed by Hancock's of New Bond Street) if they remained undefeated for three years. One of those attracted by this competition was Tom Sayers, a twenty-eight year old 11 stone Camden Town bricklayer, who in 1856 managed to scrape up the money to challenge the much heavier Paulson on his release from prison, beating him by cunning tactical skills and a final relentless battery. When he beat Aaron Jones, another big man, Sayers became 'the Little Wonder', a soubriquet justified in 1857 when he demolished the 14st 6lb veteran Bill Perry, 'the Tipton Slasher' and various other lumbering giants to become undisputed holder of the Belt.

An American challenge set the seal on the revival. John Carmel Heenan was 6ft 2ins and 14 stones and six years younger than Sayers, who had given his backers a nervous moment or two in his previous fight through lack of training. Not every newspaper approved. 'Apart from the legal question, it is a point of considerable interest to determine whether morality demands that prize-fighting be discontinued', wrote the high-minded *Manchester Guardian*. But most of the papers were full of the coming match and there was dismay when the Derby police arrested Heenan in his training quarters, binding him over to keep the peace. The *Sporting Life* criticised Heenan's managers for allowing this interruption. 'There are plenty of obscure nooks in England where he might have gone on training till doomsday.[16]

The police action meant that several weeks later, though everyone knew the fight was still on, no-one knew where or when. *The Times'* revelation on 24 January 1859 that it was to be held on 16 April, 'privately' near Mildenhall in Suffolk merely caused a change of venue, and soon the *Sporting Life* was warning its readers to be ready for a 'tremendous journey' in mid-April. Opinions were divided even amongst the authorities. On 13 April the Home Secretary, when asked in Parliament what measures he would take to prevent a breach of the peace, said he felt sure the Commissioner of Police had the matter in hand. Palmerston urged the opposition to be moderate and was commended by traditionalists for his thoroughly English character and his 'love for every manly sport'.

The eventual venue, near Farnborough on the Hampshire–Surrey border, was chosen after a deal with the South Eastern Railway Company to run a special train that would stop between stations. On 15 April *Bell's Life* gave the names of places where excursion tickets could be had – Owen Swift's, Nat Langham's, George Byers' and Harry Brunton's. The cost, three guineas, was about six times the normal fare, and the excursion began at London Bridge at 4.00 a.m., yet the railway needed all its available rolling stock – two trains with 63 carriages. The Metropolitan Police lined the track at various points to prevent the train stopping but it pulled up at an unmanned stretch near Farnborough where the crowd set off running across country, after the ring-maker and the caterers. Many fell in a ditch full of stagnant water.

The fight itself was an extraordinary affair. Sayers lost the use of his right arm early on but used his left to close one of Heenan's eyes and cut his cheek to ribbons. By round thirty-six however, Sayers was exhausted and seemed beaten: Heenan was so frustrated at not being able to finish him off that he grabbed him by the throat and as the crowd filled the ring, appeared to be choking Sayers against the ropes, which had to be cut to release him. The referee tried to stop the fight, but the crowd, which had been fending off intermittent attacks from the police, would have none of it. It limped on for five more rounds until both men slithered to the ground together.

The result was afterwards declared a draw, but no one was satisfied. In America James Gordon Bennett, the newspaper magnate, thought 'the Britons stopped the fight to save their money'. Conversely Thackeray, grow-ing lyrical about 'that little man with one hand powerless on his breast, facing yonder giant for hours' told readers of *The Cornhill* that 'the advantage was all on Mr Sayers side'. The *Saturday Review* extracted journalistic juice. 'If the British supporters did not witness exactly what they expected, they saw an even finer sight. Never in the annals of pugilism were skill, coolness, judgement, variety of resource, pluck and bottom displayed in such wonderful degree.' Yet money-scenting talk of a rematch collapsed because neither man was in any condition to face it. Sayers retired a month later, and on Derby Day was received by Princess May in the Royal Box. Replica Belts were presented to both men, who were hailed as great ambassadors and harbingers of peace by the press of Britain and America.

But the euphoria wore off and there was no great resistance when the Home Secretary gave notice that any attempt at resumption would lead to prosecution. The Commons debated the matter and called (albeit ineffectually) for the files of the South-Eastern Railway. The traditionalists were unrepentant, of course. One of the first to contribute to the testimonial for Sayers was Palmerston. Yet reality soon diminished nostalgic myth. The testimonial list closed at £3,000 and was invested for Sayers, but he was soon penniless and afflicted by an ailment which gave him a great thirst. When he appeared as a second for Heenan in 1863 he was a pathetic, useless figure. Heenan was himself never the same, and when he lost a poor slugging match against the big rough docker, Tom King, and claimed to have been drugged, public opinion moved solidly behind the abolitionists.[17]

Furthermore, though the press on both sides of the Atlantic was now the main source of sponsorship, it was clear that glamorised accounts of essentially seedy affairs were not enough. In fact sporting journalism itself was in process of change under the influence of a new breed of university men. One of the first was a young Welsh gentleman, John Graham Chambers, who after Eton and Cambridge was forced by family financial problems to turn to the organisation and promulgation of sport for a living. In 1866 he set up the Amateur Athletic Club in rented premises at Waltham Green. Club members enjoyed boxing – the gloved variety – and one of its leading lights was the twenty-two year old Marquis of Queensberry. Using Queensberry's name to add social clout, Chambers produced in 1867 rules which were to give a new lease of life to boxing in the next era. The prize-ring was not dead, but it was on its last legs.[18]

Expensively educated galley slaves

Chambers, an all-round sportsman, was one of the best 'pedestrian' race-walkers in England, but first and foremost he was a prominent oarsman, rowing twice in the Boat Race, a member of Leander and a noted sculler.

Rowing was still in the doldrums, largely because of the preoccupation of the leading clubs with the threat of professionalism. In 1853 Tom Egan, now himself a sporting journalist, felt so strongly about Cambridge University's limp attitude that he took himself off to Oxford where the amateur cause was being upheld by a new generation of Old Etonians.

That year's Boat Race drew thousands to the tow path (including 200 on horseback) and enough steam launches to endanger the myriad small boats following the crews. Cambridge lost and, duly chastened, welcomed Egan back and challenged Oxford to a rematch. Oxford suggested that this be held during the Henley Regatta which 'having clearly shown symptoms of decline, it was desirable by all means to endeavour to preserve'. All of which boded well for the true amateur spirit. However, Henley's becalmed waters were now rippled by the rise of Royal Chester who, having appointed a professional coach in 1854 and invested in new-style boats, were so successful for a time that the Henley authorities felt obliged to tighten the rules, restricting more competitions to public school and university crews.

Their reaction illustrated the convoluted thought processes by which the upholders of tradition sought to fend off the challenge of vulgarity. Chester's coach, Matt Taylor, one of the many fine professionals from Tyne and Wear worked closely with the captain of Royal Chester, J. B. Littledale, son of a Liverpool shipbuilder in designing a revolutionary new keel-less boat. After Royal Chester crews, inelegant and scarcely able to sit Taylor's boat properly in spite of his coaching, won both the Grand and the Ladies' Plate in 1856 they were ostracised socially. Yet Taylor made his name in the best circles and several similar boats were made, including one for the Oxford president, A. P. Lonsdale, built at his own expense, in which Oxford outclassed Cambridge in the following year's Boat Race. Oxford had engaged Taylor, Lonsdale reckoned, 'not to instruct us in the art of rowing but to show us the proper way to send his boat along as quickly as possible'.[19] A subtle distinction indeed.

Amateur no longer merely meant one who played games for fun: the category included many who wanted success at any price. There were men of impeccable amateur status, gentlemen by any formal standard, who nevertheless had acquired at school and college a fierce institutional pride, often bolstered by muscular Christianity, that they wore like a badge, jousting with any who carried different emblems. For others it was a mark of social status, which outsiders had to see and recognise. Many amateur oarsmen, on the other hand, often suffered from limited leisure – and sometimes money – which obliged them to choose between rowing and its social trappings. A survey in 1856 of Thames clubs showed dwindling membership all along the river (we may discount Leander's decision that same year to extend its membership from 25 to 35, scarcely an abandonment of élitism). Yet when the survey was followed up by Mr Josias Noltidge seeking recruits to a proposed London Rowing Club with modest subscriptions it was quickly launched and within five weeks had 140 members owing. This was followed in 1860 by City of London Rowing Club, started by a group of young clerks and salesmen. At first their idea was purely recreational: they would take the 6.34 p.m. horse-driven omnibus from Waterloo to Putney and form scratch crews when they got there, but two years later, expanded and renamed Thames Rowing Club, they became much more competition-minded in the spirit of the times.

These new ventures led to the disappearance of some of the smaller, struggling clubs but the survivors were stronger and more active. Throughout the country new clubs were being formed, from Agecroft in Salford to York City, enough to justify the publication in 1862 of a *Rowing Almanack*, which conveniently categorised clubs as for Gentlemen, Tradesmen and Watermen. It was competition and the stipulation of amateur status that caused trouble. Private matches within the inner circle of the universities and, the most select public schools were no longer a problem now that professional coaching was at an end. The two universities nevertheless began to take the Boat Race as seriously as any professionals. Tom Egan's reinstatement at remorseful and repentant Cambridge led to renewed belief in what was becoming known as the 'orthodox English' style of rowing. Meanwhile Egan had acquired a fervent disciple at Oxford, Edmond Warre, who in 1860 became a master at Eton and took over the coaching of rowing.

By this time the muscular Christianity that imbued the new model public schools in the wake of Dr Arnold was taking hold even in the older ones, though there was even less *dirigisme* in the development of school games at Eton and Harrow than in the new foundations, not least because of the reactionary attitude of influential Old Boys who had grave doubts about such new-fangled ideas as making games compulsory. The enthusiasm came from young schoolmasters, convinced, as were their contemporaries who actually went in to the church, that games, and team-games in particular, were a splendid and necessary way of preparing young gentlemen for leadership whilst imbuing them with patriotic, chivalric and Christian virtues. In fact, their model was the pre-Christian notion of a healthy mind in a healthy body. This was the credo of Drummond Levy, the master who composed the 'Eton Boating Song' for the school in 1865 and of Dr Warre who laboured for many years, as housemaster and eventually headmaster, to establish Eton as the cornerstone of British rowing.

So although rowing was, and would remain a minority sport it was a very powerful minority. Schools began to measure themselves by the number of Blues (i.e. representatives in the annual Boat Race) they achieved and colleges began to look out for good oarsmen in choosing students. Old Blues who became dons (as university teachers liked to be called) or found benefices nearby were eager to assist with coaching. The gruelling discipline the coaches demanded, though a masochistic necessity, evoked hostility from outsiders. Trollope, who went to riverless Harrow, admitted rowing to his list of selected sports but mainly, it seemed, so as to crack wise about the mindless Spartan regime it required. Amongst the foremost critics of the modern approach was F.C. Skey, an eminent surgeon and popular public lecturer. Skey disliked the modern sporting cult and especially rowing, asserting that it inflicted the greatest cruelty of any animal in any sport. Trollope, replying to Skey's criticism, did so in a highly skittish fashion, casting doubt on the mentality of people who would subject themselves to such torture for sport. He was particularly scathing about the collective nature of its classical mode, eights (the team approach so admired by adherents), which he reckoned suppressed individuality and required the disciplined servitude of the galley.[20]

Gentlemen and 'peds'

The changed status of team-games, rising from the mobbish mayhem of folk football through the more individualistic and genteel cavortings of early cricket to sanctification in university rowing, was indeed one of the most remarkable phenomena of the Victorian age. Rugged individualism was still admired: pugilism retained its appeal to the public schools because of the basic British belief that fists were the best way to settle arguments, but, just as in rowing sculling was always suspect to the purists, so team-games were thought good for the character. It followed that track and field athletics, however conducive to healthy non-violent competition, tended to bear the taint of individualism. Some field events also bore the stamp of bucolic or even Celtic idosyncrasy, and track events in particular were associated with gambling.

This was no modern vulgarisation: indeed, there was a long tradition of gentlemanly involvement in pedestrian feats of one kind or another, for wagers. Beauclerk had been as adroit on the old furlong track at Lord's as on the cricket field. But in the newer urban centres crowds were drawn by popular heroes like Blackburn Mick, the hero of a meeting described with more enthusiasm than art in a Preston broadsheet:

> On the first day of December eighteen hundred and forty five,
> Some thousands came to Bell view with hearts all fine,
> To see these gallant heroes bold, come and strip unto the skin
> To try their best for fifty pounds, which of them could win.[21]

These were gate-money affairs, often in fields adjoining public houses, with plenty of beer and bookmakers taking bets and star attractions in exotic costumes contending against the local lads.

Field events, by contrast, were survivals of feats of strength and agility which had not remained part of aristocratic training or leisure pursuits, or attracted their patronage to any great extent, and, since they were unspectacular, were less susceptible to commercial exploitation. Their re-emergence owed much to the revival of Scottish Highland culture typified and stimulated by Victoria's annual visits to Balmoral and by railway access to a field sports paradise for her English subjects. It was part of a glamorisation assisted by the novels of Sir Walter Scott and the invention of the tartan kilt (by a Lancashire industrialist) which had been adopted by the lowland gentry as badges of ethnic identity. In the same spirit the Braemar Royal Highland Gatherings, first organised after Waterloo to raise money for relatives of war-victims, offered an opportunity for the lairds to show off their finery to the English court and the assembled crowds.

The competitions at these Gatherings and their counterparts and imitators at lesser Highland meetings, the Border Games in Southern Scotland and the Lakeland Games in North-west England were plebeians interested in prize-money as well as honour, and the events were stylised versions of traditional contests – tossing the weight, throwing the hammer, tossing the caber, moun-tain-top racing, sometimes with hurdles to be leapt, pole-vaulting for dis-tance, long-jumping and the Border specialism 'hitch-and-kick'. In Ireland, where tradition went back to the legendary Tailtean Games (dating from royal sports around 2000 BC and defunct since around AD 1180) it survived in such events as hammer-throwing – a ball and chain said to derive from hurling a wheel – leaping and hopping, which found its way into the triple jump; but there were no revivals amongst the ascendancy. Here and in England, where casting the stone had become putting the shot and village sports featured the highly popular tug-of-war, the meetings were of decidedly plebeian tone.[22]

In England, furthermore, they were often loosely organised, attached to fairs, race-meetings or seasonal festivities where drink flowed freely. Middle class and religious apprehensions were offset, however, by gratification that athletic contests were gradually replacing the old, barbaric amusements and there were soon a host of regular, organised well-publicised events, with prizes drawing competitors from far a field.[23] Existing sporting clubs, particu-larly cricket and rowing clubs, often held athletic sports meetings as diversions and money-raising activities. Ulverston Cricket Club, for instance, helped popularise pole-vaulting for height, West London Rowing Club held sports meetings as off-season fitness training for the members.

Not surprisingly, in view of their individualistic nature and mixed origins, track and field athletic events were not held in high regard in the public schools. Events like hare-and-hounds and paperchases, essentially ways of making fitness training tolerable by making a game of it, were as far as they usually went. There was, however, growing interest in academic and pedagogical circles in the classical ideals of achieving the balanced development of mind, soul and body exemplified by the Olympic Games. The Olympic idea was rescued from the political, Merrie England image of Captain Dover's Cotswold spectaculars by such scholarly works as J. H. Krause's *Die Gymnastik und Agonstik der Hellenen* (The Physical Recreation and Contests of the Greeks) published in 1848.[24] Another influence was that of the army's officer training establishments which introduced an early version of the modern fashion of track and field athletics meetings, first at Royal Military College, Sandhurst, and then on a bigger scale at Royal Military Academy, Woolwich, which held annual meetings between 1849 and 1853. A less high-minded but profound influence came from a group of high-spirited undergraduate at Exeter College, Oxford. In 1850 the annual College point-to-point steeplechase known as 'the Grind' was so disappointing, because of the quality of the 'screws' hired for the occasion, that one contestant said he could have jumped the course better himself. He and his friends went on to devise a human steeplechase, for fun, and this grew into a full-scale Exeter Autumn meeting. The steeplechase – a two mile race with 24 jumps – was a sweepstake (£1 each, 10s forfeit) and there were flat-race sweepstakes over a mile, quarter-mile, '300 yards and a distance', 100 yards, 140 yards over hurdles and a 'consolation stakes for beaten horses'. The Exeter became an annual event, soon other Oxford colleges followed suit – with less horsey versions – and by 1856 St John's and Emmanuel at Cambridge were also holding athletics meetings, and Trinity College, Dublin, held one in 1857. By 1864 there were annual contests between Oxford and Cambridge – rough affairs by all accounts.[25] In 1866 the meeting ended in disorder following a dead-heat which brought competitors, spectators and bookmakers into conflict, 'the sound of which, dinning into the midnight', Clement Jackson an athletics-minded Oxford don, reckoned he could still hear many years later.[26]

It was to be some time before foot-racing could shake off the clinging tendrils of gentlemanly wagers and the vulgarian professional 'peds' they so much loathed. The Beauclerk style lived on in influential, colourful figures like E. H. Budd, best known as a cricketer but also a talented 'spirter' in his youth. His reminiscences are revealing about the social limits within which the code of honour was deemed to operate. When his sister rebuked him for having run against a person for whom the stake was an object his excuse was that he had done so only to teach him a lesson, like a debased self-conscious version of Orlando and the wrestler, Charles. He made a point, whenever he saw a chance to put such professionals in their place, of running in his street clothes, in contrast with such as the 'Brighton Shepherd' who paraded in a smock frock for publicity purposes but removed it just before a race to reveal aerodynamic vest and drawers.[27]

Publicity was important to the 'peds', and exotic costumes and personae were part of their stock-in-trade. Everyone had a flowery nickname. Bill Lang, landlord of the Royal Oak in Manchester with his own track alongside, was 'the Crow Catcher', his great rival Jack White was 'the Gateshead Clipper'. Best of all, however, was the Canadian, Louis Bennett, known as 'Deerfoot' because he was part Red-Indian, who was the great commercial success of 1860, giving rise to many imitators. The more flamboyant 'peds' were known collectively as 'Wild Indians' and they took their place in gentlemanly demonology along with the sham captains of steeplechasing.

Sharp practice was expected of them, and much deplored. But it was not unknown amongst the gentlemen. Budd recounts gleefully how he deceived a young Etonian to win a bet. And *Sportascrapiana*, which devoted a whole chapter to what it called 'Fleet of foot', took a markedly unamateurish stance. After detailed advice on such matters as the spacing of spikes in running shoes the anonymous expert author dilated on tactics with much more emphasis on gaining an advantage than on fair play. Starting by mutual consent was preferable to starting by pistol which left too much in the hands of referees. This involved two competitors at the starting line facing each other each trying to sense when the other was about to take off and beating him to it without incurring a penalty. Skill at this showed the difference between a professional and a novice. He went on to discuss the state of the art of 'spirting'. He was a good man who could do 100 yards in 10.5 seconds and a 'clinker' who could do it in 10. It was extremely rare for anyone to do better, and if you had a man capable of 10 seconds you could win £10,000 with him at Sheffield, the leading pedestrian centre.

There were hopeful signs, however, for apart from young dons like Clement Jackson and his friend Montague Shearman, the better rowing clubs were also trying to create a purer atmosphere. In 1867, for instance, Thames Rowing Club inaugurated a paperchase that rose from its beginnings as a training outing to become a celebrated cross-country event. There was promise of better things furthermore in the formation of all-round athletics clubs like Mincing Lane Athletics Club (1863) ancestor of London Athletics Club, which catered for young professional and businessmen. And at a higher social level there was Chambers' Amateur Athletic Club, one of whose avowed objects was to keep out the 'peds' and wild Indians.

Notes

1 For the emergence of the class system see H. Perkin, *The Origins of Modern English*

Society, 1780–1880, London, 1969. For the effects of the industrial revoltuion see P. Mathias, *The First Industrial Nation*, London, 1969 and, with particular reference to the shift towards commerce, E. Hobsbawm, *Industry and Empire*, London, 1968. For regional differences see H. Kearney, *The British Isles*, Cambridge, 1989 and, on economic matters, E. Richards, 'Regional Imbalance and Poverty in Early Nineteenth Century Britain' in R. Mitchison and P. Roebuck (eds.), *Economy and Society in Scotland and Ireland*, Edinburgh, 1988, pp. 193–207. For religion see G.S.R. Kitson Clark, *The English Inheritance*, London, 1950.

2 E. Longford, *Victoria RI*, London, 1964, p. 295.

3 J. Roussmarière, *America's Cup 1851–1983*, London, 1988, p. 14. See also I. Dear, *The America's Cup*, London, 1980, on which this account mainly draws.

4 *British Sports and Pastimes*, London, 1868. The book consists of a series of essays that originally appeared in Trollope's *St Paul's Magazine*, of which he was editor and much of which he wrote himself. The contributors to the book are not named, so Trollope is credited with authorship.

5 *Hansard*, 11 July 1853, quoted in W. Vamplew, *The Turf*, London, 1976, p. 204.

6 Vamplew, *The Turf*, pp. 102–3; see also R. Mortimer, *The Jockey Club*, London, 1958, pp. 95–6.

7 Vamplew, *The Turf*, p. 98; Mortimer, *Jockey Club*, pp. 107–10. The occasion was Lord Redesdale's Light weight Racing Bill (1866) providing that no horse should carry less than 7 stone.

8 Mortimer, *Jockey Club*, p. 102. For Hastings and Chaplin see H. Blyth, *The Pocket Venus*, London, 1966. For Chaplin and the Prince of Wales see C. Hibbert, *Edward VII*, London, 1975.

9 8 November 1854.

10 H.R. Sargent, *Thoughts Upon Sport*, London, 1894, p. 135.

11 *British Sports*, p.4.

12 *A Sportsman of Limited income*, pp. 137–153.

13 Trollope, *British Sports and Pastimes*, pp. 130 157, 168–9

14 Ibid., pp.185–6

15 Sargent, *Thoughts Upon Sport*, p 303.

16 A. Lloyd, *The Great Prize Fight*, London, 1977, pp. 72–4.

17 Ibid., pp 90–164, passim.

18 See article on Chambers by G.L. Boase in *Dictionary of National Biography*.

19 C. Dodd, 'Rowing', in T. Mason (ed.), *Sport in Britain*, Cambridge, 1989, p 281

20 Trollope, *British Sports and Pastimes*, pp. 226–256.

21 Full version in L. James (ed.), *Print and the People, 1819–1851*, Harmondsworth, 1978, p. 138.

22 For the origin of the various field events see R.L. Quercetani, *A World History of Track and Field Events*, Oxford, 1964, The caber is a tree-trunk or thick pole. Hitch-and-kick was an idiosyncratic kind of high-jump with a football.

23 A detailed account of the social currents in the sporting life of mid-Victorian Lancaster is given in M. Speak, 'Social stratification and Participation in Sport' in J.R. Mangan (ed.), *Pleasure, Profit and Proseleytism*, London, 1988, pp. 41–63.

24 The words 'athletic' and 'athlete' had been in use since the seventeenth century, but were somewhat obscurantist until 'athletic' began to be used (a) to describe all-round sporting clubs like Chambers' and (b) in discussion of trends in the schools and universities: e.g. Mark Pattison 'pretending to think that cricket, boating and athletics, as now conducted, are only recreations: *Suggestions on Academic Organisation*, 1868; *Daily News* 'The controversy about athleticism at the universities and public schools', 24 November 1870 (*OED*).

25 H.A. Harris, *Sport in Britain*, London, 1975, pp. 46–7.
26 P. Lovesey, *The Official Centenary History of the Amateur Athletic Association*, London, 1979, p. 41.
27 C.A. Wheeler, *Sportascrapiana* (2nd edn), 1868.

CHAPTER ELEVEN

Judicious bottle-holding: glimpses of modernity

1851–66

It was an indeterminate age politically, with the combatants of the next era Gladstone and Disraeli still searching for distinctive themes. The values of the septuagenarian Palmerston, applied commonsensically to practical issues rather than visionary schemes, were what counted. The Crimean experience had few lasting effects. The person to emerge with most credit from the war and the one who best showed how to turn its lessons to peace-time advantage was Florence Nightingale. The admiration she evoked did nothing to challenge male supremacy – she was quite indifferent to talk of women's rights – but it helped to draw attention to female characteristics of which men were only dimly aware. Charitable works, writing books and dedication to humane causes were still the main outlets for female talent.

Specifically feminist advances, such as reform of the marriage and divorce laws came in fitfully and far from equitably. More substantial change came from industrialisation. Factory work added substantially to the opportunities of working class women. It gave many of them not only more economic independence but leverage in persuading husbands towards smaller families. For the least fortunate it offered a better alternative to prostitution which had assumed frightening proportions by mid-century. Less helpful – either to the feminist cause or society in general – was the cult of the lady which came with prosperity. Work of any sort – notwithstanding Miss Nightingale – was not thought genteel. It was the charms, not the occupations, of the various fictional heroines that gripped the imagination of the age; from old favourites like Scott, Jane Austen and the Brontes to new writers like Dickens, Thackeray, George Eliot, Meredith and Trollope. The perfect lady was ornamental and gracious but supposedly delicate and not to be exposed to physical challenge at work or play.

A modest intrusion

In sport women's historic role was that of handkerchief-fluttering spectators. Times were beginning to change, especially amongst the younger generation. The early pioneers of women's education had more serious things on their minds than organising athletic activity. Nevertheless the schools built up by graduates of the Governesses' Benevolent Association like the redoubtable Miss Buss, Head of North London Collegiate School from 1850, and Miss Beale, Head of Cheltenham Ladies College from 1858, produced girls of independent spirit unwilling to be deterred by meaningless convention from pursuing innocent and enjoyable activities like the games they played with their brothers in school holidays.

Meanwhile, however, the cause of female emancipation was not helped by the controversy about rational dress that followed the visit of Miss Amelia Bloomer in 1851 – not a good time for American liberals to come to England. The serious aspects of her campaign were submerged by the ridicule which greeted the pantaloons, called after her but modelled by her colleague, Libby Millar. *Punch* made the most of the opportunity. The crinolines which true ladies wore for truly lady-like athletic activities such as dancing allowed a little relief from the steel-and-whalebone tight lacing of the forties, for the new style made largish waists seem smaller, and below the waist the layers of petticoats were replaced first by horsehair frames, then by steel hoops and air tubes. Yet whatever the quirks of fashion, corseting was still necessary and the lower half of the body had to be concealed from view.

This posed particular problems on the hunting field. With a few exceptions, mostly royal, active hunting for women had for centuries meant first hawking and then hare-coursing. Riding itself normally meant side-saddle since it was not thought proper to draw attention to the bifurcation of the lower limbs, but riding at speed, though unusual, was not unknown. There was, for instance, the unconventional wife of Colonel Thornton, himself an eccentric Yorkshire squire, who issued an elaborate and public challenge to a Mr Bromford in 1805 to a race for 'four hogsheads of Coti Roti, pp and 2,000 guineas, h-ft.' over the York course. When Mr Bromford declined, choosing to pay the forfeit, Mrs Thornton took on the professional jockey, Buckle, instead.[1] But foxhunting became a difficult proposition once it involved jumping hedges, not least because early side-saddles had only two upright pommels between which the right, forward, thigh was inserted while the left had only a stirrup for support.

Because of this, and for reasons of etiquette, very few women appeared on the hunting field in early Victorian times. Those that did were a mixed lot. There was a small group of independent-minded wives and daughters of the leading hunts such as the Countess of Craven, the Marchioness of Salisbury, Lady Eleanor Lowther and the four daughters of the Earl of Darlington; one or two professional equestriennes and riding teachers; and the occasional mistress of the outdoor type. But when the first faint glimmerings of the liberation of women appeared – characteristically in the upper reaches of society – some of the first indications were to be seen in the fashionable hunts.

Assisting the process was an advance in technology, which added a third downward-sloping pommel to the saddle against which the left thigh could be pressed: this gave a more secure seat and also allowed the rider to jump off when in trouble. Safety stirrups and non-slip girths helped as well and before long there came the safety habit, designed to come off in an emergency: long sers underneath would preserve decency even in a crisis.[2] (Though this not always prevent exhibitionism or prurient speculation: it was rumoured that the notorious 'Skittles' wore white frillies.) Some of the more dubious newcomers were amongst the best riders. 'Skittles' herself – so called because she had once worked in a Liverpool bowling alley – frequently, in her capacity as current mistress of the Earl of Fitzwilliam, rode with the Quorn in the sixties. Her riding skills infuriated Lady Stamford, wife of the Master, as much as her flamboyant presence, possibly because Lady Stamford herself had an equestrian background (some said she had worked in a circus). In general, however, the new recruits were welcomed and fitted in surprisingly well.

Most commentators, including Trollope, remarked with approval upon the improved atmosphere in such things as swearing and uncouth manners. There were, of course, complaints from serious hunting men that some women presumed on their sex by pushing through gaps, jumping on hounds and committing other breaches of the code, and worst of all when they got into trouble gentlemen were obliged to offer assistance, which meant falling behind in the chase. But the new trend was set and more and more women followed it, first in the shires then in less fashionable terrain.

Compared with English ladies, American women were vulgar, chauvinists thought, and French ones were decadent. The French reputation for iniquity was as bad as ever. A new source of annoyance now arose over the velocipede. No-one had yet properly solved the problem of translating up-and-down or to-and-fro leg movements into wheeled propulsion, and even for men it required real, unencumbered athleticism to work the early machines. A British designer, William Sawyer, had shown a model at the Great Exhibition and later made one for the Prince of Wales (his Commercial Model, on sale in 1860, cost £17 2s 6d). But the French went ahead in both design and production of four-, three- and two-wheeled machines, and it added insult to injury to learn that Parisiennes taking up the new vogue were prepared to take the principles of rational dress far beyond what any English lady would contemplate.[3]

The poor French got no compensatory credit for the entirely decorous vogue of the late 1850s and 1860s, croquet. This was a version of *jeu de mail*, the mallet game, which was probably taken by French nuns to Ireland, where it flourished in the early nineteenth century and whence it came to England in 1852. There were no croquet mallets in the sports equipment on display at the Great Exhibition, and croquet seems to have been regarded as purely a ladies' diversion until Lord Lowther, now the Earl of Lonsdale, took it up a few years later. Yet by 1858 letters and articles began to appear in *The Field* about it, arousing much debate about its origins and the proper rules of play. John Jaques, an ivory-turner of Hatton Garden, who had seen the game on a business trip to Ireland, was the first manufacturer of high-quality equipment (sets could cost as much as twenty guineas) and it was he who issued the first rules.[4]

Croquet, the first open air ball-game to be considered suitable for mixed play, clearly filled a niche. The frontispiece to *Mr Punch's Pocket Book for 1862* showed the possibilities for mild titillation: a cartoon by John Leech had 'Fanny . . . placing her pretty little foot on the ball' and proceeding to croquet her male opponent. It was perfectly suited to the decorous display of crinolined charms, especially when the skirt was underpinned by the anti-Aeolian, an elaborate wire device to control billowing. Soon croquet was all the rage. New clubs were founded in superior places like Worthing (1865) and Bedford (1866). Jaques' print orders for sets of rules increased from 25,000 in 1865 to 65,000 two years later. Other manufacturers, including John Wisden the cricket expert and James Buchanan an archery specialist, began to supply equipment, and before long sets were available for as little as fifteen shillings. At the other end of the scale the Viceroy of India played with a mallet of solid ivory, and at home the cynosure of fashion was the Earl of Eglinton, the fabulously rich and open-handed Anglo-Scottish peer who had twice been Viceroy of Ireland. Eglinton's reconstruction of a medieval tournament in 1839 reputedly cost between £30,000 and £40,000. Croquet players wore red boots at Eglinton Castle.

Ice-skating, weather permitting, was also considered a suitable sport for ladies. They were set a dignified example by the gentlemen of the exclusive London Skating Club, founded in 1842, which was dedicated to figure-skating of a stately, not to say statuesque kind. (Speed-skating chiefly flourished in the Fens amongst the lower orders.) The club's prestige was greatly enhanced when Prince Albert agreed to become its patron, and he showed great interest in the introduction of the all-iron skate from America in 1850. The mild English climate was the biggest obstacle. A possible answer was the wheeled roller skate which was developed in New York in 1863, but its very accessibility gave it overtones of vulgarity which cast doubts on its suitability for ladies.[5]

Golf discovers England

No such criticism could be levelled at golf but the time was not yet ripe for ladies to be admitted to its mysteries. The coming of the railway to St Andrews in 1852 ushered in a new era and set the seal on the club's success, but there was no disposition to rush headlong into modern fashion. For instance, the Alma Mater of golf saw no occasion yet to employ a professional. The fashion crept in nevertheless. Already the new club, Prestwick, had in 1851 lured away Tom Morris from St Andrews to lay out and maintain the greens at a wage of fifteen shillings a week. Prestwick also were the first to put forward the idea of a national tournament. The resulting competition, for pairs of gentlemen golfers, was held at St Andrews but it was won by Blackheath, who at once styled themselves 'the Champion Golf Club of the World'. The experiment was not repeated.

Prestwick nevertheless tried further competitive innovations on their own course – first a match-play singles competition for gentlemen and then, despite lack of support from other clubs, a stroke play competition for professionals for a challenge belt costing thirty guineas. It attracted only eight entries and the following year, 1861, it became open to gentlemen. This first Open Championship fared little better and it was dominated in its early years by two professionals, Willie Park and Tom Morris. The R and A remained somewhat aloof from these goings on as befitted their seniority. Though Blackheath and the Honourable Company retained their own rules – and did so until the late 1880s – the other clubs, including Prestwick, adopted the St Andrews code. And the R and A's finances were in such a healthy state that by 1867 they felt able to support the proposition that Tom Morris be invited back to St Andrews 'as a professional Golfer' at a salary of fifty pounds a year with a twenty pounds allowance for greenkeeping tools and equipment.[6]

Furthermore, though they did not seek missionary status, it was thrust upon them. For it was an R and A member, General Moncrieffe, visiting his cousin, Rev J.H. Gossett, vicar of Northam in the west of England, who famously cried, 'Providence obviously designed this for a golf links!' on first seeing the nearby North Devon coast. The comparison with

> stout Cortez when with eagle eyes
> He star'd at the Pacific–

is irresistible. Mr Gossett aided the divine plan, improvising two or three holes over which he played with his sons and a few friends. By 1864 there was enough interest amongst the local gentry to form a club. The Hon. Michael Rolle was elected president, Tom Morris came down to advise on lay-out, and the Devon and West of England Golf Club was set up with a Scottish professional and greenkeeper, Johnny Allan.[7]

The club members held no clear title to the links land and the local farmers who were accustomed to graze their cattle there resented intrusion. It was not practical to build a clubhouse so at first the members changed in a bathing machine. However, villagers' resistance gradually melted: those who were not already working for the golfers or their friends looked forward to new employment for caddying, catering and the like, and the club gradually established settlers' rights and moved smoothly on its way to the accolade of 'Royal' status.

Blackheath by contrast had persistent problems of land ownership. The course was on common land, the people had always been free to walk over it or to play other games or picnic there if they wished. The Enclosure Act of 1845 reduced the size of the common and the resulting expansion of housing put what was left under pressure. Wimbledon Common remained relatively less spoiled and in 1865 Lord Elcho started a golf club there for his London Scottish Rifle Volunteers (one of the county and regional associations set up to try to remedy weaknesses shown by the Crimean War). As time went on civilian friends were allowed to join the club, but when, after Lord Elcho's departure, the new Commanding Officer insisted upon all these club members conforming to military jurisdiction the civilians split off and formed their own club, using the same course, as they were entitled to do. So London was a crowded scene. Housing generated an insatiable demand for land. Great tracts of Epping Forest, Hampstead Heath and Wandsworth Common as well as Blackheath had been built on before the Metropolitan Commons Act of 1866 began to check the encroachment.

Cricket: a question of values

Golf did not qualify for inclusion in Trollope's select list, though he thought it all very well in its way. Ethnic origins apart, however, and notwithstanding his strictures on rowing, he rated individualistic encounters less highly than team activities. Even rackets, which he regarded as the greatest man-to-man game yet invented (no doubt because of its association with Harrow) did not receive the accolade. Nevertheless it was acquiring a glossier image. The Prince's Club, which built a closed court in 1853, became the fashionable centre, though the Harrovian Sir William Hart-Dyke, who in 1862 for the first time took the championship outside the Fleet and King's Bench prisons, maintained to the end of his life that open-court was better. Real tennis, the ancestor game, also enjoyed a resurgence. In London, both MCC and the newly formed Prince's Club had courts and Brighton was also a flourishing centre. The revival was assisted in 1863 when Edward Tompkins, the Oxford professional, brought the thirty year supremacy of the veteran French champion Edward Barre to an end. Tennis had been one of the first intervarsity contests and both Oxford and Cambridge were strongholds. Soon after staging the 1859 encounter against Cambridge, Oxford's Oriel Street Court became a lecture theatre. This still left two, however, and at Cambridge they were even able to build new courts – one at Parker's Piece, and two at the new Grange Road cricket ground.[8]

Cricket was, of course, on Trollope's select list of sports though he deplored many of its modern features, such as the advent of the All-England XI. In the good old days professionals 'were proud of being asked to play. They came up to Lord's and earned their five pounds for winning a match. They were civil and contented.' Then 'in an evil hour for cricket' Old Clarke had conceived his money-making scheme, exercising the 'quasi-episcopal function' of 'propagating cricket in distant parts'. This might have done some good initially, perhaps, but any benefit had been far outweighed by the rush of other professionals to mine this rich seam.[9]

There had certainly been a gold rush. As early as 1852 a disagreement between Clarke and John Wisden, a senior colleague, led to the formation of a rival group, the United England XI. The split is usually ascribed to Clarke's stinginess, but in fact few of the All-England regulars left him or showed signs of going back to MCC. Nor, for some years, did the rivalry between the two elevens have any adverse effects. Clarke himself finally split with MCC in 1854 when he declined to put selection for Players versus Gentlemen before an All-England commitment, and when he died in 1856 All-England voted to continue on the lines he had introduced. This was highly inconvenient for MCC, but otherwise beneficial. The two elevens put their opposition to the benefit of the game, and from 1857 played an annual match that soon became the highlight of the season. The funds went to a newly-created Cricketers' Fund Friendly Society.

The first of the multitude of imitators of the two elevens did little harm either, for Charles Lawrence's United All-Ireland venture was dependent on visits from English teams to Dublin. There were very few Irish clubs. A few had been started by ascendancy landlords in country districts in the 1820s, but it was first the military connection at the Phoenix Club and then Trinity College, Dublin, that set such standards as there were before modern clubs like North of Ireland (1859) came into being.[10] They were inspired by All-Ireland, which lasted from 1856 to 1861, when Lawrence, touring Australia, was persuaded to stay on as coach by the Albert Club at Redfern, Sydney. But in England it was soon another story. Two new teams calling themselves New All-England XI were set up in 1858, both Surrey-based and both – despite the brief resurrection of one of them in 1862 as Another New All-England – of short and sour duration. Another breakaway group played twice in 1864. A number of northern ventures – a New England XI of 1860, another England XI of 1862 and An Eleven of the North of England of 1863 – were equally evanescent but further debased the currency.

Even so the first reaction did not take the form of support for MCC or a rush to join the embryonic county clubs, but rather of frivolous gentlemanly anarchy. Already in 1845 some of the livelier spirits at the Canterbury Festival had thought up the idea of an élite club without subscriptions or the burden of a ground that would play any team of gentlemen at any country house that would entertain them. They called the club I Zingari, the Gypsies, and they soon had imitators and rivals, all with fancy names. The relatively serious Quidnuncs of Cambridge University (1851) and Harlequins of Oxford (1852) were followed by the Free Foresters from the Midlands (1856), the Band of Brothers from Kent (1857), Incogniti, Eton Ramblers, Butterflies, Yorkshire Gentlemen, and Emeriti (for Catholics), and soon they were joined by innumerable groups – Perambulators, Etceteras, Knickerbockers, Accidentals, Inexpressibles, Anomalies, Gnats, Active Fleas, Caterpillars, Grasshoppers, Limits, Jolly Dogs, Odds and Ends – who annoyed Trollope as much as Old Clarke did.

In this battle for the soul of cricket the standard of play was less important then keeping the professionals in their place and, some thought, this was best done by not playing against them, thus avoiding comparison. The policy failed – as it was later to do in Association football, driving gentlemanly footballers into the Rugby camp – but the quest for amateur purity made the attempt necessary. It was not solely an English phenomenon, though in Ireland the division between gentlemen and players was of lesser importance than that between the cricket players and the rest: ascendancy types regarded cricket as a badge of ethnic purity or at least of goodwill. And there were variations on the theme in Scotland and Wales.

In Scotland, for instance, the game had first been introduced by the army sent to quell the 1745 rising, and the earliest match of note took place on the Earl of Cathcart's estate in 1785. The gentry who played the game did so for gambling purposes, as in England, but with less enthusiasm. By mid Victorian times, however, there was an Edinburgh coterie, fed by Old Boy rivalry (the High School and Edinburgh Academy had played against each other annually since 1815 and there was a famous match – on Bruntsfield Links – in 1849). Perhaps the visit of the All-England XI in 1845 encouraged the game to spread; whatever the reason it certainly did spread, socially as well as geographically. On the evidence of Stirling, a small town at the apex of the Glasgow–Edinburgh–Stirling triangle, and its environs, cricket was the fastest growing of all sports at this time, outstripping curling, Highland Gatherings, bowling and quoiting, and maintaining its position (save only for the new craze, soccer) thereafter. Only the top layer, MCC and the professionals, was missing.[11]

In Wales a slightly different picture emerges from the scanty records. Cricket was being played in Swansea in 1780 but we can say little more about the early days except that, as in Ireland and Scotland, the army and the gentry were the mainstay. Monmouthshire, border territory, fielded the first county side in 1825 against Breconshire, matching the pattern, it not the standards of the English counties. And thereafter the county theme, much concerned with amateur purity, is evident alongside urban developments similar to Scotland.

Thus there were prominent town clubs at Dolgellau (1841) Ynysgerwn and Maesteg (1846) and in 1848 the Swansea club laid out £2,000 for the first phase of the development of the St Helen's Ground, which became one of the finest athletic stadia in Britain. The game spread from the sixties as in Scotland, and the north in particular was soon studded with clubs – Bangor, Llandudno, Wrexham, and, most celebrated later, Colwyn Bay. The north was given a strong amateur stiffening by the products of Rydal and Ruthin schools, and everywhere the clubs owed much to the goodwill and sometimes sponsorship of the landed gentry.

Concern with social status was evident in the county clubs formed in mid-century: Montgomeryshire (1855) restricted membership to gentlemen and Carmarthenshire (1860) specifically excluded tradesmen. The distinctive event, however, was the formation of the South Wales Cricket Club in 1859 by Captain George Homfray. This was a nomadic affair whose activities centred on visits to London, to play Gentlemen of Surrey at the Oval or MCC at Lord's. On one memorable occasion when they played I Zingari, bristling with MCC notables, South Wales were bolstered by the presence of E.M. Grace of Gloucestershire and his sixteen year old brother, W.G. All the Grace brothers played at times for South Wales, who no doubt paid generous expenses, and a little later W.G., then famous, was to visit Neath with the United South of England XI, another splinter group. He was bowled without scoring by a local professional.[12]

Money could be a source of unity as well as division and it was money that motivated the first of the overseas tours that were afterwards hailed by traditionalists as the cornerstone of Empire. The invitation from Mr Pickering, formerly of Eton and Cambridge, now of Montreal, that led to a five match tour of Canada and the USA in 1859 was, through the good offices of Mr Edmond Wilder, President of the Cricketers' Fund, fulfilled by a combined team from the two professional elevens. Their leaders, George Parr of Nottingham, successor to Old Clarke, and John Wisden of Sussex were partners in managing a cricket ground at Leamington. The players, guaranteed £50 for the two month trip on top of their expenses, actually cleared £90. Soon afterwards Messrs Spiers and Pond, proprietors of the Café de Paris, Melbourne, seeking an attraction to tour the Antipodes and failing to interest Charles Dickens, turned to cricket.

The image of Australia was not good. Until 1840 every state had received its quota of convicts, and although when the law was changed to prevent their being assigned to private houses and farms only Western Australia (to 1852) and Tasmania (1868) continued the practice, the stigma remained. The discovery of gold at Ballarat had aroused new interest. Still Australia was an outlandish prospect and one that few leading cricketers fancied, and it was the relatively obscure H.H. Stephenson of Surrey who agreed to get up a team for £150 a man plus expenses including first-class travel, during the winter of 1861–2.

The tour was a commercial success (Spiers and Pond made £11,000 profit, sold up and moved to London) but back home the selection of preponderantly Southern – and Surrey – men exacerbated growing regional tensions and adversely affected North versus South matches which had become attractions equal to matches between the two Elevens and Gentlemen versus Players. These tensions were intensified by the growing controversy about the bowling law which did not allow the hand to be above shoulder height at the point of delivery. In 1862 Edgar Willsher, a Kentish stalwart of All-England, who had a suspect action, was no-balled six times by an umpire believed to be under instructions from Surrey, and he and his fellow-professionals walked off the field in protest. George Parr and his allies refused to play in matches involving Surrey Players in 1863.

Throughout all this MCC's leadership – or lack of it – was widely condemned. The *Sporting Life* led a campaign for a Cricket Parliament that would supersede MCC and would include practical men of business. It got nowhere. MCC was not only the traditional source of legislation but the biggest employer of professional bowlers. By 1866 they had 12, 4 at £2 a week and 8 at 30s for the May to July period, with additional fees for umpiring, scoring or playing in matches, whereas of the counties only Surrey employed any ground staff. Most clubs recruited players on a match basis – in the emergent Yorkshire, for instance, £5 was the fee, regardless of venue, with no expenses or travel costs. Local club professionals in the early 1860s might be on as little as 2s 6d a game.

Nevertheless commercial opportunities were rapidly eroding MCC's monopoly position. That winter Parr agreed to a proposal from Melbourne Cricket Club (where a former Nottinghamshire colleague was a professional) for a tour for £250 a man plus expenses. For an eight month stint this compared favourably with the average wage-earner's £37 a year or the skilled worker's £90 a year – good enough to attract the Surrey 'cracks' Julius Caesar and William Caffyn, and to persuade a young Gloucestershire doctor, E.M. Grace, to flout convention and serve under a professional captain in an all-professional team.

Despite MCC's belated change of the laws to allow overarm bowling there were more bitter clashes, withdrawals, overlapping fixtures and general bloody-mindedness between northern and southern factions in 1864. The creation of the United South of England XI that winter seemed like the last straw. Whilst MCC vacillated the counties quarrelled amongst themselves. In 1865, after a disputed victory at the Oval, Surrey refused to play Notts and five recalcitrant Yorkshire professionals, who had been suspended for one match, were reinstated against Nottinghamshire and then refused to go to the Oval for the return with Surrey.

MCC were much criticised for their feebleness by friends as well as enemies, and there was more talk of replacing them. But at last they were stung into action when in 1866 the northern players seceded at the last moment from the two elevens match which was played, as the secretary recorded, 'for the benefit of Professional Cricketers, the ground being given to them for the purpose.' 'Gratitude', he added laconically.[13] There were also withdrawals from North versus South and Gentlemen versus Players. Finally MCC announced that henceforth they would only choose for MCC and all matches at Lord's those players 'willing to play together in a friendly manner'. There were still a few troubles to come, but normal – that is feudal – relationships were about to be resumed.

Football: a game for gentlemen

No such coarse professional considerations beset the pioneers of modern football which was by now one of the very emblems of the new public school spirit. When G.E.L. Cotton (portrayed as a sympathetic young master in *Tom Brown's Schooldays*) became head of Marlborough in 1852 he found the school, though only nine years old, already a hot bed of poaching, trespass and general licence. The following year in a Circular to Parents he proposed not only a reformed teaching syllabus but also a programme of organised games. These he justified as a way of keeping boys out of mischief and inside the school grounds, encouraging them to spend time and money on 'wholesome' recreation. He did not, of course, propose compulsion. Control of games was still the prerogative of senior pupils as an extension of the fagging and prefectorial systems. However, what Cotton could do was appoint young enthusiastic games players as masters and then infiltrate the system.

That same year Edward Thring, a fervent Christian and games-player from Eton, took over a struggling grammar school at Uppingham. He himself played football, cricket and fives with the boys and gave priority to acquiring playing fields, a swimming pool and even a gymnasium (an unheard of continental thing). It was an eventful year at Harrow, too. The fifth and sixth formers formed a Philathletic Club for organised games. The headmaster, Charles Vaughan, though he had no intrinsic interest in games, supported the club as a potential aid to the monitors through whom he was seeking to establish order and control. These monitors – an innovation that disturbed such distinguished old Harrovians as Palmerston – were ex-officio members and it was they who brought in compulsion, which the headmaster would have hesitated to introduce on his own.

Many were won over by the moral uplift the new games cult brought. As a footballing handbook noted: 'a generous feeling of rivalry in Houses and Forms sprang up . . . the public houses were emptied of their thoughtless occupants, and all the vicious amusements were abandoned'.[14] Soon enthusiasts for athleticism were growing rhapsodical, not only about games for their own sake (as Thomas Hughes in 1857: 'the whole sum of schoolboy existence gathered up into one straining, struggling half-hour, a half hour worth a year of common life') but about their ennobling effect on the English character, as in the *Quarterly Review* of October that same year: 'The Isthmian games of our public schools do much to make England what it is'.[15] As well as claiming character-building features – games were variously said to encourage loyalty, unselfishness, team-spirit and a sense of honour – which was dubious enough, sceptics thought, it was even suggested that playing games stimulated mental activity.

The issue was obscured by the stupefying rigid classical curriculum that still prevailed in the most renowned schools, but the Public School Commission that reported in 1864 found them disappointing, and their critics blamed this, at least in part, on over-emphasis on athleticism. There were exceptions, notably Marlborough – though this owed something to the corrective bias towards scholarship of Dean Farrar, author of school stories like *Eric, or little by little* (1857), an assistant master who succeeded Cotton as head. And a Scottish newcomer showed what could be done on the basis of *mens sana in corpore sano*,[16] H.H. Almond of Loretto.

Almond completed his own education at Balliol College, Oxford, which he hated but where he honed his philosophy, compound of enthusiasm for Empire, the philosophies of John Stuart Mill and Herbert Spencer, and, not least, a fervent Protestantism. He came to teaching accidentally, having failed to gain entrance to the Indian Civil Service, and after a spell at Merchiston (where he introduced cricket, importing an English professional for the purpose) purchased Loretto, then an obscure private school at Musselburgh, and began to put his own strong convictions into practice. The truly radical side of these was his introduction of functional clothing – shorts, open-necked shirts, sensible boots, flannels for games, fresh air, cold baths and changing after exertion – and the fusion of healthy exercise with attention to scholarship. Less admirable, perhaps, was the over-regulated, tightly-scheduled regime and his fervent, somewhat masochistic, Christian code in which healthy bodies were consecrated as 'a living sacrifice to God', and enduring pain and facing danger were desirable skills best learned on the football field.[17]

Football, at this stage, was not so much a single game as an array of roughly similar tribal codes preferred by different public schools. Teams at Cambridge in the 1850s usually played the Harrow-style compromise code agreed under Henry Malden. The Malden rules were re-issued in Cambridge in 1856. But the Rugbeians, whose game included not only handling and running with the ball but also hacking, had their own disciples. Since Arnold's early success Rugby School boys were in great demand as schoolmasters, especially in the newer schools – Marlborough, Wellington, Haileybury, Cheltenham and Clifton. And, when the Gladstone family and its wealthy friends in the Liverpool district got up a football match in 1856 as an ideologically superior alternative to hare-coursing, the rules were largely determined by a young guest, Richard Sykes, a sixth former at Rugby. This match, twenty a side, styled Rugby versus the World, led to the formation of the Liverpool Club and three years later, when Sykes went to work in Manchester, to an almost equally prestigious club there.[18]

Meanwhile, at only slightly lower social level, rules which specifically excluded hacking and picking up the ball were being adopted by a new club in Sheffield. In 1854 the Sheffield Cricket Club leased a site in Bramall Lane from the Duke of Norfolk and the following year a football match was held. One of the players, William Prest, together with a group of friends, mostly Collegiate School Old Boys, decided to form a separate football club and its first rules were issued in October 1857. Its committee members were young technologists, businessmen and future captains of industry (including the son of Edward Vickers, founder of the famous firm), merchants and solicitors. Clubs with such membership tended to set the pattern in particular localities and there were soon fifteen clubs in Sheffield playing these rules, though there was still scope for variation: for a time, for instance, 'rouges' or touch-downs were allowed in Etonian fashion owing to the influence of an Old Etonian master at the Collegiate School.[19]

But wherever they could the Rugbeians, fervent in their own cause, and bridling at the prospect of generally accepted rules evolving from Harrow-style, stuck out for their own code. It was an uphill struggle. Of the many new London clubs only Blackheath, formed from an earlier local private school Old Boys' club in 1861, Richmond (also 1861) and Hampstead (1866, predecessors of the Harlequins) followed the Rugby tradition, whereas Epping Forest (1859) led a much bigger group including Crystal Palace (1861), Barnes and Civil Service (1863) that followed modified Cambridge rules.

The majority cause was aided when in 1862 Eton and Harrow Old Boys took part in an eleven a side match at Cambridge that led the following year to new rules for the university club which forbade hacking and handling the ball. Soon afterwards Old Harrovians and Etonians dominated a meeting called at the Freemason's Tavern, Lincoln's Inn Fields to form an association and settle rules for competition.

Most of the new London clubs – Kilburn No Names; Barnes; War Office; Crusaders; Forest; Crystal Palace; Surbiton – favoured Harrow–Cambridge-style rules, but Blackheath and three local private schools, keen Rugbeians, resisted. When the meeting stalled, it was decided to consult the leading schools; but none of them was willing to give up their present rules. There was also a cross-current in the peculiarly British social stream. Oxford had not so far shown much interest in the new vogue and Oxford men were always likely to be doubtful of joining something in which Cambridge was taking the lead. As an Oxford undergraduate put it in a letter to the *Sporting Life* that November: 'these London meetings were not attended by people or clubs of sufficient consequence to cause their suggestions to be generally acted upon'.[20]

By this time, however, the new Cambridge rules had been printed and the Harrovian J.F. Alcock of Forest proposed their adoption, subject to amendments that might be negotiated. This was vehemently opposed by F.W. Campbell of Blackheath, a passionate advocate of hacking and handling, who took exception to a letter from the Sheffield Club describing such techniques as more like Cornish wrestling than football. He thought hacking in particular part of the true public school spirit: 'if you look into Winchester records you will find that in former years men were so wounded that two of them were actually carried off the field'. Nowadays, he reckoned, there were too many people coming into the game who had not had the benefit of public school training. The president of the emergent Association, a Mr Pember, not himself a public schoolman, courteously demurred. Campbell persisted: 'if you do away with it [hacking] you will do away with all the courage and pluck of the game, and I will be bound to bring over a lot of Frenchmen who could beat you with a week's practice'.[21]

This patriotic appeal got him nowhere, so the Rugbeians went their separate way. At first they had a hard time of it, especially in London, where there was a distinct shortage of opponents. And elsewhere, apart from prestigious strongholds in Lancashire, most of their support was in or near the Celtic fringes. The violent image was a problem. When the Lincoln Club withdrew from the Association to play Rugby-style the President commented acidly that they evidently only cared about hacking and throttling (which Lincoln hotly denied in *Bell's Life*). By contrast the London and Sheffield poles of the Association axis arranged friendly challenge matches, home and away, in the Cambridge mode with slightly different rules on each occasion to suit the home teams. The Association also won the support of a number of army regiments: the Royal Engineers in particular were enthusiastic pioneers.

But if tribal loyalties built up at school and university shaped and motivated the rule-makers' attitudes, there were other forces at work. First and foremost, and noticeable for the first time in Britain, was that of industrial workers exercising influence as players and even as club members. Secondly, there was a great upsurge of middle class missionary zeal, sometimes mingled with commercial acumen, amongst the middle classes eager to spread sport amongst the workers: sporting journalists and organisers, priests and parsons, sons of wealthy industrialists, teachers in the elementary schools, young professional men embarking on their careers in developing towns and cities, all played their part. The increasingly commercial age was well able to accommodate both these phenomena. Institutionally, the public houses and breweries retained their traditional influence, but there were new ones. The railways, for instance, showed dramatic new possibilities for transport and acted as a social catalyst.

The railway companies made specific local contributions to industrial, commercial, social and sporting developments. It was in their interests to do so but they were also influential as employers. They offered gentlemanly industrial openings for public schoolmen, and they helped to create a working class élite. North Staffordshire railway employees formed the nucleus of the future Stoke City FC: young Carthusian trainees may have influenced the choice of Association rules. This novel admixture, in unfashionable places, often invigorated old public-house-based ventures such as Crewe Alexandra, where an existing cricket club started a winter football section.

Usually the less rugged Association code was chosen. An exception was at Leeds, where an athletic club was started in 1864 after a railway clerk put an advertisement in the local paper suggesting football practice from 7.00 to 8.00 a.m. The size of the response probably swung the balance in favour of Rugby which was played twenty a side compared with Association's eleven. Five hundred enrolled at one shilling a year, many of them ready to start practice even earlier than 7.00 a.m. On the whole, however, working people preferred the less dangerous code. And working people's opinion was to be the decisive factor in soccer's ultimate success.[22] You could have got long odds against this in 1866, the year the Etonian Chambers set up his Amateur Athletic Club and the Harrovian Charles W. Alcock replaced his brother as Forest's representative on the Football Association.

Notes

1 *Morning Post*, 20 August 1865, quoted in E. Sitwell, *English Eccentrics*, Harmondsworth, 1971, p. 105.
2 R. Longrigg, 'Women in the Hunting Field', in M. Seth-Smith, *The Horse*, London, 1979, pp. 90–3.
3 For velocipedes and early cycling see A. Ritchie, *King of the Road*, London, 1975.
4 For early developments see D.C.M. Pritchard, *The History of Croquet*, London, 1981. *OED*, noting the supposed derivation of the name from a north French dialect

diminutive of (Shepherd's) crook, states that the game and name were introduced to England from Ireland in 1852, quoting *The Field* in 1858 on its particular popularity in Co. Meath.

5 See N. Brown, *Ice-skating: A History*, London, 1955.

6 Minutes of R. and A. 4 May 1867.

7 B. Darwin, et al. (eds.), *A History of Golf in Britain*, 1952, p. 141, record the well-known story; but Campbell in the same book, p. 58, gives a different version. R. Browning, *A History of Golf*, London, 1955, pp. 93–4, gives the authorised version with more details of North Devon's early struggles. For Cortez see Keats' sonnet 'On first looking into Chapman's Homer.'

8 J. Arlott, *Oxford Companion to Sports and Games*, Oxford, 1976, p. 720. For a fuller account see E.O. Pleydell-Bouverie, *Rackets*, London, 1890.

9 A more sympathetic account is A.A. Thomson, 'Lord's and the Early Champions, 1787–1865, in E.W. Swanton (ed.), *Barclay's World of Cricket*, London, 1986, pp. 10–12. For the full story see R. Sissons, *The Players*, London, 1988, pp. 3–76.

10 S. Bergin and D. Scott, 'Ireland' in Swanton, *World Cricket* p. 554.

11 N.G. Mair, 'Scotland' in Swanton, *World of Cricket*, pp. 556–7. For Stirling see N. Tranter, 'The Chronology of Organised Sport in Nineteenth Century Scotland' in *IJHS*, Part 1, vol. 7, September 1990.

12 P. Carling, 'Wales' in Swanton, *World of Cricket*, p. 559. The scoresheet of the I Zingari Match is in B. Green, *Wisden Anthology*, 1864–1900, London, 1979.

13 F.S. Ashley-Cooper and Lord Harris, *Lord's and MCC*, London, 1914, pp. 151–2. For the full story of the quarrels see C. Box, *The English Game of Cricket*, London, 1877.

14 Introduction to *Routledge's Handbook of Football*, pp. 9–10, quoted in M. Marples, *A History of Football*, London, 1954, p. 122 in an admirable chapter on 'The public School Games Cult'. For a full discussion of the phenomenon see J.A. Mangan, *Athleticism in the Victorian and Edwardian Public Schools*, Cambridge, 1981.

15 *Tom Brown's Schooldays*, p. 76. *Quarterly Review* quoted in E.C. Mack, *Public Schools and British Opinion*, London, 1938, vol. 1, p. 299. The Isthmian Games were the Corinthian equivalent of the Olympics.

16 In full 'Orandum est ut sit mens sana in corpore sano' – 'You should pray for a healthy mind in a healthy body.' Juvenal (c. AD 60–c130) *Satires* x356.

17 For Almond's life see article by T.F. Henderson in *Twentieth Century Dictionary of National Biography*, vol.! (1901–11). For his philosophy, and philosophical influences, see Mangan, *Athleticism*, pp. 48–58.

18 U.A. Titley and R. McWhirter, *Centenary History of the Rugby Football Union*, London, 1970, pp. 51–2.

19 P.M. Young, *The History of British Football*, London, 1973 edn, pp. 115–18.

20 G. Green, *The History of the Football Association*, London, 1953, p. 27.

21 Ibid., p. 29.

22 For the influence of the various social classes on the development of modern soccer see T. Mason, *Association Football and English Society 1863–1915*, Brighton, 1980.

CHAPTER TWELVE

The missionary spirit: tribal stirrings

1867–88

The trouble with progress is that it requires change. This was not an agreeable prospect to most Britishers even if their present state cried out for it. Political change, in any event, took place only at the margin. After Palmerston's death in 1865 the uneasy Liberal coalition broke up on the question of extending the franchise, and it was the Conservative Disraeli, seeing an opening, who persuaded Lord Derby to take the 'leap in the dark'. The new voters reacted by returning the Liberals. So it was Gladstone whom the Queen reluctantly summoned to form a government in 1868. He was philosophical about it. 'Very significant', he said. 'My mission is to pacify Ireland.'[1]

Ireland was indeed the main threat to the kind of ordered progress Gladstone stood for. In mainland Britain talk of revolution was just that – talk. Chartism, Republicanism and the new Marxism were not practical politics. The serious struggle was between the old landed interests and the constitutional Parliamentarian middle classes – intellectual progressives, respectable moralists, hard-nosed industrialists and so on. The House of Lords was the great bulwark of tradition, but even in the Commons a third of the 396 members came from six leading public schools. Though the size of the electorate had swelled from 1,430,000 to 2,470,000 this still only covered 60 per cent of adult males in the towns; the rural working classes had to wait until 1884 for a similar reform. By 1871 the population had grown to nearly 32 million, despite a drop in Ireland of nearly 1.2 million (to 5.4 million) mostly the result of emigration. Of the 2.6 million UK-born residents of the USA over 1.8 million were Irish. So were some 567,000 of the 23 million population of England and Wales and 25,000 of the 3.36 million in Scotland. This caused particular distress to the Scottish commissioners who complained that the influx 'undoubtedly produced very deleterious results, lowered greatly the moral tone of the lower classes, and greatly increased the necessity for . . . sanitary and police precautions.'[2] The Irish went, of course, mostly to the towns, which continued to grow, and to sprawl, greatly adding to the electoral imbalance: 3.3 million in the inner cities were represented by just 18 members.

The pyramid structure of society changed little. The economist Dudley Baxter categorised the bread-winners of England and Wales on the lines shown in Table 12.1.[3]

Anyone with £200 or £300 a year was in the boss class. Mrs Beeton's *Household Management* which first appeared at this time lists 25 categories of servant. All of them 'would enter into the establishment of a wealthy nobleman', ranging from Kitchen Maid (£9–£14 a year), Groom (£15–£30),

Table 12.1

Class	Annual income	Numbers	% (approx.)
Upper	£5000+	7,500	0.075
Upper middle	£1000–£5000	42,000	0.42
Middle	£300–£1000	150,000	1.50
Lower middle (1)	£100–£300	850,000	8.50
Lower middle (2)	Under £100	1,003,000	10.03
Skilled labour	Under £100	1,230,000	12.30
Less skilled labour	Under £100	3,819,000	38.19
Agricultural and unskilled	Under £100	2,843,000	28.43

Table 12.2

Approximate annual income	Household
c £1000	Cook, upper housemaid, nursemaid, Under-housemaid, manservant
c £750	Cook, housemaid, nursemaid, footboy
c £500	Cook, housemaid, nursemaid
c £300	Maid of all work, nursemaid
c £200–£300	Maid of all work, occasional girl

Housekeeper or Butler (£25–£50) to House Steward (£40–£80). Mrs Beeton then indicates the proper scale of domestic help for lower incomes (see Table 12.2).[4]

Inequality did not inspire revolution because industrialisation, though it enraged the political radicals and moralists, brought increased prosperity all round. Between 1850 and 1875 wages went up by 50%, 33% in real terms. There were fluctuations, of course, and unemployment, which dropped as low as 2% in 1882, shot up to 10% four years later. But those in work flourished. Cotton workers were doing well again, the wool trade was still buoyant, building, shipbuilding and engineering went on advancing, as did mining, and even agricultural workers did not fall behind. And in the 'Great Depression' which followed when Britain began to falter in face of inter-national competition most organised groups of workers were able to resist wage cuts and so became better off as prices dropped.[5]

Wages were the workers' chief concern. Better working conditions, including increased amounts of leisure, were higher priorities for philan-thropists and reformers than for the trade unions. But soon a virtuous spiral began with leisure as an incentive. The legal requirement to close the mills before 2.00 p.m. on Saturdays was bettered by manufacturers seeking to attract the best skilled workers. A Birmingham engineering firm, for instance, began to close at 1.00 p.m. as early as 1853, and eventually this became general practice in the area. London, where employers could afford to pay more and faced the biggest competition for scarce skilled staff, set the pace in negotiating shorter hours in lieu of higher wages; Liverpool, which had the lowest percentage of skilled labour of all major towns, lagged behind. Generally, however, the likes of railwaymen and other superior tradesmen had the Saturday half-day by the early sixties. The engineers and builders took the lead in securing shorter daily hours (9 hours in 1874) and the following year the Factory Act gave a 56½ hour week maximum to the cotton workers.[6]

Sabbatarianism, still a powerful force, should in theory have been strengthened by the shorter working week. In practice things worked out rather differently. The moralists were greatly concerned, furthermore, by the connection between Saturday afternoon sport and drinking. Another result of industrialisation was that the old patchwork of Feast Days was gradually replaced in the towns by holidays suited to the rhythm of the factories. Paid annual holidays came in slowly, again from top down, but the 'wakes week' phenomenon in which whole towns shut down suited the economy and ethos of the times and also the leisure industry. The first Bank Holiday, in 1871, aroused fierce controversy, but won support amongst the middle class electorate for similar, prudential reasons. By the 1880s Britain was foremost in Europe in the amount of leisure the working classes enjoyed.

Football: Association versus Rugby

It was obviously games of short duration that chiefly benefited from Saturday half-holidays, and football most of all. In Birmingham alone, for instance, the number of clubs rose from one in 1874 to 20 two years later and to 155 in 1880. Football required relatively little time, natural resources or equipment. Space was the chief requirement and for improvised games, if all else failed, the street would do as it had done for centuries. Indeed streets were important: in the growing new towns, they were natural social units, the bases for many of the new ventures. Street names joined those of church, pub, and works in the titles of football clubs.[7] In the increasingly strident competitive times the old conflicts between churches and pubs were intensified. Different churches had different views of drink, of course, and there were local complications. In Wales the non-conformist denominations 'equated rugby football with all kinds of profanity and intemperance' partly because early teams tended to change in the local pubs, but partly because rugby was the chosen sport of St David's College, Lampeter, an Anglican training college.[8]

So far, however, the most important influences on both codes of football were the tribal allegiances of the public schools. In London the early running was being made by the Football Association, and in particular the Harrovian Charles Alcock, who became its honorary secretary in 1868. Alcock, assistant editor of *The Sportsman* and compiler from 1868 of the *Football Annual*, the first of its kind, was perhaps the best and certainly the most successful of the new breed of gentlemanly journalist sports organisers. He soon secured the post of paid secretary to Surrey County Cricket Club, and embarked on making the Oval into a national sports centre.

Both football codes were to use the Oval for big matches in the next few years, but the Association took the lead. They had already held two London versus Sheffield matches, which had not only helped to clarify outstanding issues regarding the rules but had aroused public interest, and now chance opened up possibilities north of the border. The Glaswegian gentlemen who formed the Queen's Park Club in 1867 had played their first match against outside opponents (Thistle FC) with twenty a side. But then in 1869 one of their founders, Robert Smith, went to work in London, and threw in his lot with the FA. Soon afterwards Alcock placed an advertisement in the *Glasgow Herald* challenging players from Scotland, 'once essentially the land of football', to a game at the Oval in November 1870 in case 'there should still be a spark left of the old fire'. In the event the only Scottish club player chosen was Smith and the only other Scottish-born player the Hon. Arthur Kinnaird of the Old Etonians Club. The rest were gentlemanly cronies of Alcock and Kinnaird, often with scant Caledonian connections. Both teams were chosen by the FA.[9]

The leading Scottish schools – Edinburgh Academy, Royal High School, Merchiston Castle, Loretto, Fettes – fervent addicts of the Rugby code,[10] were not amused by all this and a month later *The Scotsman* published a challenge from a group of Former Pupils to any team 'selected from the whole of England'. This came at a critical time for English Rugby players. After the prestigious foundations at Liverpool and Manchester there had been a few new Northern ventures, such as Hull, Leeds, Bradford and Huddersfield, though of lesser social status and playing to local rules. Sheffield was Association-minded and so was most of the Midlands. London had some 30 clubs but they were a miscellaneous bunch and there was as yet no general agreement about the rules. The game had a violent reputation with the public at large, not least because of its adherence to 'hacking'. Matters came to a head in 1869 when controversy arose at Rugby School itself. Reports in the local press about an injury in a house match were picked up by *The Times* which added a critical leading article. Supporters claimed the account was inaccurate, but then Dr Temple, recently retired as headmaster, revealed his own misgivings about some aspects of the game, and 'A Surgeon' weighed in with further criticisms. *Punch* delivered an adverse judgement (later partially retracted) and there were widespread calls for 'instant reformation' or total abolition of this 'brutal and unmanly' pursuit. The accidental death of a player in Richmond's opening practice of 1870, though unconnected with hacking, did not help the code.[11]

Clearly, the Rugbeians had to get their act together. The secretaries of the Richmond and Blackheath Clubs in a letter to the press invited 'clubs who profess to play the Rugby game' to join them 'in forming a code to be generally adopted' and at the Pall Mall Restaurant, Cockspur Street, on 26 January 1871, 32 representatives of 21 clubs, including 8 which still survive, formed the Rugby Football Union. Its first act was to abolish hacking. Shortly afterwards its representatives went north to take on the Scots.

This game, on 27 March 1871, played at Raeburn Place, Edinburgh Academicals' ground and won by Scotland before some 4,000 spectators, not only whetted the appetites of the London men for a return but excited the envy of the Association, north and south of the border. Alcock's immediate preoccupation, however, was a competition at club level. This, the FA Challenge Cup, inspired by the Cock House competitions at Harrow, was open to all, though of the 15 entries for the 1971–2 season 13 were from London, the others being Donington, an obscure school in Lincolnshire, and Queen's Park, both of whom proved something of a nuisance. Queen's Park, exempted until the second round on grounds of distance and further privileged when their opponents, Donington, scratched, proceeded to the semi-final thanks to another bye. Then, having drawn their semi-final with Wanderers, they withdrew because they could not afford the time to come back for a re-play. So it was Wanderers who played (and beat) Royal Engineers in the first Cup Final at Kennington Oval on 16 March 1872.[12] The crowd, 2,000 or so, was, all things considered, not too bad and might have been bigger, Bell's Life reckoned, but for the one shilling admission charge.

The fact remained that a month earlier England's return Rugby Union match with Scotland had attracted to the Oval twice as many spectators at one shilling basic admission and an extra one shilling for the reserved enclosure. The Football Association at this point had only 10 Scottish clubs compared with the RFU's 32 and an expedition north of the border was clearly indicated. The first match, played at West of Scotland Cricket Club ground at Partick on 1 November 1872 against a team chosen by Queen's Park, was a success both for the gate – 2,000 – and for the missionary cause, for the Scots fought a goal-less draw and were inspired to go on to form a Scottish Football Association. (In February 1873, a month before the Scottish Rugby Union came into being.) This had only 8 members but 16 clubs entered for the first Scottish Cup in 1874, demonstrating the pull of this new-style competition.

The FA's own Challenge Cup was even more popular, especially amongst the little clubs springing up in the north and Midlands. The Cup competition was to be dominated by the southern, gentlemanly clubs for another decade or more, but times were changing. An important influence was the 1870 Education Act, which brought a great expansion of the elementary schools (the school population went up from 1.25 million to 5 million). They needed a growing number of teachers. These were not for the most part university men but products of *ad hoc* training colleges, originally set up by the churches, austere and purposeful places, predominantly lower middle class. Training college teams – in England at least – usually played Association football themselves and their diplomates were often the mainstay of early clubs, especially in industrial areas. Thus in 1873 a group of young teachers set up what was to become Sunderland FC.

It was not all a matter of the downward transmission of polite values, however. On the contrary, by the last quarter of the century the great bulk of new players came from the urban working classes on whom the public house, the factory floor and the street corner were often at least as important influences as school or church. The Association game remained the preferred game of School Board and church authorities for elementary school pupils because of its relative lack of violence, but church enthusiasm for links with senior clubs did not always endure. The Christ Church School XI, Bolton, became Bolton Wanderers in 1875 when the vicar changed his mind about letting the club use the church fields, and other famous clubs to outgrow church links were Small Health Alliance (later Birmingham FC) from Holy Trinity Cricket and Football Club, Wolverhampton Wanderers from St Luke's Church, Blackenwall, and Everton from St Domingo's Church Sunday School XI. At junior level Sheffield soon had so many local clubs based on public houses – such as Royal Oak and Burton Star – that the local Sunday Schools formed their own Association to discourage young men from stripping at public houses and playing on public house grounds.[13]

Urbanisation and new patterns of working class leisure were much less influential in Ireland. The traditions of the Anglo-Irish ascendancy, which still set the tone, were rooted in field sports. Trim races, the Duhallow hunt and Punchestown steeplechase were the highlights of the year, and the current talk was of a famous greyhound, three times winner of the Waterloo Cup, which was received at court by Queen Victoria herself. (His owner, Lord Lurgan was a lord-in-waiting.) 'With what different emotions March will hereafter be remembered by the French and by the Irish', commented the *Sporting Gazette* in 1872. 'By the Parisians it will be remembered with deep humiliation because of the occupation of their city by the Prussians – by the Irish with feelings of unmixed gratification at the unprecedented honour paid by The Queen of England to their champion of the leash – Master McGrath'.

The new footballing vogue began in 1855 at Trinity College, Dublin, where the honorary secretary of the club was a Rugbeian. Trinity abandoned hacking in 1868, three years ahead of the RFU, and this modified form of Rugby football caught on amongst the young professional and business classes in

Dublin who were the mainstay of clubs like Wanderers (founded by a Blackheath Old Boy), Merrion Square and Scott's Military Academy. There were counterparts in Cork (Cork RFC and Cork Bankers) and Belfast, where North of Ireland Club was formed in 1868 as an offshoot of the cricket club with a nucleus of Cheltenham, Marlborough and Bromsgrove Old Boys. There were soon other Belfast clubs, Queen's College (later University), Methodist College (which became a grammar school) and Windsor (which disappeared). Most of the players were Protestant, south as well as north, and a few of either kind were working class.

Trinity played North of Ireland in 1871, but both were more interested in making fixtures outside Ireland. The Northerners found themselves spiritually and socially attuned to the coterie of Edinburgh schools and colleges that carried the Rugby banner. But Trinity, along with Wanderers and the Lansdowne Club, mostly ex-Trinity men, were more oriented towards London and the RFU. So when North came back from a Scottish tour in 1873–4 with plans for an international they were chagrined to read in the *Sporting Gazette* of October 1874, 'We hear on good authority that Ireland proposes challenging England to play a match according to the Rugby Union rules.' This was followed by an announcement that Wanderers, Trinity and Lansdowne had formed an Irish Rugby Union with the Lord Lieutenant as president. That season's North versus Wanderers match was not a jolly affair and in January 1875 the institution of a Northern Football Union was announced. The quarrel was patched up in time for the subsequent fixture at the Oval, but the basis of selection, ten from the South, ten from the North, and last minute defections did not make for cohesion or success. Defeat in a Scottish fixture in 1877, this time at fifteen-a-side, emphasised how far there was to go to catch up.[14]

Public school influence was the vital factor in Wales. The earliest clubs, Blaenau Gwent (1869) and Chepstow (1870), were just across the English border and well within the ambit of the Rugby-playing schools, Cheltenham, and Clifton, to which many of the Welsh bourgeoisie sent their sons. A number of the better Welsh schools, Llandovery, Monmouth, Christ's College, Brecon, attracted young masters from England, and Cheltenham rules (which still retained hacking after the RFU decision) were often used, or at least became a basis for negotiation. Lampeter was also a powerful influence. Accident played its part: Neath (1871) was founded by a Merchistonian who had come to work there as a doctor. Elsewhere Association clubs, finding it hard to get fixtures of any social standing, switched to Rugby. Swansea did this in 1872 mainly to get fixtures with Llandovery. Llanelli, founded in 1872 as an Association club, switched three years later. Newport, after a year in the Association, also changed in 1875 so as to get fixtures with Glamorgan Rugby Club, Cardiff, which had been founded by Cheltenham College Old Boys.[15]

Similar factors influenced the spread of football in the largely non-industrial south-west of England. Clubs in Truro, Penzance, Redruth, Bristol and Gloucester were started by young public schoolmen from Marlborough, Rugby itself, the more localised Clifton and Taunton, and the crusading Cheltenham College. In small towns particularly they were obliged to make up the numbers with persons of lesser status. Many of these, like artisans in rowing, turned out to have a natural aptitude and a vocationally developed physique, a combination that challenged social hierarchies and thus the RFU. The first serious threat to its authority came, however, from the North of England, stimulated by the rival attraction in industrial areas of the Association game. In particular the Cup competition was a siren voice to the local Rugby Unions, who saw gate-money as well as glory in the concept. In Lancashire the two élite clubs, Liverpool and Manchester, dominated the scene. In the lesser, suburban clubs – Broughton, Manchester Rangers, Free Wanderers, Swinton – and in small towns like Rochdale and Wigan, the social composition of clubs might include small tradesmen, publicans and clerks as well as solicitors, merchants and other wealthy or educated pillars of society, but the influence of these clubs was small.

Yorkshire, whose broad acres were less comprehensively industrialised, housed persons at all levels of society of deeply conservative disposition, but ruggedly independent. The two main cities – in any event not so dominant as their Lancashire counterparts – were not Rugby strongholds. Leeds' allegiance had been indeterminate and Sheffield was a soccer town in which a press report of a Rugby match in 1877 concluded that it might be 'quite suitable for schoolboys who are proverbially impervious to accident, but we should have thought adults would have preferred a game with more skill and less roughing'.[16] Everywhere, and especially in the numerous smaller towns a local desire to win tended to come before social considerations. One manifestation of this was a Yorkshire Challenge Cup. This venture was not at all to the liking of the gentlemen in London. When the Calcutta Football Club disbanded in 1877 and offered the balance of its funds to the RFU to buy a Challenge Cup 'to be competed for annually in the same way as the Association Cup' the Union preferred to put up the trophy for annual competition between the gentlemen of England and Scotland.[17]

Soccer: the amateurs give ground

The FA Cup at first seemed harmless enough, in fact; Southern gentlemen and their clubs still dominated the scene. Alcock himself captained Wanderers in the 70s, and the future Lord Kinnaird played both for them and for Old Etonians. In 1875 when Royal Engineers beat Old Etonians in the Cup Final,

Major Marindin was eligible to play for both and scrupulously played for neither. Their Scottish counterparts also had claims to gentlemanly status: Queen's Park remained the dominant influence, and the newcomers Glasgow Rangers (1871) were founded by young rowing men impressed by the Eastern Club whom they saw playing on the Clyde banks. In Edinburgh, the two leading clubs were the respectable Heart of Midlothian FC (1873) and Third Lanark (1872), a fashionable regimental side. Even so there were danger signs: Hibernian (1875) was founded by Irish immigrants. But Rugby was the popular game in Edinburgh: elsewhere soccer's appeal was irresistible. In Stirling, for example, in the first decade of the new football era, 1861–71, there were already 66 soccer clubs to 22 for rugger, and in the next there were 506 to 16.[18] And with popularity came commercialism in the shape of gate-money. This together with Cup-tie fervour produced undesirable scenes even at Queen's Park, shocking the correspondent of the Glasgow Herald: 'Yelling, hooting, and calling out the players by cognomens were nothing to the coarse and vulgar pleasantries indulged in. Happily no ladies were present in the vitiated atmosphere.'[19] As less socially-elevated clubs came into being – Kilmarnock (1869) and Partick Thistle (1876), St Mirren (1877) – the threat to amateurism loomed larger.

Ireland, through socio-political accident, retained its innocence longer. During a Scottish honeymoon in 1878 John McAlery, manager of the Irish Tweed House in Belfast, invited Queen's Park and another gentlemanly club, Caledonians, to come over and play an exhibition match at the Ulster Cricket Ground, Belfast. This led to the formation of Cliftonville FC, who became the leading lights of the Irish FA (1880) which included Belfast clubs like Windsor and Albion, both of whom also played Rugby football, Knock, originally a lacrosse club, suburban teams like Oldpark, Avoniel and the socially conscious Balmoral Academy. There were also a few country members like Alexander (Limavady) a public-house-based cricket and football club in a small north coast town, and Moyola Park, feudally maintaining the rough public school traditions of its founder, Major Spencer Chichester, on whose Castledawson estate the team performed. When Ireland sustained a 13–0 defeat in their first international match at Knock in 1882 the local newspaper cheerfully commented, 'The weather was shocking, but in spite of that, there was a large number of spectators – proof that the new game is rapidly attaining popularity in our midst', adding that it could scarcely be expected that after a mere three years 'players could have arrived at such perfection to compete against . . . England, the majority of whom have played the game from boyhood'.[20]

But entrepreneurial serpents were now creeping into the English game and local pride was transmuted into a crude desire for success in the FA Cup. It

271

began in Lancashire, at a modest level at first, poaching good players and then offering them inducements – a friendly mill-owner would find a job for a good footballer and give him time off to train. Clubs with committees of business, commercial and professional types, sporting landlords and other enthusiasts saw nothing wrong in paying travelling expenses, making up lost wages – 'broken-time' payments – and even cash inducements to assemble good teams. Improved transport – railway excursions, tramways, charabancs, bicycles – had greatly improved the scope for attracting paying spectators. Gate-money was not to every club's taste, but even the most puritanical needed better amenities for the players, changing rooms and showers instead of the primitive and insanitary arrangements which involved putting street clothes on over dirty and sweaty playing kit.

The great sea-change happened, however, when clubs began to use gate-money to reward urban artisans who wanted to better themselves through sport, and to import them from foreign parts. It caused a sensation in 1878 when Darwen's millworkers reached the fourth round of the FA Cup and were drawn to play against Old Etonians at the Oval. The club committee launched a public appeal for 'the working lads of our town'. And when Darwen earned a re-play and faced another journey south the FA gave them £10 and Old Etonians themselves contributed £5. Yet in fact these 'lads of our town' included Fergus Suter and James Love, who both came from Partick, near Glasgow. The following season the local newspaper commented that Blackburn Rovers, in a match against Darwen, were well marshalled by one McIntyre 'who, we believe, is engaged as a professional'.[21]

Local supporters seem to have been more concerned about the ethics of importation than of remuneration. 'It looks as if the Blackburn men were afraid to fight out their own battles in a fair and honest manner, and if allowed it would justify other clubs in bringing down the best Scottish players to help them in important encounters', commented the *Athletic News* a new Manchester-based paper.[22] Three years later a correspondent was complaining 'I understood when I gave my mite towards purchasing the Lancashire Cup that it was for Lancashire lads alone.'[23] This view had no chance, however, against the gathering momentum of competition: a proposed ban by Lancashire FA on importing players was rejected by the clubs, who ageed merely to a two-year residential qualification and restriction of players to one club a season.

The parent FA was naturally concerned about these imports, and those like Alcock who were involved in cricket did not like foot-loose amateurs, either. But payment in what, unlike cricket, had hitherto been an entirely amateur game was an alarming prospect indeed, especially in view of cricket's recent experience. In 1881 Alcock in his *Football Annual* declared that the time had come for the subject to be given 'the earnest attention of those on whom revolves the management of Association Football'. The line he took in the FA's subsequent deliberations was that, as in cricket, professionalism should be legalised but the professionals kept under control. Sham amateurs were the worst of both worlds. Other football administrators still yearned for pure amateurism. Of the English local associations Sheffield tried to insist on no payment beyond expenses and Birmingham threatened drastic action against offenders. But they were swimming against the tide. The Scottish FA's fierce opposition to professionalism merely increased the flow of cross-border traffic.

By this time entrepreneurs like Captain Sudell, chairman of Preston North End, were openly touting for players. Nicholas Ross, captain and full-back of Heart of Midlothian, was an early recruit (1883) to Sudell's 'Invincibles of Proud Preston' who sought to topple local rivals Blackburn Rovers. Rovers had reached the FA Cup Final in 1881–2, losing to Old Etonians. Then, astonishingly, their neighbours Blackburn Olympic actually won the Cup the following year. The Town Band came out to welcome them and there was dancing in the streets. But even more amazingly Blackburn Rovers won the Cup next, not once but three times in a row. They may have been working class heroes, but they were indulged like emperors: nor were they ashamed to train, spending the week before the final tuning up at Blackpool.

All of this made a nonsense of the belated attempt at compromise by the FA in 1882, prohibiting payments beyond expenses and 'wages actually lost'. Two years later the *Sporting Life* was arguing that:

> there can be no possible objection to the recognised payment of men who cannot afford to play for amusement, and we can see no reason why the principle which exists in almost every sport should be considered detrimental to football. The sooner the Football Association opens its eyes to the fact that the recognition of professionalism is a certainty in time, the better it will be for the consolidation of the game.[24]

The point was reinforced when Captain Sudell, accused by the southern club Upton Park of fielding professionals, frankly admitted it: how else could he keep up with Blackburn Rovers? The *Preston Herald* concurred: 'Even if some of the North End team are professionals why should the London team have the right of interference?[25]

Civic pride apart, the most fervent opponents of professional football were those who felt their own status threatened by it. Thus whilst not only Alcock but the Etonians Lord Kinnaird and Major Marindin took a moderate view, N. Lane Jackson, the bourgeois founding chairman of the London FA, became an implacable opponent. Jackson appears to have conceived the idea of improving the cultural standards of the populace from a precociously early age: in his memoirs he recalled how on leaving school in 1866, finding himself marooned in the village of Edmonton he founded, with the 'help of the "county" folk', a Mutual Improvement Recreational Society for the lower orders, beginning with a library and a club-room for indoor games and branching out into football and cricket. Saturday afternoons off had not yet penetrated to rural parts so the matches were Sunday affairs. The Church of England parson, himself a sporting type, had no objection: one dissenting minister, a blacksmith in the week, was talked around: the other was ignored. The scheme worked less well for cricket – relatively unpopular but also happening at the wrong season – than for Association football which was Jackson's first love.[26] By the time of the FA's crisis the philanthropic youth had become a sporting journalist, editor of the magazine *Pastime*, businessman, organiser and handicapper. That he made his living from sport in no way altered his attitude to professionalism. In 1882 he founded the Corinthians, on the model of cricket's I Zingari, with a membership restricted to 50, no subscription fees (in order to ensure 'the right sort'), no ground, no participation in organised competitions; and of course no professionals.

In the north and midlands socially-conscious types like Charles Clegg of Sheffield (later Sir Charles and a future FA president) who had not enjoyed his own first match for England because the southern snobs looked down on north-country lawyers, thought professionalism would encourage gambling. W.H. Jope of Birmingham, who thought it would be degrading for respectable men to play with professionals, also took a strong line. Jackson led the diehards in a long rearguarded action but it came to an end in 1885 when 36 clubs, all but one from Lancashire, threatened to form a separate British Football Association.

Under Alcock's guidance the FA sought to follow the example of cricket: it banned professionals from any of its committees and introduced controls on residence and transfers but allowed them to play with and against amateurs in open competitions. This dismayed the Scottish FA who outlawed the 68 professionals registered with English clubs, and was furious when England chose a young Blackburn professional called Forest to play against them in the next international. The Scots finally agreed to let him play, provided he wore a different shirt from the rest. This suited the FA well enough. In 1886 they arranged a Gentlemen versus Players fixture and 'did their level best', the *Athletic News* complained, 'to make the pros look like pros. Dark blue jerseys savour more of the collier than anything else and the Gentlemen were clad in spotless white'.[27]

Rugby: straws in the wind

This, some felt, was the end of the road for soccer. An idealistic correspondent of the liberal *Manchester Guardian* argued that professionalism marked the end of an 'an important social movement' and thus the hope of bringing together 'all classes in football and athletics on terms of perfect equality'. Professionalism would provide a fresh excuse 'for the tendency to exclusiveness which is even now sufficiently apparent. The universities of Oxford and Cambridge have for some time picked the clubs with which they may deign to compete, and an example of this kind will be widely followed.' The way would be open for Rugby football to become the gentlemanly game.[28] This was an accurate prediction, but any tendency towards complacency on the part of the RFU was offset by events at the fringes of their own empire.

Even in Scotland, where at its Edinburgh heart Rugby was purely, indeed fastidiously, amateur, the spread of the game to the border area brought potential danger. Gala, Melrose, Hawick, Earlston, Kelso, Duns and Selkirk enjoyed the kind of popular support given to Association clubs in metropolitan Glasgow and the teams competed in a Border League Championship. Things were, however, very much worse in Wales.

There were a few socially aspirant Welsh clubs, particularly near the English border, but in the early heartland of the game, the coastal industrial belt along the Bristol Channel, the social mix and the competitive spirit transformed the situation. In 1876 Newport, utterly Anglicised, lent their support to a proposed South Wales Football Club, a joint venture with Cardiff, Aberavon, Neath, Swansea and Llanelli which tried to derive a team capable of challenging English clubs. The idea backfired. As part of the selective process they organised a cup competition whose success and popularity soon overshadowed the original notion. It now became the South Wales Union, new clubs further inland joined – Llandaff, Abergavenny, Llandillo, Aberdare, Cowbridge, Bridgend, Carmarthen – and the possibilities of gate-money were clearly demonstrated. The competition inspired primitive feelings of local pride even in superior Newport. Of the final tie against Cardiff in 1879 the *Monmouthshire Merlin* commented, 'On its becoming known that Newport had won the news was circulated throughout the town and received by many with almost frantic excitement.[29]

But Newport still had nobler aspirations and their honorary secretary, Richard Mullock, secured a fixture for a Welsh representative side against England. This took place at Blackheath on 19 February 1881. The Welsh were heavily defeated. 'Looked at from whatever point,' commented *The Field*, 'it is impossible to congratulate the Welsh Rugby Union on their first match, unless it was on their pluck in coming so far with the prospect of almost certain defeat.' There was in fact no such thing as a Welsh Rugby Union at that stage. A disgruntled correspondent of the *Western Mail* asked whether the selection had been made by the South Wales club – formally disbanded in 1880 – or 'was it a private team, got up by Mr Mullock of Newport, to do battle for Wales?'[30]

The malcontents had to retreat. On 12 March 1881 delegates from eleven clubs – Bangor, Brecon and Lampeter as well as eight southern clubs – formed a Welsh Rugby Union with Mr Mullock as honorary secretary. But the fervour of Cup-tie football had captured the West Walians. Local pride was as fierce as it had been on Christmas Day 1719, between Llandyssul and Llanwenog when Anne Beynon wished she were a boy 'to fight for the parish'. As the correspondent of the *Llanelli County Guardian*, sponsors of the Guardian Cup, put it in 1885, 'The question is not one merely of beating fifteen picked men from each of the other towns in the western district of South Wales. It means much more. It means vindicating the honour of Llanelli against her many detractors.'[31] It was the task of the Welsh Rugby Union to transmute these local passions and overcome the social tensions between west and east to construct a team that would similarly vindicate the honour of Wales. Fortunately the new game tapped a well of talent that was able to express heroic qualities emblematic of a new Welshness born of industrial growth and power.

Less happily for both the Welsh and the English Rugby Unions the well was also to be tapped (like its Scottish counterpart in soccer) by Rugby clubs in northern England, battling with each other for local pride and against the soccer vogue for gate-money. It was not long before the tradition of Welsh Rugby players 'going North' began. At first it was to Yorkshire where the Union's challenge cup had been a great success, causing great concern to the gentlemen in London. The RFU's Honorary Secretary Rowland Hill, an ultra-conservative MP, expressed his own and the RFU's anxieties: cup competitions were all very well as methods of stimulating or reviving the game in backward areas, but having achieved their objective they should be dropped. It was a matter of grave concern that 'in some districts the system had been allowed to assume very large proportions, which were responsible for many evils that had crept into the game, notably betting'.[32] The idea was blocked. But the Yorkshiremen would not go away. Indeed, as their Challenge Cup flourished, more and more clubs came into membership, more existing ones charged gate-money and some, it was rumoured, paid working class players for 'broken time' to compensate them for lost wages – the slippery slope towards professionalism.

Pot-hunting mashers and Irish nationalists

For all its paternalistic concern to avoid such pitfalls, however, the outlook of the administrators of both codes of football was inspired by a liberal idealism that was not to be found in the pioneers of older sports. The AAC issued rules in 1867 defining an amateur as a person who had never competed for money, had never taught or assisted in athletic pursuits as a means of livelihood and adding 'or is a mechanic, artisan or labourer'. This last phrase, redolent of its rowing origins, could hardly be justified in athletics and it was removed the following year. The revision made no concessions to the claims of democracy, however, for the definition now began, 'An amateur is a *gentleman*, who . . . etc.'

The AAC's new ground at Lillie Bridge in West Brompton (1869) became the venue for prestigious events such as the intervarsity match and the club staged national championships at the end of May to attract the best of the university men before the summer vacation. Most of the other competitors were public schoolmen, army officers, civil servants and others of impeccable credentials. Other clubs were less fastidious. London AC (formerly Mincing Lane) decided to admit tradesmen in 1872. Sixty members resigned in protest but the tradesmen more than compensated and the club had 900 members by 1874. Nevertheless such social issues clouded the serene skies of early competition, as in the case of W.J. Morgan, a walker. Walking, highly popular in the 1870s, had a good many gentlemanly exponents (notably Chambers himself, of course) but it required constant vigilance to see that competitors did not lift both feet off the ground together. 'Lifting' was widely regarded as a peds' trick and the AAC refused entry to their competition to Morgan, a wage-earner, and when London AC admitted him to membership some senior members threatened to reign.[33]

The AAC was the gentlemanly model for the Irish Champion Athletic Club (1872), the brain child of Harry Dunlop, formerly of Trinity, now a civil servant. The new club's Lansdowne complex had an archery ground, a croquet lawn, tennis courts, Rugby football and cricket pitches, as well as the first cinder track in Ireland. That it was an Anglophile development, as the inclusion of cricket emphasised, went without saying. Cricket itself was enjoying quite a vogue. To MCC's visits were now added those of I Zingari, entertained at the Vice-Regal Lodge. The All-England XI paid a visit to Belfast, playing on the North of Ireland Club ground which its members liked to call 'the Lord's of Ireland'. But Phoenix Park still cast its spell and the great W.G. Grace made the first of several visits to Dublin in 1873. Elsewhere in the south there were improbable outposts in places like Wicklow, where young Charles Steward Parnell was the keen if somewhat autocratic captain of the team started by his landowner father.

More irksome to the nationalistically inclined, however, was the injection of English (and Protestant) values into activities with some claim to Irish identity, like athletics. Field events in particular were still kept up at village festivals and drew crowds at town events. It was especially vexing that amongst the recruits to Dunlop's venture were outstanding Catholic athletes from the middle classes. One such was a young farmer, Maurice Davin, a great hammer-thrower and long-jumper as well as a good boxer and oarsman. His brothers Tom and Pat, champion high jumpers, were also drawn in to the ICAC circle. Tom held the 'world' record until 1874 when it was overtaken by the Hon. M.J. Brooks, an Oxford undergraduate, and Pat regained it the following year. The climax came in 1876 when ICAC challenged London AC to a match at Lansdowne Road. Tom and Pat Davin tied for first place in the high jump and Maurice delighted the crowd when, after winning the hammer, he carried three of the English team away on his back.

Davin was an innocent but his consorting with the enemy enraged his more politically-minded associates. One of these was Michael Cusack, an aspirant schoolteacher from County Clare who throughout the seventies had made a good living out of preparing candidates for the Imperial Civil Service examinations at his own crammer's shop which he rather grandly called the Civil Service Academy. Cusack happily led his school's Rugby team until the 1879–80 season when the foundation of the Irish Rugby Union added to his growing resentment of English dominance in Ireland. This increasingly inflamed his political campaigning in which he used sport as his chief battleground. A shot-putter of some renown, Cusack saw the English influence on Irish athletics – detrimental to field events, dominated by pedestrianism values – as wholly bad, and unlike Davin he was unimpressed by talk of reform.[34]

It was more than talk, although the AAC's early zeal to exclude the 'peds' had encouraged the growth of a professional circuit: as well as Sheffield there were soon regular well-attended handicap meetings in Manchester, Newcastle, Birmingham, Wolverhampton, Glasgow and, not least, Edinburgh. These meetings, arranged so as not to clash with traditional summer events such as the Lakeland, Border and Highland Games, were held in the spring and early summer and then resumed in the autumn, culminating in a Christmas meeting at Sheffield, which also staged the star event, the Spring Handicap. There was good prize money – £100 was commonplace, but the betting was a more important source of revenue. As with horse-racing, however, it was essential to have keen competition if crowds were to be attracted, and there had to be an element of uncertainty and challenge to established champions.

The different venues competed with each other, and Sheffield could no longer assume continued supremacy. Edinburgh in particular became a serious rival. Pedestrianism was so popular there that in the sixties there were three stadia all drawing good crowds. The meetings often led to disorder, however, through disputes over the judging. Powderhall Grounds, built by a syndicate in 1870, set out to raise the standards, and increase the profits. In 1871 it advertised 'GREAT SENSATIONAL ONE MILE HANDICAP!'

> The unprecedented number of 56 pedestrians *will run all at once* for this race. A spectacle never before witnessed in the Pedestrian World!

And in the three miles R. McInstray, a local favourite, took on the 'Red Indian' Diveaux Daillebout. In 1875 the sprint was billed as the world championship:

> WALLACE of THORNLEY is the MOST EXTRAORDINARY Runner that ever lived, having deprived Johnson of Stockton, Clowrey of Birmingham, Baylis of Gainsford and Jackson of Barnsley of the Proud Title of CHAMPION OF THE WORLD, which they All Held in Turn.

Powderhall's great achievement was to extend the winter season beyond Christmas and its main meeting on New Year's Day soon advanced from being a mere tailpiece to the climax of the season.[35]

In the fierce competitive world of commerce, stunts and novelties were as important as world records, and both were put before ordinary sporting values. Walking was particularly susceptible. In 1876 Powderhall matched W. Perkins of London against 'Walking Dick', a familiar figure of its Edinburgh streets, but their rivals at the Royal Patent Gymnasium Grounds drew 10,000 to see the American, E.P. Weston. Weston had first attracted notice in a six-day-and-night walk at the Agricultural Hall, Islington for £500 a side against Dan O'Leary, another American – sponsored by Sam Hague who led a black-faced minstrel troupe. Weston was backed by Sir John Astley MP, known as 'the Mate', a sporting baronet who spent money as fast as he won it. O'Leary won by some ten miles, but it was Weston the crowds flocked to see. He wore black velvet knickers, knee boots, a frilly shirt and a straw hat, carrying a riding whip with which he occasionally flicked his own flanks. If the crowd's interest flagged he would switch to walking backwards for a while or playing a silver cornet.

Powderhall tried various novelties to broaden their appeal. Pony-trotting was one that never quite caught on. Nor did matching Jack Kerr, the crack bicycle rider from London, against the ponies. Straight cycling was successful for a time, but the public taste was fickle and when the syndicate broke up after the failure of the City of Glasgow Bank in 1878 their successors were barely able to survive. They had high hopes of a new sprinting star, Harry Hutchens of Putney, who had been bringing back the crowds to the Hyde Park Grounds in Sheffield. In 1880 they proudly announced:

> HARRY HUTCHENS!!!!
> The Swiftest Pedestrian that ever trod a path is in Edinburgh!!
> The Greatest Racing ever seen out of Sheffield!!!!

cial trains were put on, including one from Sheffield, and the crowds rolled in but the great man was either not on form or did not like the odds.

Meanwhile the AAC had also been doing very well out of Lillie Bridge, where it now staged professional as well as amateur events. In 1876 it offered the Scottish miler J. McLeary £50 and half the profits of the meeting if he broke the record. Two years later the University Sports, when Brooks amazed the crowd with a high jump of 6ft 2½ins, brought in £1,100 at the gate. By 1879 the AAC's hypocrisy and subsequent loss of authority led to a serious division in the amateur ranks and London AC staged its own rival national championship meeting. The rift was healed by the initiative of three Oxford seniors, Clement Jackson, Bernard Wise and Montague Shearman, who invited representatives of the leading clubs to a meeting. At this on 24 April 1880 the Amateur Athletic Association was formed and a somewhat less élitist regime began. The 'gentleman' requirement was dropped and, of course, any reference to mechanics, artisans and labourers whilst the ban on competing for money or against professionals was retained. The AAA was, however, so fervently anti-professional that its precepts were hard to live up to, and were frequently breached, and the gambling habit persisted.

The English troubles were seized upon by Irish patriots like Cusack as evidence of moral decay from which Ireland must at all costs be kept free. He saw the answer in the revival of traditional Irish sports. He began by trying to revive hurling, which for thirty years or more had been scarcely seen in its original form. There was a milder version known as hurley, which had a vogue at Trinity and some Protestant schools, and there was even briefly an Irish Hurley Union, but it faced a serious threat from hockey which was beginning to take organised form in England. In December 1882 Cusack persuaded a number of hurley players to join a new Hurling Club in Dublin and when this split up because of political tensions he started his own Metropolitan Hurling Club with members chiefly drawn from Cusack's own Academy. Its success drew the admiring comment from a sporting magazine that 'judging by the increasing number of spectators the game is likely to become even more popular than its kindred sport, polo, or hurling on horseback.'[36]

By October 1884 Cusack was writing to *The Irishman* about 'the so-called revival of athletics' in Ireland. This, he insisted, did not originate with those who have ever had any sympathy with Ireland, or the Irish people; and he was highly indignant at restrictions which he claimed excluded 'labourers, tradesmen, artists and even policemen and soldiers' from competition. The allegation of class distinction took no account of the AAA's 1880 decision and the reference to policemen and soldiers was ironical to say the least in view of the decisions the Gaelic Athletics Association was to take. Cusack completed his wild charges asserting that with the new athletics movement there 'came a law which is as intolerable as its existence in Ireland is degrading.'

This 'law' was in fact the decision of the Irish athletics authorities to hold their meetings under the rules of the AAA:

> 'Every effort has been made to make the meetings look as English as possible – foot-racing, betting and flagrant cheating being their most prominent features . . . Swarms of pot-hunting mashers sprang into existence. They formed Harrier Clubs for the purpose of training through the winter, after the fashion of English professional athletes, that they might be able to win and pawn the prizes open for competition in the summer.[37]

The following week Maurice Davin sent in a much milder letter, defending the Harrier Clubs and pointing out the reforming efforts of the AAA, but agreeing with Cusack to the extent of calling for a rule-book of Irish games, greater emphasis on field events and a revival of Irish football as well as hurling.

In November Cusack issued a joint invitation from himself and Davin to a meeting at the Commercial and Family Hotel, Thurles. Why so obscure a venue was chosen is hard to say, but as the *Cork Examiner* put it 'the meeting was but poorly attended'.[38] Practically everyone there became an officer of the proposed 'Gaelic Association for the Preservation and Cultivation of National Pastimes', including the *Examiner*'s reporter. His long report of the meeting, giving extensive coverage to his own contribution, was not entirely adulatory but he was fulsome in his praise of the three patrons chosen for the new Association – Michael Davitt, founder of the Irish Land League, recently released from an English jail, Charles Stewart Parnell, president of the Land League, also recently jailed, and Dr Thomas Croke, Archbishop of Cashel, a fervent nationalist and supporter of the Land League, and a former professor of rhetoric.

This previous avocation could be adduced from Croke's long letter of support for the embryonic GAA. It is a masterpiece of invective, larded with sanctimony and appearing to envisage a sort of merrie Ireland full of innocent sports and sportsmen, a condition brought about by excluding everything English. As an Irish man, he wrote, he was greatly pained by

> the ugly and irritating fact that we are daily importing from England not only her manufactured goods, which we cannot help doing, since she has practically strangled our own manufacturing appliances, but together with her fashions, her accents, her vicious literature, her music, her dances and her manifold mannerisms, her games also and pastimes, to the utter discredit of our own grand national sport and to the sore humiliation, as I believe, of every genuine son and daughter of the old land.
>
> Ball-playing, hurling, football kicking according to the Irish rules, 'casting', leaping in various ways, wrestling, handygrips, top-pegging, leapfrog, rounders, tip in the hat and all such favourite exercises and amusements amongst men and boys, may now be said not only dead and buried but in

several locations to be entirely forgotten and unknown. And what have we got in their stead? We have got such foreign and fantastic field sports as lawn-tennis, polo, croquet, cricket and the like – very excellent, I believe, and health giving exercises in their way, still not racy of the soil but rather alien, on the contrary, to it as are indeed for the most part, the men and women who first imported and still continue to patronise them.[39]

Despite this eloquent, if idiosyncratic support the GAA did not at first succeed. Cusack was ousted in 1886 and then in 1888 came the decision to bar members of the Royal Irish Constabulary, which caused a split in the ranks. This apart, the GAA was in serious financial difficulties. However, it survived and undoubtedly helped to bring sport to many working class athletes – at a price. It was an irony that in Ireland professionalism was kept at bay both by rampant nationalism and by the handiness of England for those sportsmen who wanted to earn a pound or two, which Irish clubs and associations could not afford to pay. For the AAA's puritanism had so far been no more successful than the AAC's exclusiveness in stamping out betting and under the counter payments. The out-and-out professionals had to enlarge their horizons – America and Australia were big attractions – as domestic centres like Sheffield, Manchester and Newcastle got into financial difficulties. The Lillie Bridge ground was burned down by a betting gang at a professional match in 1887, a suitable end to this citadel of pot-hunting mashers.

Notes

1 R. Shannon, *The Crisis of Imperialism*, St Albans, 1976, p. 72. Cynics reckoned that what Gladstone meant was 'My passion is to mystify Ireland.'
2 E.L. Woodward, *The Age of Reform* (2nd edn), Oxford, 1962, p. 601.
3 Tables based on Baxter's *National Incomes*, 1868, in G.D.H. Cole and R. Postgate, *The Common People*, London, 1956, p. 354. The Scottish and, particularly, Irish lower classes were poorer and proportionately more numerous.
4 Isabella Beeton, *Beeton's Household Management*, London, 1961, facsimile edition, London, 1982, p. 8.
5 Cole and Postgate, *Common People*, pp. 352–3, 441–2.
6 Ibid., pp. 355–7, 598.
7 M. Marples, *A History of Football*, London, 1954, p. 170. For the transition to urban patterns of play see R.J. Holt, 'Football and the Urban Way of Life' in *Pleasure, Profit and Proselytism*, pp. 71–5; for the origins of urban clubs see T. Mason *Association Football and English Society 1863–1915*, Brighton, 1980, pp. 21–31; for earlier foundations see Young, *History of Football*, pp. 165–8 and for the variety of origins see Marples *History of Football*, pp. 165–8.
8 G. Williams, 'Image and Reality in Wales' in *Pleasure, Profit and Proseylitism*, p. 153.
9 P.M. Young, *The History of British Football*, London, 1973 edn, p. 149–53.
10 H.H. Almond, 'Rugby Football in Scottish Schools, in F.P. Marshall (ed.), *Football: the Rugby Union Game*, London, 1892, pp. 51–66.
11 E. Dunning and K. Sheard, *Barbarians, Gentlemen and Players*, Oxford, 1979, pp. 113–21.

12 Young, *History of Football*, pp. 155–6.
13 Ibid., p. 163; Mason, *Association Football*, p. 51.
14 For early Irish Rugby see J.J. McCarthy, 'International Football: Ireland', in Marshall, *Football*, E.E. Van Esbeck, *One Hundred Years of Irish Rugby*, Dublin, 1974 and S. Differy, *The Men in Green*, London, 1973.
15 For early Welsh Rugby see D. Smith and G. Williams, *Fields of Praise*, Cardiff, 1980, G. Williams, 'Rugby Union' in Mason, *Sport in Britain*, pp. 311–43, J.B.G. Thomas, *The Men in Scarlet*, London, 1972.
16 Quoted in full in Marples, *History of Football*, pp. 159–60. For local allegiances see D. Bussell, 'Sporadic and Curious' in *International Journal of the History of Sport*, September, 1988, pp. 185–205.
17 For the background to the Calcutta Cup see U.A. Titley and R. McWhirter, *Centenary History of the Rugby Football Union*, London, 1970, pp. 88–102. For Early Scottish Rugby see A.C.M. Thorburn, *The Scottish Rugby Union Official History*, Edinburgh, 1985, A. Massie, *A Portrait of Scottish Rugby*, Edinburgh, 1984.
18 N. Tranter, 'The Chronology of Organised Sport in Nineteenth Century Scotland' in *IJHS*, Part 1, vol. 7, September 1990.
19 Young, *History of Football*, p. 158.
20 M. Brodie, *100 Years of Irish Football*, Belfast, 1980, pp. 1–3 and section in J. Arlott *Oxford Companion to Sports and Games*, Oxford, 1976, p. 314.
21 *Darwen News*, 19 April 1879; 12 November 1879, quoted in Mason, *Football*, p. 69.
22 *Athletic News*, 12 November 1879.
23 Ibid., 25 January 1882.
24 15 September 1884.
25 Mason, *Association Football*, p. 73.
26 N.L. Jackson, *Sporting Days and Sporting Ways*, London, 1932, pp. 21-2.
27 21 December 1886.
28 30 November 1884, quoted in full in Young, *History of Football*, pp. 171-2
29 Smith and Williams, *Fields of Praise*, p. 1.
30 Richard Mullock also represented Wales at the inaugural meeting of the Amateur Athletic Association at Oxford in 1880. See Williams, 'Image and Identity', p. 136.
31 Smith and Williams, *Fields of Praise*, p. 5.
32 Titley and McWhirter, *Centenary History*, p. 86.
33 P. Lovesey, *The Official Centenary History of the Amateur Athletic Assocation*, London, 1979, pp. 19–23.
34 For early Irish athletics see D. Greene, 'Michael Cusack and the rise of the GAA' in C.C. O'Brien (ed.), *The Shaping of Modern Ireland*, London 1960, W.F. Mandle, 'The IRB and the Beginnings of the Gaelic Athletics Association', *Irish Historical Studies*, September 1972, and M. O'Hehir, 'The GAA: 100 Years, Dublin 1984.
35 See D.A. Jamieson, *Powderhall Grounds and Pedestrianism*, Edinburgh, 1943 esp. pp. 24–48, for an account of the period.
36 *Illustrated Sporting and Dramatic News*, Dublin, 22 March 1884. See Chapter 14 below for the origin of the joke (hockey on horseback) forty years earlier. Hurley, described as a modification of hockey, is outlined in G.A. Hutchinson, *Outdoor Games and Recreations*, London, 1893. The reference, together with off-prints of the documents in the early history of the GAA, was circulated by the Gaelic Athletic Association in 1984 to commemorate its centenary.
37 11 October 1884.
38 8 November 1884.
39 Letter to Cusack, 18 December 1889, printed in *The Nation*, 27 December 1884.

CHAPTER THIRTEEN

The missionary spirit:
Barbarian delights

1867–88

The slackening pace of industrial revolution in Britain allowed Germany and America to seize the economic lead. One reason for the slackening was the belief that easier money was to be had from commercial investment than industrial production: another was the cushion of cheap raw materials from colonial possessions; but the main one was the failure of the managerial and professional classes to take seriously the technological challenge British industry now faced. There was, indeed, in the public schools and in Oxford and Cambridge, whose prestige was never higher, hostility to the values of industry and the unrefined prosperity it brought.

By now the sharp, spiritual edge had gone from the reforms sparked off by Thomas Arnold at Rugby. His son Matthew (minor poet, inspector of schools, social and literary critic) rejected conventional Christian values. For him the admired virtues were of 'sweetness and light'. These qualities, he claimed, were once possessed by the upper classes (the Barbarians, as he called them, distinguishing them from the middle class Philistines and the lowest, biggest group, the Populace). But the Barbarians had so squandered their inherent sweetness and light in pursuit of wealth, grandeur, power and pleasure that all they had left was a passion for individual liberty and a taste for field sports. At the other extreme the Populace – part aspirant, part rabble – promised only anarchy. In between, the Philistines, though trapped in 'the prison of Puritanism', remained powerful, and the best hope was that they could overcome their narrow prejudices and embrace 'right reason', a distillation of the best culture ever known and exemplified by the grace and charm of Oxford.[1]

This mandarin view of society and culture was at odds with the flexible, pragmatic approach that had sustained the nation over the years. Arnold was admired chiefly by those who could afford snobbery: those who could not followed the tenets of the apostle of self-help, Samuel Smiles, who saw education in a sterner light, as a route to occupational advance and a basis for intellectual and spiritual betterment.[2] There were a few – too few – like Lyon Playfair, successful factory manager, professor, civil servant and government minister, who tried to steer the ancient universities into applied science and technology, but with no success. The great debate of the day was between Jowett, Master of Balliol, who saw the university as an extension of public school, a training ground for the governing classes pursuing the ideal of a healthy mind in a healthy body, and Mark Pattison, Rector of Lincoln, who argued for more attention to scholarship and research, in suitably respectable subjects of course. Humane and literary studies were seen as the hallmark of a gentleman, which was a very important thing to be.

Jowett's views prevailed, adding great weight to those of the public school men who saw no significant difference between Thomas Hughes and Thomas Arnold. Sport was the great character-builder on which the nation depended to train its leaders. Team-games in Hughes' eyes were infinitely superior to individual ones. The young master in *Tom Brown's Schooldays* gives pride of place to cricket: 'The discipline and reliance on one another, which it teaches, are so valuable', he tells Arthur, a convert to the new way of looking at sport '. . . It merges the individual in the eleven; he doesn't play that he may win but that his side may.' Yet an exception had to be made for boxing: fighting with the fists was the British way of accepting responsibility.[3]

Boxing: the gloves go on

This philosophy, still active enough to be put forward by a speaker in a House of Lords debate in 1991, only needed regulation to fit the Victorian scheme of things. From 1867 the annual sports meetings of AAC included outdoor boxing contests at three weights, and Chambers persuaded a Cambridge contemporary, the eighth Marquis of Queensberry, to present challenge cups and to give his name to new rules for the contests. There were some innovations: gloves were compulsory; rounds (three) lasted three minutes followed by a minute's rest; and umpires awarded points for style. Fixed rounds, replacing the conventions of the prize-ring where time could be called by the drop of a knee, put a premium on skill and footwork rather than brute force and gamesmanship; and the prohibition of 'in-fighting' cut out spoiling, wrestling tactics. Traditionalists disapproved, dreaming up all manner of fanciful reasons. Harry R. Sargent thought the introduction of gloves a doubtful blessing: he feared 'hammer-and-tongs' aggression in which a man could repeatedly hit an opponent hard in the face without breaking his own knuckles.[4] In fact the very opposite was intended: in one of the early bouts at Lillie Bridge a Mr J. Anderson was disqualified 'for fighting'.

The Queensberry rules were, however, by no means intended to apply only to amateurs: before the amateur section there were twelve rules for 'Contests of Endurance'. These said nothing about the length of contests nor did they provide for referees' adjudication, so the winner was the one who stayed on his feet longest. (Rule 5 provided that 'A man hanging on the ropes in a helpless state with his toes off the ground, shall be considered down.') The major change proposed was the use of 'fair-sized boxing gloves'. This did not appeal to every promoter, and modern boxers had to be ready to fight with or without gloves. The current British champion, Joe Goss, begged the question by taking himself off to America. The more far-sighted looked to the possibil ties of legalised contests and of renewed links with gentlemen amateurs. Jem Mace, the former champion, spent his later years demonstrating the potential of glove-fighting and in Australia in 1879, aged fifty, he sparred with A. N. 'Monkey' Hornby, Harrovian captain of Lancashire Cricket Club, who was touring with Lord Harris's XI.[5]

New and congenial occupations sprang up for ex-pugs. Every amateur sports club worth its salt had a Professor of Boxing. New clubs devoted solely to boxing sprang up, at first mainly of an élitist kind, but soon as part of the missionary work of such ventures as the Regent Street Polytechnic, established in 1882 by Quintin Hogg (philanthropist sugar magnate, friend and fellow Christian team-mate of Lord Kinnaird in the 1870 international soccer match). The polytechnic's clientele were mostly lower middle class, whereas the university settlements, begun in 1884, involved groups of dedicated graduates living in urban working class areas. Both aimed to enrich young men's lives athletically as well as spiritually, socially and intellectually. Boxing, as character-builder, also appealed to clubs based on the YMCA, developing beyond its earlier scope, church clubs and other charitable Boys' Clubs, and works' sporting clubs. Working Men's Clubs were slower to accept boxing, for ethical reasons, but contests were highly popular with their members.

The Amateur Boxing Association, founded in 1880, in the familiar fashion – by a group of influential members of the leading clubs – took on the task of co-ordination and control. Its first president was none other than Mr J. Anderson and it is noteworthy that, unlike the Queensberry original, the ABA's rules did not forbid 'fighting'. They were determinedly amateur, however, though without attempting to exclude the working class. Their championships were immediately popular and the ABA's influence spread quickly – Dublin BC affiliated in 1884 and Cardiff three years later. They were models of decorum.[6]

By contrast the professional game was as sordid as it had ever been. The Americans now ruled the roost and the tone was set by the larger-than-life 'Boston Strongboy', John L. Sullivan, who preferred bare-knuckles and persistent prosecution. The upholders of the prize-ring tradition in Britain were led by a dissolute set of amateurs who modelled themselves on earlier sportsmen. The most notorious was George Baird, heir to a Scottish industrial fortune, who styled himself Squire Abingdon. Like his heroes Baird was a fine rider; he kept a hundred horses in training and prepared himself for his own races by 'wasting' on brandy and soda. He was the foremost remaining patron of cock-fighting, staging spectacular mains at his country house near Newmarket, where he was ready also to match his bull-terrier, Donald, against all-comers and to gamble on any other vicious animal sport. (Ratting was one of his urban pleasures, and his most celebrated exploit was to let a bag of rats loose at the theatre where his mistress, Lilly Langtry, was playing. Less well-known is that in 1893, by which time Mrs Langtry was the friend and former mistress of the Prince of Wales, he beat her up.) This self-consciously Regency recidivist also surrounded himself by toughs and was given to roaming the streets with a gang of prize-fighters, Barrymore fashion.

One of these was Charley Mitchell, who had the talent but lacked the weight, physical or moral, to reach the top. Mitchell fought John L. Sullivan twice; first in New York in 1883 where he knocked the champion down before being knocked out of the ring, then at Baron (Nathan) Rothschild's estate at Chantilly where he back-pedalled and used the knee-drop for thirty-nine rounds to secure a draw (Madison Square Garden was packed for a third encounter but Sullivan turned up too drunk to fight). Another of Baird's acquaintance was Hugh Lowther whose brother's death later took him from bankruptcy to immense wealth and the title of Lord Lonsdale. Lowther was a scapegrace, one of whose milder exploits was to fight with Sir George Chetwynd in Hyde Park over the honour of Mrs Langtry, and who was more than once sent abroad on cooling-off missions. His early tribulations, which had taught him the art of survival, probably saved him from going the same way as Baird who died in the nineties after one week-long blind too many.

Instead Lonsdale lasted another half a century living on to become the darling of press and people, 'the sporting Earl'.[7] It was in this guise that he contributed a piece to the popular newspaper *The People* in the early 1930s claiming that in a private match in New York he had knocked Sullivan out, wearing gloves, as he said, to prove that a man could hit just as hard with them as without. It was this kind of support, together with the mounting problems of avoiding prosecution, that eventually reconciled the fans to gloved contests. The last bare-knuckle championship bout in England was in 1885 when Jem Smith, who like most of his contemporaries could fight in either style, defended his title against Davis. It was like a faint copy of Sayers versus Heenan. Passwords were given to 'safe men' at sporting pubs, and some of those setting off from the rendezvous in a Soho café to the depths of East Anglia in the small hours carried fishing rods and shotguns to disguise their intentions. The constabulary were indeed bamboozled long enough for Smith to retain his title, but there were very few spectators: the game was clearly no longer worth the candle.

Nostalgia still sent frissons down the spine of some enthusiasts, however. One of the less probable was George Bernard Shaw, who in 1886 wrote a novel, *Cashel Byron's Profession*, in which the hero was a prize-fighter, a gentlemanly by-blow. It is a work of no great literary merit and the melodramatic story is unoriginal, but the background distilled from the works of Egan, Dowling and company in the Reading Room of the British Museum, gives a feeling of authenticity. There is an episode, for instance, in which a group of ladies – though protesting – allow themselves to be escorted to a gloved contest at the Agricultural Hall. The phenomenon of the delectable shiver, reminiscent of the wrestling scene in *As You Like It* and central to the chivalric code throughout the ages, was given added spice on this occasion by the knowledge amongst the menfolk that the gloved exhibition was only an appetiser for the bare-knuckle affair to come.

In fact in late Victorian times the ladies' blushes had to be spared whether they liked it or not. The gladiatorial contests staged from 1886 by the Pelican Club – glove-matches between professionals for an elite audience over brandy and cigars after dinner – were barred to women. Queensberry was one of the founder members. Sir John Astley, 'the Mate' was chairman and Lonsdale was chairman of its Boxing Committee. Other members included two Dukes, Manchester and Hamilton, two actor-managers, Fred Terry and George Edwardes, and two entrepreneurs, the money-lender Sam Lewis and Billy Harris, the sausage king. Away from this dazzling metropolitan vortex the culture that created the type of professional favoured by the Pelican Club was also part of a male world, with its own version of chivalry.

Gloved contests brought legal, cheap entertainment to the new urban working classes. For the contestants they brought little material reward but they offered a chance of celebrity and a better, less random, proving-ground than the fairground or the street. The London ghettos, Strathclyde, northern England, South Wales, Belfast and Dublin provided the stream of contenders for recognition. The mines and iron-works had their own network of championship and contention, echoing the old prize-ring, though with light-weight gloves and Queensberry rules. Conan Doyle's *The Croxley Master* (set in northern England, though it could equally have been in parts of Wales or Scotland), paints a romantic picture which has all the ingredients of the British sporting myth.

First, we have an updated version of the old Establishment view that bloodsports were a better outlet for working people than the 'march of intellect'. The spectators slouch out from their work with their fox-terriers and lurchers at their heels.

> Warped with labour and twisted by toil, bent double by week-long work in the cramped coal-galleries, or half-blinded by years spent in front of white-hot fluid metal, these men still gilded their harsh and hopeless lives by their devotion to sport. It was their one relief . . . Literature, art, science, all these things were beyond their horizon, but the race, the football match, the cricket, the fight, these were things which they could understand . . . Sometimes

brutal, sometimes grotesque, the love of sport is still one of the great agencies which make for the happiness of our people. It lies very deeply in the springs of our nature, and when it has been educated out, a higher, more refined nature may be left, but it will not be of that robust British type which has left its mark so deeply on the world.

Next we have the patrons: the mine-owners, the publican, the bookmaker – horse-dealer, and the 'young blood of twenty' heir to a fortune' down for the vacation from Cambridge. There is a hierarchy of spectators: seats were five shillings, three shillings and a shilling ('with half-price for dogs'!) The takings, deducting expenses, were to go to the winner 'and it was already evident that a larger stake than a hundred pounds was in question'. And we have the referee from London who notices that the hero – an impoverished medical student – is wearing the Anonymi Cricket Club tie and warns him, 'You realise that you're a professional pug from this onwards' and is mollified to be told it is a once-for-all occasion.[8]

Rowing: amateurs and gentlemen

It was now becoming clear that for all their defects, professional sportsmen, with unlimited time at their disposal, were likely to reach a higher standard than amateurs, and it was they who attracted spectators. It was still possible, however, in a sport like rowing, where the towpath was not easy to turn into a gate-money area, for the leading amateurs to prevail. All that had to be done was to expunge the taint of professionalism from gentlemanly competition. At first this was attempted through club membership: thus in 1868, when W. B. Woodgate (of Radley and Brasenose but a sculler and therefore suspect) was accused of professionalism, the Henley stewards ruled that since he was a member of Kingston, an amateur club, he must be an amateur.[9]

Their reliance on such criteria was undermined by the advent of American crews. This had begun decorously enough with Harvard who showed every sign of gratitude for the stylistic lessons they learned, but interlopers appeared in 1878. That April a gathering of leading oarsmen had met at the Leander Club rooms in Putney, to try to define amateurism, deciding to debar oarsmen who were 'employed in or about boats'. The Henley stewards adopted this safeguard only to find that they had accepted an entry from the Shoe-wae-cae-mettes, a crew of French Canadian lumberjacks. The Shoes got as far as the final of the Stewards' Cup, drawing outraged comments from *Bell's Life* (now edited by Tom Egan) – ' "bucketing" would be a mild term in describing their stroke' and 'some of the crew did not receive the plaudits bestowed on them with that becoming modesty which is generally inseparable from true merit'. The stewards at once adopted a more specific version of the Leander code, making it plain that anyone who was or ever had been a mechanic, artisan or labourer was ineligible, and the Shoes entry for 1879 was declined.

But there had been other threats to English gentlemanly supremacy. Another American entrant, Columbia College, New York, had actually won the Visitors' Cup, and that same year a group of clubs – Leander, Oxford and Cambridge, Thames, Kingston, London, Royal Chester, Twickenham, and Trinity, Dublin – set up a Metropolitan Rowing Association with the aim of forming national crews to face foreign challenges at Henley or elsewhere. That nothing came of this may be attributed to confusion of purpose rather than decreasing xenophobia. The Henley stewards refused entry in 1882 to four store clerks who had been three times American Amateur Champions. In May the MRA changed its name to Amateur Rowing Association and in June declared its first object to 'maintain the standard of amateur oarsmanship . . . of the UK'. That it had its priorities right seemed to be confirmed when another American crew attracted adverse publicity.

The British press had first of all been very much on their side when Cornell University embarked on their declared mission of conquering Europe and especially Henley. The stewards had telegraphed New York seeking further proof of their amateur status, but Cornell set off anyway. Since they had travelled 3,000 miles they were eventually allowed to enter the Stewards' Cup. This, to the great relief of the authorities, they comprehensively lost. Cornell blamed the notoriously unfair course but since they went on to lose elsewhere in Britain and Europe, even the American newspapers remained unconvinced. One, remarking on the continued failure of US crews in England, commented, 'Let us accept the fact that rowing is not and cannot be made an American sport and urge young men to waste no time on it.' The conclusion was premature and the explanation less fundamental: one of the crew had been selling races.[10]

This can scarcely have surprised the ARA which by now was thoroughly convinced of the need to batten down the hatches. The first rules went much further than any previous ones in defining amateurism: they added to the list of those barred anyone 'engaged in any menial duty'. They also tried to debar anyone belonging to a club of which any other member had ever infringed any tenet of amateurism, though this mercifully proved impractical. The Times was sarcastic: 'The outsiders, artisans, mechanics and such like troublesome persons can have no place found for them. To keep them out is a thing desirable on every account. Let no base mechanic arms be suffered to thrust themselves in here.'[11] But the ARA was scornproof, armour-clad in its rectitude, and stuck to its guns for over fifty years. Its arrogance drove idealists like the Polytechnic authorities to take the lead in founding clubs for young amateurs from the lower middle classes, and eventually to start a separate organisation. This was hardly conducive, of course, to the proclaimed objective of maintaining the higher standards of British rowing, and the socially-oriented rules and the consequent exclusion of skilled performers and coaches further weakened the British effort against the lesser breeds.

Yachting: amateurs but not gentlemen

Exclusiveness was having a similar effect in yachting. In February 1866 *Hunt's Yachting Magazine* declared its confidence that after a period of lunacy 'putting sterns where bows had been and almost, we might say, vice versa' British yacht design was as 'nearly approaching to perfection as possible'. There seemed no reason, when little Clyde-built cutters of 25 tons could voyage to Australia, why our leading yacht clubs could not organise 'a fleet of powerful schooners to cross the Atlantic and wake up Uncle Sam in the Bay of New York'. The clubs themselves were more cautious. Even when the American *Sappho*, seeking to wake up John Bull, was beaten by four yachts in a set-to round the Isle of Wight it was only Mr James Astbury, from the Royal Harwich Yacht Club, business man and aspirant MP, who felt emboldened to issue a challenge to the New York Yacht Club.

He cut little ice in the best circles. The American journal *Spirit of the Times* commented, 'We are sorry to hear that some ill-feeling prevails in England in regard to Mr Astbury. We are told that many English yachtsmen say that he made the match to render himself prominent and catch popularity, and they hope the Cambria will be defeated.'[12] It was worse than that. Some sought to explain Astbury's antics by allegations that he was of Canadian origin. Whatever the cause, Astbury's 1870 challenge for the America's Cup was characterised by protracted and bitter legalistic wrangling before, during and after the race. The RYS averted its eyes, but Astbury rose in popular British esteem by racing and beating the press mogul James Gordon Bennett's *Dauntless* in a pick-up encounter across the Atlantic. And though his Cup challenge failed (or perhaps because it failed) there was much sympathetic support for Astbury amongst the cheering American crowds around the finish.

The sympathy continued for a time during the increasingly ill-tempered exchanges with the New York Yacht Club as Astbury arranged a return for 1871. But he lost the support of the American press when, after losing again, he accused the NYYC of 'unfair and unsportsmanlike proceedings'. The club returned all the trophies he had presented; he issued a pamphlet roundly abusing them: they protested to his sponsoring club. It was to be fourteen years before there was to be another challenge, and for some this distasteful episode merely showed how intrinsically undesirable competition was. When the Yacht Racing Association was formed in 1875 it attracted only 17 clubs out of the 49 – not including the RYS, or Royal Thames. The division led the YRA to boycott the regattas of the leading clubs, and it was not until 1882 when on the death of the Earl of Wilton the Prince of Wales, who was president of the YRA, was asked to become Commodore of the RYS, that normal diplomatic relations were resumed.

The truce coincided with renewed hopes that a suitable (i.e. rate-cheating) design had been found to beat the Yankees. Unfortunately by the time of the challenge the Americans had changed their rating rules and built several yachts capable of taking advantage of the new ones, whereas *Genesta*, the British entry, got a very poor time allowance. There was no question this time of the breeding of the challenger, for Sir Richard Sutton of the RYS was the son of a famous Master of the Quorn, unbelievably rich and every inch a gentleman – indeed perhaps too much so for some tastes. 'He assumes an air of superiority, as if we had everything to learn from him, while he could not possibly learn anything from us', wrote one American yachting correspondent, adding a vicious thrust: 'Finding faults with the New York Club course . . . may accord with English ideas of sportsmanlike conduct, but it looks to the American eye more like querulousness and a purely business propensity to haggle.[13]

Happily Sir Richard made amends, first by losing after some splendid racing, and then by taking his defeat graciously. Indeed when offered one of the series of races by disqualification after collision he magnanimously declined, saying 'We want a race, not a walk-over.' And he won all hearts by even refusing to accept payment for his broken bowsprit. Anglo-American relations were further improved by another popular British loser in 1886. William Henn, a retired naval lieutenant, took his wife with him on the trip as well as several dogs and a pet monkey. *Galatea*'s saloon was furnished with potted palms and a leopard skin rug. The Anglo-Irish Henn was really a cruising man and he made it clear that the RYS was unlikely to mount further challenges: 'The Club hardly thinks the game is worth the hunting,' he told reporters. 'It is a long trip over here in the first place, and then you miss a whole racing season abroad.'[14]

So it was left to Royal Clyde to pick up the gauntlet in 1887. The challenger, James Bell, was a Glasgow businessman, and the designer of his boat *Thistle* was a Scot, G.L. Watson, whose earlier *Madge* had been the prototype of the frustrated rate-cheater *Genesta*. This time in the customary disputatious pre-race period Watson tried to keep his designs secret, which may have been a wise precaution but which caused outrage when *Thistle*'s own dimensions turned out to be slightly different from the specification. An even sourer note was struck by the allegation after the British defeat that John Barr, the highly-experienced professional skipper, had sold out to the enemy. Barr later settled in America where professionalism was respected.

In Britain, the owners of these grand yachts were entirely dependent on their professional crews to do the actual sailing, and on cash bonuses to win races. According to a later pundit, Lord Dunraven, when the Largs Club on the Clyde ordered cork life jackets to be worn at all times in the interests of safety, they had to rescind their decision because 'the men filled their jackets with shot instead of cork, in order that by sitting up to windward, and acting as shifting ballast, they might give their boats an advantage when sailing on a wind'.[15] The Corinthian clubs, for smaller boats, virtually alone in encouraging actual sailing by amateurs, faced the usual problems of definition. The Portsmouth Club, founded in 1880, originally ruled that 'no person shall be considered an amateur who has at any time engaged in the navigation or sailing of a yacht for pay'. This unfortunately deprived the club of an important source of membership and it hastily amended it to exempt officers of the Royal Navy or mercantile marine. Happily not many plebeians were in a position to take their place amongst the small yacht-owning classes where such distinctions needed definition.

Hunting: a matter of standards

Landlubbers were more vulnerable to democratic incursion, even on the hunting field as rising costs took their toll. Subscription packs were now almost universal – the *Rural Almanack* of 1874 listed 122 against 14 maintained privately – but subscriptions fell far short of the necessary resources, whilst introducing a jarring note of vulgarity. Big subscribers demanded too much deference, and the rest paid far too little, often no more than £25. Visitors were rarely asked to pay but some fox-hunts were seriously considering introducing 'capping' just like common harriers.

Things weren't what they used to be, yet even diehards had to concede that subscription packs had some advantages over penurious yet still exclusive family packs. Unfortunately, though, under the open system many took on masterships for the wrong reasons. The callow often resigned once the cost of their social aspirations was borne in upon them, just as they were learning the job. Others were vastly experienced but rootless. Some tried to live off their guarantees and were reduced to skimping on feed and giving the hunt servant 'plugs' to ride, thus losing respect and authority.[16]

There was still a fortunate elite. The ninth Duke of Beaufort took up fox-hunting in 1868, with great style and generosity, and his Belvoir pack became famous. The Quorn, after the demise of the egregious Marquess of Hastings, was rescued by Mr Coupland (1870–84) who attracted Tom Firr, the greatest huntsman of the day, from Lord Eglinton. The Pytchley had the fifth Earl Spencer, and the regenerate Henry Chaplin cherished the Burton. The Brockleby had the Earls of Yarborough or their surrogates. The 18th Lord Willoughby de Broke created a new pack for the Warwickshire in 1870. The ninth Earl of Coventry brought his private pack to the Croome in 1873. The revitalised South Notts pack was bought by the eighth Earl of Harrington in 1882. Mr William Orkley sustained the Atherstone. The Bicester had Lord North, the South Oxfordshire Lord Macclesfield. In Wales the munificent Williams-Wynn tradition was carried on by Sir Watkin's nephew from 1885. In Scotland the Dukes of Buccleuch and the lavish but tyrannical Eglintons carried the torch.

Some moneyed men sought to maintain aristocratic values. The Rothschilds were scarcely *nouveaux-riches*, but they were foreign barons of the Austrian Empire – and Jewish to boot. Yet Lionel and Meyer, grandsons of the founder of the great banking house, were exemplary Masters, gracious hosts, tactfully discreet and helpful members of the Prince of Wales' circle. Lionel's love of tradition even extended to a pack of staghounds in Buckinghamshire, taking over a moth-eaten royal tradition in splendid fashion. Meyer was prominent on the Turf and also a generous and popular Master of the Whaddon Chase. Indeed the bourgeois Trollope, one of 'that numerous band of sportsmen who rode with the Baron', was, as he says in his *Autobiography* (1883), so disillusioned with Rothschild's successor, Mr Selby Lowndes, whom the sixth Duke of Grafton allowed to return on Meyer's death in 1874, that he went back to his old, less fashionable haunts in Essex.

It was a sign of the times that organisation and legislation eventually penetrated such rarefied, non-competitive circles. Territorial disputes were common but the rich, spoilt petulant hunting grandees were usually content to have them settled by an informal committee under Lord Redesdale at Boodle's Club where the leading MFH were wont to foregather. This was to change. Part of the Quorn territory had fallen into the hands of Sir Bache Cunard, son of the founder of the shipping lines, and Mr Coupland wanted it back; ugly scenes ensued between the two factions. The case was referred to Boodle's but Sir Bache proved highly resistant to arbitration. Another blow to the old order came in 1880 when the MFH establishment fell out – temporarily – with the Boodle's management and left in a huff. With the old informality gone the Duke of Beaufort wrote to all MFH asking them to join a new, representative body. Recognition by the Master of Fox Hounds Association thereafter became a caste mark and even the most pig-headed were gradually persuaded of the virtues of conformity.

Collective strength was to be increasingly required – eventually against government intervention, but more immediately against farmers and shooters. Wire fencing and the increase of sheep farming were the biggest nuisances. Wire was quicker and cheaper than orthodox fencing, though an influential MFH – like Lord Willoughby de Broke in Warwickshire in the seventies – could often persuade farmers against it. Yet most farmers used it to fill gaps in hedges, and after 1882 when barbed wire came in from the USA it became even more dangerous. Some farmers used it for economy, others for spite. Some were encouraged by landowners who wanted to protect their pheasant shoots.

The shooting men were coming into their own. In all but the best hunting territories, which were mostly grass or on empty hill terrain, coverts were closed off to hounds, sometimes until Christmas, sometimes year round. Foxes were shot without a qualm. There were some areas, like Norfolk, where co-existence was the thing, but there were many where open or concealed hostility prevailed. The fierce resentment fox-hunting men felt against shooters was often either subdued or sublimated into ritualised complaints against the vulgar debasement of sporting values by farmers, railway companies, industrialisation and so on. Tensions were exacerbated by the blatant enthusiasm for shooting exhibited by the heir to the throne.

His own shoots at Sandringham were memorable orgies of destruction. Princess Alexandra's letters recalled 'days of wonderful shooting' in the sixties and in particular one famous day when Edward's personal bag was '229 head of game, of which 175 were pheasants'. The humbler partridge bred well in Sandringham's sandy environment and as many as 3,000 had been accounted for in a day. Rabbits were even more readily available: the record was 6,000. The Prince was a devotee of the vulgar battue, which more sporting shooters deplored. One such critic reckoned the ones he attended cost 'little less than one hundred pounds an hour' (so that half an hour's shooting would cost about the same as a working man's annual wage).[17] Guests' coarse-fibred expectation of enormous 'bags' was looked at askance by the fastidious: so too was exulting in the kill, almost as much as not being careful to kill, and not wound. Similarly the code deplored callousness towards beaters. Idstone of *The Field* referred to 'the familiar sight of a little group around one or more of their body who owes his life to the thickness of his head, and is made fit to be shot at again by half-a-crown and a pull at one of the gentlemen's flasks'.[18]

Deer-stalking had introduced a new and grisly sporting fashion. Mounted stags' heads were now to be seen in all the best country houses and shooting boxes, and their size and antler-point count were matters of keen social competition, but it had become such a contrived affair of lying low until targets were driven past that *Punch* suggested the hardest part was staying awake. The relatively civilised alternative of target shooting – which was at least patriotically inspired and killed no living creature for practice – was making

steady progress. The Elcho Shield competition offered £200 in prizes ea
year. The National Rifle Association's contests at Wimbledon attracted such
crowds – 2,000 in 1888 – that a new site was needed, and Bisley, opened by
Queen Victoria herself, brought much-needed relief. Nevertheless, the sport-
loving Prince of Wales, though proud of his Rifle Brigade buttons, preferred
the battue or the occasional deer-stalk at Abergeldie.

Unlike his father, the Prince of Wales did not enjoy the more contemplative
pleasures of fishing. The sport underwent a great expansion, however, beginning in the sixties when the urban middle classes discovered the idyllic and
socially-superior world of game fishing. The quest for suitably exclusive
waters took them from London to the rivers to the north and west, from
Birmingham to the Severn, from Liverpool to Wales from Manchester to the
Lakes and from Newcastle to Northumberland. Scotland and its salmon were
the pinnacle of social distinction and a source of tension between English
townee visitors and local countrymen. The introduction of excise licences in
1879 did little to curb the demand.

A much bigger expansion took place in coarse fishing, initially amongst the
less affluent middle classes amongst whom clubs began to be established in
order to organise access to waters to negotiate fishing rights and, of course, to
exchange fishing stories over a glass of beer. Both they and the fly-fishermen
were troubled by the intrusion of more and more working people. Sometimes
the workers had been there first. When the better sort of Whitby sought to
restrict the River Esk for salmon and sea trout fishing in the sixties local miners
objected that it interfered with their established right to fish there, forcing the
concession of a small area for the miners' use, rescinded in 1868 when it
transpired that they were selling the fish. Ten years later the columns not only
of the élitist *The Field*, but also of the *Fishing Gazette* which was to make much in
later years of the ennobling influence of angling on the lower orders, were
filled with complaints by those imbued with the Isaac Walton spirit about the
rowdy behaviour of working class members of new clubs. For some clubs
working class membership was itself an issue: for instance Hull's Wilkinson
Angling Association split in the 1880s over this question.[19]

Temperance and the Sabbath were other causes of friction. It was notable
that many of the new clubs took their names from public houses – two
celebrated ones were the Stanley in London and the Rockingham in Leeds –
and a lot of others called themselves Brothers after friendly societies which
were themselves associated with pubs. There were some temperance (which
usually meant teetotal) clubs, but they were very much in the minority. The
sabbatarians were not pleased with the fishermen either. As early as 1860 the
Friendly Anglers decided to make Sunday their main fishing day, and even
when the Saturday half-day brought more leisure the lure of the early morning

excursion train and a whole day in the country proved irresistible. And if, as sometimes happened, the whole family went, the effect on church-going was even more significant. A curious side-effect in some areas was the survival of Saint Monday. Sheffield, after London the leading angling centre, was the outstanding example. There the skilled workers in small cutlery and engineering shops were in a good position to influence the arrangement of working hours to suit themselves and could afford the extra days off. Saint Monday remained the big fishing day until the turn of the century.[20]

A Parliamentary Committee were told in 1878 that there were two hundred angling societies in Sheffield and only one of them temperance. Most of them furthermore were for coarse fishing and addicted to competition, which was thought highly vulgar amongst the salmon and trout brigade, especially since there were prizes and, inevitably, gambling. Yet by and large angling was thought one of the more acceptable working class pursuits. As the *Fishing Gazette* put it: 'Angling has long been a pastime much practised by miners, furnacemen, and others engaged in industrial occupations in the Midlands, and a love for the contemplative man's recreation has done much to tone down the taste for more vicious forms of amusement.'[21]

Racing: the National Hunt Committee and its problems

The Queen doubtless wished for some such moderating influence on the Prince of Wales, for his incessant quest for pleasure – yachting, banquets, balls, garden parties, secret trips to Evans' Music Hall, baccarat, and above all the races – were a constant source of anxiety to her. Marriage and fatherhood had done nothing to steady him down. Nor had Victoria forgotten or forgiven the Nellie Clifden affair. Consequently, Disraeli's request in 1868 that the Prince be allowed to return to Ireland for a short holiday was not well-received. For one thing Victoria saw no point in diplomatic visits there: the disaffected Irish would never grow used to English rule. But Disraeli was persuasive, and it was too late before she learned that Punchestown races was a major feature of the visit.

Ireland, however troublesome, was a paradise for horse-lovers of all kinds. Hunter-breeding was now of great importance and the Royal Dublin Society's International Horse Show, first held in 1864, was building up a fine reputation. One of its sporting by-products was an early form of show-jumping. Both 'high' and 'wide' leaping events were held in 1865 and by 1876 the Royal Agricultural Society's show at Islington had taken up the idea. Entry was confined to horses in the show classes and the competition was judged – by MFHs – according to style, not height, distance or speed.

As for hunting, deer-hunts were actually on the increase in Ireland, harrier packs were numerous, and despite the shortage of quarry in some places fox-hunts were enjoyable affairs. Horses and hounds were strong, willing and cheap. Fences were unknown and when wire, for cheapness, began to replace banks and walls at least it was not hidden in hedges. Neither the railway nor industrial sprawl had darkened the scene. Indeed there was only one blot on the landscape. When the Land League began its campaign, financed by Irish emigrants to the USA, hunts were obvious targets. Harry R. Sargent was deeply upset by the attacks on Lord Waterford's Curraghmore. 'During the season 1880–81 unpleasant manifestations began to be shown . . . by certain sections of the farmers' and the following year Waterford and his friends were 'absolutely stoned out of it' by a mob 200 strong who ran through some of the hounds with pitchforks.[22] Vowing never to surrender, Waterford went to stay with his kinsfolk at Badminton until the trouble died down, and when they continued sold his pack.

The Land League caused the cancellation of Punchestown races in 1882, but they were restored the following year, and three years later Lord Drogheda was able to invite the prince back again to receive the plaudits of a loyal crowd. The organisation of Irish racing differed from that in England. First there were three times as many steeplechasers as Flat racehorses, and second Lord Drogheda was the head of both National Hunt and Flat racing branches. By contrast the English National Hunt Committee was still very much on trial so far as the Jockey club was concerned. Diehard MFHs like George Payne were also concerned about its coarsening influence. However, with the early support of Mr W. G. Craven and the Earl of Suffolk and afterwards of the Duke of Beaufort and the Earl of Coventry, the Committee gradually began to raise standards.

Relationships with local hunts were crucial – and highly unpredictable. It was important for the credibility of steeplechasing that horses entered for the many competitions for hunters should actually be genuine hunters, and MFH were asked to certify them. This did not work very well, for while some were conscientious others handed out certificates freely. The trouble was that hunting was not the best form of training for the new style of steeplechasing and genuine hunters rarely made good steeplechasers. Some of the best performers over jumps were, in fact, flat-racers that had not quite made the grade: they would be tried in hurdle races – a hybrid, somewhat suspect new category – and if they showed talent for jumping put in for steeplechases. So stewards were required to look beyond certification, seeking detailed information about horses that had run on the Flat after the age of two.

There was just as much trouble over the provenance of riders. The initial controversy about defining gentlemen had modulated into more elaborate distinctions. Below gentlemen riders there were now four categories (a) farmers with at least 100 acres, (b) qualified riders, persons of gentlemanly background who nevertheless rode more or less full-time, specially licensed, (c) yeomen who could ride at their own regimental meetings, and (d) professionals. Theoretically none but the professionals were supposed to ride for money, but this was just a theory.

The good 'gentleman' rider was a rarity and could name his own price, in cash or in kind. A few, like Mr Crashaw, rode for love of the game or were friends or relations of owners or trainers like the Hon. George Lambton, brother of Lord Durham, or Captain Coventry who rode for his brother Arthur. Some like 'Mr Thomas' (Thomas Pickernel) 'Mr Edwards' (Edward Ede) or Mr J.M. Richardson could name their own terms but were very good value. Others were more trouble than they were worth. 'You had to put them on ten pounds,' Bridges recalled, 'and if they lost, as they frequently did by disobeying orders, or having no knowledge of pace, they wanted money to get home, and very likely to have a night in town on the way'. A few, like Mr E.P. Wilson, took the honest course and became qualified riders.[23]

The Irish National Hunt Committee avoided bureaucracy but invited criticism by introducing in 1877 a system whereby 'gentlemen' riders were elected annually by the Committee from proposals made by their own number, or by MFH and a few others in the inner circle. By English standards this seemed to allow a certain laxity, a sensitive point during a sustained period of Irish domination in National Hunt racing, which included three successive Grand National winners. There could be no complaints about the first. Garrett Moore, who rode it, was the son of its owner and breeder, a rough diamond but no professional – indeed he soon retired as a result of hell-raising and mounting weight problems. But the next two were won by Harry Eyre Linde, the leading breeder and trainer in Ireland, a man so professional that he had replicas of the Grand National fences built near his stables at the Curragh. His rider Tommy Beasley, was supposedly Linde's racing manager and his brother Harry an assistant trainer.[24]

Linde's sharp tactics were demonstrated in 1882 when shortly before the National he sold a horse, Seaman, for £2,000 to Lord 'Hoppy' Manners, of Eton and the Guards, who had never ridden in a steeplechase before. The word was that Linde knew the horse was unsound and in fact it went lame taking the last fence. Fortunately 'Hoppy's' languid appearance belied him and he held Seaman up fractionally ahead of Linde's own entry, ridden by Tommy Beasley. Lord Manners, shortly to become Master of the Quorn, rode in only one other steeplechase, the Grand Military Gold Cup which he also won, before retiring undefeated. Such triumphs of gentlemanly amateur virtue, though heart-warming, were rare and becoming rarer.

Racing: the world of Fred Archer

Meanwhile, on the highly-professional Flat, despite the tremors caused by the scandals of the Marquess of Hastings and afterwards the Duke of Newcastle and Lord Westmorland, who had also got into Padwick's clutches, the Jockey Club continued on its oligarchic way. It made history in 1871 by admitting its first Jew. Camels might find it hard to get through the eye of a needle but the fabulously rich Meyer Rothschild, with the aid of his friend the Prince of Wales, charmed his way inside the magic circle. Another sign of the times was the opening in 1875 of Sandown Park race-course, in the London suburbs. Sandown was an enclosed course, with turnstiles and an admission charge, but unlike previous gate-money ventures it was a great success. Though it was to be a challenge to the established order its first effect was helpful to the Jockey Club.

For some time there had been criticism of the many low-level race meetings, especially around London. Admiral Rous was particularly scathing about the 'wretched £30 plates and small prizes' at these places. They drew few good horses and the promoters – local bookies and publicans – supplied most of the runners. Their attraction was that they were free and they offered opportunities for legal, on-course, betting. The railways had greatly assisted 'the movement of bands of indolent roughs' to depressing affairs like Harrow, Kingsbury, West Drayton, Croydon, Lillie Bridge and deplorable ones like Enfield, Bromley and Streatham. Riots, attacks on defecting bookies, and robberies by rival race-gangs were commonplace.[25]

Mr George Anderson – of skating fame – had long pressed for legislation to curb these grotty places. The Jockey Club, to fend off state interference, had imposed a minimum of 300 guineas a day in added prize money on course authorities, and this had helped close a few down, but something more positive was required. Sandown's success and renewed pressure from Anderson brought in the 1879 Metropolitan Racecourses Act, requiring minimum standards of amenity and conduct and stirring the Jockey Club into bringing in a licensing system. There were soon entrepreneurial imitators of Sandown – Kempton Park, Gatwick, Hurst Park, Lingfield – run on commercial lines for the benefit of spectators. The Park courses were a new phenomenon – they were convenient to railway stations; they had good grandstands, catering and other facilities; they offered programmes designed to interest the public not the owners; owners had to pay higher entrance fees but prize-money was greater. By 1866 Sandown was offering the richest prize-money for a single race in England – £10,000 added – for the Eclipse Stakes. Kempton and Manchester followed Sandown's lead and the challenge to the establishment slowly gathered momentum.

The world was shifting around the Jockey Club as the logic of the sport's dependence on gambling unfolded. Scandals apart, the latest crop of young aristocrats included some who looked to racing for a living. The Prince of Wales, for his part, showed that even the highest rank could not only stoop to consort with but actually prefer the society of rich cronies who were not always chivalric heroes underneath their smooth exteriors. Despite his cultivation of sycophantic money men he was not yet able to launch himself into ownership on the Flat. Advised by Lord Marcus Beresford, however (younger brother of the Marquess of Waterford who had emerged from a raffish youth through a modest career as a gentleman rider to try his hand at a racing manager), he acquired a couple of chasers in 1878.

Less aristocratic but more successful was Captain James Machell, son of a clergyman who had married an heiress of no longer profitable acres. After Rossall School he joined the army, using his service in Ireland to advance his knowledge of horseflesh. This progressed so fast that when his Commanding Officer refused him leave to go to the 1863 St Leger he resigned his commission and set up at Newmarket. He had only one three year old at first, but it did very well for him. He soon attracted patronage including that of Henry Chaplin for whom he trained Hermit, winning £70,000 in the celebrated 1867 Derby. He became racing manager to 'Hoppy' Manners and was also helpful to a number of aristocratic newcomers to the Turf, including Lord Aylesford, who, like Chaplin, was a friend of HRH. During this time he had been building up his own stable, and when the Earl of Lonsdale, Hugh Lowther's older brother, decided to take up racing Machell sold him thirty-five of his own horses and stayed on to manage them. This so infuriated Lowther that he challenged Machell to a card game – losing £18,000 which he did not have.

Trainers themselves, though still seen as tradesmen, often became extremely rich, and once-humble families grew into flourishing dynasties. The mantle of the Days of Daresbury fell on to John Day's son-in-law, Tom Cannon, whose three sons all became top jockeys. Training was now a frequent objective of successful and intelligent jockeys, and if weight problems – a penalty of prosperity – kept them off the flat, they could get experience in National Hunt racing. Sam Darling, Richard Marsh, John Porter and Arthur and Walter Nightingall, future trainers of distinction, all served this apprenticeship. William Archer, rider of the Grand National winner of 1858, set up his elder son, Charles, as a trainer: the other, Fred, became the richest and most famous jockey the Turf had ever known.

Fred Archer was first the protégé and then the son-in-law of Matthew Dawson, one of three successful Newmarket sons of a Scottish trainer. Matt Dawson had never been a jockey but started, aged twenty, as a salaried trainer for Lord Eglinton. Setting up on his own he was fortunate to secure the

patronage of Lord Falmouth, a rich and unusually honest owner. Their partnership flourished and by 1885 Dawson was investing his money in an old
manor house and filling it with a collection of racehorse paintings. But in the
eyes of the sporting public both were of infinitely less importance than Fred
Archer.

All the leading jockeys got their share of admiration. Of all the professional
sportsmen they undoubtedly earned the most, though it is hard to know how
much, since in the nature of their trade so much came from presents and
back-handers which were not usually disclosed. Almost certainly by the 1880s
eight or ten leading jockeys were earning, above board, over £5,000 a season,
about a hundred times the earnings of most working men. This apart they
were cult figures, lionised in society, cultivated by aristocratic ladies, featured
on picture postcards and followed closely by the sporting press. Fred Archer
was, in modern idiom, a superstar. A 'damned, long-legged, tin-scraping
young devil', Matt Dawson called him when first engaging him as an apprentice in 1867. He was champion jockey from 1874 for thirteen years in succession, winning 2,471 races out of 8,004. Moreover he was master of the big
occasion.[26]

The great champion was, in fact, illiterate, a challenge to conventional
wisdom, suggesting that literacy is essential only to those without talent.
More to the point Archer showed that if you were talented enough you could
afford to be honest, or at least treat honesty as an optional extra. Such
peculiarities, together with the adulation that came with success, made him
somewhat arrogant. He also stopped at nothing to win. This made him the
man to follow and he never let the punters down. He was richly rewarded.
The distinguished medical man, Sir James Paget, whose aid he had called on to
overcome an injury just before the 1880 Derby, was surprised to learn in the
course of conversation that their annual income, £8,000, was about the same.

The following year Archer became Dawson's partner and two years later
disappointed dozens of female admirers by marrying his daughter. Special
trains were put on for the crowds who came to the wedding. The story was
denied a happy ending as Archer's wife died in childbirth, and he cracked
under the strain. There were persistent rumours that he had pulled his horse
in the 1883 Derby because he had backed his brother Charles' entry, and the
rumours were revived the next year when Lord Falmouth suddenly gave up
racing. In 1885 his new patron the Duke of Portland, hearing that Archer
intended to go into partnership with 'Squire' Abingdon Baird, peremptorily
forbade him to do so. Archer returned his retainer. This was a profound shock
to the Establishment.

Archer became intensely moody as 'wasting' became a bigger and bigger
problem and in 1886, not yet thirty, he shot himself. Yet he had given a new

tatus to jockeys. The feudal relationship remained, but the leading jockeys were so sought after that they no longer had to depend on single patrons. The Earl of Suffolk felt strongly that the Jockey Club should take action to control the situation, protesting at the inordinate incomes – £100,000 a year or more riders could make. But if the owners had become capitalistic why should not the jockeys? Like it or not the Turf, which had become an industry, had to obey the rules of the new era. Soon multiple retainers and the virtual impossibility of buying the loyalty of these all-important little fellows made the situation very much worse, leaving the owners and the Jockey Club with only the trappings of power.

Here was a startling example of how rich men's sport could endanger social stability and the preservation of the class system. The Jockey Club did not like it. Bourgeois critics saw it as a threat to civilised values. 'In all probability,' wrote one critic, 'the three principal jockeys of England will earn, or at any event receive, more money in a year than the whole professional staff of a modern university.'[27] But the ordinary man, the potential threat to the established order, identified with Fred Archer, quote apart from whether or not he won a few pounds backing him. And if the industry was part of the dream-world of wealthy folk seeking an escape from reality, it also offered an avenue of hope to small working class boys who wanted to rise above their environment.

Becoming an apprentice jockey was very much a working class ambition, partly because it usually meant forgetting about schooling (the 1870 Education Act was a nuisance but it could be got round) and partly because the under-nourished had a better chance of making the required weight. The job required commitment as well as physical courage and endurance. Apprentice-ships were long and poorly paid – Archer had nine guineas a year at first rising to thirteen in his fourth and fifth years, plus his keep and the occasional present for a race-ride. Only a small proportion went on to become jockeys: for those who had to settle for the life of a stable lad it was a pound a week and their keep with tips for 'doing' a winner. There was still a ladder of oppor-tunity. A good head lad could aspire to £400 or £500 a year. This again was not for everyone. Many had to settle for the arduous, obsessive world of the racing stables, and the occasional pickings from inside information. They found it more fulfilling than working in a factory.

Notes

1 *Culture and Anarchy*, London, 1869.
2 His best-selling *Self-Help*, London, 1859, was re-issued (ed. A. Briggs), London, 1958.
3 A. Briggs, 'Thomas Hughes and the Public Schools' *in Victorian People*, Harmonds-

worth, 1965, p. 60, T. J. L. Chandler, 'Games at Oxbridge and the Public Schools' *IJHS*, September 1991, pp. 171–201.

4 H. R. Sargent, *Thoughts Upon Sport*, London, 1894, p. 310.
5 See Chapter 15 below for another example of Hornby's virility.
6 S. Shipton, 'Boxing' in T. Mason (ed.), *Sport in Britain*, Cambridge, 1989, pp. 78–88.
7 For Lonsdale see D. Sutherland, *The Yellow Earl*, London, 1965.
8 *The Conan Doyle Stories* (one volume edition) London, 1929, pp. 24–5, 29.
9 R. D. Burnell, 'The Amateur Rowing Association 1882–1982' in *British Rowing Almanack*, London, 1982, pp. 42–3, C. Dodd 'Rowing' in T. Mason (ed.), *Sport in Britain*, Cambridge, 1989, p. 279–87.
10 G. Gipe, *The Great American Sports Book*, New York, 1978, pp. 72–3.
11 Dodd, 'Rowing', p. 285.
12 I. Dear, *The America's Cup*, London, 1980, p. 67.
13 Ibid., p. 73.
14 Ibid., p. 76.
15 'Yachting' in Earl of Suffolk and Berkshire et al. *The Encyclopaedia of Sport*, 1897–8, vol. II.
16 See R. Longrigg, *The History of Foxhunting*, London, 1975, pp. 125–140, 141–152, on which this account is largely based.
17 Idstone Papers, London, 1872, Extract in E. Parker, *The Shooting Weekend Book*, London, 1934, p. 257.
18 Ibid., p. 259.
19 J. Lowerson, 'Brothers of the Angle', in J. A. Mangan (ed.), *Pleasure, Profit and Proselytism*, London, 1988, pp. 105–29, and 'Angling' in Mason, *Sport in Britain*, pp. 12–43, on which this section is largely based.
20 Saint Monday was the jocular term given to Mondays taken off after a weekend's drinking.
21 26 April 1890, quoted in Lowerson, 'Brothers', p. 108.
22 Sargent, *Thoughts Upon Sport*, pp. 39–40, gives a full account of the episode.
23 J. A. Bridges, *A Sportsman of Limited Income*, London, 1910, p. 202.
24 Sargent, *Thoughts Upon Sport*, Chapter VIII gives a useful account of the period.
25 W. Vamplew, *The Turf*, London, 1976, pp. 75 et seq.
26 For Archer see J. Welcome, *Fred Archer: His Life and Times*, London 1967. A good short account is in G. Lambton, *Men and Horses I Have Known*, London, 1924, pp. 6–7.
27 L. H. Curzon, 'The Horse as an Instrument of Gambling', *Contemporary Review*, no. 30, 1978, in *Racing and Steeplechasing*, London, 1886.

CHAPTER FOURTEEN

The missionary spirit: Philistine perspectives

1867–88

Matthew Arnold had the morose satisfaction of seeing many of his gloomier forebodings become reality. The Philistines did not in sufficient numbers – or with sufficient seriousness of purpose – embrace 'right reason'. In Oxford itself, as in the public schools that fed it, games assumed enormous importance and often seemed to weigh more than intellectual or moral considerations. The Revd C.L. Dodgson (Lewis Carroll) was particularly severe on the cricketers who now monopolised the Parks:

> One selfish pastime grasps the whole domain
> And half a faction swallows up a plain.[1]

Arnold's work as an Inspector of Schools had frequently taken him on trips to study continental methods. He commented caustically to the Taunton Commission in 1868 that the cult of the body in English public schools was characteristic of the way industrial societies confused ends with means. Gymnastics would serve the nation's purpose better than games, particularly for working class boys, but it seemed unlikely that the public school Old Boy would agree. Nor indeed did many headmasters. There were exceptions. Almond, for instance, was impressed by Herbert Spencer's progressive ideas of physical education (though he did not share Spencer's enthusiasm for extending it to girls). Another of Almond's mentors, Archibald MacLaren, who kept a gymnasium in Oxford, helped shape the fitness training programmes being devised for the British army. Thring, who had a foreign wife, was an adherent of the continental luminaries Guts Muths and Johann Jahn, seeing a place for Swedish 'free movement' as well as exercises in lance, dagger, sabre or foil. But it all seemed joyless and alien to most Britishers.

Buds of virtue

By the same token, if they could make a game of it, they were willing to try anything. Consider swimming, for instance. It had generally been held in low regard, more of a safety precaution for rowing men than an occasion for competition. There were ancient and modern historical reasons. The Greeks encouraged swimming as part of military training, but their medical writers were not all in favour of it and it was not one of the organised competitive sports at the Olympics and similar festivals. Swimming appealed to the sybaritic side of the Romans, as well as being a military asset, but again it was not a feature of organised sport. The contest in *Beowulf* was an underwater

307

virility test rather than a game. Bathing was looked at with extra suspicion in the middle ages; many thought plagues were brought by sea. At the Renaissance Erasmus derided it as a 'frog's life': Shakespeare wrote of 'little wanton boys that swim on bladders'.[2] Later writers on etiquette commended it as a suitable accomplishment for gentlemen, and there were even advocates of sea-bathing for health purposes. Immersion in the waves became fashionable in the eighteenth century as a result of royal adventures with bathing machines at Weymouth, but Strutt in 1801 noted that swimming was 'by no means so generally practised with us in the present day as it used to be in former times.'[3]

Harry R. Sargent, later in the century, commented frankly on the unpopularity of swimming compared with other 'manly exercises'. 'In the generation before my own it was little practised in Ireland, nor was it, I think, in England.' Indeed, he added: 'Beyond having a bathe in hot weather I am afraid our fathers were not over-fond of immersing themselves in water at all; nor was the matutinal tub considered a necessity to a gentleman in his preparation for the day. Even in my own boyhood [the 1850s] many could not swim.'[4] The weather, polluted rivers and the absence of privacy discouraged outdoor bathing. In the new industrial, urban era, furthermore, indoor swimming was associated with the sanitisation of the poor. (Hence the British usage 'swimming baths' compared with American 'swimming pool'.) Liverpool, though far behind other towns in playing field provision, had had a swimming bath as early as 1828 and under the Baths and Washhouses Act of 1846 built no fewer than 9 indoor and 4 outdoor baths in the next 25 years. This added nothing to the social standing of the recreation or its claims to recognition as a sport.

Yet there were some middle class and lower middle class enthusiasts for it, and swimming clubs began to appear in the bigger towns in the 1860s. They were usually able to negotiate private sessions, once or twice weekly at the municipal baths, but this was some way short of ideal. In London there were superior baths at the German Gymnasium and it was there that the Metropolitan Swimming Clubs Association was founded in 1869. Though it organised a mile race from Putney to Hammersmith that same year, it was at first concerned mainly with teaching swimming as a safety measure and health-giving exercise. A lyrical contribution to the *Gentleman's Magazine* in October 1870 entitled 'Swimming for the Million' (the million or so that made up the classes as distinct from the masses) reckoned that it was ideal for captains of industry and commerce, with the 'double advantage of developing the forces of the muscles whilst it contributes largely to strengthening those of the nervous system, and through it the operations of the mind'. Soon the MSCA was organising championships at various distances and concerning itself with the definition of amateurism.

A more potent early influence on competitive swimming was Matthew Webb, called 'Captain' because of his service in the Merchant Marine, who performed the amazing feat of swimming the English Channel in 1875. It was a well-advertised venture, and he was accompanied (in a lugger) by a bevy of special correspondents, including the ubiquitous J.G. Chambers, and sustained as he swam by 'cod-liver oil, beef tea, brandy, coffee and strong old ale'.[5] He received a handsome testimonial to supplement his winnings of £125. Public adulation did not bring Captain Webb the profits from exhibitions for which he had hoped, and he met his death eight years later in an attempt to swim the turbulent waters at the foot of Niagara Falls. But his channel-crossing fired public imagination. However, swimming seemed to have little commercial potential, though the public was much interested in a race from London Bridge to Woolwich in 1880 between a man and a dog called Now Then. (The dog won.) The Amateur Swimming Association, which superseded the MSCA in 1886, was obviously above this kind of thing. It set high standards of amateurism but with no vestigial traces of bygone privilege: respectability was all. This was scarcely enough to inspire public school headmasters to go to the lengths of raising funds for the considerable expense of building a pool. The river (if they had one) had to suffice. Expense apart, swimming's individualistic record-breaking, somewhat freakish image told heavily against it as a moral force.

Another ancient military training exercise, hockey, appears to have been no more than a rustic knockabout game in Britain until the nineteenth century, with few identifiable references to it in the records. The mysterious cambuca has already been discussed. In the Statute of Galway it is far from certain whether the reference is to a stick for playing hockey or simply to a hooky stick. And thereafter there is virtual silence. The poet Cowper in a letter of 1785 mentions a boys' game called hockey that consisted in 'dashing each other with mud, and the windows also', which sounds like the real thing, but Strutt in 1801 does not refer to hockey, or shinty, which was the Scottish version, and only incidentally to bandy – which was a more general name for scrabbling a ball about with sticks – in his remarks on golf.[6] Holloway's 1838 definition of hockey – 'game played by several boys on each side with hawkey-bats and a ball' – also implied juvenile rusticity in the Cowper mode.[7] Yet four years later when a returned oriental traveller described the game of the Chaugan, polo, as 'hockey on horseback' he must have been confident that his readers knew what the pedestrian version was.[8] In 1848 Malden was citing the threat from hockey then in vogue at Cambridge as a reason for trying to codify the rules of football, but nothing seems to have come of it and in 1857 Chambers's *Information for the People* is dismissively vague on the subject: 'Shinty in Scotland,

Hockey in England and Hurling in Ireland seem to be very much the same outdoor game.'

In this vague anarchic limbo, ignored by sixth form levees and the like, some adult clubs enjoyed a whackabout. The Old Blackheathen Football Club (1858), private school Old Boys and their friends, who later as Blackheath took the lead in the struggle to preserve hacking and similar emblems of virility in football, also played a rugged form of hockey on a pitch on the heath some 270 yards by 70 yards, using rough sticks and a cube-shaped ball of solid rubber. In politer mode the Teddington Cricket Club started a hockey section in 1871, using the smoother and smaller outfield of their ground for an eleven-a-side game played with a cricket ball. The idea of such a winter outlet also attracted cricket clubs in the fashionable suburbs of Richmond, Wimbledon and Surbiton, and this appears to have begun the emergence of hockey from its makeshift origins.

Teddington and the other cricketing offshoots began regular fixtures, gradually refining the rules to introduce conventions like not stopping the ball with the hands or raising the stick above the shoulder: the scoring circle, a device to discourage wild swipings at the ball from mid-field, was first used in a game between Teddington and Surbiton in 1876. In 1883 Wimbledon published a set of rules and three years later representatives of seven London clubs and Trinity College, Cambridge met to form the Hockey Association. Blackheath, as in football, went their own way, but unlike its counterpart in Rugby the Hockey Union came to naught. In 1890 Bell's *Handbook of Athletic Sports* gave hockey 'a foremost place' amongst games that had 'come into fashion of late years', adding that it was not new 'as probably everyone who has been at school in the past thirty years can testify'. It did not mention the Blackheath version.

Hockey was not a game of physical contact and once it had shed the cruder conventions it was to prove surprisingly suited to women. Young tomboys in families living in houses with spacious lawns played in knockabout versions with their brothers in school holidays, and alumnae of the new girls' schools afterwards recalled playing improvised games with suitably shaped sticks cut from trees. More orderly versions, emulating the footballing men students, were organised at the new women's college, Lady Margaret Hall, which opened at Oxford in 1870. By 1887 the first ladies club was formed, at Wimbledon. The dramatic aftermath, first securing independence of and then outclassing the men, lay in the future, and meanwhile Wimbledon was earning renown for a quite different game.

Lawn tennis and some of its rivals

The convoluted story of lawn tennis began with a proposal in 1868 for an All-England Croquet Club. Croquet was currently much discussed in the columns of *The Field*. Its editor, J.H. Walsh, had trained as an eye-surgeon but like so many young men of his class at that time was attracted to sports writing and organisation. Under the pen-name Stonehenge he first made his name as a writer on horse, dog and hound, with a little falconry for the nostalgic and occasional forays into rowing and fencing, and swiftly trod the pontifical path to the editorship of *The Field*. Amongst its correspondents was a kindred spirit, also a surgeon, Henry Jones, known as 'Cavendish' and primarily an authority on indoor games. Both he and Walsh were deeply interested in the possibilities of croquet.

The acknowledged expert was, however, one Walter Whitmore, who had left Oxford without a degree, tried the Civil Service and thereafter sought to augment his £40 a year private income by inventions, such as a patent boot-lacer, as well as by sports journalism and organising. It was Whitmore who devised the first rules for croquet, published in *The Field* in 1866, and his subsequent series of articles formed the substance of a book, *The Science of Croquet*, published that year. And it was Whitmore who organised, and himself won, a championship in 1867. Amongst those he overcame was the skilled but nervous Dr Prior whom Whitmore prevailed upon to write (under the name Meliora Spero – I hope for better things) to *The Field* in May 1868 proposing an All-England Club.

So far so good. The idea was taken up with enthusiasm. Walsh chaired the inaugural meeting which elected Whitmore honorary secretary and authorised him to find a suitable ground. Before long, however, the Committee, suspecting Whitmore of seeking to feather his own nest, relieved him of office. At first he declined to go, and when he eventually departed he made a great deal of fuss and started a rival club. So in 1869 there were two national croquet championships, with the opposing factions airing their views at great length in the columns of *The Field* and its competitor *Land and Water*. Accusations and counter-accusations, claims of falsified minutes and such-like evidences of bad faith flew around.

Walsh and *The Field* struck a decisive blow when they acquired a ground at Worple Road, Wimbledon, in 1871 and most of Whitmore's allies left his National Croquet Club and rejoined the All-England. Whitmore's contributions to *Land and Water* grew shriller as he became more desperate. He refused to accept defeat, starting a Grand National Croquet Club which he inaugurated at a spectacular event at Aldershot, including a race meeting, a cricket match between the garrison and MCC, a sham fight with 1,700 troops and a series of splendid balls and dinners. But both he and croquet were on their way out. Whitmore's death in 1872 restored harmony to the scene but the vogue lasted barely another year, during which more spirited rivals took its place.

One of these, an indoor racket game, was called Badminton after the Duke of Beaufort's estate, where it was supposed to have been invented about 1870 by high-spirited guests, confined indoors by the weather, who improvised a competitive game with the implements of the old game of battledore and shuttlecock. In battledore and shuttlecock, which dates back at least to the early sixteenth century,[9] the idea was to keep the shuttle in the air back and forth between two players. By the nineteenth century this decorous pursuit was restricted to children (it was a childhood favourite of Queen Victoria) and the innovation which made it an adult sport in the modern idiom was trying to make the other player miss. Furthermore the use of a shuttlecock rather than a ball made it both suitable for indoor play and for ladies. That it originated at Badminton was disputed even at the time. But it was an attractive name with socially superior connotations, which had been applied since about 1845 to a refreshing drink of claret, sugar and soda water; and no doubt the game was played there, particularly by officers on leave from India, for as *Cassell's Handbook* pointed out, Badminton had been 'fully patronised in Calcutta and Madras long before the good folk at home had any idea that sport could be had out of it'. Its first rules were published in Poona about 1870. Badminton was, of course, well suited to indoor play in a mess hall after dinner, and the idiosyncratic shape of its court, narrowing at the centre like an hour-glass was presumably designed to allow access through side doors without dismantling the net.[10]

Shuttlecocks were, however, no use out of doors and there were many attempts to devise a bat and ball game that could be played on a lawn. Outdoor versions of tennis had been played almost as long as the original: One of the variants, *longe paume*, was played five-a-side as 'bord and cord' in Elizabethan times:[11] as field tennis it was described as a current vogue in William Hickey's *Memoirs* in 1763 and as threatening to 'bowl out cricket' in the *Sporting Magazine* in 1793.[12] It appeared under another name, long tennis, in Urquhart's translation of Rabelais in 1653 and was mentioned in Douglas Walter's *Games and Sports* in 1873. Interest in its possibilities was revived with the introduction of rubber balls (Goodyear's invention of vulcanisation in 1838 greatly improved their possibilities) and there were reports of fashionable parties where such a game was played around 1864, at Sir Walter Scott's Roxburgh estate and on the Revd Lord Arthur Harvey's rectory lawn in Suffolk. The most systematic approach was made, however, in the superior environs of Birmingham where in 1866 Major T.H. Gem and his friend J.B.

Perera played a game they first called Pelota, after the Basque version of *jeu de paume*, and afterwards lawn rackets. With two local doctors they played a doubles version at the Manor House Hotel, Leamington Spa, and by 1872 they had formed a club and printed 'Rules of Lawn Tennis'.[13]

The game Gem and Perera played had a four-foot-high net and a rectangular court, it could be played with a racquet, a fives bat or the bare hand and there was a gentler version for ladies. It was soon superseded by rival versions, including some by suppliers of equipment alive to the commercial possibilities. Several boxed sets with rules appeared in the shops, offering special features. Some evidently sought to oust the exotic newcomer Badminton and there were references to 'improved wingless lawn tennis' and 'the new Indian lawn game'. There was much correspondence in the sporting journals about the various claims to authenticity and originality.

The one that most deftly caught the tide was that of Major Walter Wingfield, late of the 1st Dragoon Guards, who had recently returned from service in China to a spell with the Montgomeryshire Yeomanry. A socialite with inordinate pride in his ancestry, he first tried out his ideas at a Christmas party at Nantclwyd in 1873. It had the high sagging net and hour-glass shaped court of Badminton but it was played with a rubber ball – ideal, Wingfield reckoned, for frosty days when the ground was too hard for hunting and the best of the shooting was over. The following March he was persuaded to market it: he called it 'Sphairistike' (a characteristically pretentious coinage from the Greek for ball-play) adding Lawn Tennis for the uninformed. For five guineas his boxed set included poles, pegs, mallet and netting, described as 'A New and Portable Court for Playing the Ancient Game of Tennis'.

This odd hybrid soon outstripped in popularity other versions, including that of Mr J.H. Hale, Sussex cricketer and founder-member of the All-England Croquet Club, though his had a rectangular court. However, in his second edition that same summer Wingfield was able to include in his colourful publicity commendations from the *Army and Navy Gazette*, which called it 'a clever adaptation of tennis to an ordinary lawn piece of ground',[14] and from other prestigious publications, noting that amongst the first to acquire sets had been the Prince of Wales, the Crown Princess of Prussia and the Tsarevitch of Russia. Between July 1874 and June 1875, 1,050 sets were sold, mainly to the aristocracy. Before long Wingfield abandoned the trade name, which people tended to shorten to 'stické' pronounced 'sticky', as altogether too undignified, and called the game lawn tennis which he now claimed to have invented and of which he hoped to secure exclusive rights.

He was to be disappointed. Between March 1874 and May 1875 *The Field* devoted many columns to discussion of the rules, method of scoring (rackets and real tennis), size and shape of court, dimensions of net and type of ball.

The All-England Croquet Club was persuaded by Henry Jones in February 1875 to set aside a ground for lawn tennis, a shrewd move, despite the somewhat premature decision to invest £25 on purchasing equipment and preparing the ground for Wingfield's version. By this time J.M. Heathcote, the outstanding real tennis player of his generation, had persuaded MCC to provide courts for the lawn variety at Lord's. The Committee, after seeing demonstrations of Wingfield's and Hale's versions, set up a sub-committee with Heathcote as chairman, to determine what rules they would follow. Heathcote's chief interest was in the ball, about which he had theories, and the flannel-covered, hollow rubber ball he favoured was the major factor in giving lawn tennis the potential to become a sport rather than a mere pastime. His sub-committee – for what reason is not clear – opted for Wingfield's high sagging net and hour-glass shaped court and was persuaded by Hart-Dyke, the rackets player, to use the hand in-hand out method of scoring favoured – on the rackets model – by Badminton players and by Wingfield.

This fitted in well with the plans of the All-England Croquet Club, which was glad of the imprimatur of such an august body as MCC and, as the stické craze continued, not only provided four more courts for lawn tennis but changed its name to the All-England Croquet and Lawn Tennis Club. This was Wingfield's finest hour. His stické was also popular with the army (who presumably saw it as an outdoor version of Badminton) and it had found its way through casual social contact into the United States. But by the following year when the All-England Club, assisted by *The Field*, organised 'a lawn tennis meeting open to all amateurs . . . entrance £1 1s' the Rules Committee, which included Julian Marshall, a rackets champion at Harrow but the self-appointed custodian of the traditions and values of real tennis, abandoned the hour-glass court and chose the tennis system of scoring.[15]

For all the solemn debate about rules this first Wimbledon Championship was a somewhat casual affair. The event was not advertised until a fortnight beforehand so the organisers were perhaps fortunate to attract 22 entries. Similarly only two hundred spectators watched the Final (admission one shilling) but since it had been postponed twice, once to avoid clashing with the Eton versus Harrow cricket match, and once because of rain, this was perhaps to be expected. The net profit, augmented by the sale of nets, posts and guy ropes at thirty shillings a set, was £10. More to the point, for this was by no means a commercial venture, the objections of the rackets players to the scoring system were silenced when the event was won in 1877 by a former Harrow rackets player, Spencer Gore, and again in 1878 by another, P.F. Hadow, a young tea planter who had taken up lawn tennis only when he came on leave that summer.

This happy informality also allowed the following year's winner, J.H.

Hartley, a clergyman serving in Yorkshire, who had not expected to reach the finals and had made no arrangements for a curacy, to return home, take his services on the Sunday and come back at the crack of dawn on Monday to meet the deadline. There was, of course, no question of Sunday play for a gate-money event, but the new vogue led some private clubs into error. In the west London suburb of Bedford Park the local paper waxed indignant on the subject in 1880: 'If lawn tennis on Sundays is right at the Bedford Park Club, may it not be claimed that billiards, bagatelle, bowls and even skittles would be proper at the surrounding public houses.'[16]

Serious sportsmen had other objections. Spencer Gore himself expressed grave doubts whether anyone who had 'played really well at cricket, tennis or even rackets' would ever take up lawn tennis, the monotony of which 'would choke him off before he had time to excel in it'.[17] But simpler minds, capable of dedication to the mundane, got a great kick out of the new game and as the interested parties struggled for its soul its idiosyncratic earlier features were gradually shed. MCC and All-England, who produced joint rules for some years, periodically reduced the height of the net until in 1882 the present 3ft 6in was determined.

Whatever harmony prevailed in these deliberations there was no such sweetness and light within All-England itself. Its internal wranglings had little to do with the nuances of sporting legislation. The basic problem was that Henry Jones was doing very well out of the bath houses he had constructed out of old sheds on the Worple Road site, and Walsh, feeling himself more and more side-lined, became so cantankerous in his resentment that he was voted out of his position as honorary secretary. He struck back with venomous attacks in *The Field*, and when the Committee remonstrated, Walsh retorted that 'he was Editor of *The Field* and could do what he liked. They might go hang themselves.' This was recorded with relish by Jullian Marshall, the new secretary, who turned out to be even more pompous and arbitrary from the beginning than poor old Walsh had eventually become.

There was no disagreement, however, that the hour had struck for croquet. In 1882 the Croquet Championships, which had realised only seven shillings profit in the last two years were abandoned and in 1884 the word croquet was dropped from the club's title. Lawn tennis, by contrast, was big business: by this time every spa and watering place worth mentioning had a lawn tennis club and All-England saw itself as a towering eminence above them. It severed its connections with MCC in 1883 and took on the mantle of supreme law-giver. Under Marshall's administration this soon led to total disregard, if not contempt, for any outside considerations and many outsiders were consequently considerably miffed.

Amongst them was N. Lane Jackson, who was profitably deploying his talents as handicapper, organiser and publicist of the many tournaments that were arranged by the leading clubs. The arrangements for these were a topic of great fascination for a wide range of people, including Charles Dodgson (Lewis Carroll), a mathematics don by avocation, who in 1883 produced a treatise called *Lawn Tennis Tournaments, The True Method of Assigning Prizes with a Proof of the Fallacy of the Present Method*. But Jackson was the leading practitioner and his reputation was greatly enhanced by his organisation of a successful tournament for the London AC. He lent his support to the formation of a Lawn Tennis Association to co-ordinate the proliferating fixtures and tournaments and was chagrined to find that it was treated in cavalier fashion by the imperious Julian Marshall. That Marshall, before assuming control at All-England, had been a contributor to Jackson's magazine *Pastime* was an extra irritant.

Marshall's idea of consultation was to meet representatives of the clubs once a year, announce his plans and leave the others to fit in around them. Jackson, unwilling to clash openly with Marshall for prudential journalistic reasons, enlisted the aid of a front man, but he, the gentlemanly Major-General Bartlett of Exmouth, proved too 'half-hearted and apologetic' and Marshall demolished his protests at the annual meeting. Fortunately for Jackson, however, Marshall over-reached himself and made enemies of great social weight. In 1887 when H.S. Scrivener, president of the Oxford University Club, asked if his match at Wimbledon could be postponed because it clashed with the annual fixture against Cambridge, Marshall sent a brusque postcard reply: 'Impossible to excuse you. Why don't you alter the date of your 'Varsity match?' Scrivener and his friend George Hillyard, all-round sportsman and future pillar of Wimbledon, were soon powerful recruits to Jackson's plan. They revived the LTA and out-manoeuvred Marshall in the subsequent skirmishing.

Life became easier for everyone when Marshall peremptorily dismissed a gardener, involving the club in paying damages, and was obliged to resign. It was agreed that the LTA should become the governing body but that the All-England Club should retain control of the Wimbledon championships. All-England thereby got much the more prestigious and lucrative side of the bargain, and was thereafter generously financed to retain its élitist traditions. Amateurism was taken for granted (though Dodgson's essay is firmly anchored to the principle of competing for prizes, which, as in athletics could take the form of ornamental clocks, silver salvers and such-like) and was controlled as in golf by the test of social acceptability through election to membership. In the superior suburbs where lawn tennis was played this was no problem. There were a few professionals, but they were either equipment salesmen demonstrating their wares by giving coaching lessons or groundkeepers and court attendants, not much more advanced socially than the Roman pilicreps, and there were as yet no professional tournaments even in the United States, that beckoning land of opportunity.

The role model for the emergent lawn tennis player was Willie Renshaw, Wimbledon champion from 1881 to 1886, who with his twin brother Ernest, his partner in many doubles finals and his opponent three times in the singles, showed that the new game was no mere pastime but a serious sport, worthy of being taken up as the first string to a man's bow, and certainly no mere 'pat-ball' as the cricketers were inclined to call it. The Renshaws were Cheltenham College boys, but needless to say their prowess was acquired mainly in the holidays, on the local covered court or in the winter at Cannes. Lawn tennis had no appeal to the public schools' muscular Christians.

Indeed it soon became established as a highly suitable sport for the modern woman. Long dresses with voluminous skirts (and corsets) were a handicap, of course, and some felt at first that it was too strenuous for ladies. By 1879, however, All-England (during the period of association with MCC) were claiming in their advertisements that 'the exercise required to enjoy the game is not in any way of an exhausting character and affords the gentler sex a training in graceful and charming movements' and a ladies magazine was suggesting a suitable garb: 'a cream merino bodice with long sleeves edged with embroidery, skirt with deep kilting, over it an old-gold silk blouse-tunic with short wide sleeves and square neck'.[18]

The demands of competition were soon to put even greater strains on modesty. That same year of 1879 the prestigious FitzWilliam Club in Dublin included a women's event in its championships. The winner, Miss May Langrishe, one of two beautiful sporting daughters of Sir Hercules Langrishe, Master of the Kilkenny Hunt, was only fourteen and not temperamentally too anxious about convention, but when eventually Wimbledon introduced a women's event in 1884 decorum was to the forefront. Miss Maud Watson, who beat her sister in the first final and won again in 1885, was a model of respectability and the more accomplished Miss Blanche Bingley, who became Mrs George Hillyard, dressed for tennis as if she were going to church. Even the prodigious Charlotte 'Lottie' Dod, who burst on to the horizon in 1887 and as a fifteen year old was allowed to wear calf length skirts, and who later argued against restrictive sportswear for women, never went so far as to advocate 'rational dress'. Lawn tennis was not that sort of a game.

Golf: England takes notice ✗

It was a sign of the times, however, that women were in at the start of this new sporting vogue. In golf on the other hand, whose patterns had been set in the eighteenth century, few women had appeared since Mary, Queen of Scots had reputedly shocked the conventional by playing golf and pall-mall in the fields at Sefton soon after the demise of her husband, Darnley. We may discount the resolution of the Musselburgh Club in 1810 'to present by Subscription a new Creel and Shawl to the best female golfer who plays on the annual occasion on 1st January . . . to be intimated to the Fish Ladies by the Officer of the Club' as a Hogmanay frolic for the amusement of the gentlemen.[19] In the Victorian era ladies (still less Fish Ladies) were not generally welcomed on golf courses even as spectators: they were thought incapable of remaining silent or standing still at critical moments. All clubs, sporting and social, were essentially male strongholds and golfers greatly enjoyed the amenity of a masculine retreat.

It is surprising, therefore, to find the far from radical R and A acquiescing in, if not actively encouraging the first Ladies' Golf Club, formed at St Andrews in 1867, and the fact that the links was common land probably influenced the situation. Legend has it that the wife of a prominent member sought to lessen the tedium of waiting for him to finish a round by practising putting on a bit of land used by the caddies for that purpose. Such social exposure being thought inappropriate, a more secluded spot was set aside for the pioneer and her friends. Be that as it may by 1872 the St Andrews Gazette and Fifeshire News could proudly report that 'the Ladies Golf Club is an institution that was born in the soil of St Andrews and made its struggle for existence there . . . Its remarkable success has led to the introduction and culture of golf in England and elsewhere.'[20]

The article went on to explain that, of course, 'the wielding of a club assumes a milder sway of the gentler sex and has never yet extended beyond the simple stroke of the putting green'. This was no doubt also true of pioneering English clubs like North Devon, which had 47 lady members in 1868 and of the London Scottish and Wimbledon Ladies Clubs started in the 1870s. Two decades were to elapse before ladies, including Lottie Dod, began whacking the ball about in earnest and in public, but it is hard to believe that a few of them at least were not practising in secret.

Serious golf, though, was indisputably masculine in the meantime. It was also dominated by the Scots and, worse, by their professionals. The Open Championship was just beginning to find its feet. In 1868 Young Tom Morris at the age of seventeen beat Old Tom, his father, to win the Belt, repeating the feat twice more in succession, bringing new standards of play and a dashing style and winning the Belt outright. The event then lapsed for a year but was revived in 1872 with the presentation of a cup to be competed for at St Andrews, Musselburgh and Prestwick in turn. Young Tom won again twice running and looked as if he might win it for ever, but he died in 1874, though not without attracting the attention of Wimbledon, still in contention with

Lord Elcho's London Scottish and anxious to make a name for themselves, who sought him as professional.

The R and A was now revered, much as MCC was in cricket, by golfers in England and indeed everywhere (save perhaps the Honourable Company in Edinburgh), an interesting example of the way antiquity and superior social status had imposed an ascendancy code above the claims of nationalism in Britain since the Norman conquest. Normally this worked in favour of England, but, for reasons we shall consider presently, the usual fashion-makers, London and the public schools and universities, were somewhat out of things in the early days of English golf. The next, and most influential, pioneering club, improbably, was in a small fishing village near Liverpool.

In May 1869 a Mr J. Muir Dowie, with Scottish blood and an eye for a golf links, sent out a circular letter inviting recipients to join a proposed club with a subscription of ten shillings a year, meeting at the Royal Hotel, Hoylake. In the eighteenth century this had been the resort of fashionable bathers, but the fashion and the hotel had since declined and only the nearby race-course, ancient but remote and outmoded, remained of its former glory. George Morris, Old Tom's brother, was summoned from St Andrews to lay out the course, leaving his son, Jack, as professional, stoically making balls in a loose box at the hotel during the lonely hours until membership improved. Happily the son of the owner of the hotel, John Ball, was a quick learner of the new game, his enthusiasm increased by victory in the first competition that October, in which well-wishers from Blackheath, Manchester and North Devon took part.[21]

Liverpool did much to re-assert the prestige of the amateur golfer as a player rather than just a social figure. This was a difficult proposition now that the Open was launched, showing professional dominance for all to see, and it took some time. After some years of successful local competition, eventually, in 1885, the club issued invitations to a Grand Open Amateur event. It at once encountered the problem of defining amateur status, hitherto a matter for local decision. The difficulty, as in rowing and athletics, was not with out-and-out professionals, still a small group; they knew their place. But there was a growing number of Scottish players, several of them good enough to win the Open itself, who had other jobs but played golf to augment their earnings.

Such a one was Willie Fernie, champion in 1883, a St Andrews plasterer who travelled to tournaments in the donkey cart he used for work. Jack Simpson of Elie was a stonemason, David Brown a slater and Jack Burns a plasterer. (Their trades were the result of cautious parents not wishing their boys to take up golf without 'something to fall back on': several were apprenticed to Andrew Scott, a golf-addicted master-plasterer. Most were members of the St Andrews Golf Club, which shared the common with R and A, founded in 1865 as the echanics' Golf Club.)[22]

So the entry of Douglas Rolland, an Elie stonemason, for Liverpool's inaugural meeting in 1885, caused consternation. His entry was refused, on the grounds that he was a professional, since, having come second in the previous year's Open, he had taken a money prize. The consequent embarrassment that John Ball, junior, son of the pioneering hotelier, had come sixth in the 1876 Open aged fourteen, and had pocketed the ten shilling prize, was relieved by the expedient ruling that accepting prize-money did not confer professional status if the acceptance had been more than five years earlier and the acceptor under sixteen. Thus protected from vulgar artisans the Liverpool event was a great success and the following year the R and A agreed that it should become the official amateur championship, alternating each year between an English and a Scottish venue.

As previously mentioned, the early growth of golf in England, unlike other games, owed very little to London influence and nothing at all to that of the public schools. It was, of course, intrinsically too individualistic to appeal to the pundits of athleticism, outside its native land at least. Nor would it have been an economic proposition for the schools to acquire sufficient land to construct a course. Hence, as in tennis, it was in school holidays that those public school boys fortunate enough to have access to a nearby course learned the game. One such, Horace Hutchinson, a precocious member of North Devon and later a prolific journalist, did much to introduce golf to Oxford and to inaugurate the inter-versity match in 1878.

Land was also an obstacle to expansion in London where virtually the only suitable spaces were those protected by the Municipal Commons Act. So there was little activity outside Blackheath – seven holes, lacking in privacy, scarred by gravel-pits, laced by roads and footpaths and open to picnickers – and the only marginally better Wimbledon, until Clapham (1873) and a decade later Epsom, Epping Forest and Tooting Bec. Londoners inevitably found themselves looking father afield. It was a couple of frustrated Wimbledon members who acquired land near Deal on which the club that became Royal St George's was founded. The resorts themselves began to take notice as they competed for superior visitors. Eastbourne (1887) quickly attracted 500 members. Much better progress was made further north, however, particularly along the Lancashire coast, where Liverpool had showed the possibilities of the terrain. The West Lancashire Club (1873), which exploited the dunes at Blundellsands, was essentially a local Liverpool development but the splendid stretch to the north, within railway reach of Manchester as well as the populous industrial hinterland, was ripe for exploitation. Formby (1884) and Southport and Hesketh (1885) preceded the illustrious Lytham (1886) and Birkdale (1889).[23]

The Irish were much better endowed with suitable land, though again it was in the north that the game first seriously took hold. In November 1881 *The Field* announced the formation of the Belfast Golf Club at a meeting presided over by the mayor. The course was located at the Kinnegar in nearby Hollywood, by kind permission of Captain Harrison, JP, and *The Field's* reporter commented, 'from personal knowledge of the spot we can vouch for its capability of being converted into a first class golfing arena'. Belfast was involved in the setting up of two other fine courses, at Portrush and Newcastle in 1888 and 1889, each of them inaugurated by local aristocrats and dignitaries and each favoured with a visit from Old Tom Morris, without whose imprimatur no club could hope its course to be admitted to the first rank.

Belfast's first captain was Thomas Sinclair (later the Rt Hon.) who had returned from a holiday at St Andrews to seek further instruction in the art from a master at the Royal Belfast Academical Institution who was a native of Musselburgh. Some of the early members had not played before and one of the founders reputedly took 200 to get round in the first annual competition. It was five years before a native Irishman, George M. Shaw, won the trophy. It was Scots, too, who inspired the foundation of the first southern club, at the Curragh in 1883, shortly after the posting there of the 71st Regiment of the Highland Light Infantry. Scottish blood still coursed in the veins, furthermore, of the future Lieutenant General Sir Henry D'Oyley Terrens, CB, born in India of an old Londonderry family, who was Officer Commanding Cork District between 1881 and 1884, where golf was reputedly inaugurated, though no formal club seems to have emerged. And in 1885, Scottish exiles led by Mr John Lumsden, manager of the Provincial Bank, started the Dublin Club, based in Phoenix Park, maintaining friendly relations with the military who had played there earlier and securing the patronage of the Lord Lieutenant.[24]

Unemployed legs, tricycles and penny farthings

It was the Anglo-Irish Harry R. Sargent who best encapsulated the ebullience of the British as they embarked on their self-appointed task of spreading their sporting skills, organising ability and ethical values throughout the globe, not only in the colonies but everywhere that her armies and businessmen carried the flag. Even Europe was not immune and the environment was no obstacle. 'That the British excel all other nations in manly exercise no-one cany deny', wrote Sargent, adding by way of explanation, 'for to us all games and pastimes come easy.' As an example he took skating: 'with only a very few days in the year to practise this invigorating pastime we have, taking them all round, as good performers on the ice as any to be found in any of the countries where skating is the principal means of locomotion'.[25]

The fashionable venue for skating, weather permitting, was the lake in the grounds of the Royal Toxophilite Society in Regent's Park. ('The Tox' was a deeply traditional survival from 1781, as interested in the antiquarian aspects and social possibilities of archery as in competition.) There the top-hatted gentlemen of the Skaters' Club besported themselves. The patronage of HRH the Prince of Wales did not, alas, give the same guarantee of respectability as that of his father had done. Skating parties, like shooting parties and hunting parties, were sometimes occasions for the flightier sort of female to flaunt her charms. 'Skittles' herself was an accomplished skater. She was also to be seen on the voguish new roller-skating rinks in London and Tunbridge Wells that sought to exploit the invention of ball-bearing skates in the USA, but no real lady would venture into such places. Even the Skaters' Club, which had highly respectable counterparts in Glasgow and Edinburgh, was sufficiently suspect for HRH, with whatever motive, to encourage Princess Alexandra, an accomplished skater, to perform only in private.

There were elaborate social distinctions even in this evanescent pursuit. At the lowest level was the bucolic Fenland addiction to the crude pleasures of competition, improvised races that attracted heavy betting. Two families, the Smarts and the Sees, conducted a local vendetta and their intermittent encounters aroused great local excitement: the cheating and rough tactics were a by-word. Suitable conditions on the Cam during the 1870s happily attracted a superior class of skater, for whom figure-skating was the thing. Amongst them was J.M. Heathcote, the tennis player, who, as Colonel of the Huntingdonshire Rifle Volunteers, encouraged skating as an aspect of military preparedness. It is to the great credit of James Digby, a Cambridge journalist, that he managed to bring together these disparate elements. Emulating his metropolitan counterparts he saw an opportunity to corner this peripheral and intermittent market by founding a somewhat grandly named National Skating Association.

Despite a cool reception initially he persisted, and in 1880 his Association was able to boast an Ice Figure Committee, chaired by the awe-inspiringly dignified H.E. Vandervell of the Skating Club and including George Anderson, MP, who wrote about skating under the *nom de plume* of 'Cyclos', and J.M.'s brother, C.G. Heathcote, HRH, who had earlier been evasive about becoming a patron, now sent a £5 donation, though he decided that for the time being, the patronage of the Princess of Wales had better be withheld. The problem of the speed-skaters was tackled next. In 1880 George 'Fish' Smart became the first professional champion and a separate amateur championship was launched in 1881. Mild winters then prevented further championships, and thus further scandals, until 1887.[26]

It was not only the manifest and vulgar problem of speed-skating that threatened British standards, however. British figure-skating comprised a series of separate, unconnected figures. Alas, the continentals, sometimes reportedly to the strains of music, were linking figures together with many small circles and narrow curves. Their greatest sin, according to Mr Montague S. Monier-Williams in that essential guide, the Earl of Suffolk and Berkshire's *Encyclopedia*, was using 'the bent employed knee and the non-quiescent unemployed leg'. He summarised the correct (i.e. British) way of skating as follows:

1. Body to be held strictly upright.
2. Employed leg to be kept straight.
3. Unemployed leg to be carried behind the employed, whenever possible the heels being approximated.

That British skaters fell foul of such tactics confirmed Harry R. Sargent's assertion, for it was in essence a self-fulfilling prophecy. The British were best at sport so anything unBritish that prevailed was not true sport. In any event Sargent's example was a mere rhetorical flourish from one who basically regarded snow and ice as an interruption of hunting. He also regarded the craze for cycling as 'an infringement on the prerogative of the horse'.[27] No doubt he took comfort, nevertheless, from the fact that in 1868 when Velocipedomania was still a largely French affair, it was a British resident, James Moore, who won the first public race in Paris and the following year the first road-race from Paris to Rouen against over 300 locals.

The machine Moore rode, popularly known as the Boneshaker, was, however, a French creation. The enlarged front wheel with pedals attached to it, the latest and most advanced design, was so popular that the factories of Pierre Michaux, a Parisian coach-builder, were turning out 400 machines a year. It was when Michaux ran into trouble by the loss of his chief mechanic to the USA and arguments over patents that Rowley B. Turner, Paris agent of the Coventry Sewing Machine Company, took a Boneshaker home and persuaded his uncle, the manager, to start making them. The Franco-Prussian War obliged the firm, now styled the Coventry Machinists' Company, to concentrate on the English market. The managing foreman, James Starley, produced the improved design called the ordinary bicycle (the 'penny farthing').

Nevertheless the bicycle became increasingly popular for leisure as well as competition. There was soon an Amateur Bicycling Club, mostly university men, and in 1870 the Pickwick in London (named in honour of Dickens who had just died) was followed by the Edinburgh and Surrey. Oxford, Cambridge and London University Clubs followed. By 1874 there were seven clubs in London and twenty-two elsewhere. Their membership was small and somewhat exclusive, mainly because of the athleticism required, but also because decent bicycles were not cheap. Starley's improved Coventry Gentleman's bicycle cost £16 in 1875. Still the sport was so well established that the following year a Bicycle Union (later the National Cyclists' Union) was formed to further the interests of road-using bicyclists.

H.J. Lawson had produced a bicycle with two wheels of more equal and moderate size in 1874, but it was eclipsed for a time by Starley's even more manageable Coventry Tricycle first brought out in 1876. This seemed a great advance to the better sort; it was more dignified, and it offered a solution to the problem of ladies' costume. Long skirts were not suited to bicycles, which had high cross-bars, and the tricycle or the 'sociable' in which two ladies or a gentleman and lady could sit alongside each other, were the refined choice. However most men preferred the new safety bicycles. The tricyclists had to rely on snob appeal, seeking members for a proposed Tricycle Union by emphasising the social superiority of those who choose them over the vulgar bicyclists. But the bicyclists started to become even more vulgar in 1884. J. Durley of Wolverhampton offered The Working Man's Friend at £4 10s, and the following year came Starley's Rover bicycle with chain, rear-wheel drive, diamond shaped frame and nearly equal-sized wheels, the first recognisably modern machine. Tradesmen, shop assistants and clerks flooded into the bicycle clubs – and the middle classes dropped out apart from school teachers and a few doctors.

The same social decline overtook cycle-racing. In 1877 the Hon. Ion Keith-Falconer, younger bother of the Earl of Kintore, Arabic scholar and future missionary, became the president of the London club after a glittering career at Harrow and Cambridge. In 1878 in a two mile race at Cambridge Keith-Falconer raced (and beat) the professional champion, John Keen, without infringing his amateur status. In June 1882 he cycled from Land's End to John O'Groats in just under thirteen days and a month later won the Bicycle Union's fifty miles amateur championship at Crystal Palace.

Time-trials were the customary alternative to road-racing, which was illegal. Nevertheless it happened at first, just like coach-racing in earlier days, but the crowds and commercial interests became too blatant and the authorities clamped down. There were in any event better commercial opportunities in track-racing. The earlier professional events were held in general sports arenas like the Star Grounds, Fulham or the Aston Cross Grounds, Birmingham, but soon special cycle tracks were built: Paddington – ash, Herne Hill – ash with wooden battens, Manchester – shale, and Coventry – gravel, in addition to many grass tracks. Cycle-races began to attract great crowds, not just in England but in Glasgow and Edinburgh and at the Lansdowne complex in Dublin where Mr W.F. Blood rode a historic mile in three minutes eight seconds in 1875.[28]

The first road-race in France had included four women competitors and eventually bolder spirits in England began to defy public opinion by demonstrating their athleticism. Few thought cycling a suitable pursuit for ladies though. There were those who thought the whole exercise capable of severe structural damage to the pelvis, but most criticism focused on the question of clothing, Mrs King, secretary of the Rational Dress Society, designed a cycling costume consisting of a long jacket and baggy trousers, but when Miss Jessie Chance wore it in 1883 to achieve her record-breaking 114 miles in a day she aroused fierce and prolonged criticism. Straddling a cross-bar was just as bad as straddling a horse and nothing like as socially prestigious. Harry R. Sargent spoke for all right thinking horsey people when he declared 'I do hate the sight of a cycle, whether it be a "bi" or a "tri".[29]

Notes

1 'The Deserted Parks' 1867 in *The Works of Lewis Carroll*, London, 1965, p. 947.
2 *Henry VIII*, Act III, ii.
3 J. Strutt, *Glig-garmena angel deod: or The Sports and Pastimes of the People of England*, London, 1801); new edition 1903, reprinted Bath, 1969, p. 73.
4 H.R. Sargent, *Thoughts Upon Sport*, London, 1894, p. 301.
5 Article by T. Seccombe in *Dictionary of National Biography*.
6 *Strutt, Sports and Pastimes*, p. 98. His editor of 1901 inserted several paragraphs alluding to its similarity to hurling and possible Irish origins in the distant past.
7 W. Holloway, *A Genteel Dictionary of Provincialisms*, London, 1838.
8 G. Vigne, *Travels in Kashmir*, London, 1842. For ancient polo see E.B. Tylor, 'The History of Games', *Fortnightly Review*, London, 1879, reprinted in E.M. Avedon and B. Sutton-Smith, *The Study of Games*, New York, 1971, p. 67, in which he argues that polo was the original and hockey 'dismounted polo'. The modern game was brought back to England from India around 1870, by the 9th and 10th Hussars. It was played on Hampstead Heath amongst other places in London, where it attracted fashionable attention. The first organised club was that of the Royal Horse Guards, who played at Lillie Bridge but it was superseded in 1875 by Hurlingham. For long the preserve of London Cavalry regiments (W.S. Churchill in *My Early Life* writes of his passion for it) provincial clubs with civilian members were started – the first in Monmouthshire, the best in Sussex – in the seventies by officers retired or on home leave from the army. See F. Herbert 'Polo' in Earl of Suffolk, and Berkshire et al, *The Encyclopaedia of Sport*, 1897–8, vol. II.
9 I trow all wyll be nought
Nat worthe a shyttle cocke'.
John Skelton, *Why come ye not to Court?*, c1522, 1.356.
10 Both J. Arlott, *Oxford Companion to Sports and Games*, Oxford, 1976, p. 37 and J.A. Cuddon, *MacMillan Dictionary of Sport and Games*, London, 1980, p. 75, attribute the shape to the geography of Victorian drawing rooms and this is the usual explanation. See N.B. Redford, *Badminton*, London, 1954.
11 'In this square they . . . played, five to five with the hand ball, at bord and cord (as they tearme it), J. Nichols, *Progresses and Pageants of Queen Elizabeth*, vol. 4, p. 19, quoted in Strutt, *Sports and Pastimes*, p. 82.
12 See note 17, Chapter 6.

13 The following account is based on a variety of sources including Aberdare, op cit, Jackson, op cit, J.M. Heathcote et al. *Tennis, Lawn Tennis, Badminton, Rackets and Fives*. Badminton Library, London, n.d., G.W. Hillyard, *Forty Years of First Class Lawn Tennis*, London, 1924, A.W. Myers, *Fifty Years of Wimbledon*, London, 1926, L. Tingay, *100 Years of Wimbledon*, London, 1977.

14 *Army and Navy Gazette, XV*, p. 154, in *OED* as first use of 'lawn tennis'. *OED* also records 'stické' as still in use in 1910.

15 Myers, *Fifty Years of Wimbledon*, p. 58.

16 *Acton, Chiswick and Turnham Green Gazette*, 28 May 1880, quoted by H. Walker, 'Lawn Tennis' in T. Mason (ed.), *Sport in Britain*, Cambridge, 1989, p. 248.

17 Myers, *Fifty Years of Wimbledon*, p. 35. They also retained the 'second chance' service, a feature that still survives.

18 P. Cunnington and A. Marsfield, *English Costumes for Sports and Outdoor Recreation*, London, 1969, p. 92.

19 Minutes of the Club, 14 December 1810, quoted by E.B. Wilson 'Women's Golf' in B. Darwin, *et al.*, *A History of Golf in Britain*, 1952, p. 222. Hogmanay, thought to be of plebeian origin, was a popular custom in southern Scotland and northern England in the seventeenth century.

20 21 August 1872, quoted in Wilson, 'Women's Golf', pp. 222–3.

21 Darwin, History of Golf, pp. 142–3. R. Browning, *A History of Golf*, London, 1955, p. 102.

22 Darwin, p. 145. *History of Golf*.

23 The first Welsh clubs, Aberdovey (1892) and Harlech (1894) are of slightly later date but Welsh golfers in the modern era have in included many great players. For the problems of land, and many other interesting social questions see the various books of Geoffrey Cousins: *Golfers at Law*, London, 1958, *Golf in Britain*, London, 1975, *Lords of the Links*, London, 1977.

24 W.H. Gibson, *Early Irish Golf*, Naas, 1988, pp. 39–47.

25 Sargent, *Thoughts Upon Sport*, p. 302.

26 N. Brown, *Ice-skating: A History*, London, 1955, passim.

27 Sargent, *Thoughts Upon Sport*, p. 299.

28 Sources include Ritchie, op cit, R. Watson and M. Gray, *The Penguin Book of the Bicycle*, Harmondsworth, 1978; biographies of Falconer and Starley in *Dictionary of National Biography*.

29 Sargent, *Thoughts Upon Sport*, p. 299.

CHAPTER FIFTEEN

The missionary spirit: 'Imperial fiddlestick'

1867–88

Shrewsbury

The belief that games were an essential preparation for leadership and that the British were uniquely gifted in both grew with the prosperity that flowed from earlier industrialisation. Succeeding generations had discovered that financial dealings brought quicker and easier profits than attempting to keep up with technological challenge. In this they were cushioned by the haphazard collection of overseas territories that people were beginning to call the Empire in which raw materials abounded and cheap labour was ripe for exploitation. Gladstone, whose successful first administration ended in 1874, was a free trader in the Prince Consort style, and his unromantic attitude contrasted sharply with the blatant emotionalism of the Conservatives. The proclamation of Queen Victoria as Empress of India in 1876 was a highly popular move.

Shortly afterwards a contributor to the *Nineteenth Century* questioned Gladstone's commitment to the cause, arguing that 'if our Empire beyond the seas is to be undone of our own free will, we shall have not only to re-write our history but to re-model our character as a nation.'[1] The great man's reply was magisterial, 'The sentiment of Empire may be called innate in every Briton. If there are exceptions they are like those of men blind or lame among us.'[2] Nevertheless he expressed concern lest conviction might lead to 'excess'. There was indeed room for caution: the claims of Empire – in particular protecting the route to India – were inflaming old passions. With Disraeli buccaneering in the Near East and the Queen urging the government to declare war on Russia anything could happen. A music hall song expressed the national mood:

> We don't want to fight,
> But by Jingo! if we do,
> We've got the ships, we've got the men
> And got the money too.

The men, it might have added, were sportsmen. A decade later J.E.C. Welldon, Headmaster of Harrow, could write, 'In the history of the British Empire it is written that England has owed her sovereignty to her sports.'[3] This extravagant view was no isolated eccentricity. Indeed it has survived the years as part of the modern orthodoxy articulated by Sir Robert Ensor in 1936: 'the development of organised games . . . on any reckoning may rank among England's leading contributions to world-culture'.[4] (The hyphen is significant.) And at the time of imperial crisis few doubted that cricket was the jewel in the crown.

Cricket: the quintessence

Cricket was, in Thomas Hughes' much quoted phrase, 'more than a game . . . an institution'. It was 'the birth right of British boys old and young, as habeas corpus and trial by jury are of British men'.[5] Its spiritual force, ever since Pycroft, had been attested not only by the cricketing metaphors for the spiritual life, which were as plentiful in Victorian days as hunting metaphors had been in the middle ages, from the One Great Scorer to the Straight Bat, but in the astonishing number of clerical practioners – the church cricketant as it has been happily described.[6]

When, in 1867, John Lillywhite used the important phrase 'not cricket', meaning unfair play, he referred to appealing unnecessarily to the umpire.[7] In fact in first class cricket the umpires were relatively unimportant, at least when gentlemen were involved. From their origins as hirelings employed by the great patrons to supervise the workings of the code of honour they were now ciphers subordinate to the public school captains who led most sides in important matches. We shall see later that some great players took advantage of their position, undermining the umpires and breaking the ethical code cricket was supposed to embody. First, however, we should note that the public schools did not always set a good example.

At the Eton versus Harrow match, the acme of sporting fashion, the spectators' fervour could lead to unseemly conduct. In 1873 MCC issued a manifesto expressing pained displeasure: 'Such scenes . . . would not occur if the partisans of both schools were to assist the authorities in checking the immoderate expression of feeling at the conclusion of the match'. The correspondent of *The Times*, though not wishing to be alarmist ('It was just like a rough game, such as football, and was, as far as the boys went, just as harmless'), was also critical of the crowd's comments. ' "Well hit!" and "Well bowled!" are fair cries enough, but "Well fielded!" when the adversary misses a catch, and "Well asked!" when the umpire gives his decision in favour of the batsman, are to put it mildly, errors in taste and judgement.'[8]

Eton were coached in those days by a young master, R.A.H. Mitchell, who dedicated the next thirty years of his life to the cause. He was one of a new breed who got a Blue four years running. During the 1870s and 1880s this happy band included, at Oxford S.E. Butler, C.J. Ottoway, R.D. Walker, the Hon. George Harris, E.F.S. Tylecote, M.C. Kemp, H.V. Page, and K.J. Key, and at Cambridge the Hon. C.G., Hon. Revd E., and Hon. A. Lyttleton, C.I. Thornton, W. Yardley, A.P. Lucas, D.Q. Steel, A.G. Steel, C.T. Studd and the Hon. Ivo Bligh. The renown of these players, many of whom captained or played for the counties or England, and many of whom were capped in other sports, encouraged the colleges to look for athletic prowess rather than academic distinction in their students and the schools to vie with each other in their tally of Blues.

The new generation of amateurs included some who regarded country house cricket as lacking in competitive edge, too frivolous for such a noble game. Foremost amongst these was the Hon. George Harris, whose father, Lord Harris, reconciling the warring factions in Kent in 1869, became the first president of a new county club, of which George, in his first year at Oxford, became captain. It was one of several new ventures that were changing the face of cricket, ironically by reviving the old feudal loyalties though in modern, organised competitive guise. The railways brought in new spectators and the newspapers soon – to the chagrin of traditionalists – began to publish not only players' averages but an unofficial championship table.

Kent did not figure at the head of any of these league tables, basically because they lacked a solid professional core. Nor did Sussex, who lacked distinction amongst the amateurs too. Nor at first did Surrey, in spite of their sound finances. C.W. Alcock took over the post of Secretary at the Oval in 1872 (£200 a year) and soon built up a membership of 1200, yielding an income of £3,500 annually. Alcock was a powerful influence on the emerging county system, steering it in a different direction from that of soccer. In 1873, with his own FA Cup only a year old and still impeccably amateur, he opposed MCC's suggestion of a cricket equivalent (with an obvious eye to the travelling circuses which were still active) since an MCC cup might become a precedent for Cup matches in other places and so discourage existing county cricket in which, of course, the professionals were more docile.

Middlesex, invincibly amateur and improvident under the leadership of V.E. and R.D. Walker, two of eight Harrovian brothers all members of the Southgate Club, did not achieve the success their dashing play deserved. Nor did Lancashire, also utterly amateur.

In Yorkshire anarchy was succeeded by schizophrenia. In 1864 the old Sheffield-based club that bore the county banner was upstaged by a superior faction based in York, with patrons such as the Duke of Devonshire, the Earls of FitzWilliam, Harewood and Effingham, Viscount Milton and the munificent Lord Londesborough. Thereafter the county club had two playing sections, the Yorkshire Gentlemen and a professional eleven who competed in the championship. It was led successively by Roger Iddison, a mercenary who also played for Lancashire, J. Rowbotham about whom little is known, the rough-hewn Ephraim Lockwood known as 'Mary Ann', and Tom Emmett who claimed to have – and to have earned – the reddest nose in cricket. Louis Hall, recruited in 1873, was a lay preacher and a teetotaller, said to be the first who ever played for Yorkshire.[9]

Significantly the two counties who dominated the early championship did so by professionalism, the one honestly, the other hypocritically. Nottinghamshire remained as unashamedly professional under what George Parr the first captain called 'Committee cricket' as under Old Clarke; and his successors W. Oscroft, Richard Daft (owner of a small brewery and a sports shop but too scrupulous to draw expenses as an amateur) and Alfred Shaw, a cricketing genius and rather muddled entrepreneur, followed the tradition. Less gloriously the other leading county, Gloucestershire, was heavily reliant on amateurs, two of whom spent their summers playing cricket and made more money out of it than the professionals. E.M. Grace, 'the Coroner', was paid secretary, and awarded himself and his younger brother, W.G., 'the Doctor' lavish expenses, not always over the counter. Both were to be the subject of official scrutiny but both adopted a lordly attitude. W.G. was well aware he was above such petty consideration, secure in public adulation. In 1871 W.G.'s average was 78, more than twice that of the next man, Richard Daft.

Grace abounding

Both W.G. and the Hon. George Harris were members of an MCC team which toured Canada that winter at the invitation of the Montreal Club. MCC's secretary, R.A. Fitzgerald, was heavily facetious about it in his book, *Wickets in the West* (1873). The Montreal gentlemen had first explained 'where Canada was and who the Canadians were. The precaution was necessary as great ignorance prevailed in England at the time respecting its colony.' Of the actual tour *The Times* also struck a slightly patronising note:

> The British Lion has consented to 'walk round and show his muscle' to the Canadians, and he has done so to some purpose, making exceedingly short work, as might have been foretold, of the very weak teams the colony could bring into the field . . . still, the recollection of how the English force came, saw and conquered is bound to stimulate the game in Canada and teach the rising generation how [battle] fields were won.[10]

W.G. was ready to carry the flag to more distant fields. For a price, that is. He had been asked to take a team to Australia in the winter of 1872–3, but the £1,500 fee he asked was more than the colonists could afford. However, they had raised the money by the following winter. W.G. made it a honeymoon trip, no doubt an enchanting as well as profitable experience for his new wife. The team, which included W.G.'s younger brother, Fred, was not as strong as it might have been because of the rather stingy terms he offered to the professionals – £150 plus £20 expenses and second class travel. The tour was only a limited success. For one thing those inhabitants who were not lost in starry-eyed admiration for all things English thought the great cricketer small-minded, too inclined to wrangle over small points of the game.

At home, by contrast, though many instances of his excessive keenness to win and the reluctance of umpires to give him out were recorded and are still recounted, they are usually thought rather amusing, the amiable foibles of a larger than life character.[11] It was hardly in the 'spirit of the game' – another phrase cricketers freely used – either to invoke a legal point or to impose on the poor umpire as he did in a North versus South match in 1878. When Barlow, the Lancashire professional, having blocked the ball, playfully tapped it to him and made as if to run (merely to amuse the crowd) W.G. appealed for hitting the ball twice. A.G. Steel, recording the incident, added '– and out Barlow had to go – a lesson which he never forgot'.[12] And when, in the Test Match of 1882, the Australian S.P. Jones, having completed a run 'and thinking wrongly but very naturally, that the ball was dead, went out of his ground' to repair the pitch Grace removed the bails and the umpire again had to give him out. This incensed the Australians, but as Wisden put it, 'There was a good deal of truth in what a gentleman in the crowd remarked, amidst some laughter, that "Jones ought to thank the champion for teaching him something.' "[13] In Francis Thompson's nostalgic poem about Lord's matches in the seventies W.G. is recalled as 'The long-whiskered Doctor, that laugheth rules to scorn.'[14]

It was James Lillywhite, leading twelve professionals on a commercially sponsored tour in 1867, who by agreeing to play an extra match against a combined Australian XI inadvertently made history, for it was subsequently dubbed the first Test Match. Several things obscured the significance at the time. Australia won, no gentlemen were involved and, in fact, the Commonwealth of Australia was not created until 1901. So far as most people in Britain were concerned Australia was a collection of colonies to which convicts were sent.

So the arrival of a touring team from Australia in 1878 was regarded with curiosity rather than sporting anticipation. There had been an aboriginal tour ten years earlier in which players with soubriquets such as 'Bullocky', 'Dick-a-Dick', 'Tiger', 'Twopenny' and the like entertained the crowds to boomerang throwing and similar feats of strength and skill as an additional attraction to the cricket. This may explain why when the ultra-white D.W. Gregory and his team took the field against Nottinghamshire someone in the crowd called out, 'Why, they ain't black!' Though they lost to Nottinghamshire the visitors later beat a strong MCC side, dismissing them for 33 and 19, W.G. Grace getting 4 and 0. The crowds rolled in for later fixtures including one against the Players of England which attracted some 5,000 spectators at a shilling a time on each of two days and enriched the Australians by £36 a man.

The match had originally been scheduled to take place two weeks earlier, but the leading English players, led by the Nottinghamshire professionals

Alfred Shaw and the twenty-two year old Arthur Shrewsbury refused to play because they had asked for £20 and were offered only £10. Nottinghamshire was old Clarke country and the new generation of professionals, who still played for the All-England XI in exhibition matches, were already upset that the United South of England XI, built round the Graces, got the cream of the limited fixtures remaining for this type of cricket – and the profits.[15] Shrewsbury in particular resented the outworn distinctions preserved by MCC between Gentleman and Players – the amateurs were called 'Mr' whilst the pros were addressed simply by their surnames, for instance – and the situation was exacerbated because the profit-taking Australians were classed as amateurs and were given the distinctions. Few professionals were impressed by MCC's protestations that they always adhered strictly to the rules over amateur expenses or by their pious but incriminating resolution that in future no-one who was paid over the odds would be selected to play for the Gentlemen in their annual matches against the players.[16]

Subsequent events confirmed the sceptics' suspicions. In Gloucestershire that winter a special meeting of the County Club had to be called to investigate various charges of irregularity involving the Grace family. E.M., the secretary, was accused of general malpractice in his handling of the Club's accounts: in particular it was revealed that he had submitted a bill for the team's expenses which the host club, Surrey, had refused to pay. Compared with the standard out-of-pocket expenses of £4 10s, E.M. had claimed £15 for W.G., £11 for G.F., and £20 for himself (Midwinter, the senior professional was down for £10).[17] The row blew over, but it provoked great cynicism. So too, that summer, did the first of several testimonials to W.G. At a ceremony at Lord's he was presented, after glowing tributes from the aristocracy, with a cheque for £1,400, as an aid to purchasing a medical practice.[18]

Meanwhile the imperial cause was being advanced by the Hon. George Harris, now Lord Harris, who led an expedition to Australia in the winter of 1878–9. It was originally intended as an all amateur affair, but the three Walker brothers of Southgate and Middlesex had to drop out when a fourth brother died, and the team was completed by the two Yorkshire professionals Tom Emmett and George Ulyett, who were expected to do most of the bowling chores. The tour ended in sensational fashion after an episode in which the crowd swarmed on the pitch in a match against New South Wales.

The problem lay in Lord Harris' choice of umpire. The custom then was for each side to choose one. Unlike England Australians usually used amateur umpires, but Harris had hired one, bringing him furthermore from Victoria, New South Wales' traditional enemies. The man started well enough (though he gave his Lordship an extra 'life') but trouble erupted when he ruled against Billy Murdoch, the local hero. There were shouts of 'change the umpire' and

'Go back, Murdoch!' and the New South Wales captain protested. Then sections of the crowd rushed on the field and made as if to attack the umpire. Harris interposed his noble person and a 'larrikin' hit him with a stick. 'Monkey' Hornby, the pugilist, seized the offender and frog-marched him to the pavilion, and the two pros armed with stumps protected his Lordship from further indignities. 'Nothing but convicts' one of them muttered.

Harris refused to leave the field so that New South Wales could not claim the match by default: 'I determined to obey the laws of cricket', he explained afterwards. The hooligans eventually withdrew and play was about to restart when the sight of the offending umpire, whom Harris refused to change, inflamed tempers again and there were several more invasions of the pitch before close of play when Harris eventually left the field. That evening the New South Wales officials and the Sydney ground authorities apologised profusely, and Lord Harris seemed appeased. The Australian press grovelled. 'What will they say in England?' asked *The Australian*, whilst the *South Australian Chronicle* observed, somewhat inaccurately 'Such a scene had never before been witnessed on a cricket ground.'[19]

The game resumed on the Monday and the English XI won by an innings before a small and subdued crowd. There the matter might have ended had not his Lordship written a long, acrimonious account of the affair to a friend, giving a one-sided version of events and had not this account appeared in the *Daily Telegraph*. Indeed Harris did not readily forgive the outrage. When an Australian touring team arrived in England that summer it was not welcomed and only the persistent tact and diplomacy of C.W. Alcock finally saved the day. He prevailed upon his Lordship to lead an England XI against the tourists at the Oval. It was, Harris recalled in his memoirs, a surprisingly strong team bearing in mind that 'some of the amateurs were on the moors'. The Graces were there in force and England won what was afterwards declared the first Test Match in England before record crowds of nearly 45,000.[20]

Gentlemen and players

Lord Harris spent much of his subsequent career as a colonial administrator, notably as Governor of Bombay where he imposed the disciplines of cricket on the natives with scant regard for religious and other local customs.[21] He later claimed that cricket had done more to consolidate the Empire than any other influence and he was proud of his part in it. Harris' attitude was, let us be clear, not unusually racist. Racism was taken for granted. He simply regarded cricket as God's playing field and himself as the custodian of cricket values. Thus in England he opposed lax residential qualifications in the counties, especially when Kent seemed disadvantaged, he opposed suspect bowling actions, and he defended as natural the distinction between gentlemen and players, hotly opposing what in later years he was to define as Bolshevism in cricket.[22]

The New South Wales episode occurred at a turning point in the English county scene. Serious-minded amateurs in the Harris mould were beginning to get a grip on things. The combative Wykehamist John Shuter greatly improved Surrey's fortunes when he took over the captaincy in 1880, as did the pugnacious Harrovian A.N. Hornby in Lancashire. Yorkshire took a little longer but eventually in 1883 found a true disciple of Lord Harris in the Hon. M.B. Hawke who, aged twenty-three and still up at Cambridge, took on the nine drunks and a chapel parson who formed the rest of the team and began to sort them out, dismissing Edmund Peate, an England bowler for overdoing the insobriety. Even Nottinghamshire tried to instil true amateur values through their honorary secretary, Captain Holden, Chief Constable of the County, known as 'Hell-Fire Jack'.

Captain Holden's task was unenviable, however, and he met his match in Shrewsbury. In the winter of 1881–2 Shrewsbury and Shaw, with their business partner James Lillywhite, made a lucrative trip to Australia, marred somewhat by a scandal involving George Ulyett and another player, Selby, who were accused of taking bribes to lose a match. Interestingly *The Times* declined to join in the parrot-cries denouncing professionalism as the root cause but compared the English system unfavourably with that of the Australians. Welcoming the Australian tourists of 1882, its long leading article hoped they would 'inspire our too highly-organised system of matches with fresh life'. It complained that 'cricket here is made more of a business than in Australia where men wear cricket proficiency lightly, as a flower'. This was not just a matter of professionalism: in England both amateurs and professionals 'made a business of the game in the sense that for a certain time during the year they do nothing else'.[23]

During the season it had been borne upon the public for the first time that English supremacy had to be demonstrated not just assumed. The press took England's defeat, at full strength, in sporting fashion. 'Well done, Cornstalks, whipt us fair and square', began a poem in *Punch* and the *Sporting Times* published a mock-obituary lamenting the death of English cricket, and announcing that the body had been cremated and the ashes taken to Australia. The only serious breach of the sporting code, in fact, came from 'the Champion', W.G., in the incident noted earlier, which was much worse than Wisden suggests. The Australians were generous enough in victory not to dwell on it, but, according to Spofforth in an account he allowed to be published only after his death, W.G. had fielded the ball and pretended to give it to the bowler before running Jones out, which was definitely 'not cricket'.[24]

The authorities were more interested in professional misdemeanours. Lord Harris, as part of his campaign against illegal bowling actions refused to play Lancashire that summer unless they dropped Jack Crossland, a rough lad whom they had hired in spite of his Nottinghamshire birth, a circumstance which also persuaded Nottinghamshire to refuse to play against Lancashire. It proved difficult to convict Crossland of throwing, basically because the professional umpires were reluctant to take such a bold step as to no-ball him on their own initiative. When Harris told Bob Thomas, the most respected umpire of the day, that they should do something about the proliferation of throwing, Thomas replied, 'My Lord, the umpires are going to do nothing. It is you gentlemen who are going to do it.'[25] The gentlemanly code was not impregnable to gentlemanly rivalry, however: the will to win was strong. In the end Crossland was forced out of cricket not because of his action but because he had infringed the rules of residence.

Believers in the gentlemanly code had their faith restored that winter when Old Etonian the Hon. Ivo Bligh, the future Lord Darnley, took a side to the Antipodes to resume the challenge. It was a happy moment when a group of fashionable young Melbourne ladies burnt a bail, put the ashes in a little urn and presented them to the dashing Ivo. The other side of the coin appeared when the following summer Shrewsbury and two other Nottinghamshire players refused to play against Murdoch's Australian tourists for the £10 fee offered by the Yorkshire Committee – advised by Hawke – for a Players' game at Sheffield. This in turn provoked reaction when Shrewsbury, Shaw and Lillywhite returned with an all-professional team to what Shaw called 'the Land of the Golden Fleece' in 1884–5.[26] It was evident, wrote Wisden, that Murdoch's men 'were animated by a feeling of bitter hostility towards Shaw and his party'. The tour was characterised by disputes, players' strikes and reprisals by the establishment. At a luncheon during one representative match which had been ruined by withdrawals the Attorney-General of South Australia, the Hon. C.C. Kingston, sternly criticised Murdoch and his men 'who appeared to sink everything for monetary considerations.[27]

Murdoch's XI indeed attained a place in Australian official demonology similar to that of Old Clarke in early times in England. In 1886 the superior Melbourne Cricket Club decided the time had come for it to organise a civilised tour to England in 1886. Alcock warmly welcomed the development.

> This is the first Colonial team that has visited us since that other gallant body of Colonists was ranged beneath our flag in the Soudan . . . Their trip, let us hope, will be free from the usual dismal squabbles about gate money, about amateur and professional rank, about the distinctions of 'Mr' and 'Esquire'. The Team is under new management and is organised on new and non-mercenary principles.[28]

The Melbourne Club, however, went a little too far when it tried to pre-empt a further tour of Australia by Shrewsbury and company that winter and the sporting press heatedly debated the propriety of Australians sponsoring their own opponents. Major Wardill went to the lengths of asking MCC to select a team for him, but the Premier Club declined to get involved and the field was left clear for the mercenaries, to Shrewsbury's grim satisfaction.

He made very little profit this time, however, partly because the Melbourne crowds showed little interest either in the tourists or their own undistinguished Australian XI. Only Sydney drew the crowds, and the long-headed Shrewsbury sought to spike the Melbourne Club's guns by hiring the Sydney ground for matches in a projected tour in 1887–8. Melbourne, this time with the tacit approval of MCC, were busily recruiting players for a higher-class project. With this in mind they engaged G.F. Vernon, the Middlesex amateur, to sign up players on their behalf. The emphasis was to be on the gentlemanly approach. Shrewsbury, alive to this danger, signed a few amateurs of his own, including as captain C. Aubrey Smith, later Sir Aubrey, who was to become a Hollywood movie actor famous for his portrayals of English dignitaries in epics about the British Raj. Melbourne's riposte was to sign up no less a personage than the Hon. M.B., now Lord, Hawke together with such fine amateurs as the fast bowler Walter Read, the new star A.E. Stoddart, pleased to accept a lucrative commission to offset lost income from the Stock Exchange, and the dashing Sir Timothy O'Brien, a true Anglo-Irish swashbuckler.

Such recruits, advertised in astute advance publicity, led to the local press referring to Vernon's team as 'the English amateurs'. Shrewsbury retaliated by renewed efforts to sign amateurs 'so as to knock the wind out of the sails of the Melbourne Club'. (He was also, through his agents in England, recruiting players for a Rugby Union tour, a venture that was to lead to allegations of amateurs taking money.) He arranged for his team to be advertised as Gentlemen of England 'same as the MCC do' and the two parties embarked on an unedifying and unprofitable competition for the favours of the Australian public.[29] It was a fitting irony that the two teams should agree to cut their losses and combine to play an Australian XI, and that when they did so the leading Victorian players refused to take part.

Britain, warts and all

Crickets' unresolved tensions, working themselves out in competition for the Antipodean missionary concession, were a microcosmic emblem of the national situation. Britain was at a cross-roads. She had come a long way since the Roman intrusion but once she had trodden the commanding heights of economic prosperity, technological achievement and imperial power the atmosphere became too rarefied for comfort and the right way forward no longer seemed quite so clear. Indeed in some cases idealism led to disillusion.

In 1886 Alfred, Lord Tennyson, the cynosure of the Establishment, shocked his admirers by expressing doubts about progress and its promulgators. The wondrous vision of sixty years before had been a mirage:

> 'Forward' rang the voices then, and of the many mine was one;
> Let us hush this cry of 'forward' till ten thousand years have gone.[30]

If, he went on, social evils could not be eradicated without 'wallowing in the trough of Zolaism' it was time for reappraisal. The 'tonguester' politicians were clearly neither competent nor trustworthy. It was this that particularly stung Gladstone, who had only recently secured the peerage for Tennyson, and he replied publicly with a catalogue of the advances that had been made in recent times.

In fact another name for 'Zolaism' was realism and the British experience had not prepared its intellectuals and artists for reality. Progress was one thing, democracy something else entirely. Romanticism, born of prosperity and conquest, had suffused Victorian literature with a rosy hue. Tennyson himself was often an escapist, albeit one with a guilty conscience. Even the novelists who moved to the centre of the literary stage assumed a conventional social structure and an ordered progression through enlightenment, not revolution or any other mass movement.

Similarly the basic social function of sport and games as an institutionalised preparation for life had got lost in a xenophobic welter of high-flown assertions about the intrinsic virtue of the British approach and question-begging assumptions about its contribution to British superiority. J.E.C. Welldon, the headmaster of Harrow mentioned earlier, was in no doubt about the superiority of the British to the continentals, nor about wherein it lay. This was not, he allowed, in brains, industry or the science or apparatus of war but in 'the health and temper which games impart . . . The pluck, the energy, the perseverance, the good temper, the self-control, the discipline, the co-operation, the esprit de corps, which merit success in cricket or football, are the very qualities which win the day in peace or war.'[31] The implication was that these lesser nations (he mentioned France and Germany in particular) ought to save themselves a lot of trouble, knuckle under and try to be more like the British. In fact such was the reluctance of other nations, notably the Germans, to accept this paradigm that it had to be put to the test in two world wars. This apart, as more and more nations found opportunity and inclination to take up sport and claimed their share of success, Britain was obliged to retreat into face-saving claims of greater organising ability, innovative leadership, skill and judgement in rule-making, ethical standards in refereeing and, of course, sportsmanship.

But that was for the future. Meanwhile, as we have seen, the John Bullish self-image served the nation well in its formative days. The inordinate pride taken by Britons of all classes and persuasions in their sporting achievements, and the chauvinistic conclusions they drew, helped to hold the nation together when it faced external threat. Sport also helped avert the kind of political revolution other European nations experienced, by providing a safety valve, escape, sublimation, socially acceptable outlets for strong aggressive or sexual drives. It was a trickle-down process but one in which the trickle was bound to happen, especially when gambling was involved, even under the old system of patronage. And as commercialism increased, so did upward mobility.

There is little doubt either that in the making of Britain sport was an important influence on the separate nations that comprise the United Kingdom. It was not always a unifying influence, at least on the surface: in this it was a microcosm of the complex political and social relationships of the alliance. Of the many examples, great and small, of conflict the most obvious was in Ireland, the last to join and the first to break away. The English – and a good many Anglophiles in the three other countries – deplored the GAA's rejection of British sporting traditions in the 1880s. But Archbishop Croke's clarion cry was a derivative – a call to fight fire with fire. And other sports, notably racing and rugby, have risen above politics as the tournament did in the middle ages.

These latter examples remind us of the nature of the union, like the nature of organised sport, a coming together of the top people in mutual self-interest, drawing the lower orders in after them (sometimes with unforseen consequences). Amongst this ascendancy – the English taking over the reins from the Normans, with Scottish, Dutch and German admixtures at strategic times – the terms British and English have tended to be interchangeable, sometimes synonymous. In the archetypal game of cricket, for instance, the national team has always been known as England, despite the inclusion of distinguished Scottish and Welsh players. (We may discount the solitary Irishman as not statistically significant.)[32] In his imperialistic rhetoric Mr Welldon, as we have seen, equated British with English, using both indiscriminately in the same sentence. Nor is this merely an annoying English habit: the Scottish man of letters, Andrew Lang, actually substituted 'English' for 'British' in paraphrasing Thomas Hughes: 'Cricket ought to be to English boys what Habeas Corpus is to Englishmen, as Mr Hughes says in *Tom Brown*.'[33] And at another level the home internationals in football have provided an outlet for aggressive nationalistic feelings that arguably might otherwise have shown themselves in ɔre serious conflict.

Sport, in fact, is essentially a conservative influence, deriving from its primal function as a survival mechanism. Sometimes, of course, in sport as in politics, extreme conservatism can manifest itself in fascistic, National Front behaviour (and this, notwithstanding the publicity given to the Union-Jack-faced youths in soccer crowds is not solely the prerogative of the lower classes). But for all the shame this brings to sport and to the nation it is a less characteristic emblem of the social effects of sport than that of players battling it out with ferocity on the field and then having a drink together afterwards – a good example, incidentally, of the trickle-down effect of commercialisation: this behaviour, associated with public school attitudes, is found nowadays not only amongst bourgeois amateur ruggermen but amongst highly professional soccer stars who flit restlessly from club to club and country to country in search of money. Hooliganism, besides being relatively infrequent, is also uninfluential: mindless mobs in sport – again as in politics – do not make policy, and only imprudent politicians try to make use of them.

These modern developments were hidden in the mists of futurity from the earnest empire builders, amateurs and 'shamateurs', entrepreneurs and aspirant working class players of the 1880s. For British society there was to be change in plenty in the decades to come – so much, indeed, that change sometimes appeared even to liberals to be a threat to conscious purpose and planned reform. The choice increasingly seemed to be between order and its due processes and the chaos threatened by dangerous irrational forces, often of alien origin, from within or without. In the struggle that ensued, sportsmen and their honour code, leavened gradually by women's subtler values, were, for all their faults, undoubtedly on the side of the angels.

Notes

1 Edward Dicey, 'Mr Gladstone and our Empire', *Nineteenth Century*, September 1877.
2 Nineteenth Century, September 1878.
3 Quoted in J.A. Mangan, *The Games Ethic and Imperialism*, London, 1986, pp. 35–6.
4 *England, 1870–1914*, Oxford, 1936, p. 164.
5 Hughes, *Tom Brown's Schooldays*, Chapter 7, 'Tom Brown's Last Match', in a conversation between Tom, now captain of the eleven, Arthur, his *protégé*, and the young master (the Cotton prototype) who is sympathetic to, but not yet experienced in, the game's mysteries.
6 The title of a poem by Norman Gale (In *Cricket Songs*, 1894) of which the chorus is 'I bowled three curates once,
With three consecutive balls!'
7 *Cricketer's Companion*, p. 13: 'Do not ask the umpire unless you think the batsman is out; it is not cricket to keep asking the umpire questions.' Pycroft had earlier (1851) used it in the sense of 'not cricket as it should properly be played', *Cricket Field*, Chapter 9, p. 210. See *OED* for the development of the figurative use.
8 21 July 1873.

9 By Lord Hawke in his memoirs, *Recollections and Reminiscences*, London, 1924.

10 1 October 1872.

11 The literature on Grace is voluminous. Some examples are A.G. Powell and S. Canynge Cape, *The Graces*, Hunstanton, 1948. B. Darwin, *W.G. Grace*, London, 1934, A.A. Thomson, *The Great Cricketer*, 2nd edn, London, 1968: and his own book *'W.G.': Cricketing Reminiscences and Personal Recollections*, London, 1899.

12 'W.G. Grace' in B. Green (ed.), *Wisden: An Anthology 1864–1900*, London, 1979, p. 962.

13 B. Green, *Wisden*, p. 678.

14 'At Lords' in *Poems*, ed. T. Connolly, New York, 1941, and numerous anthologies: famous for its refrain 'O my Hornby and my Barlow long ago!'

15 P. Wynne-Thomas, *Give Me Arthur*, London, 1985, p. 12.

16 Ibid., p. 15.

17 *The Times*, 14 January 1879 in M. Williams (ed.), *Double Century: 200 Years of Cricket in The Times*, London, 1985, p. 75.

18 ibid., p. 76. To commemorate his hundredth hundred in 1895 a 'shilling fund' testimonial started by the *Daily Telegraph*, raised 'the better part of £10,000' (£5,000 plus according to the *Dictionary of National Biography*). Recalling this, a journalist on the *Telegraph* afterwards quoted the editor, Sir John Le Sage, as saying that W.G. was 'perhaps the most handsomely paid of any public servant: 'And believe me' he added, 'Grace so carefully counted the number of shillings as they were acknowledged in the columns of the paper, that he knew, to the last bob, what would be handed over to him.' B. Bennison, *Giants on Parade*, London, 1936, p. 130.

19 *Wisden*, 1880, B. Green, *Wisden*, pp. 818–22.

20 Lord Harris is perhaps best approached through his own memoirs, *A Few Short Runs*, London, 1921, which inter alia reproduces his celebrated piece in *The Times* on the distinction between amateurs and professionals (22 January 1909, also in Williams, *Double Century*, pp. 150–2).

21 For Harris in India see E. Docker, *History of Indian Cricket*, Delhi, 1976.

22 See *The Cricketer*, 19 August 1922, quoted in D. Birley, *The Willow Wand*, London, 1979, p. 56.

23 20th May 1882 in Williams, *Double Century*, pp. 82 4.

24 Letter from E.C. Sewell to *The Times*, 17 August 1926, reprinted in M. Williams (ed.), *The Way to Lords*, London, 1983, pp. 44–2.

25 A familiar story, quoted in P.C. Standing, *Cricket of Today*, Edinburgh, 1902, vol. 1, p. 65, in an interesting chapter 'The unfair bowling question'.

26 Wynne-Thomas, *Give Me Arthur*, p. 45.

27 *Wisden*, 1885, quoted in B. Green, *Wisden*, p. 829.

28 *Cricket*, April 1886, quoted in Wynne Thomas, *Give Me Arthur*, p. 54.

29 Wynne Thomas, *Give Me Arthur*, pp. 76–98, which also includes discussion of the first rugby tour of Australia.

30 'Locksley Hall Sixty Years After'.

31 Mangan, *Games Ethic*, pp. 35–6.

32 Sir Timothy O'Brien, mentioned above as a member of Vernon's touring side to Australia, played in 5 Test matches for England between 1884 and 1895–6 and also played for Ireland between 1902 and 1907.

33 Introduction to R. Daft, *Kings of Cricket*, London, 1893.

INDEX

aboriginal cricketers, 332
Acts of Union
  Ireland (1800), 54, 174
  Scotland (1707), 107, 121
  Wales (1536, 1542), 57
Aelfric, Abbot, 13, 50
Agincourt, battle of, 41
Agricultural Hall, Islington, 279, 289, 298
agriculture, changes in, 65, 83, 130, 142, 153,
  181–2, 228, 288
Albert Edward, Prince of Wales, 228,
  229–30, 248, 249, 296–7, 298, 301, 302,
  313, 322
Albert, Prince Consort, 201–3, 207–8, 224–5,
  227, 228, 229
Alcock, C. W., 260, 265–6, 272–3, 274, 330,
  334
Alcuin of York, 13
ale-houses, 57, 78, 80, 85, 86, 88, 92, 112
  see also inns, public-houses
Alfred, King of Wessex, 13–14
Allardyce, Barclay, ('Captain Barclay'), 165
All-England cricket teams; 18th century,
  141, 149; 19th century XIs and imitators,
  217, 252–3, 255–6
All-England Croquet and Lawn Tennis
  Club, 314–15
Almond, H. H., 257, 307
Amateur Athletic Association, 280, 282
Amateur Athletic Club, 236, 242, 260, 276,
  278, 280, 282, 286
Amateur Boxing Association, 287
amateurism, 6, 68, 190, 232, 237, 271–4, 275,
  276–7, 280, 286–7, 291, 319–20, 330–1,
  336, 340
Amateur Rowing Association, 287, 291–2
Amateur Swimming Association, 309
America, 65, 95, 141, 142, 163, 195, 208, 215,
  227, 228, 249, 254, 282, 285, 296, 308, 317
Americans, 129, 165, 167, 168, 225–6, 234–6,
  247, 248, 287–8, 290–1, 292–4
America's Cup, 225–6, 292–4
amphitheatres, 10, 109, 118, 119
Anderson, George, 301, 322
angling: see fishing
Anglo-Normans, 11, 15, 30, 37, 44, 50
Anglo-Saxon sport, 12–15
animal baiting, 10, 14, 59, 63, 64, 79, 86, 94,
  117, 118, 134, 157, 175, 206
Anne, Queen, 103–6, 130
Apperley, Charles, 'Nimrod', 178, 179, 206
Arab horses, 78, 87, 90, 101, 103, 110
Archer, Fred, 302, 303–4
archery, 12, 18, 20, 31, 34, 35, 37, 42, 44, 50,

52, 53, 55, 58, 60, 61, 63, 67, 68, 79–80,
  249, 277
army, influence of
  Cromwell's Major Generals, 86–8
  facilities, 116, 196
  military games, 2, 4, 15–16, 17–18, 22–4,
    27–8, 31–2, 33–4, 38–9, 41, 52–3, 69–70
  officers as amateurs, 184, 231, 232, 294,
    300
  physical training, 231, 242, 307
  recreations of officers, 101, 102, 148, 153,
    154–5, 158, 159, 164, 168–9, 176, 183–4,
    190, 212, 231, 253, 259, 267, 270–1 313
  Renaissance thought, 55–6, 59–60
Arnold, Matthew, 285, 307
Arnold, Thomas, 209–10, 258, 285–6
Arthur, King, 17–18, 23, 30, 32–3, 38
Artillery Ground, London, 67, 116–17, 120,
  121, 123, 141
ascendancy
  Anglo-Irish, 142, 154, 157–8, 224, 231–2,
    253, 268–9, 271, 277
  Anglo-Norman, 37
  Anglo-Scottish, 76, 83, 186, 223, 240, 249,
    266
  Anglo-Welsh, 169, 178, 253–4, 275, 299,
    300, 301
  English, 40, 44, 50, 57, 65, 121, 142, 167,
    232, 285, 331, 334, 339
  Norman, 16, 30–1, 35
Ascham, Roger, 61
Ascot, 103, 117, 155, 161, 168, 181, 184, 201,
  203, 205, 211, 212
Astbury, James, 292–3
Astley, Sir John, 279, 289
athletics, 3, 239–42, 243n, 257, 275, 276–82
Augustine, St, 11, 209
Australia, 129, 252, 254–5, 282, 332, 333–4,
  335, 336, 337
axle-tree tossing, 36, 43, 53

back-staff: see quarter-staff
Badminton estate, 132, 312
Badminton, game of, 312, 313, 314
Baird, George ('Squire Abingdon'), 287–8,
  303
'ball, famous game of', 21
Ball, John, 319, 320
balls, 3–4, 10, 41, 43, 50, 51, 52, 62, 78–9, 93,
  218–19, 221n, 312
Balmoral, 208, 240
bandy, 36, 114
Bannockburn, battle of, 33
bans on sport: see legislation

Barclay, Andrew, 61–2
barons, medieval, 15, 16, 18, 19, 20, 21, 22,
    27–9, 30, 33, 66
Barry, Richard, Lord Barrymore, 145, 155,
    179, 183, 230, 288
Basilicon Doron, 76, 81, 82, 88
Bath, 95, 104, 136, 160
baths, Roman, 10–11
battledore and shuttlecock, 312
Battle Royal, 119
battues, 175, 207, 233, 296
Beale, Miss Dorothea, 246
bear gardens, 84, 92, 106
bears, 9, 14, 20, 63, 79, 80, 84, 86, 94, 157
Beauclerk, Lord Frederick, 149, 161, 177,
    178, 192, 214, 239, 241
Beaufort
    5th Duke of, 132, 166
    7th Duke of, 176
    9th Duke of, 294, 295, 299
Becher, Captain, 184, 192, 206
Becket, Archbishop Thomas, 19–20
Beckford, Peter, 133, 207
Bede, the Venerable, 11, 79
Beeton, Isabella, 263–4
béhourds, 28, 30
Belcher, Jem, 159
Belfast, 174, 220, 223, 269, 271, 277, 289, 321
Bell, James, 293
Bell's Life, 206, 209, 232, 235, 290
bells, silver, 62, 77
Belt, Championship, 234
Belvoir hounds, 111, 132, 179
Bendigo (William Thompson), 208–9
benefit of clergy, 31, 45n, 66
Bennett, James Gordon, 235, 292,
Bentham, Jeremy, 152, 202
Bentinck, Lord George, 184–5, 203–4, 229
Beynon, Anne, 113–14, 276
Beowulf, 12, 13, 77, 308
Beresford, Lord Marcus, 302
Berkshire, 117, 179, 201
bicycles, 248, 323–5
Bingley, Blanche, 317
Birmingham, 153, 158, 223, 264, 265, 268,
    274, 278, 324
Black Act, 108
Blackburn Mick, 239
Blackburn Rovers FC, 272–3
Black Death, the, 35, 37, 44
Blackheath; golf, 78, 138, 219, 250–1, 320;
    hockey, 310; rugby, 258–9, 267, 275, 310
Blackwood's Magazine, 186, 193
Bligh, Hon Ivo, 336
Blood, W. F., 324
Bloomer, Amelia, 247
Blucher, General, 168
boars, 9, 13, 16, 18

Boat Race, the, 212–13, 237–8
Boke of St Albans, 54–5
Bolton, 3rd Duke of, 110, 111, 139
Bolton Wanderers FC, 268
Boodle's Club , 295
bookmakers, 204, 229, 230, 241, 290, 301
'bord and cord', 51, 312
Border Games, 240, 278
Borrow, George, 208, 209
Bosworth, battle of, 45, 50
Bouchier, Richard, 89
bowls, 36, 42–3, 44–5, 50, 51–2, 57, 58, 60, 68,
    79, 80–1, 86, 89, 91, 94, 117, 123, 138–9,
    148
boxing, 10, 51, 68, 102, 109, 117, 118, 119,
    123, 144–5, 155–7, 166, 168–9, 174,
    193–6, 208, 234–6, 239, 286–90 *see also*
    prize-fighting
Boyne, battle of the, 101
bribery and corruption, 123, 141, 146, 148–9,
    177, 180, 203–4, 229, 230–1, 242, 300
Bridges, J. A., 210, 234, 300
Brighton, 143, 144, 145, 153, 155, 159, 160,
    161, 163, 215, 251
Bristol, 88, 143, 145, 153, 158, 159, 194, 270
Britain, ancient, 1, 5, 6–7, 9–12
'broken time payment', 273
Broughton, Jack, 5, 109, 118, 119–20, 123
Broughton's rules, 119–20
Buccleuch, 5th Duke of, 178, 187
Buckle, F., 180, 247
Budd, E. H., 241–2
bulls, 9, 20, 64, 79, 80, 157, 161, 175
Bunbury, Sir Charles, 136, 146
Bunyan, John, 91
Burke, James 'Deaf', 208
Burns, Robert, 139, 152
Burton Hunt, 176, 230, 295
Burton, Robert, 80
Buss, Miss Frances Mary, 246
Byerley Turk, 101, 110
Byron, Lord, 152, 155–6, 193

caber-tossing, 36, 24
caddies, 93
Caffyn, William, 255
caiche-ball, 77
calcio, 69
Calcutta Cup, 270
Calvin, John, 56, 65, 159
Cambridge University, 49, 80, 85, 149,
    190–2, 210–13, 236, 237–8, 241, 251,
    257–9, 275, 316, 324, 335
cambuck, 36, 51, 309
cammock: *see* cambuck
camogie, 36
campball, 83, 103, 115
Campbell clan, 62, 69, 76, 122

Index

Canada, 167, 254, 331
Cannon, Tom, 302
Canterbury festival, 216
capitalism, growth of, 34–8, 49–50, 65–6, 95,
    100, 120, 129, 135, 142, 153, 173–4,
    224–5, 233–4, 289–90
Cardiff, 174, 223, 269, 287
cards, 53, 57, 68, 143, 302
Carew, Richard, 69–70
Carnegie, George Fullerton, 186
Carroll, Lewis: see Dodgson, Revd C. L.
Carthusians, see Charterhouse
Castiglione, Baldassare, 59, 60
Caunt, Ben, 208–9
Cavanagh, John, 197
Cavendish, William, Duke of Newcastle, 87
Celts, 5, 10, 69, 167, 239
Chamberlayne, Edward, 102
Chambers, John Graham, 236, 242, 260, 277,
    286, 309
Chance, Jessie, 315
Chaplin, Henry, 229–30, 295, 302
Chapman, George, 70
chariot-racing, 10
Charles I, 82–5, 139
Charles II, 88–95, 100
Charles V, Emperor, 56, 60
Charlton Hunt, 111
Charterhouse, 139, 188, 211, 260
chase, rights of, 17, 19
Chaucer, Geoffrey, 40
cheating, 51, 91–2, 144, 146–9, 162, 165, 169,
    176, 203, 204, 227, 229, 242, 303, 329, 335
Cheltenham, 184, 231, 269, 270, 317
    College, 216, 258, 260, 317
    Ladies' College, 246
Cheney, John, 110
chess, 30
Chester, 42, 62, 77, 114, 192, 212, 237
Chesterfield, Earl of, 123
Chetwynd, Sir George, 288
Chifney, Sam, 146, 180
chivalry, 15, 17–18, 23, 27–45, 55, 56, 70, 77,
    289
Christian, Dick, 179
Christianity and the sporting code, 12, 13,
    15, 17, 19, 23, 27, 35, 45, 209–10
Christian Socialism, 189, 209–10, 228
Christmas, 51, 53, 58, 63, 86, 113, 278
Church, attitude to sport of
    games, 11, 36, 42, 43, 56–7, 61, 78–80, 112,
        114, 265
    horse-racing, 92
    hunting, 13, 15, 17, 29
    tournaments, 18, 20, 23, 27
Church of England, 57, 65, 91, 100, 142,
    223–4, 265, 268, 274
Civil War, 81–4

Clapham Common, 320
Clarence, Duke of, later William IV, 156–7,
    160, 169, 185
Clark, William, 216–17, 252, 253, 331
Claudian, 9
Clegg, J. C., 274
Clephan, Luckie, 117
clergy, pre-Reformation
    upper, 11, 13, 19–20, 29, 36, 42, 43
    lower, 13, 16, 36, 38, 40, 43, 54, 62
Clermont, Council of, 17
Clifden, Nellie, actress, 228, 258
Clifton College, 258, 269, 270
Cliftonville FC, 271
Clinker, v. Clasher and v. Radical, 179, 180
cloish, 36, 52, 57
closh: see cloish
Cloth of Gold, Field of the, 56
club-ball, 36, 61
Clydeside, 153, 223, 289
Cnut, King, 14–15, 17
coaching (driving) 86, 143, 163
coaching (training), 143–4, 163, 191, 211–13,
    216, 237
Cobbett, William, 175
Cockburn, Sir Alexander, 229
cock-fighting, 10, 20, 36, 64, 84, 86, 94, 106,
    117, 123, 134, 145, 157, 161, 174, 206,
    208, 287
cock-penny, 20, 25n, 134
cock-shy, 88, 94, 112, 134
codes of honour, 3, 5, 12, 113–14, 276
    chivalric, 18, 23, 27–8, 70, 79
    18th & early 19th century, 102, 104–6, 113,
        129–30
    Norman, 15–16
    public school, 189, 209–10, 238, 256–7
    Renaissance, 51, 67–8, 76
    Victorian, 227, 230–1, 232, 241–2, 248, 289
coffee-houses, 117
Coke, Thomas, Earl of Leicester, 130, 175,
    177
colonies, 82, 95, 106, 115, 285, 336
commercialism
    catering, 118–19, 158, 183, 206, 213,
        215–16
    equipment, 51, 52, 58, 78, 118–19, 133,
        157, 213, 214, 218–19, 249
    licensing, 23, 68
    organising, 183, 207, 216–17, 236, 252,
        255, 274, 311, 315–16, 332, 333, 336–7
    playing facilities, 87, 89, 117, 118–19, 315
    services, 110, 135, 136
    spectators, 67, 92, 106, 116, 117–21, 141,
        148, 151, 177, 192, 194, 197, 215–16, 242,
        270–2, 277, 278–9, 289, 301, 314, 323–4
    sponsorship, 138, 212, 236, 254–5, 275,
        332

transport, 205, 206, 235, 272, 288
common land, 83, 115, 130, 251, 320
Commonwealth period, 84–8, 91
competition, grip of, 107, 109, 130–6, 174–9,
    183, 216–17, 218, 234, 252, 270, 314–15,
    317, 318, 319–20, 322–3, 329–30
Compleat Angler, The, 55, 87
Cooper, George, lawyer, 167
Cooper George, pugilist, 169–70
Corinthians, 163, 165, 194, 274, 294
Corinthian sailing clubs, 234
Cork, 14, 137, 269; RFC, 269
Cornell University, 291
Corn Laws, 173, 201, 228
Cornwall, 67–8, 69–70, 85, 259, 270
Cotswold 'Olympicks', 81, 84, 241
Cottesmore Hunt, 132, 230
Cotton, Charles, 89, 91
Cotton, G. E. F., 210, 256
Coupland, Thomas, 294–5
coursing, 13, 35, 64, 81, 130, 164, 183, 207,
    231, 247, 268 *see also* hare-hunting
courte paume, 51
Coventry, 323, 324
Coventry, 9th Earl of, 295, 299
Cowes, 185, 225, 227
coxing, 211–13
Craven, W. G., 232, 299
creag' (possibly early form of cricket), 32
Creçy, battle of, 35
Crewe Alexandra cricket and football clubs,
    260
Cribb, Tom, 165, 167, 193, 194
cricket, 5, 32, 36, 45*n*, 60, 71, 73*n*, 84, 86, 93,
    103, 106, 112, 117, 121, 157–8, 161, 162,
    169, 170*n*, 240, 260, 289, 307
    All-England XIs and imitators, 217,
        251–6, 277, 333
    colonies, 329–37
    county, 139, 216–17
    country house, 252–3
    Hambledon era, 139–141
    Ireland, 277, 282
    Lords and MCC, 147–9, 177, 192, 213–15
    patrons, 106, 115–17, 120, 121, 123, 138,
        145, 216
    public school, 209–10, 257, 329
    Scotland, 253
    Test, 332, 335–7
    University, 329
    Wales, 114, 253
Crimean war, 227, 231, 246, 251
Crockford, William, 165, 181, 204
Croke, Archbishop Dr Thomas, 281–2
Cromwell, Oliver, 84–8
Cromwell, Thomas, 57
croquet, 36, 78, 248–9, 260–1*n*, 277, 282,
    311–14, 315

cross-bow, 16, 31, 34, 52, 57, 61, 64
'crossing',
    in boxing, 123, 141, 156
    in cricket, 140–1, 162, 177
Cruikshank, George, 166, 167, 168, 169, 195
Crusades, 17, 22, 23, 30
Crystal Palace, 203, 258, 324
cudgels, 81, 85, 109, 110, 112, 117, 119, 174,
    214
Cumberland, 16, 180
Cumberland, Henry, 2nd Duke of 135, 137,
    143, 144
Cumberland, William Augustus, Duke of,
    118, 119, 120, 121, 122, 135–7
Cunard, Sir Bache, 295
curling, 138–9
Curragh, the, 111, 154, 300, 321
Curraghmore Hunt, 299
Cusack, Michael, 278, 280–2
cycling, 248, 323–5

Daffy Club, 195–6
Daft, Richard, 331
daggers, 31, 32, 66
dancing, 20, 56, 59, 62, 63, 77, 79, 80, 91, 106,
    247, 281
Daniels, Revd W. B., 175, 176
Dark, James Henry, 214, 216–17
Darley Arabian, 103, 110
Darwen FC, 272
Davenant, Sir William, 94
Davin, Maurice, 278, 281
Davitt, Michael, 281
Dawson, Matthew, 302–3
Day, John, 184, 230, 302
debtors' prisons, 196–7, 251
de Coverley, Sir Roger, 104–5
deer-carts, 111, 122
'Deerfoot' (Diveaux Daillebout), 279
deer-hunting, 15, 16, 19, 20, 29, 32, 38,
    39–40, 54, 59, 64, 76, 77, 86, 107, 108,
    111,122, 130, 170, 208, 298–9
deer parks, 38, 77, 87
deer-stalking, 177, 296–7
De La Warr, Lord, 111
de Mandeville, Bernard, 108
democratisation, 195, 197, 202–3, 206–7,
    208–9, 212–13, 238, 239–40, 241–2,
    250–1, 253, 264–5, 268–70, 274–7, 286–7,
    291–2, 294, 297–8, 304
Derby, 10, 61, 114
Derby, the, 136, 155, 168, 181, 203–4, 205,
    229, 230
Derby
    12th Earl of, 134, 136, 148, 183
    14th Earl of, 206, 224–5, 228, 229
de Saussure, Cesar, 109, 112
destriers, 15, 20, 78, 87

de Valbourg, Henri Misson, 102, 109
Devonshire, Duke of, 110, 134, 330
d'Ewes, Sir Symonds, 80
dice, 3, 11, 18, 38, 42, 52, 57, 68
Dickens, Charles, 196, 202, 246
discus, 46
disorder, 18, 31, 37–8, 45, 50, 58, 62, 66–7,
    79, 85, 88, 103, 107, 112, 153, 166, 174,
    181, 210, 241, 301, 334, 346
Disraeli, Benjamin, 115, 141, 142–3, 146,
    202, 224–5, 246, 298
Dissenters, 91, 100, 104, 107, 153, 158, 175,
    223–4, 265, 274
Dod, Charlotte 'Lottie', 317, 318
Dodgson, Revd C. L. (Lewis Carroll), 307,
    316
dog-fighting, 208, 287–8
Doggett, Thomas, 109
dogs, 9, 10, 13, 29, 35, 38, 39, 53, 59, 63–4, 77,
    105, 108, 111, 131, 132–3, 135, 161, 175,
    177, 178, 233, 287, 295
dog-tossing, 88, 94
Donnelly, Dan, 169–70, 193
doping, 165, 166, 230
Dorset, 3rd Duke of, 139, 140–1, 147
Dorset, cricketing sons of 1st Duke of, 116
Dorset, Marquess of, 50
Dover, Capt Robert, 81, 241
Dowling, Vincent, 193, 194, 289
Doyle, Sir Arthur Conan, 289–90
Draper, Squire William, 111
drink, consumption of, 17, 20, 21, 25n, 51,
    76, 77, 92, 138, 144, 162, 165, 178, 179,
    186, 233, 240, 287–8; by boxers, 165,
    169–70, 193
  disapproval of, 106, 123, 177, 233, 257,
    265, 268, (lower orders), 20, 31, 43, 51,
    57, 80, 85, 92, 162, 214, 265, 297–8
  gin, 108, 111–12, 123, 177, 233, 257, 265,
    268
  see also ale-houses, inns, public-houses
Drogheda, 7th Earl of, 231
Dublin, 14, 158, 169, 223, 228, 269, 277, 287,
    289, 298, 317, 331
Dublin horse show, 101, 298
Duhallow Hunt, 179, 268
Dunn, Willie and Jamie, 219
Dunraven, 4th Earl of, 294
D'Urfey, Tom, 113–14
Durham, 73, 174, 183, 192

earls, as royal lieutenants, 14, 20, 27–9, 31,
    33, 35, 44, 50
Eastbourne Golf Club, 320
Easter sports, 20, 36, 53, 92
Eclipse, 137
economic benefits and costs of sport, 9, 22,
    35, 37, 42–3, 52–3, 56, 67, 68, 78, 86–7,

    94, 101–2, 103, 106, 117–18, 129, 131–2,
    173, 226–7, 232–4, 240, 296, 303–4
Edinburgh, 79, 121, 138, 158, 213, 218, 253,
    266, 267, 269, 271, 275, 278, 322
  schools, 257, 260, 266
Education Act (1870), 267–8, 304
Edward I, 28, 30–1
Edward II, 32–3
Edward III, 33–7
Edward VI, 62–3
Edward the Confessor, 15, 16
Edward, the 'Black Prince', 36, 37
Egan, Pierce, 166–7, 168–169, 193–194
Egan, Thomas S., 212, 238, 289, 290
Eglinton, Earl of, 219, 249, 295
Elcho, Lord, 251, 297
Elizabeth I, 63–76
Ellenborough Act, 159
Ellis, William Webb, 189
Elyot, Sir Thomas, 59–60, 62
Emmett, Tom, 330, 333
Empire, British, 328, 333, 334, 340
enclosure movement, 82–3, 87, 95, 115, 130,
    149n, 153, 251
entrepreneurism, 110, 117–18, 138, 160, 183,
    206, 216–17, 252, 271–3, 278–9, 330, 335
English
  language, 40, 49
  literature, 66, 281
Ensor, Sir Robert, 328
Epping Forest, 251, 320
Epsom, 136, 149n, 155
Erasmus, Desiderius, 49, 50–1, 53
Essex, 18, 38, 84, 112, 115, 156
Essex, Earl of, 67
Eton, 49, 118, 139, 140, 144, 145, 149, 154,
    157, 160, 161, 188, 189, 190, 191, 192,
    193, 196, 211, 232, 236, 238, 256, 258,
    260, 266, 270, 306
Eton v Harrow, 314, 329
Evelyn, John, 86, 88–90, 94
Everton FC, 268
Exeter, 43, 177
Exeter College, Oxford, 241
Exeter, Earl of, 87

F.A. Challenge Cup, 267, 270, 271–3, 330
fagging, 209–210
fair play, 292–3, 329, 332, 335, 340n
  see also Fayre Lawe
fairs and festivals, 11, 17, 21, 38, 56, 61, 109
falconry, 35, 39, 54
  see also hawks
Falmouth, 6th Viscount, 303
Fancy, the, 166, 171n, 174, 234
farmers, 5, 19, 49, 76, 115, 164, 168, 233, 250,
    295–6, 300
Fasten's E'en, 10, 62, 113

Fayre Lawe, 5, 64, 76, 132
Felix (Nicholas Wanostracht), 215
fencing, 3, 31, 58, 77
Fens, the, 38, 83, 102–3, 118, 322
feudalism, 15, 16, 20, 21, 22, 37, 49, 57, 76, 304
field events, 240, 277
Field, The, 248, 296, 297, 314–15, 321
Figg, James, 109, 118
fishing, 9, 13, 38, 55, 133, 161, 208, 224, 233–4, 297–8
Fitzgerald, R. A., 331
FitzNeale, Richard, 19
FitzStephen, William, 20–1, 36, 77
FitzWilliam Club, Dublin, 317
fives, 156, 196
Fives Court, 156, 169
Flanders, 17, 22, 34, 49, 53,
fly fishing, 133, 234, 297–8
football, 10, 20, 32, 36, 38, 42–3, 52, 60, 61–2, 69, 70, 77, 79, 81, 85, 88, 102, 103, 106, 112, 208, 256–60, 289
    Association, 253, 259–60, 265–74, 340
    early clubs, 258–60
    early stylised, 62, 69, 81, 113, 117, 118
    & gilds, 20, 42, 61, 62
    Ireland, 268–9, 271, 281
    mass, 10, 20, 61, 115, 157, 187
    public school, 5, 187, 188, 209–211, 256–60, 265–7
    Rugby, 188–9, 265–70, 274–6, 277, 337, 340
    Scotland, 42–3, 45, 52, 62, 69, 113, 138, 187, 266–7, 271, 275
    Wales, 114, 265, 269, 275
Football Association, the, 258–60, 265–6, 267, 274
foot-racing footmen, 93, 109, 118
Forbes, Duncan, 122
Forest, the, 5, 16–17, 19, 20, 22–3, 29, 82, 95, 107
Forest Charter, 29
Formby Golf Club, 320
Fox, Charles James, 143
fox-hunting, 13, 18–19, 54, 59, 88, 111, 131–3, 149n, 154, 161, 164, 176–7, 178–9, 207, 230, 232–3, 247–8, 294–5, 298–9
Frampton, Trigonwell, 101–2, 103, 110
France, 17, 30, 33, 65, 67, 128, 142, 147, 152–79, 268; *see also* French, the
Francis I, King of France, 56
Frederick Louis, Prince of Wales, 115–16, 119, 120, 125n, 128
Free Trade, 173, 184, 328
French the, 23–4, 28, 43, 55–6, 100, 110, 122, 209, 259, 338
    & bicycles, 323
    & cricket, 32, 147, 193
    & croquet, 248

& fencing, 66
& hunting, 39–40
& pall mall, 75
& Rugby football, 259
& tennis, 43, 50–1
Froissart, Jean, 35, 55
Fulco, Archbishop of Rheims, 13

Gaelic Athletic Association, 280–2, 339
Gage, Sir William, 115
Galway, Statute of, (1527), 309
gambling, 2–3, 31, 43, 51, 84, 85, 86, 91–3, 104, 112, 116, 120, 154, 161, 162, 181, 204, 207, 214, 229, 230, 231, 239, 278, 279, 280, 281, 298, 302, 339
game birds, 18, 59, 105, 207–8, 296
gamekeepers, 108, 131, 159, 175
Game Laws, 95, 108, 131, 182, 207, 233
games cult in public schools, 210, 256–7, 307
gaming laws, 106, 120, 157, 204, 229
Gaston, Comte de Foix, 39–40
gate money, 120, 156, 164, 177, 205, 206, 239–40, 267, 270, 272, 290, 314
Gaveston, Piers, 32–3
Gay, John, 133–4
Gem, Major T. H., 312–13
gentlemen, 5, 12, 146, 209, 232, 234, 250
    participation in sport, 59–60, 63, 81, 87, 89, 101, 120, 139–40, 144, 145–6, 155–6, 188, 205, 214–15, 217, 226–7, 238, 239, 241–2, 250, 252–3, 256–60, 265–6, 268, 270–1, 291–2, 292–4, 294–6, 310, 329–37
'gentlemen and players', 68, 89, 93, 112, 140–1, 145, 180
    cricket, 214–17, 250–6, 329–37
    football, Association, 270–74
    football, Rugby, 274–6
    golf, 319–20
    lawn tennis, 316–17
    rowing, 290–1
    yachting, 294
Gentlemen Golfers, Edinburgh, 117, 123, 158
gentlemen riders, 205–6, 231–2, 299–300
Gentlemen v Players
    cricket, 252, 255, 256, 274, 333, 334–7
    football, 274
Gentlemen's Magazine, 110, 120, 308
Geoffrey of Monmouth, 17–18, 23, 27, 166
George I, 106–11, 128
George II, 111, 118–25, 128
George III, 128–9, 131, 142–3, 145–6, 153, 158
George IV (also Prince of Wales and Prince Regent), 143, 144–6, 152–3, 155, 165, 168, 169, 173, 181, 185
George of Denmark, Prince, 103
Germany, 11, 17, 56, 168, 193, 285, 308, 338, 339

gilds, 20–1, 42, 61, 62
gin, 108, 111–12, 123, 143, 195
Giraldus Cambrensis, 15, 19
girls, 20, 70, 81
Gladstone, William Ewart, 228, 246, 258, 328, 338
Glamorgan, 117, 284
Glasgow, 62, 121, 138, 153, 158, 178, 220, 223, 228, 253, 266, 271, 278, 293, 322
Glorious Revolution, the, 100
Gloucester
  1st Earl of, 18, 27
  6th Earl of, 27
  7th Earl of, 27–8
Gloucestershire, 117, 254, 255, 270, 331
Godolphin Barb, 110
golf
  Scotland, 36, 43, 45, 51, 78, 93, 117, 122, 123, 158, 186, 217–19, 249–50
  England, 138, 219, 250–1, 317–20
  Ireland, 139, 321
  women, 317–18
Gore, Sir Ralph, 111
Gore, Spencer, 314–15
Gourlay, 218–19
Grace, E. M., 254, 255, 331, 333, 334
Grace, G. F., 331, 333, 334
Grace, W. G., 254, 277, 331–2, 333, 334, 341n
Grafton,
  1st Duke of, 102
  6th Duke of, 295
grammar schools, 20, 68–9
Grand National Steeplechase, 206, 300
Great Exhibition, 203, 224–5, 248
Greece, 3–4, 11, 77, 307
Greene, Robert, 70
Greenwood, the, 33–4
Gregory, Pope, 11
Greville, Charles, 165, 176, 184, 203–4
grooms, 32, 92, 115
Grosvenor, 1st Earl, 135, 136
grouse, 131
guilds: see gilds
Gully, John, 160, 162, 165, 181, 194
gymnastics, 59, 209, 256, 307, 308

Hale, J. H., 313–14
Hall, Edward, 57
Hambledon, Hampshire, 139–41, 192
Hambleton, Yorkshire, 110
Hampshire, 15, 16–17, 139, 215, 216
hammer-throwing, 81, 240, 278
handball, 36, 38, 61, 68, 196
Hanger, Colonel George, 145–6, 175
hare-hunting, 10, 13, 18, 38, 40, 54, 59, 106, 107, 130, 133, 176, 179; see also coursing
Harlequins Club, 253, 258
harrier clubs, 281

Harrington, 8th Earl of, 295
Harris, Hon. George, later 4th Baron, 178, 287, 330, 333, 334, 336
Harrison, William, 65
Harrow, 68, 188, 192, 196, 210, 211, 216, 238, 251, 256, 258, 259, 260, 261, 267, 324, 328, 338
Hart-Dyke, Sir William, 251, 314
hastiludes, 27, 33, 45n
Hastings, 4th Marquis of, 230–1, 294, 301
hats as prizes, 162
Hawke, Hon. Martin, later 7th Baron, 335–7
Hawker, Colonel Peter, 174
hawking, 13–14, 31, 35, 52, 54, 55, 59, 63, 76, 77, 86, 87, 247
hawks: see hawking
Haxey Hood game, 10
Hazlitt, William, 175, 193, 194, 195, 196–7
Heart of Midlothian FC, 271
Heathcote, J. M., 314, 322
Heenan, John Carmel, 234–6
Henley-on-Thames Regatta, 212–13, 237, 290
Henn, William, 293
Henry I, 17
Henry II, 18–22
Henry III, 27–30
Henry IV, 39–41
Henry V, 40–1
Henry VI, 43–4, 49
Henry VII, 49–55
Henry VIII, 55–62
Hertfordshire, 20, 77, 177
Hibernian FC, 271
Hickey, William, 137
Hickman, Tom, 194
Highland Games, 240, 253, 278
Highlands, Scottish, 9, 44, 76, 121, 122, 142, 177, 223–4, 240
Hill, Rowland, 276
Hillyard, George, 316
hobby (horse), 78, 96n
hockey, 32, 36, 61, 91, 211, 280, 309–10
Hockley-in-the-hole, Clerkenwell, 106, 122
Hogarth, William, 109, 122
Hogg, Quintin, 287
holidays, 11, 20, 85, 102, 265
Holland, 49, 50, 53, 65, 78, 82, 89, 142, 154, 339
Homer, 3, 4, 12, 36
'honnête homme', 5, 168
Honourable Edinburgh Company of Golfers, 158, 186, 218, 250, 319
Hornby, A. N., 287, 334, 335
horse-breeding, 76, 78, 87, 90, 101, 103, 110, 111, 132, 135–6, 178, 182, 183, 229, 298, 302
horsemanship: see horses

horse-racing, 10, 13, 18, 20, 53, 55, 62, 77, 81, 86, 87, 90, 92, 101, 103, 110, 134–7, 147, 154, 164, 168, 169, 174, 201, 229, 247, 298–304
horses, 12–13, 20, 32, 55–6, 59, 63, 77–8, 82, 88, 132, 161, 203, 225, 247, 298, 323
hound-breeding, 13, 16, 105, 108, 132, 137, 179
Howard, Sir Edward, 87
Hughes, Thomas, 189, 209–10, 257, 286, 329, 339
Huizinga, Johan, 5
Humphreys, 'Gentleman' Richard, 144–5, 155
hunting
    early, 2, 4, 9, 13
    medieval, 15–17, 18–19, 20, 29, 32, 38, 39–40
    Tudor, 52, 54, 55, 59, 63, 64, 65
    17th century, 76, 77, 82, 86, 87, 88, 95
    18th century, 103, 107, 108, 111, 114, 130–3
    19th century, 154, 161, 164, 176–7, 178–9, 207, 224, 230, 232–3, 247–8, 294–5, 298–9
    Ireland, 19, 179, 231, 232, 298–9
    Scotland, 52, 178, 295
    Wales, 114, 179, 295
    see also deer-, hare-, fox-hunting
hurling, 10, 36, 37, 61, 69–70, 85, 157–8, 280, 281, 310
Hutchens, Harry, 279
Hutchinson, Horace, 320

I Zingari, 252, 254, 274, 277
incomes, 21, 31, 34, 44, 58, 68, 82, 83, 85, 91, 95, 101–2, 110, 130, 134, 137, 146, 149, 158, 177, 179, 202, 214, 218–19, 228, 263–4, 300, 331, 337
India, 129, 143, 153, 227, 249, 312, 334
industrial advance, 129–30, 153, 202–3, 229
inns, 52, 57, 78, 80, 109, 117–18, 132, 146, 161, 164, 176, 183
    sporting inns, 93, 109, 117–18, 121, 127, 139–40, 148, 163, 196, 216, 319
see also ale-houses, public houses
Ireland, 9, 12, 14, 15, 22, 31, 35, 44, 50, 57, 65, 76, 82, 83, 95, 101, 111, 121–2, 142, 145, 153–4, 158, 167–8, 173, 182, 201–2, 223–4, 263, 308, 317, 339;
    archery, 37, 61
    athletic sports, 240, 277–8, 280–82
    bowls, 220
    boxing, 145, 169–70, 193, 287
    cricket, 86, 158, 252, 253, 282, 337
    croquet, 248, 282
    football, 32, 61, 113, 281
    football, Association, 271
    football, Rugby, 268–9, 281
    golf, 321
    hockey, 61, 280
    horses, 101, 132, 136–7, 148, 154, 298–9
    hunting, 19, 179, 231, 298–9
    hurley, 280
    hurling, 37, 61, 280, 281
    quoits, 37
    steeple-chasing, 206, 231–2, 299, 300
    yachting, 137, 231
Irish Champion Athletic Club, 277–8
Irish Football Association, 271
Irish Hurley Union, 280
Irish Jockey Club, 231, 299
Irish National Hunt Committee, 300
Irish Rugby Union, 269, 278
Irving, Washington, 175
Italy, 22, 34, 66, 67, 69, 110

Jackson, Clement, 241, 242, 280
Jackson, 'Gentleman' John, 145, 155–6, 168–9, 193, 195
Jackson, N. Lane, 273–4, 315–16
Jacob, Giles, 108
Jacobins, 153, 159, 166
Jacobites, 100, 101, 108, 121, 122
James I of England (VI of Scotland), 51, 76–82
James I of Scotland, 42
James II (also Duke of York), 89, 93, 100
James IV of Scotland, 52
javelin throwing, 209
Jenyns, Soames, 147
Jersey, 5th Earl of, 181, 184
jeu de paume (tennis), 36, 43
Jews, 155–6, 301
Jingoism, 328
Jockey Club, 5, 123, 135–7, 146, 154, 159, 166, 181, 184, 203–4, 205, 227, 229, 230, 232, 299, 301–2, 304
jockeys, 92, 180, 183, 205, 302–4
John Bull, 174–5, 193, 227, 339
John of Salisbury, 19
John, King 24
Johnson, Samuel, 81, 142, 143, 144
Johnson, Tom, huntsman, 111
Johnson, Tom, boxer, 144
Jones, Henry, 311, 314–15
Jones, S. P., 332, 335
Jonson, Ben, 66
'Jorrocks', 181–3, 207
journalism, 138, 166–7, 168–9, 178–80, 186, 193–4, 224, 235–6, 260, 265–6, 273, 274, 275, 280, 309, 311–16, 334–5
jousting, 18, 28, 53, 55–6, 63, 77, 80, 81
Jowett, Benjamin, 285–6
jumping, 20, 51, 55–6, 63, 77, 80, 81, 240, 278, 281

Keats, John, 193, 250
Keith-Falconer, Hon. Ion, 324
Kennedy, Lord, 176, 179–80
Kent, 5, 16, 20, 43, 84, 93, 112, 115, 117, 139, 141, 147, 164, 192, 193, 198, 215, 216, 217, 252, 255, 330, 334
Kilkenny, Statute of, 37
Kilmarnock FC, 271
Kinnaird, Hon. Arthur, later Lord, 266, 270, 273
knappan, 70
knighthood, 5, 15–16, 17, 21, 22, 23, 29, 30, 31, 33–5, 53, 56
Knighton, Henry, 35
Knox, John, 65

Labourers, Statute of, (1351), 35
Lade, Sir John, 143–4
Lakeland Games, 240, 278
Lambert, William, 161, 177
Lambton, Hon George, 300
Lampeter, St David's College, 265, 269
Lancashire, 16, 78, 80, 129, 153, 160, 239, 259, 266, 270–3, 272, 274, 287, 320–1, 330, 334, 335, 336
lance, throwing the, 18, 20, 37
    see also spears
Land League, 299
Langham, Nat, 234, 235
Langrishe, May, 317
Langtry, Lily, 288
Lansdowne Dublin
    rugby, 269
    sports complex, 277–8
Laud, William, Archbishop, 83
laudanum, 112, 123, 230
lawn tennis, 277, 282, 311, 312–17, 316 (Association)
Leander Club, 190, 211, 236, 237, 290
leap-frog, 81, 281
Leeds, 223, 260, 266, 270
legislation on sport
    (1285), 31
    (1314), 32
    (1337), 34
    (1349), 35
    (1367), 37
    (1369), 35
    (1388), 38
    (1401, 1409, 1410, 1414), 41
    (1424), 42
    (1457), 43
    (1471), 45
    (1474), 44
    (1477), 44
    (1491), 52
    (1511), 55
    (1526), 56

    (1528), 57
    (1541), 58
    (1572), 66
    (1618), 80
    (1625), 83
    (1649–60), 85–6
    (1740, racing), 110
    (1853, racing), 229
    class-based legislation, 49–50, 56–7, 58, 60, 66, 68, 78–80, 131–2, 182
Leicestershire, 132–3, 175, 180, 294–5
Leith, 77, 93, 117, 138, 158, 186, 218
Lillie Bridge, 277, 280, 282, 286, 301
Lillywhite, James, 332
Lillywhite, John, 329
Lillywhite, William, 'the Nonpareil', 215
Linde, Harry Eyre, 300
Lindsay, Sir David, 62, 77
Liverpool, 158, 174, 183, 184, 205–6, 223, 228, 258, 265, 270, 308, 319–20
Llandovery, 269
Llandyssul, 113–14, 276
Llanelli RFC, 275–6
Llanwenog, 113–14, 276
Locke, John, 128
loggats, 36
London, 11, 19–20, 28, 31, 33, 34, 35, 57, 58, 68, 79, 82, 84, 86, 92, 93, 94, 95, 102, 109, 111, 112, 117–18, 147–9, 163, 173, 196, 208, 223, 251, 258–9, 289, 308, 320
London Athletic Club (Mincing Lane AC), 242, 277, 278, 280
London Skating Club, 322
long bow, 31, 34, 41, 44, 52, 58, 61
longue paume, 51, 312
Lonsdale
    4th Earl of, 168, 248, 288, 302
    5th Earl of, 288, 289, 302
Lord's cricket ground, 164–5, 177, 214, 252, 254, 333
Lord, Thomas, 148, 169
Loretto, 257, 266
Love, James, 120
lower middle class, 224, 260, 268, 287, 308
lower orders, 20, 21, 29–32, 33–6, 42–3, 49, 52, 57, 61–2, 68, 78–81, 83–4, 91–3, 102, 106, 109, 110, 114–20, 138, 140–1, 144–5, 147, 155–6, 157–8, 162, 165, 169–70, 180, 188, 194, 197, 204, 206, 208–9, 211–12
    see also clergy, lower; working class; lower middle class
Lowlands, Scottish, 49, 76, 122, 142, 240
Lowther, Viscount, see Lonsdale, 4th Earl of
Luddites, 166, 168, 173
Luther, Martin, 56
Lytham Golf Club, 320

Macaulay, Thomas Babington, 84

Index

MacDonald clan, 76, 101
Mace, Jem, 287
Machell, Captain James, 302
Magna Carta, 27, 29
magnates, 6, 18, 19, 21, 23, 27–9, 38
Malden, Henry C., 211, 258, 309
Malory, Sir Thomas, 53, 55
Malthus, Revd Thomas, 158
Manchester, 79, 138, 158, 163, 173, 185, 202, 223, 242, 258, 270, 282
Manchester Guardian, The, 235, 275
Mann, Sir Horatio, 139–40, 148
Manners, Lord Henry, 300, 302
Manton, Joseph, 175–6
'march of intellect', the, 174, 193
Marindin, Major Sir Francis, 271, 273
Markham, Gervase, 78, 101
Marlborough, 210, 256, 257, 269
Marlborough, Duke of, 101, 103, 106
Marsden, Thomas, 192
Marshall, Julian, 314–16
Martial, 9
martial arts, 31, 59, 67
Mary, Queen of England, 63
Mary, Queen of Scots, 65, 318
Marylebone Cricket Club, 148, 149, 161–2, 164–5, 169, 177, 214, 216–17, 251–7, 277, 314–15, 319, 329, 330, 332, 337
Mason, Jem, 184, 206
Master McGrath, 268
Masters of Foxhounds Association, 232–3, 294–5
Masters of Defence, Corporation of, 58, 67, 79, 92, 119
May games, 53, 80
Mayhew, Henry, 208
Melbourne, Viscount, 182, 201
melees, 23, 119
Mellish, Harry, 154, 160, 163, 164, 179
Mellitus, Bishop of London, 11, 209
Melton Mowbray, Meltonians, 132–3, 176
Mendoza, Daniel, 145, 155–6
mens sana in corpore sano, doctrine of, 11, 77, 285
Merchant Adventurers, 49, 65
merchant companies, 35, 65, 82, 95, 143
Merchant Taylors School, 43, 69
Merchiston Castle School, 266, 269
Methodism, 157, 159, 173
Metropolitan Commons Act, 251, 320
Metropolitan Swimming Association, 308–9
Meynell, Hugo, 132–3
middle class, 79, 142, 160, 224, 248, 260, 268–9, 273–4, 278, 280, 285, 287, 291–2, 297–8, 304, 308, 311–16, 319–20, 321
Middlesex, 20, 116, 216, 330
Middlesex, Earl of, 116
Mill, John Stuart, 257

Millar, Libby, 247
Mitchell, Charley, 288
Mitford, Revd John, 192–3
Molineaux, Tom, 165–6, 167
monasteries, 11, 13, 16, 36, 57, 61, 196
monks: *see* monasteries
Monmouth School, 269
Monmouthshire, 17, 231, 253
monopolies, 20, 22, 34, 78, 81, 85, 86, 93
Montgomeryshire, 254, 313
Moore, Thomas, 193
Morgan, W. J., 277
Morley, Thomas, ???
morris dances, 80, 85
Morris, 'Old' Tom, 218–19, 249–50, 318, 321
Morris, 'Young' Tom, 318, 319
Morrison, Fynes, 66
Mulcaster, Richard, 69–71
Mullock, Richard, 275–6
Murdoch, Willam, 333–4, 336
muscular Christianity, 6, 213, 237–9, 256–7, 287
music, 31, 55–6, 63, 66, 80, 281
Musselburgh, 43, 117, 138, 158, 186, 218, 219, 257, 318
Mynn, Alfred, 192, 217
Mytton, Jack, 179, 183, 230

Nash, Beau, 104
National Hunt Committee, 231, 232, 299–300
nationalism in sport, 12, 17, 27–8, 30–1, 37, 39–41, 47, 50, 51, 55, 57, 66–7, 83, 113–14, 142–3, 174–5, 210, 307, 319, 321, 338, 339
  athletics, 240, 276–8, 280–2
  boxing, 118–19, 155, 165, 167, 169, 170, 209, 234–6, 288
  cricket, 147–8, 157–8, 192–3, 277, 329, 334, 335
  cycling, 323
  fencing, 58, 66–7, 119
  football, 266, 268, 271, 275–6
  golf, 36, 138, 319
  horse-racing, 110–11, 206, 231
  hunting, 39–41
  hurling, 157–8, 280
  rowing, 290–1
  tournaments, 23, 27–8, 32–3, 38
  yachting, 225–6, 227, 292–3
navy, influence of, 55, 82, 89, 137, 154, 185, 196, 201, 229–30, 232, 294
  see also Clarence, Duke of (William IV, 'the Sailor King'); Rous, Admiral
Neate, Bill, 194
Neath RFC, 275
Nelson, Horatio, Admiral Viscount, 154, 159

Newcastle, 2nd Duke of, 102, 128
Newland, Richard, 116–17, 120, 140
Newmarket, 77–8, 82, 90, 101, 102, 103, 110, 123, 135, 144, 146, 155, 165, 205, 225, 302
Newport RFC, 269, 275
newspapers, 104, 106, 135, 138, 224
New York Yacht Club, 292–3
Nightingale, Florence, 246
Norfolk, 16, 35, 107, 118, 131, 148, 175, 192, 233, 296
Norfolk, Duke of, 64
Normans, 5, 15–19, 22, 30, 37, 43–4, 319, 339
North Devon Golf Club, 250, 261n, 318
North of Ireland CC, 252, 277
North of Ireland RFC, 269
North–South divide, 57, 71, 129, 153, 180, 188, 193, 223–4, 259, 267, 272–6
Norwich, 14, 76
Nottingham, 148, 177, 208, 209, 216–17, 254, 255, 256
Nottinghamshire, 16, 216–17, 332–3, 335, 336
Noulton, 'Paddy', 191, 212
nouveaux-riches, 120, 129–30, 137, 207, 229, 232, 293, 302
novelty, quest for, 135–6, 137–8, 166, 179–80, 206, 216–17, 279–80
Nyren, John, 140–1
Nyren, Richard, 140

Oaks, the, 136, 155
O'Brien, Sir Edmund, 111
O'Brien, Sir Timothy, 337
O'Kelly, Dennis, 136–7, 144, 184
Old Berkeley Hunt, 164
Old Etonians FC, 270, 272
Oliver, Tom, 184
Olympic Games, 4, 241, 307
Open Championship, golf, 250, 318, 319
Oppian, 9
Orford, 3rd Earl of, 130
Osbaldeston, George, 'the Squire', 160–3, 175–7, 183, 184–5, 190, 195, 209
Oval, the, 266–7, 272, 330, 334
Oxfordshire, 16, 43, 109, 129, 209
Oxford University, 32, 49, 190–2, 211–13, 230, 231, 237–8, 241, 251, 259, 275, 285, 307, 310, 316, 330

pageantry, 17, 28, 33, 38, 49, 53, 55, 56
Paine, Thomas, 146
pall mall, 36, 51, 78, 89
Palmerston, Viscount, 182, 202–3, 209, 227–8, 236, 246, 256, 263
papacy, attitude to sport of, 11, 16, 17, 22, 27, 45, 55, 57, 66
Paris, Matthew, 28
Parliament, 37–8, 40, 44, 49, 78, 82, 83–4, 86, 89, 95, 103, 107, 108, 128, 129, 157, 162, 181, 182, 229
Parnell, Charles Stewart, 277, 281
Parr, George, 254, 255, 331
Partick Thistle FC, 271
partridge, 59, 105, 131, 208, 296
patronage of sport, 41–2, 62, 66, 77, 90, 92–3, 109, 112, 115–17, 122, 123, 135, 138, 139–141 144–5, 146–9, 156–7, 160, 165, 169, 192, 193, 194, 205–6, 218–20, 234, 236, 287–9, 294–5, 304, 313, 339
Patterson, Revd Dr Robert 219
Pattison, Mark, 285
Peacham, Henry, 81
Pearce, Hen, the 'Game Chicken', 159, 160
Peasants' Revolt, (1381), 37
pedestrianism, 239–42, 278–80
Peel, Sir Robert, 182, 201
Pelican Club, 289
Pembroke, Earl of, 15, 19
Pepys, Samuel, 88–90, 94
Perera, J. B., 313
Perkins, William, 80
Perthshire, 10, 62
pheasant, 59, 105, 131, 175, 208, 233, 296
Philip of Burgundy, 50
Phoenix Park, Dublin, 252, 277
Pickernel, Thomas, 300
Picts, 11, 12, 14
pigeon-shooting, 176
Pigott, Charles, 135, 146
Pilch, Fuller, 192, 215, 217
pilicreps, 4, 317
Pitt, William, the elder, Earl of Chatham, 128
Pitt, William, the younger, 143, 145, 153, 158–9
Plantagenet, Edward, 40
play-days, 69
plays, 42, 85, 86, 92, 95
pleasure gardens, 118, 122, 137
Plough Monday, 113, 125n
poaching, 16, 18, 29, 52, 108, 131, 157, 159, 164, 166, 175, 209, 256
poetry, 23–4, 31, 40, 53–4, 66, 95, 113, 120
polite manners, growth of, 61–2, 81, 84, 104–6, 110, 115–16, 118–20, 134, 147–8, 156, 157, 160, 176, 182, 187–8, 191–2, 201–2, 206, 208, 210, 228, 267–8
polo, 282, 283n, 309, 325n
Polytechnic, Regent St, 287, 291–2
Pond, John, 123
Pope, Alexander, 105, 109
population, 21, 34, 57, 65, 82, 121, 142, 158, 173, 201, 223, 263
Portland, 6th Duke of, 303
Powderhall Grounds, Edinburgh, 278–80
Powlett, Revd Charles, 139–41

Presbyterians, 76, 142, 175
Preston North End FC, 273
Prestwick Golf Club, 219, 249–50
Princes of Wales, *see under* (1) Frederick
    Louis, (2) George IV, (3) Albert Edward
Prince's Club, 251
printing, 53–4, 152, 166
prize-fighting, 67, 68, 79, 92, 106, 109, 118,
    119, 123, 193–6, 208, 234–6, 286–90
prizes, 135–6, 144, 190, 205, 206, 212, 231–2,
    234, 236, 240, 250, 278, 281, 298, 320
professionals, 21, 60, 68, 91, 92, 109, 111,
    115, 148, 164, 177, 186, 191, 192, 205,
    211, 214, 215, 216–17, 226–7, 237,
    249–50, 251–3, 255, 272, 275, 276, 282,
    287–9, 293–4, 300, 302–4, 316–17,
    319–20, 330–1, 333, 336
protective clothing in cricket, 214–15
Protestants, Protestantism, 76, 83, 100, 104,
    109, 140–1, 223–4
public houses, 156, 160, 194, 196, 197, 206–7,
    208–9, 215–16, 234, 239–40, 242, 257,
    260, 265, 268, 288, 297–8
    see also inns, ale-houses
public schools, 139, 186–9, 196, 209–11,
    238–9, 240–1, 256–60, 277, 285–6, 306–7
pugilism *see* boxing, prize-fighting
Pugilistic Club, 169, 194, 195
Punch, 207, 247, 249, 296, 335
Punchestown races, 231, 268
Purday, Thomas, 207, 233
Puritans, 64, 70, 76, 79, 80, 83, 84, 85–8, 91,
    100
Pycroft, Revd James, 148, 162, 164, 213–14,
    215, 329
Pytchley Hunt, 295

quarter-staff, back staff etc, 58, 67, 68, 109
Queensberry , Duke of, 'Old Q', 111, 160,
    169
Queensberry, 8th Marquis of, 236, 286, 289
    rules, 236
Queen's Park FC, 266–7, 271
Qui Tam Act, 106, 204
quintain, 17, 24*n*, 28, 81
quoits, 36, 37, 38, 253
Quorn, the, 132, 176, 178, 179, 230, 248, 293,
    294–5, 300

rabbits, 19, 38, 83, 208, 296
racism, 155, 157–8, 165–6, 176, 179, 209, 259,
    336
racket, racquet(s), 50–1, 156, 196, 251,
    314–15
railways, 182–3, 201, 202, 205, 207, 232–3,
    235–6, 249, 259, 260, 288, 300, 301
ram hunt, Eton, 118
Randall, Jack, 193–4

Ranelagh, 118, 122, 137
Rangers FC, 271
rapier, 66–7
ratting, 208, 288
regattas, 137–8, 149*n*, 190, 212–13
Renshaw twins, Ernest and William 317
Richard I, 22–4
Richard II, 37–9, 40
Richard III, 45
Richmond, Bill, 165
Richmond
    2nd Duke of, 111, 112, 115, 116,
        120, 123
    4th Duke of, 139
    5th Duke of, 184, 204
    6th Duke of, 434
Richmond Park, 82, 107–8
RFC, 258, 266, 267
Robertson, Allan, 218–19
Robertson, David, 186, 218
Robin Hood, 33–4
Rockingham, Earl of, 136
Rolland, Douglas, 320
Roman Catholicism, 57, 65, 66, 79, 81, 83,
    100, 101, 111, 121, 142, 153, 158, 174,
    182, 223–4, 253, 277–8
Romans, Rome, 1, 3–4, 6–7, 9–10, 77, 307
rope-climbing, 59, 86
Ross, Captain Horatio, 176, 177, 179–80
Rothschild, Baron Nathan, 288, 295
Rothschild, Baron Lionel, 295
Rothschild, Baron Meyer, 295, 301
Round Table, 23, 28, 30, 85
Rous, Vice-Admiral the Hon. Henry,
    229–30, 232, 301
rowing, 161, 190–1, 206, 210, 211, 236–9,
    240, 277, 290–1
Rowlands, Fothergill, 231
Rowlandson, Thomas, 196
Royal and Ancient Golf Club, 186, 218–19,
    249–50, 318, 319–20
Royal appelation, sports clubs, 185, 186, 250
Royal Chester Boat Club, 237
Royal Clyde Yacht Club, 293–4
Royal Engineers FC, 259, 267, 270
Royal London Yacht Club, 225
Royal Military Colleges, Sandhurst and
    Woolwich, 241
Royal Society, 95
Royal Yacht Squadron, (the Yacht Club
    1815–20, Royal Yacht Club 1820–3),
    225–6, 292–3
rugby football, 210–11, 258–60, 265–70,
    274–6, 337, 340
Rugby Football Union, 267, 268, 270, 276
Rugby School, 178, 188–9, 196, 209–11, 252,
    258, 266
rules of games and sports, 119–20, 120–1,

123–4, 141, 169, 189, 210, 227, 242, 258–9, 266–8, 281, 286, 288–9, 291–2, 292–3, 305, 339
running, 10, 12, 51, 59, 63, 81, 92–3, 162, 239–42
Russell, Revd Jack, 177, 207
Russia, 167, 169, 227, 328
Rutland, 3rd Duke of, 111, 132

Sackville family, 116, 120, 123
St Albans, 45, 149, 183, 184
St Andrews, 117, 123, 186, 218–19, 249–50, 318, 319
St Leger, the, 136, 164, 181, 302
Saint Monday, 298
Sandown Park, 301
Sandwich
  1st Earl of, 89 Sandwich
  4th Earl of, 121
Sargent, Harry R., 231, 234, 286, 299, 308, 321, 323
Saturnalia, 11, 61
Saviolo, Vincente, 67, 68
Sayers, Tom, 234–6
Scone, 10, 138
Scotland, 9, 11–12, 14, 30, 32, 33, 35, 37, 40, 46, 56, 65, 76–7, 80, 82, 85, 95, 100–101, 121–2, 138, 142, 153, 173, 223–4, 263, 310, 322, 339
  athletic sports, 36, 240, 257, 278–80
  bowls, 138–9, 219–20
  cricket, 253
  croquet, 249
  curling, 138, 139
  fishing, 83, 208, 234
  football, 10, 42, 52, 61–2, 69, 187
  football, Association, 266–7, 271, 274
  football, Rugby, 266–7, 275
  golf, 43, 53, 93, 117, 123–4, 138–9, 158, 186, 217–19, 249–50, 317–20
  horse-racing, 77
  hunting, 178
  Sunday sport, 83, 86, 139
  tournament, 37–38
  yachting, 293
Scott, Bill and John, 180
Scott, Sir Walter, 187, 246, 312
Scottish Football Association, 267, 274
Scottish Rugby Union, 267
Scrivener, H. S., 316
scutage, 18
Sefton, Earl of, 206
Shaftesbury
  1st Earl of, 193
  7th Earl of, 202
Shakespeare, William, 66, 308
sham amateurs, 207, 231, 242, 254, 273, 300, 331, 333, 340

Shaw, Alfred, 331, 333, 336
Shaw, George Bernard, 288–9
Shearman, Montague, 242, 280
Sheffield, 148, 177, 192, 223, 242, 258, 270, 274, 278, 279, 282, 298
Shelley, Percy Bysshe, 152, 167–8
shinty, 36, 310
Shoemakers' Company, 42, 62
Shoe-wae-cae-mettes, 290
shooting, 77, 95, 131, 161, 164, 175–6, 207–8, 224, 233, 296–7
  'shooting flying', 5, 105, 175
shot-putting, 36, 51, 278
shovel-groats, 81, 112
show-jumping, 298
Shrewsbury, 188, 211
Shrewsbury, Arthur, 333, 336, 337
Shrovetide, 10, 20, 42, 61, 87, 94, 113, 134, 187
Sidney, Sir Philip, 66
Silver, George, 67
skating, 20, 89–90, 249, 321–3
'Skittles, (Catherine Walters), 248
Slack, Jack, 123, 144
Slindon, 116–17, 140
Small, John, 140
Smart, George 'Fish', 322
Smiles, Samuel, 285
Smith, Adam, 129, 134–5, 143, 152, 229
Smith, Jem, 288
Smith, Thomas Assheton, 175, 179–80, 185
Smithfield, 20, 21, 93
smock-races, 81
Smollett, Tobias, 138
social change, 49–50, 53, 57, 67–71, 83, 95, 100, 128–30, 130–6, 141–2, 147–8, 175–6, 179, 182–4, 188–9, 191–2, 194, 196–7, 201–3, 205–6, 209–10, 215–16, 224, 227–9, 232–4, 246, 259–60, 267–8, 270–4, 274–6, 285–6, 289, 294–8, 304, 322–5
social distinctions, 3, 20, 22, 29–30, 31, 33–4, 101, 137, 141–2, 160, 192, 202, 204, 224, 226–7, 303–4
  in sport, 77, 78–81, 91–2, 94–5, 138–9, 157–8, 162–3
  archery, 31, 34
  athletics, 239–42
  ball-games, 38, 57
  bowls, 58, 68, 89
  cricket, 112, 115–16, 120, 139–41, 213, 251–4, 335–7
  fishing, 297–8
  football, 188, 268–70
  golf, 138–9, 186, 250
  hawking, 35, 38, 54
  hunting, 19, 38, 87–8, 105–6, 130–1, 178–9, 232–3, 294–5
  rowing, 189–90, 211–13, 236–8

skating, 322
swimming, 308
tennis, 68, 89
yachting, 185, 226–7
Southport, Hesketh, Golf club, 320
South Wales Cricket Club, 254
South Wales Rugby Club, 275
Spain and Spanish affairs, 50, 55, 65, 142, 163, 165
spas, 95, 104, 136, 313, 315
spears (lances), 4, 13, 15, 20, 28, 31, 59, 61, 67, 82
Spectator, The, 104–5, 106, 118
spectators: *see* commercialism
Spencer, Herbert, 257, 307
Spenser, Edmund, 66, 68
Sphairistike, 313–14
Sportascrapiana, 242
Sporting Life, The, 235, 255, 259, 273
Sporting Magazine, The, 163, 178, 179, 190
sporting parsons, 161, 174–7, 213–14, 233, 274
Spring, Tom, 194–5, 196, 198*n*
squires, 83, 86, 91, 95, 105, 115, 160, 162, 174–7
Stamford, Lady, 248
Star and Garter, Pall Mall, 121, 123, 141
Starley, James, 323–4
Statute of Artificers (1563), 65–6
Statute of Labourers (1351), 31, 34, 35, 37
Statute of Winchester (1285), 31, 34
Stead, Edwin, 112, 115, 116
Steele, Richard, 66
steeple-chasing, 132, 159, 179, 183, 205–7, 231–2, 241, 299–300
Stephen, King, 17, 18
Stephenson, H. H., 255
Stevenson, George, pugilist, 119
Stick-ball: *see* club-ball
Stirling, 253, 261*n*, 271
Stoddart, A. E., 337
Stoke City FC, 260
stone, casting the, 18, 20, 36, 38, 43, 51, 240, 281
stool-ball, stobbal, stowball, stopball, 71, 102
Stow, John, 64, 66, 112
Strabo, 9
Strutt, Joseph, 1, 36, 157, 158, 308, 309
Strype, Revd John, 112
Stubbes, Philip, 64, 70, 79
Stubbs, George, 135
subscriptions (hunting), 132, 176, 252–3, 294
Sudell, Captain W, 273
Suffolk, 16, 118, 175
Suffolk, 17th Earl of, 299, 304, 323
Sullivan, John L., 287–8
Sunday sport, 68, 79, 83, 84, 85–6, 91, 104, 106, 108, 208, 265, 268, 297–9, 315
Sunderland FC, 260
Surbiton, 310
Surrey, 84, 112, 115, 116, 139, 164, 217, 252, 254, 255, 256, 266, 330, 333, 335
Surrey, Earl of, 144
Surtees, Robert Smith, 182, 206–7
Sussex, 64, 84, 112, 115, 216, 330
Sussex, Earl of, 144
Sutton, Sir Richard, 175, 293
swanimotes, 22, 107–8
Swansea, 223, 253–4, 269, 275
sweating, 50, 60
sweepstakes, 135–6, 183
Swift, Jonathan, 103, 109
swimming, 12, 32, 51, 59, 63, 88, 209, 307–9
sword-and-buckler, 58, 66–7
sword-fights, 10, 12, 20, 31, 53, 58, 59, 66–7, 68, 79, 92, 109, 110
    see also fencing, prizefights

Tailtean Games, 240
Tankerville, Earl of, 139, 141
Tatler, The, 104, 106
Tattersalls, 135, 204
Taylor, Matthew, 237
team games, 60–1, 209–10, 251, 265–60, 286
Teddington, 310
Temple, Sir William, 101
tennis, 36, 41, 43, 50–2, 57, 58, 60, 63, 68, 71*n*, 79, 81, 86–7, 88–9, 91, 117, 196, 251, 314–15
    see also lawn tennis
Tennyson, Alfred, Lord, 201, 338
Thames, River, 89–90, 109, 134, 137–8, 190, 211, 213, 237–8, 308, 309
Thames measurement, 226
Thames Rowing Club, 238, 242
Thames Yacht Club, Royal, 185
Theobalds, Herts, 77, 90
Thompson, Francis, 332
Thring, Edward, 256, 307
tilting, 53, 63, 77
Times, The, 144, 146, 148, 184, 225, 230, 266, 329, 331, 335
tip-cat, 91, 97*n*
tobacco, 85, 177, 204
Tom Brown's Schooldays, 189, 209–10, 256, 286, 339
Tooting Bec, 320
Tories, (later Conservatives), 95, 100, 104, 106, 128, 129, 182, 201, 223, 224, 263, 328
tournaments, 5, 17–18, 20, 22–3, 27–8, 31–41, 52, 53, 55–6, 60
Town Malling CC, 215–16
Townshend, Viscount, 106, 130
Toynbee, Arnold, 6
trade, 2, 5, 9, 14, 20, 22, 34, 44, 49, 65, 82, 83,

121, 130, 153, 173, 201, 223–4, 228
trades unions, 174, 202
Trafalgar, 259
trainers, horse, 102, 180, 205, 300, 302–3
Treatyse of Fysshinge with an Angle, 55
Trevelyan, George M., 6
Trim races, 268
Trinity College, Dublin, 241, 252, 268, 277
Trollope, Anthony, 226–7, 232–4, 246, 248,
    251, 253, 295
tumbling, 59, 77
Turberville, George, 64
Turf, the, 6, 134–7, 145, 146, 159, 165, 166,
    185, 201, 203, 224–5, 229, 299–300, 301–4
    see also horse-racing, Jockey Club
Twici, William, 39

Ulster, 14, 30, 82, 83, 142, 154, 174, 224
Ulyett, George, 333, 335
umpires, 112, 333, 336
universities, 81, 210–11, 228, 275, 280, 285,
    329
Uppingham School, 68, 256
urbanisation, 20, 21, 22, 29, 95, 111, 164, 173,
    223–4, 239, 265, 268

Vandervell, H. E., 322
vaulting, 51, 55, 63, 80, 240
Vauxhall, 118, 135
Victoria, Queen, 201, 203, 208, 224, 227, 229,
    240, 263, 268, 297, 298, 312, 328
villeins, 21, 38
Villiers, George, Duke of Buckingham, 78,
    82
Villiers, Lord Francis, 229

wages, 35, 82–3, 93, 95, 102, 140, 153, 177,
    181–2, 202, 214, 218–19, 228, 263–4, 276,
    296, 298, 303–4, 309–10, 333
    see also incomes
Wales, 9, 11, 14, 15, 22, 30, 31, 35, 40, 44, 50,
    57, 142, 153, 159, 168, 173, 223–4, 297,
    325n, 339n
    athletic sports, 236
    bandy, 114
    bowls, 220
    boxing, 289
    cock-fighting, 63
    cricket, 114, 253–4
    football, Association, 269, 275–6
    football, Rugby, 265, 269
    horse-racing, 110, 168, 231
    hunting, 114, 179, 295
    knappan, 70
    Sunday sport, 79
walking, 236, 277, 279
Walpole, Horace, 135
Walpole, Sir Robert, 107, 109, 111, 118, 119,

130
Walsh, J. H., 311, 315
Walton, Izaac, 55, 87
Wanderers RFC, 269
war(s), 2, 5, 13, 14, 15–16, 18–19, 22, 35, 41,
    44–5, 55–6, 95, 338
    Civil, 81–4
    Crimean, 227, 231, 246
    Hundred Years, 33–4
    Napoleonic, 153–70
    Nine Years, 101
    of the Roses, 44, 49, 50
    Seven Years, 128
    Spanish Succession, 103
Ward, Jem, 195
Ward, William, 192, 214
Warre, Dr Edmund, 238
Warren, rights of, 17, 18, 19, 38
Waterford, 5th Marquis of, 231, 299
Waterloo, battle of, 169–170
Waterloo Cup, 183, 268
watermen, 93, 109, 137, 191, 212–13, 238
Watson, G. L., 293
Waymark, Thomas, 115
Weatherby, James, 136
Webb, Captain Matthew, 309
Welldon, J. E. C., 328, 338
Wellesley, Arthur, Duke of Wellington, 154,
    158, 166, 167, 169, 174, 181
'Welsh main', 64
Welsh Rugby Union, 275–6
West Lancashire Golf Club, 320
Westminster School, 139, 188, 189, 190, 211
Weston, F. P., 279
Whaddon Chase Hunt, 295
Whigs (later Liberals), 182, 201, 223, 263
White Conduit Fields, 112, 117–18, 147, 148
White, Gilbert, 108, 131
White, Thomas 'Shock', 141
Whitmore, Walter, 311–12
wild-fowling, 38, 131, 208
Wild Indians, 242, 279
Willes, John, 162, 178
William I, the Conqueror, 15–17
William II, 17
William III and Mary, 100–3
William IV, 156, 181, 185, 191, 201
William of Malmesbury, 16
William of Newburgh, 22
William the Marshal, 23, 27
Willoughby de Broke, 18th Baron, 295, 296
Wilton, 3rd Earl of, 184, 224–5
Wimbledon
    croquet, 311–15
    golf, 251, 320
    hockey, 310
    lawn tennis championships, 314–17
Winchester College, 49, 131, 139, 189, 190,

191, 192, 196, 211
Winchilsea, Earl of, 140, 147, 148
windball, 81
Windham, William, 144, 157, 160
Windsor, 30, 34, 35, 38, 161
    Forest, 103, 106, 107
    Great Park, 122
Wingfield sculls, 190
Wingfield, Walter, 313–14
Wisden, 332, 336
Wisden, John, 249, 252, 254
Wolsey, Thomas, Cardinal, 56–7
Wolverhampton Wanderers FC, 268
wolves, 9, 13, 19, 54
women, 17–18, 20, 59, 71, 106, 110, 246–9,
    289, 310, 317–18, 325
Woodforde, Revd James, 131, 134, 139
Woodgate, W. B., 290
Wordsworth, Charles, 191
Wordsworth, William, 152, 194
working class, 142, 162, 177, 228, 242–2, 250,

260, 264–5, 272, 278, 280–1, 282, 289–90,
    291–2, 297–8, 301–4
working hours, 152, 202, 264–5
wrestling, 3, 10, 20, 31, 32, 53, 55–6, 59, 63,
    67–8, 77, 81, 92, 106, 112, 117, 259, 281
Wynn, Sir Watkin Williams, 169, 178

Yacht Club, the (later Royal Yacht Club and
    then Royal Yacht Squadron), 185
Yacht Racing Association, 293
yachting, 89, 137–8, 185, 225–7, 231, 292–4,
    298
yeomen, 31, 34, 45n, 52, 71, 83, 93, 95, 105,
    115, 116, 122, 140–1, 300
Yorkshire, 16, 111, 119, 161, 188, 247, 276
    county cricket, 216, 256, 330, 335, 336
    rugby 266, 270, 276, 314, 333
Young, Arthur, 157

Zingari, I. *see* I. Zingari

TIME BLASTERS
BACK TO THE ICE AGE

Scott Nickel
illustrated by Enrique Corts

Librarian Reviewer
Katharine Kan
Graphic novel reviewer and library consultant

Reading Consultant
Elizabeth Stedem
Educator

Raintree
SCHOOLS LIBRARY SERVICE

983

536039-1

www.raintreepublishers.co.uk
Visit our website to find out
more information about
Raintree books.

To order:
☎ Phone 0845 6044371
🖹 Fax +44 (0) 1865 312263
✉ Email myorders@raintreepublishers.co.uk

Customers from outside the UK please telephone +44 1865 312262

Raintree is an imprint of Capstone Global Library Limited, a company incorporated
in England and Wales having its registered office at 7 Pilgrim Street, London,
EC4V 6LB – Registered company number: 6695582

Text © 2008 by Stone Arch Books
First published in paperback in the United Kingdom
by Capstone Global Library in 2011
The moral rights of the proprietor have been asserted.

Art Director: Heather Kindseth
Graphic Designer: Brann Garvey
Editor: Laura Knowles
Originated by Capstone Global Library Ltd
Printed and bound in China by Leo Paper Products Ltd

ISBN 978 1 406 21844 2 (paperback)
14 13 12 11
10 9 8 7 6 5 4 3 2

British Library Cataloguing in Publication Data
A full catalogue record for this book is available from the British Library.

Disclaimer
All the Internet addresses (URLs) given in this book were valid at the time of going to press.
However, due to the dynamic nature of the Internet, some addresses may have changed, or
sites may have changed or ceased to exist since publication. While the author and Publishers
regret any inconvenience this may cause readers, no responsibility for any such changes can
be accepted by either the author or the publisher.

CONTENTS

Cast of characters 4

Back to the Ice Age 6

About the author and illustrator 34

Glossary 35

More about the Ice Age 36

Discussion questions 38

Writing prompts 39

Find out more 40

MUM

DAD

CAVEMAN

5

Why do I need a babysitter? I'm almost an adult!

You're in Year 5, David.

Yeah, but I think I saw a chin whisker this morning.

That's wonderful, but you're still getting a babysitter.

But, Mum!

Thanks for coming, Pamela.

Call us if you have any problems.

Don't worry. They're in good hands.

Okay, you pipsqueaks, don't bother me, or I'll lock you in the cupboard!

SLAM!

But first bring me a snack.

She's the worst babysitter in the world.

Yeah, we're doomed!

8

She's gone! The creepy babysitter is gone!

Hurray!

Oh no! I think my brother's time machine remote was here!

His machine could have taken her anywhere into the past or the future!

We have to go after her!

CALLUM'S ROOM

My parents will go mental if the babysitter's gone when they get back.

Luckily, the time machine has a system to track the remote controller.

Look, there she is!

11

15

This time travel thing is a pretty cool trick.

Aren't you scared?

Scared?

No way.

I'm 16 and a half years old.

Nothing scares me.

RROAR!

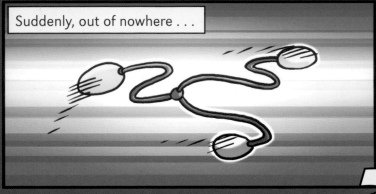

Suddenly, out of nowhere . . .

Oops! Not quite far enough. We're at the first American Thanksgiving in 1621!

Try it again, short stuff!

Mmm... the smell of their turkey is making me hungry...

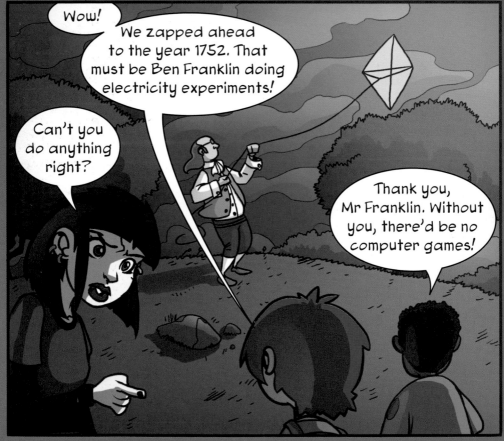

24

25

RRUUMBLEE

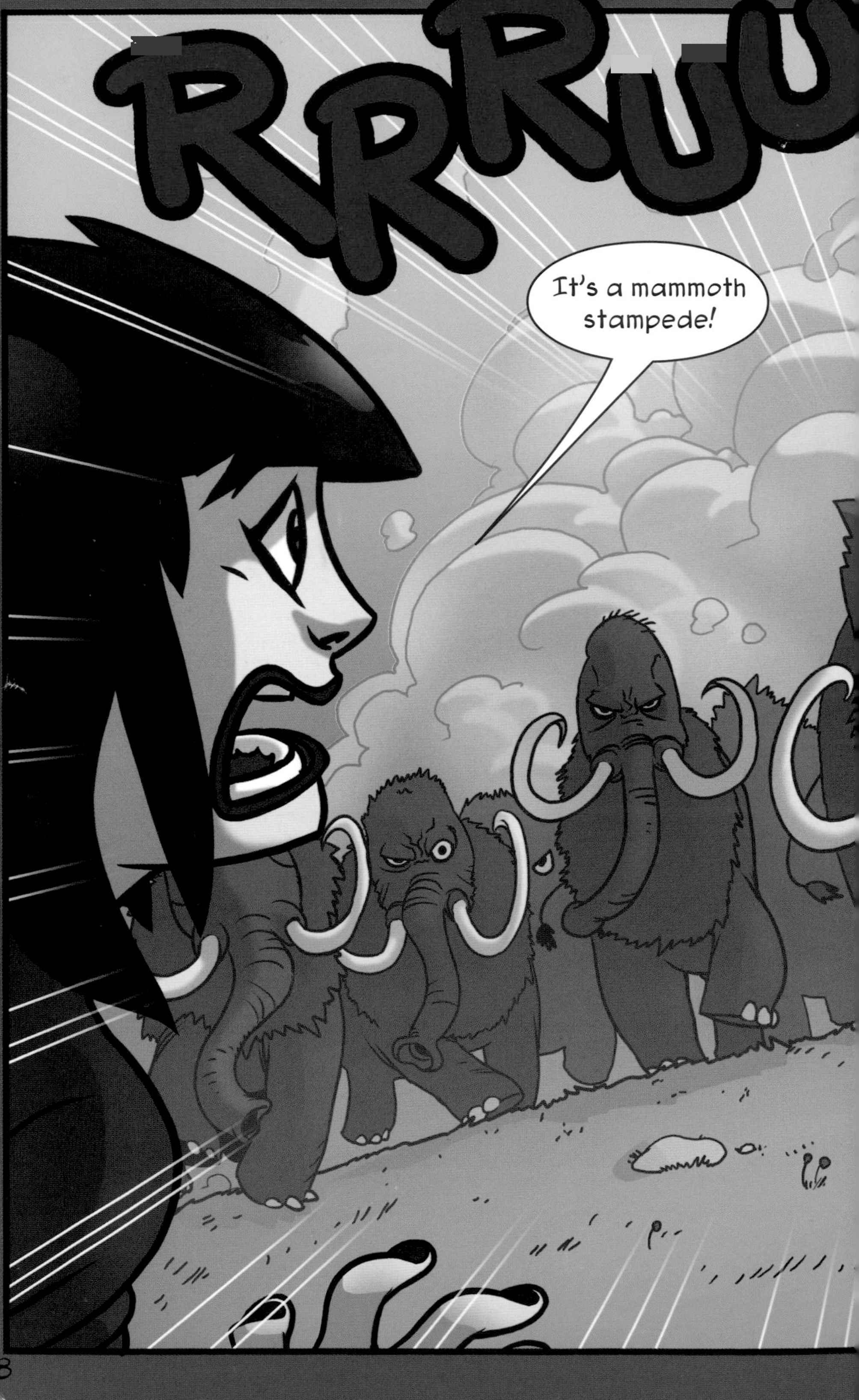
RRRUU
It's a mammoth stampede!

MBLLEE
Unless we want to become prehistoric pancakes, we need to get out of here.
Now!

THE END

ABOUT THE AUTHOR

As a child, Scott Nickel wanted to be a comic book writer or a mad scientist. Now he gets to do both. In his secret literary lab, Scott has created more than a dozen graphic novels featuring time travellers, zombies, robots, giant insects, and mutant dinner ladies. Scott's *Night of the Homework Zombies* received the 2007 Golden Duck award for Best Science Fiction Picture Book. When not creating his own crazy comics, Scott squeezes in a full-time job as a writer and editor of Garfield comic books.

ABOUT THE ILLUSTRATOR

Enrique Corts became a professional illustrator at the age of 19, working on short stories for a Spanish comic magazine. After finishing his art studies, he entered the graphic design and advertising world, spending endless hours chained to his computer. Later, he worked as a concept artist in the United Kingdom on computer games such as *Worms 3D, EyeToy Play 3*, and *Play 4*.

GLOSSARY

butterfingers clumsy person who often drops or lets things slip through their hands

exchange student person living and studying in another country to experience a different culture and learn the language

Ice Age period of time in history when ice covered large parts of Earth

mammoth elephant-like animal that lived during the Ice Age and had long tusks and shaggy hair

pipsqueak insulting word referring to an unimportant or small person

prehistoric time before historical events were written down

rascal mischievous or cheeky person, often a child

sabre-toothed tiger tiger-like animal that lived during the Ice Age and had long, pointy teeth. Never call a sabre-toothed tiger a "pipsqueak"!

MORE ABOUT THE ICE AGE

If you think winter is cold, just imagine living during an Ice Age! During the Ice Age, sheets of ice more than a kilometre thick covered much of North America, Northern Asia, and Europe. Here are a few more facts about this chilly time in history.

Earth has experienced many ice ages in its past. Some of them have lasted for millions of years. The most recent ice age began around 110 thousand years ago and ended around 12 thousand years ago.

Large glaciers, or ice sheets, covered nearly one-third of Earth during the Ice Age. Even today, some of this ice still hasn't melted in Greenland and Antarctica.

As ocean water froze, sea levels dropped more than 100 metres. Many areas that are now under water would have been dry land. In fact, during most of the Ice Age, Britain was not an island. It was connected to the rest of Europe by land.

As the huge glaciers of the Ice Age grew, they carved out canyons and valleys and pushed up hills and ridges. When the glaciers eventually melted, they left behind many lakes and swamps, and sea levels rose.

Many large animals, such as woolly mammoths and sabre-toothed tigers, roamed the Earth during the Ice Age. When the ice melted, these animals, also known as megafauna, became extinct. Today, scientists are still discovering their fossils.

You might think that temperatures during the Ice Age must have been extremely cold. Actually, much of Earth that was not covered by ice sheets was only a few degrees colder than today.

DISCUSSION QUESTIONS

1. David and Ben didn't like their babysitter, Pamela. So why do you think they went back in time to save her life? Explain your answer.

2. Each page of a graphic novel has several illustrations, called panels. What is your favourite panel in this book? Describe what you like about the illustration and why it's your favourite.

3. What do you think should happen to David? Should he be punished or rewarded for going back in time to save the babysitter? Explain your answer.

WRITING PROMPTS

1. In this story, a caveman travels with David and Ben back to the present time. What happens next? Does the caveman learn to fit in at school? Do the boys send him back to the Ice Age? Write down your ideas.

2. Mammoths and sabre-toothed tigers are both extinct animals. Ask an adult to help you find information about another extinct animal. Describe what the animal looked like, where it lived, and what it ate.

3. Make a list of three things you would pack for a journey back in time. Would you want to take photographs of woolly mammoths or show ancient Egyptians how to play computer games? Explain each item you would take with you, and why.

Books

100 Things You Should Know About Prehistoric Life,
Camilla de la Bedoyere, Rupert Matthews, Steve Parker
(Miles Kelly Publishing, 2007)

Prehistoric Scary Creatures, John Malam
(Book House, 2008)

Websites

Find out about some of the strange animals that lived
during the ice age:
**www.enchantedlearning.com/subjects/mammals/
Iceagemammals.shtml**

Check out mammoth facts on the National Geographic
Kids website:
**kids.nationalgeographic.com/Animals/
CreatureFeature/Mammoths**